# The Dog Lover's Companion to Washington DC

3RD
EDITION

**Katie Githens**

AVALON
TRAVEL

# THE DOG LOVER'S COMPANION TO WASHINGTON DC
## THE INSIDE SCOOP ON WHERE TO TAKE YOUR DOG

Published by
Avalon Travel
1700 Fourth Street
Berkeley, CA 94710, USA

Avalon Travel
a member of the Perseus Books Group

Printing History
1st edition—October 1998
3rd edition—May 2009
5 4 3 2 1

ISBN-13: 978-1-56691-712-4
ISSN: 1540-3300

Editor: Naomi Adler Dancis
Series Manager: Shaharazade Hussein
Copy Editor: Valerie Sellers Blanton
Designer: Jacob Goolkasian
Graphics Coordinator: Elizabeth Jang
Production Coordinator: Elizabeth Jang
Map Editor: Kevin Anglin
Cartographer: Kat Bennett

Cover and Interior Illustrations by Phil Frank

Printed in USA by RR Donnelley

## ABOUT THE AUTHOR

Katie Githens and her four-legged research assistant, Denali, have experienced a lot together. Denali is the puppy love-child of a roommate's purebred German shepherd and a neighbor's Dalmatian. She wiggled her way into Katie's life a few weeks before her college graduation in 2005. With a journalism degree in hand, the duo boarded a transcontinental flight from the West Coast to Washington DC.

Prior to moving to DC, Katie honed her writing skills at *The Aspen Times* and *Los Angeles Sports & Fitness* magazine. Katie and Denali happily sniffed out this writing project, and together they've spent months searching in and around DC for the doggone highlights of the nation's capital. Katie, herself a trail hound, has appreciated the opportunity to write about a topic close to her heart, while exploring new and familiar terrain. Denali's research for this book involved sharpening her own expertise on the relative ground speed of Mid-Atlantic squirrels.

Katie lives in Arlington, Virginia, with her husband Mike Githens (and Denali, of course). When not following Denali's nose, Katie works as a technical writer and editor in support of the U.S. Environmental Protection Agency.

*To Mike and Denali, my little family.*

# CONTENTS

# Beyond the Beltway . . . . . . . . . . . . . . . . . . . . . . . . . 289

# Resources . . . . . . . . . . . . . . . . . . . . . . . . . . . . . . . . 313

# Index . . . . . . . . . . . . . . . . . . . . . . . . . . . . . . . . . . . . 335

# Washington DC Area Map

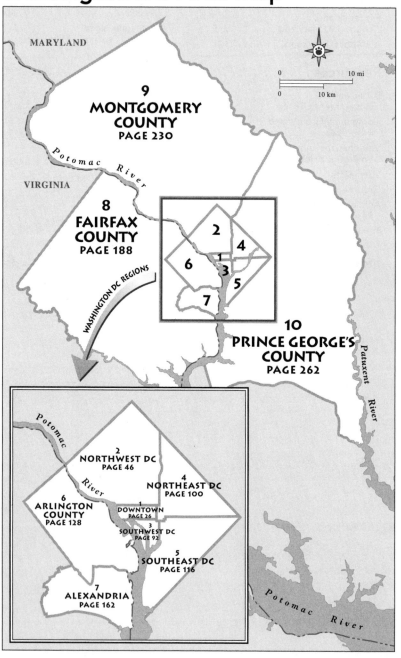

MARYLAND

9
MONTGOMERY
COUNTY
PAGE 230

Potomac River

VIRGINIA

8
FAIRFAX
COUNTY
PAGE 188

WASHINGTON DC REGIONS

0   10 mi
0   10 km

2

4

6
1
3
5

7

10
PRINCE GEORGE'S
COUNTY
PAGE 262

Patuxent River

Potomac River

2
NORTHWEST DC
PAGE 46

4
NORTHEAST DC
PAGE 100

6
ARLINGTON
COUNTY
PAGE 128

1
DOWNTOWN
PAGE 26

3
SOUTHWEST DC
PAGE 92

5
SOUTHEAST DC
PAGE 116

7
ALEXANDRIA
PAGE 162

Potomac River

# Introduction

*If you want a friend in Washington, get a dog.*

Harry S. Truman

Folks in Washington DC are known for being a serious breed—passionate about our causes, dogged about our career paths, and busy to a fault. The District's white marble monuments and conservative federal work attire only add to this prevailing culture of serious people pursuing serious matters. Luckily, it's nothing a wet lick in the face and a wagging tail can't cure.

While the District of Columbia ranks lowest in its percentage of dog owners compared to the nation's 50 states, the 1 in 5 residents who do keep pet companionship are a rambunctious, good-natured bunch. As one popular bumper sticker says: "Wag more, bark less." You could argue that those four furry legs keep us dog people better grounded than our neighbors.

In a place where pups and politics collide, it might have come as no surprise when Republican presidential nominee John McCain, with his menagerie of four dogs—and 20 other pets—had a "hair" of a lead with pet owners the summer before the 2008 presidential election. Or that President Barack Obama promised his daughters a dog at the conclusion of his bid for the White House. From Richard Nixon's cocker spaniel Checkers to Lyndon Johnson's beagles Him and Her to Bill Clinton's chocolate Labrador Buddy, the First Pet has had an undeniable role in shaping politics and softening the Commander-in-Chief's public persona. (Ironically, Truman was one of the few presidents who didn't keep pets; he even turned away a puppy sent to the White House as an anonymous gift!)

But no matter who's marking the White House lawn, my steadfast research assistant Denali, a German shepherd-Dalmatian mutt (either a "Germatian" or a "Damnation," depending on how many TV remotes she has chomped recently), is the first to attest you don't have to be Top Dog to feel at home in Washington.

Like many pooches and people living and visiting in DC, we're not originally from here. Denali joined my life one month before I graduated from a California beach college. Named after the largest mountain in North America (she was the largest pup in her litter), Denali foresaw our career path leading us to Mount Whitney, Pike's Peak, Mount Rainier, and of course Alaska's peaks... but Capitol Hill? Not long after she was born in my bathroom, we waved good-bye to the Pacific Ocean and found ourselves flying east. By the time the transcontinental flight landed, I had resigned myself to joining the cement-bound, dog-eat-dog world of broke, young professionals in the District. Denali didn't think her prospects looked much brighter from inside the cargo hold.

Thankfully, our pessimism proved ill-founded. Although Washington DC is more formal than Denali's beach town birthplace, it is unquestionably a doggy kind of town, with plenty of green space, natural beauty, and community for two-legged and four-legged newcomers. With noses to the ground, we quickly discovered parks and trails to explore that are closer to our front door here than they ever were in Malibu. Slowly but surely I began to catch Potomac Fever, and by the grin on Denali's face after rolling, again, in a dead fish along our favorite riverside trail, I guessed the feeling was mutual.

Now, several years later, the forecast for Fido is even sunnier. While for decades our nation's capital languished without a single official public dog park, Hill hounds are howling with delight as a new era is upon us. At the writing of this book, the DC Department of Parks and Recreation has sanctioned three fenced-in dog parks to be constructed in the coming months and opened a temporary dog park, with more permanent parks sure to follow.

In part fueled by the Internet's ability to link up strangers with a common interest (Northern Virginia Chihuahua Meetup Group, anyone?), the District and its environs offer numerous opportunities to make new friends with fellow mutts. With this guidebook in hand, you'll find the choicest off-leash exercise areas, biscuit bakeries, pet parades, doggy daycares, fur-friendly cafés, and Rover-welcoming hotels. DC might seem all buttoned up, but with a little digging, you'll find places to let your fur hang out and sniff out new discoveries.

# The Paws Scale

At some point, we've got to face the facts: Humans and dogs have different tastes. We like eating oranges and smelling lilacs and covering our bodies with terrycloth robes. They like eating roadkill and smelling each other's unmentionables and covering their bodies with horse manure.

The parks, beaches, and recreation areas in this book are rated with a dog in mind. Maybe your favorite park has lush gardens, a duck pond, a few acres of perfectly manicured lawns, and sweeping views of a nearby skyline. But unless your dog can run leash-free, swim in the pond, and roll in the grass, that park doesn't deserve a very high rating.

The lowest rating you'll come across in this book is the fire hydrant 🔥. When you see this symbol, it means the park is merely "worth a squat." Visit one of these parks only if your dog just can't hold it any longer. These parks have virtually no other redeeming qualities for canines.

Beyond that, the paws scale starts at one paw 🐾 and goes up to four paws 🐾🐾🐾🐾. A one-paw park isn't a dog's idea of a great time. Maybe it's a tiny park with only a few trees and too many kids running around. Or perhaps it's a magnificent-for-people national park that bans dogs from every inch of land except paved roads and a few campsites. Four-paw parks, on the other hand,

are places your dog will drag you to visit. Some of these areas come as close to dog heaven as you can imagine. Many have lakes for swimming or hundreds of acres for hiking. Some are small, fenced-in areas where leash-free dogs can tear around without danger of running into the road.

In addition to finding paws and hydrants, you'll also notice an occasional foot symbol ◖● in this book. The foot means the park offers something special for the humans in the crowd. You deserve a reward for being such a good chauffeur.

*The Dog Lover's Companion* is not meant to be a comprehensive guide to all of the parks in the DC metro area. If I included every single park, this book would be larger than the Congressional budget. Instead, I tried to find the best, dog-friendliest, and most convenient parks. Some neighborhoods and counties have so many wonderful parks that Denali and I ran ourselves ragged deciding which to include and which to leave out. Other areas had such a limited supply of parks that, for the sake of dogs living and visiting there, I ended up listing parks that wouldn't be worth mentioning in other chapters.

Navigating the District of Columbia can be perplexing if you're used to the basic grid system. Architect Pierre L'Enfant had grand visions for the Federal City. As a result, you'll probably spend at least an afternoon cursing his fancy Frenchman rotaries and grand promenades while trying to drive to a new part of town. There's an ongoing joke that he designed the city in order to confuse invaders… which in modern times might as well be every new White House intern, Congressional page, and federal contractor hire. But there is a system, and once you learn it, driving in the nation's capital becomes much easier.

Washington is divided into four quadrants: Northwest, Southwest, Northeast, and Southeast. (The chapters in this guidebook are organized in a similar fashion.) The north–south axis is North and South Capitol Street, and the east–west axis is the National Mall and East Capitol Street, with the U.S. Capitol at the center. As soon as you learn that 7th Street *NE* is in exactly the opposite side of the city as 7th Street *NW*, you're well on your way.

To help you along in your quest for the perfect pooch playground, whether local or far-flung, I've provided specific directions to all the parks listed in this book from the nearest major highway, city, or town. Although I tried to make this as easy as possible, signposts can be confusing. Both Northern Virginia and Maryland insist on naming byways with both numbers and names (e.g., Lee Highway is Route 29 is VA-29). I highly recommend picking up a detailed street map before you and your dog set out on your travels.

# Transportation

Washington DC is famous for its efficient and clean public transportation. Before moving to the Mid-Atlantic we had never heard of anyone not owning a car, whereas here, with the ease of traveling by Metro bus and rail, taxi, or bicycle, it's somewhat commonplace. This is all great, green, and commendable... until Bruiser wants to go to Great Falls Park.

The issue of public transportation can be a sore spot with District dog owners. We have one friend who has threatened to attach a trailer/child carrier to her commuter bicycle to schlep her puppy around the city. Another woman admitted the only reason she purchased a car was to transport her pooch.

Small dog owners have a paw up in the situation. Washington Metropolitan Transit Authority (WMATA or, more often, Metro) trains and buses allow dogs in "a secure container as long as there is no possibility that the pet can get free." This includes over-the-shoulder, dog-specific carrying cases (*not* backpacks, a WMATA representative emphasized). For bigger breeds, it's more complicated. One woman we met had tried jury-rigging a kennel on wheels for her Australian shepherd to ride Metro, but it was too stressful for either of them to wish to try again. The Virginia Railway Express and Maryland Transit Authority have similar policies, allowing only small pets in closed containers unless they are service dogs.

The good news for car-free dog owners is that many car-sharing programs, such as Zipcar, allow pets and can be a reasonable alternative to renting or owning a car, especially with the fluctuating price of gas these days. And dog-friendly taxis are not so hard to find. The *Resources* section contains more pointers on pet-friendly transportation, including an emergency vet tech pet taxi.

For the lucky dogs who can take a car ride at whim, I've tried to include suggestions for parking in congested areas. Many of the places Denali and I sniffed out have ample parking, particularly outside the District limits. But if you're headed to the National Mall or popular Potomac River getaways, you'll just have to be patient, or whenever possible, consider walking. Your pup will sleep better than ever.

# He, She, It

In this book, whether neutered, spayed, or au naturel, dogs are never referred to as "it." They are either "he" or "she." I alternate pronouns so no dog reading this book will feel left out.

# To Leash or Not to Leash...

This is not a question that plagues dogs' minds. Ask just about any normal, red-blooded American dog whether she'd prefer to be on leash or off during a park visit, and she'll say, "Arf!" (Translation: "Duh!") No question about it, most dogs would give their canine teeth to frolic about without that cumbersome leash.

Whenever you see the running dog 🐕 in this book, you'll know that under certain circumstances, your dog can run around in leash-free bliss. Fortunately, the greater DC metro region is home to dozens of such parks. The rest

of the parks require leashes. I wish I could write about the parks where dogs get away with being scofflaws. Unfortunately, those would be the first parks the animal control patrols would hit. In Washington DC the stakes are particularly high: If the U.S. Park Police tickets you for having your dog off-leash while on federal land, which constitutes an estimated one-third of the District, you'll be looking at a $25 ticket—and a permanent mark on your criminal record.

Also, just because dogs are permitted off leash in certain areas doesn't necessarily mean you should let your dog run free. In national forests and large tracts of wild land, unless you're sure your dog will come back when you call or will never stray more than a few yards from your side, you should probably keep her leashed. An otherwise docile homebody can turn into a savage hunter if the right prey is near, or your curious dog could perturb a rattlesnake or dig up a rodent whose fleas carry bubonic plague. In pursuit of a strange scent, your dog could easily get lost in an unfamiliar area. (Some forest rangers recommend having your dog wear a bright orange collar, vest, or backpack when out in the wilderness.) And there are many places where certain animals would love to have your dog for dinner—and not in a way Miss Manners would condone.

Be careful out there. If your dog really needs leash-free exercise but can't be trusted off leash in remote areas, she'll be happy to know that a growing number of tidy, fenced-in dog exercise areas permit well-behaved, leashless pooches.

# There's No Business Like Dog Business

There's nothing appealing about bending down with a plastic bag or a piece of newspaper on a chilly morning and grabbing the steaming remnants of what your dog ate for dinner the night before. It's disgusting. Worse yet, you have to hang onto it until you can find a trash can. And how about when the newspaper doesn't endure until you can dispose of it? Yuck! It's enough to make you wish your dog could wear diapers. But as gross as it can be to scoop the poop, it's worse to step in it. It's really bad if a child falls in it, or—gasp!—starts eating it. And have you ever walked into a park where few people clean up after their dogs? The stench could make a hog want to hibernate.

Unscooped poop is one of a dog's worst enemies. Public policies banning dogs from parks are enacted because of it. At present, a few good Washington DC parks that permit dogs are in danger of closing their gates to all canines because of the negligent behavior of a few owners. Opposing the campaign for new dog-friendly places in the city are some angry District residents who have made dogs out to be the second weapon of mass destruction—in large part because of the unsavory arsenal that irresponsible dog owners leave behind. A worst-case scenario is already in place in some parts of the country—dogs are banned from all parks. Their only exercise is a leashed sidewalk stroll. That's no way to live.

Just be responsible and clean up after your dog everywhere you go. (And, if there's even a remote chance he'll relieve himself inside, don't even bring him into hotels or stores that permit dogs!) Anytime you take your dog out, stuff plastic bags in your jacket, purse, car, pants pockets—anywhere you might be able to pull one out when needed. Or, if plastic isn't your bag, newspapers will do the trick. If you don't enjoy the squishy sensation, try one of those cardboard or plastic bag pooper-scoopers sold at pet stores. If you don't like bending down, buy a long-handled scooper. There's a scooper for every preference. And if you have a backyard, be sure to clean up there, too. The U.S. EPA has identified dog poop as a significant source of pollution in waterways, so do your doody duty to prevent sending it downstream in the Potomac River and Chesapeake Bay watersheds.

A final note: Don't pretend not to see your dog while he's doing his bit. Don't pretend to look for it without success. And don't fake scooping it up when you're really just covering it with sand. I know these tricks because I've been guilty of them myself—but no more.

# Etiquette Rex:
# The Well-Mannered Mutt

While cleaning up after your dog is your responsibility, a dog in a public place has his own responsibilities. Of course, it really boils down to your responsibility again, but the burden of action is on your dog. Etiquette for restaurants and hotels is covered in other sections of this chapter. What follows are some fundamental rules of dog etiquette. I'll go through it quickly, but if your dog's a slow reader, he can read it again: no vicious dogs; no jumping on people; no

incessant barking; no leg lifts on bicycles, backpacks, human legs, or any other personal objects you'll find hanging around parks; dogs should come when they're called; dogs should stay on command.

But even if Dog is your co-pilot, he is not infallible. Dogs make mistakes, too. While Denali is very obedient about coming when called, all bets are off if a squirrel or cat crosses the street. Do your best to remedy any problems. It takes patience and it's not always easy. Also recognize that not all dogs are cut out for off-leash play in dog parks. Breaking up a dogfight is nobody's idea of a good time, so be honest with yourself about your furry best friend's foibles. If you need professional help, the *Resources* section of this book includes contact information for some trainers and behaviorists.

# Safety First

A few essentials will keep your traveling dog happy and healthy.

**Beat the Heat:** If you must leave your dog alone in the car for a few minutes, do so only if it's cool out and you can park in the shade. Never, ever, ever leave a dog in a car with the windows rolled up all the way. Even if it seems cool, the sun's heat passing through the window can kill a dog in a matter of minutes. Roll down the window enough so your dog gets air, but also so there's no danger of your dog getting out or someone breaking in. Make sure your dog has plenty of water.

You also have to watch out for heat exposure when your car is in motion. Certain cars, like hatchbacks, can make a dog in the backseat extra hot, even while you feel OK in the driver's seat.

Try to time your vacation so you don't visit a place when it's extremely warm. Dogs and heat don't get along, especially if the dog isn't used to heat. The opposite is also true. If your dog lives in a hot climate and you take him to a freezing place, it may not be a healthy shift. Check with your vet if you have any doubts. Spring and fall are usually the best times to travel.

**Water:** Water your dog frequently. Dogs on the road may drink even more than they do at home. Take regular water breaks, or bring a heavy bowl (the thick clay ones do nicely) and set it on the floor so your dog always has access to water. I use a non-spill bowl, which comes in really handy on curvy roads. When hiking, be sure to carry enough for you and a thirsty dog.

**Rest Stops:** Stop and unwater your dog. There's nothing more miserable than being stuck in a car when you can't find a rest stop. No matter how tightly you cross your legs and try to think of the desert, you're certain you'll burst within the next minute... so imagine how a dog feels when the urge strikes, and he can't tell you the problem. There are plenty of rest stops along the major freeways. I've also included many parks close to freeways for dogs who need a good stretch with their bathroom break.

How frequently you stop depends on your dog's bladder. If your dog is constantly running out the doggy door at home to relieve himself, you may want to stop every hour. Others can go significantly longer without being uncomfortable. Watch for any signs of restlessness and gauge it for yourself.

**Car Safety:** Even the experts differ on how a dog should travel in a car. Some suggest doggy safety belts, available at pet-supply stores. Others firmly believe in keeping a dog kenneled. They say it's safer for the dog if there's an accident, and it's safer for the driver because there's no dog underfoot. Still others say you should just let your dog hang out without straps and boxes. They believe that if there's an accident, at least the dog isn't trapped in a cage. Dogs enjoy this more, anyway.

I'm a follower of the last school of thought. Denali loves sticking her snout out of the windows to smell the world go by. The danger is that if the car kicks up a pebble or bothers a bee, Denali's nose and eyes could be injured. So far, she's been OK, but I've heard of dogs who needed to be treated for bee stings to the nose because of this practice. If in doubt, try opening the window just enough so your dog can't stick out much snout.

Whatever travel style you choose, your pet will be more comfortable if he has his own blanket or bed with him. Consider bringing a faux-sheepskin blanket for your dog. At night in the hotel, the sheepskin doubles as the dog's bed.

**Planes:** Air travel is even more controversial. Denali has weathered two transcontinental flights, both with great trepidation for the both of us. If I hadn't been moving from L.A. to Washington DC (the other flight was for a monthlong trip that Denali surely needed to attend), I would rather have driven the distance or left her at home with a friend. I've heard too many horror stories of dogs suffocating in what was supposed to be a pressurized cargo section, dying of heat exposure, or ending up in Miami while their people go to Seattle. There's just something unappealing about the idea of a dog flying in the cargo hold, like he's nothing more than a piece of luggage. Of course, many dogs survive just fine, but I'm not willing to take the chance unless absolutely necessary.

If you need to transport your dog by plane, try to fly nonstop, and make sure you schedule takeoff and arrival times when the temperature is below 80°F and above 32°F (most airlines have restrictions to this effect, anyway). You'll want to consult the airline about regulations, required certificates, and fees. Be sure to check with your vet to make sure your pooch is healthy enough to fly.

The question of tranquilizing a dog for a plane journey causes the most contention of all. Some vets think it's insane to give a dog a sedative before flying. They say a dog will be calmer and less fearful without a disorienting drug. Others think it's crazy not to afford your dog the little relaxation she might not get without a tranquilizer. An all-natural remedy (e.g., a supplement of St. John's Wort, chamomile, and other herbal ingredients) such as many specialty pet stores sell might also be worth considering. Discuss the issue with your vet, who will take into account the trip length and your dog's personality.

# The Ultimate Doggy Bag

Your dog can't pack her own bags, and even if she could, she'd probably fill them with dog biscuits and chew toys. It's important to stash some of those in your dog's vacation kit, but here are other handy items to bring along: bowls, bedding, a brush, towels (for those muddy days), a first-aid kit, pooper-scoopers, water, food, prescription drugs, tags, treats, toys, and—of course—this book.

Make sure your dog is wearing her license, identification tag, and rabies tag. On a long trip, you may even want to bring along your dog's rabies certificate. Some parks and campgrounds require rabies and licensing information. You never know how picky they'll be.

It's a good idea to snap a disposable ID on your dog's collar, too, showing a cell phone number or the name, address, and phone number either of where you'll be vacationing, or of a friend who'll be home to field calls. That way, if your dog should get lost, the finder won't be calling your empty house.

Some people think dogs should drink only water brought from home, so their bodies don't have to get used to too many new things. I've never had a problem giving my dog tap water from other parts of the state, nor has anyone else I know. Most vets think your dog will be fine drinking tap water in most U.S. cities.

# Bone Appétit

In some European countries, dogs enter restaurants and dine alongside their folks as if they were people, too. (Or at least they sit and watch and drool while their people dine.) Not so in the United States. Rightly or wrongly, dogs are considered a health threat here, although many health inspectors say they see no reason why clean, well-behaved dogs shouldn't be permitted inside a restaurant.

Fortunately, you don't have to take your dog to a foreign country in order to eat together. Washington DC is full of restaurants with outdoor tables, and many of them welcome dogs to join their people for an alfresco experience. The law on outdoor dining is somewhat vague, and you'll encounter many different interpretations of it. In general, as long as your dog doesn't go inside a restaurant (even to get to outdoor tables in the back) and isn't near the food preparation areas, it's probably legal. The decision is then up to the restaurant proprietor. Many, many sidewalk cafés in DC abide by the "tie her outside the patio fence" rule; just find a table on the patio edge and you'll more or less be able to share a meal together.

The restaurants listed in this book have given us permission to tout them as dog-friendly eateries. But keep in mind that rules can change and restaurants can close, so I highly recommend phoning before you set your stomach on a

particular kind of cuisine. Since some restaurants close (and most suspend outdoor dining) during colder months, phoning ahead is a doubly wise thing to do. If you can't call first, be sure to ask the manager of the restaurant for permission before you sit down with your sidekick. Remember, it's the restaurant proprietor, not you, who will be in trouble if someone complains to the health department.

Some fundamental rules of restaurant etiquette: Dogs shouldn't beg from other diners, no matter how delicious the steak looks. They should not attempt to get their snouts (or their entire bodies) up on the table. They should be clean, quiet, and as unobtrusive as possible. If your dog leaves a good impression with the management and other customers, it will help pave the way for all the other dogs who want to dine alongside their best friends in the future.

## A Room at the Inn

Good dogs make great hotel guests. They don't steal towels, and they don't get drunk and keep the neighbors up all night. Washington DC is full of lodgings whose owners welcome dogs. This book lists dog-friendly accommodations of all types, from motels to campgrounds to elegant hotels—but the basic dog etiquette rules are the same everywhere.

Dogs should never be left alone in your room. Leaving a dog alone in a strange place invites serious trouble. Scared, nervous dogs may tear apart drapes, carpeting, and furniture. They may even injure themselves. They might also bark nonstop and scare the daylights out of the housekeeper. If at all possible, just don't do it.

Only bring a house-trained dog to a lodging. How would you like a houseguest to relieve himself in the middle of your bedroom?

Make sure your pooch is flea-free. Otherwise, future guests will be itching to leave.

It helps to bring your dog's bed or blanket along for the night. Your dog will feel more at home and will be less tempted to jump on the hotel bed. If your dog sleeps on the bed with you at home, bring a sheet or towel and put it on top of the bed so the hotel's bedspread won't get furry or dirty.

After a few days in a hotel, some dogs come to think of it as home. They get territorial. When another hotel guest walks by, it's "Bark! Bark!" When the housekeeper knocks, it's "Bark! Snarl! Bark! Gnash!" Keep your dog quiet, or you'll both find yourselves looking for a new home away from home.

For some strange reason, many lodgings prefer small dogs as guests. All I can say is, "Yip! Yap!" It's really ridiculous. Large dogs are often much calmer and quieter than their tiny, high-energy cousins.

If you're in a location where you can't find a hotel that will accept you and your big brute, it's time to try a sell job. Let the manager know how good and quiet your dog is (if he is). Promise he won't eat the bathtub or run around and shake all over the hotel. Offer a deposit or sign a waiver, even if they're not required for small dogs. It helps if your sweet, soppy-eyed pooch is at your side to convince the decision-maker.

You could sneak dogs into hotels, but I don't recommend trying it. The lodging might have a good reason for its rules. Besides, you always feel as if you're going to be caught and thrown out on your hindquarters. You race in and out of your room with your dog as if ducking the dogcatcher. It's better to avoid feeling like a criminal and move on to a more dog-friendly location. In these situations, it's helpful to know that just about every Motel 6 permits one small pooch per room; some have more lenient rules than others. A healthy percentage of Travelodge and Best Western lodgings permit pooches. And all of the Kimpton Hotels and most Westins and Loews are very dog-friendly. Space precludes me from listing all the locations, but if you find yourself in a town anywhere in the United States, and you don't know where to look for a dog-friendly lodging, those are good starting points.

The lodgings described in this book are for dogs who obey all the rules. I provide a range of rates for each lodging, from the least expensive room during low season to the priciest room during high season. Most of the rooms are doubles, so there's not usually a huge variation. But when a room price gets into the thousands of dollars, you know we're looking at royal suites here.

Some lodgings charge extra for your dog. If you see "Dogs are $10 (or whatever amount) extra," that means $10 extra per night. Some charge one fee for the entire length of a dog's stay, and others ask for a deposit—these details are noted in the lodging description. A few places still ask for nothing more than your dog's promise that she'll be on her best behavior. So, if no extra charge is mentioned in a listing, it means your dog can stay with you free.

Also included in this book are websites for those lodgings whose site names aren't too long and convoluted. (When the URL takes up more space than this sentence, I generally don't include it.) Not all lodgings have a website, but when they do, it can be very helpful in deciding where to stay. Sites often provide lots of details, photos, and a way to reserve online. But generally, when staying with a pooch, it's a good idea to reserve by phone so you can let the staff know you'll be bringing your beast.

# Natural Troubles

Chances are your adventuring will go without a hitch, but you should always be prepared to deal with trouble. Make sure you know the basics of animal first aid before you embark on a long journey with your dog.

The more common woes—ticks, poison ivy, and skunks—can make life with a traveling dog a somewhat trying experience. Ticks are hard to avoid in many parts of the greater DC metro region; in fact, the Mid-Atlantic has one of the highest prevalence of ticks in the country. They can carry Lyme disease, so you should always check yourself and your dog all over after a day in tick country. Don't forget to check ears and between the toes. If you see a tick, just pull it straight out with tweezers, not with your bare hands. Denali and I had at least one unfortunate run-in with a bed of nymphs (young ticks) that had us leery of forested undergrowth for weeks.

The tiny deer ticks that carry Lyme disease are difficult to find. Consult your veterinarian if your dog is lethargic for a few days, has a fever, loses her appetite, or becomes lame. These symptoms could indicate Lyme disease. Keep your dog on an anti-flea and -tick medication. Some vets recommend a new vaccine that is supposed to prevent the onset of the disease.

Poison ivy is also a common menace. Get familiar with it through a friend who knows nature or through a guided nature walk. Remember, "Leaves of three, let them be." Dogs don't generally have reactions to poison ivy, but they can easily pass its oils on to people. If you think your dog has made contact with poison ivy, avoid petting her until you can get home and bathe her (preferably with rubber gloves). If you do pet her before you can wash her, don't touch your eyes and be sure to wash your hands immediately.

If your dog loses a contest with a skunk (and she always will), rinse her eyes first with plain warm water, then bathe her with dog shampoo. Towel her off, then apply tomato juice. If you can't get tomato juice, try using a solution of one pint of vinegar per gallon of water to decrease the stink instead. Other wildlife to watch out for are black bears, particularly if venturing into the Shenandoah Valley, and if walking near the Potomac River, keep an eye out for black rat snakes, which are typically shy but big enough to give anyone a fright.

Finally, talk to your veterinarian about giardia and leptospirosis. Humans become infected with giardia when they drink water containing the parasite

*Giardia lamblia*, but in rare cases you can acquire it from something as seemingly innocuous as a doggy kiss to the face after your pooch has drunk from a contaminated stream. Signs of giardia include diarrhea, stomach cramps, and nausea. Leptospirosis, or "lepto," is a contagious bacterial disease of dogs and other mammals that can cause high fever, severe headache, vomiting, and, if left untreated, kidney damage or liver failure. Both can be quite serious and are worth educating yourself about.

## Ruffing It Together

Whenever we go camping, Denali insists on sleeping in the tent. She sprawls out and won't budge. At the first hint of dawn, she tiptoes outside (sometimes right through the bug screen) as if she'd been standing vigil all night. She tries not to look shamefaced, but under all that hair lurks an embarrassed grin.

Actually, Denali might have the right idea. Some outdoor experts say it's dangerous to leave even a tethered dog outside your tent at night. The dog can escape or become bait for some creature hungry for a late dinner.

Many state parks require dogs to be kept in a tent or vehicle at night; some county parks follow suit. Other policies are more lenient. Use good judgment.

If you're camping with your dog, chances are you're also hiking with him. Even if you're not hiking for long, you have to watch out for your dog's paws, especially those who are fair of foot. Rough terrain can cause a dog's pads to become raw and painful, making it almost impossible for him to walk. Several types of dog boots are available for such feet. It's easier to carry the booties than to carry your dog home.

Be sure to bring plenty of water for you and your pooch. Stop frequently to wet your whistles. Some veterinarians recommend against letting your dog drink out of a stream because he could ingest giardia or other internal parasites, but it's not always easy to stop a thirsty dog.

# A Dog in Need

If you don't currently have a dog but could provide a good home for one, I'd like to make a plea on behalf of all the unwanted dogs who will be euthanized tomorrow—and the day after that and the day after that. Animal shelters and humane organizations are overflowing with dogs who would devote their lives to being your best buddy, your faithful traveling companion, and a dedicated listener to all your tales.

Need a nudge? Remember the oft-quoted words of Samuel Butler: "The great pleasure of a dog is that you may make a fool of yourself with him and not only will he not scold you, but he will make a fool of himself, too."

# DISTRICT OF COLUMBIA

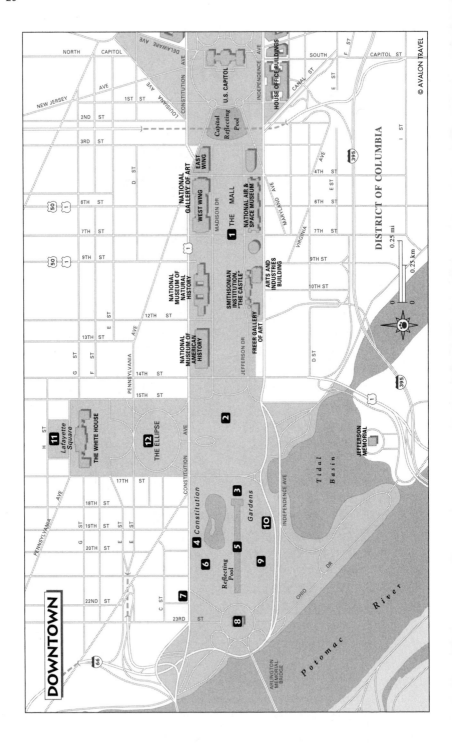

**CHAPTER 1**

# Downtown

At times it seems Washington DC has a magnetic force, drawing an incredibly diverse crowd of citizens and foreigners to its center. Lucky travelers who bring furry companions on their patriotic pilgrimage will discover that some of the best sights in DC can be seen with a leash in hand.

If you live here or have visited before, you know, Republican or Democrat, one thing holds true in Washington: All tour buses lead to the National Mall. Indeed, judging by some city maps and guidebooks, it would be easy to believe that Downtown and the National Mall *were* the capital, all of it, despite the fact they constitute only a small portion of the 10-mile square identified by our first president.

As for District residents, it never hurts to be a tourist for a day in your own city, especially when your stomping grounds are Washington DC. Many families stuck taking a "staycation" have been surprised to find it more

## PICK OF THE LITTER—DOWNTOWN

BEST PARKS
**National Mall,** National Mall (page 29)
**Constitution Gardens,** National Mall (page 33)

BEST MEMORIAL
**Washington Monument,** National Mall (page 31)

BEST WAY TO REST TIRED PAWS
**Capitol Pedicabs,** National Mall (page 33)

BEST PLACE TO EAT
**Poste,** Downtown and Penn Quarter (page 40)

BEST PLACES TO STAY
**Hotel Monaco,** Downtown and Penn Quarter (page 40)
**The Madison,** Downtown and Penn Quarter (page 41)
**The Fairmont,** Foggy Bottom (page 44)

enjoyable than fighting I-95 traffic away from the Capital Beltway. In this chapter you'll find the best places to walk, eat, and stay Downtown with your hound.

While dogs are not welcome in the Smithsonian museums or the sculpture gardens lining the Mall, the nation's favorite front lawn holds numerous free public events, such as the summertime "Screen on the Green" movie showings, and is a destination in its own right. This grassy "Grand Avenue" is an ideal spot for strolling, jogging, and people-watching with your pooch. Penn Quarter and Downtown proper supply a taste of the big city for urbanite pups but are always within five to 10 blocks of open spaces for those dogs who get city-saturated in half a day.

Closer to the Potomac River, Foggy Bottom has numerous hotels that cater to canines tucked between tidy row homes in cheerful colors. What's more, street parking, a rarity Downtown, is usually easier to find near the federal buildings located between 21st and 23rd Streets NW. Paid parking garages are also available in the city (Altman's Parking: www.altmansparking.com; PMI: www.pmi-parking.net; Colonial Parking: www.ecolonial.com).

For our purposes, Downtown and the National Mall will include the area east of the Potomac River, south of M Street NW and Massachusetts Avenue NW, west of 1st Street NW, and north of Independence Avenue SW.

# National Mall

Our nation's capital has a wealth of green space, but none is more iconic than the National Mall. Each year, an estimated 24 million tourists from around the world walk this expansive lawn spanning from the U.S. Capitol to the Washington Monument. To Denali's delight, a world of smells collides here, too. What an early District resident once called a "mere cow pasture" has become one of the most active recreational spaces in the country, today busy with herds of people rather than cattle (to the disappointment of Australian cattle dogs across Washington).

The memorial parks beckon beyond the Washington Monument and stretch nearly to the Potomac River. Your lucky leashed compatriot is permitted in all memorials except inside the domes of the Lincoln and Jefferson Memorials and the interior of the Washington Monument. In this section you'll find a selection of patriotic sights worth sniffing out in the area east of the Potomac River, south of Constitution Avenue, west of the Capitol, and north of Independence Avenue.

### PARKS, BEACHES, AND RECREATION AREAS

#### 1 National Mall

🐾🐾🐾🐾 ◀▶ (See the Downtown map on page 26)

America's favorite front lawn is in the heart of what the *Washington City Paper* has jestingly billed "Fannypakistan," but the Mall isn't just for tourists. Its

### DIVERSION

**Howl-y-wood in the Park:** For free outdoor cinema that the furriest members of the family can attend, head down to the summertime **Screen on the Green** on the National Mall. Presented by HBO on a giant 20- by 40-foot screen, the outdoor film festival celebrates a decade in 2009. Remember to bring your own chairs or blankets, refreshments (including a dog bowl), and a leash. People start staking out spots as early as 5 P.M., so it pays to get here early. Pack a picnic and hang out until the screening begins at dusk, usually between 8:30 and 9 P.M. on Mondays July–August. If the weather turns nasty, screenings may be canceled. Located on the Mall between 4th and 7th St. NW; 877/262-5866.

## DOG-EAR YOUR CALENDAR

If Fido can work a crowd, there's no place finer than these National Mall festivals.

**St. Patrick's Day Parade:** Dress Barney in a green sweater to celebrate the Blarney Stone. March; Constitution Ave.; 202/637-2474; www.dcstpatsparade.com.

**White House Easter Egg Roll:** Tickets are required to enter the South Lawn, and this is really a kids' event, but dogs can observe from the sidewalk. March; White House and the Ellipse; 202/456-7041; www.whitehouse.gov/easter.

**Smithsonian Kite Festival:** Maybe Snoopy can help Charlie Brown fly one successfully at last. Late March; National Mall; 202/633-3030; www.kitefestival.org.

**National Cherry Blossom Festival Parade:** DC's flagship springtime festival is always packed. Mind the puppy paws. April; Constitution Ave.; 877/442-5666; www.nationalcherry blossomfestival.org.

**Earth Day:** Live music, eco-action, and green technology exhibits to please Mother Earth. Canines concerned about climate change can join the greenfest. April; National Mall; www.greenapplemusicfestival.com.

**Rolling Thunder Motorcycle Rally:** Put those Harley doggy riding-goggles to good use. More than 250,000 bikers riding from the Pentagon to the Capitol pay homage to POW/MIA veterans. May; 908/369-5439; www.rollingthunder1.com.

---

approximately two-mile length of open landscape almost makes up for the tiny studio apartment you and Boomer have tried to squeeze yourselves inside. Architecture geeks will delight while walking past the nearly dozen Smithsonian museums that line either side of the promenade, while their dogs search for hot dog nubs discarded in the grass by passersby. Denali's choice route usually leads us under the shade of the 200-year-old American elm trees bordering either side of the Mall. If we detour from a straight march down to the Lincoln Memorial and back, we usually approach the most distinctive Smithsonian building, which was also the first constructed: the red sandstone, Norman-style headquarters, better known as "the Castle," in which the Smithsonian Institution founder is entombed (no dogs allowed). Without having ever stepped foot on American soil, British scientist James Smithson bequeathed his entire fortune to the United States "to found at Washington, under the name of the Smithsonian Institution, an establishment for the increase and diffusion of knowledge."

On the north side of the Castle, Denali enjoys touring the four-acre

**National Memorial Day Parade:** Patriotism on parade and a big thank you to servicemen, women, and canines. May; Constitution Ave.; 703/302-1012 ext. 227; www.national memorialdayparade.com.

**Smithsonian Folklife Festival:** A two-week celebration of contemporary living cultural traditions. June–July; National Mall; www.folklife.si.edu.

**A Capitol Fourth:** Independence Day Parade and concert. Be sure to bring the pupster home before the fireworks kick off. July; National Mall and Constitution Ave.; www.pbs.org/capitolfourth.

**National Book Festival:** Celebrate the joys of reading, or reading aloud to your furry friend. Late September; National Mall; www.loc.gov/bookfest.

**Humane Society Walk for the Animals:** Take a stroll to end pet homelessness. The $25 walk entry fee benefits the Washington Humane Society and the Humane Society of the United States. The event also includes an adoption center, $35 microchip clinic, canine agility course, best-dressed canine contests, yoga with your dog, and a beauty and the bark grooming station. October; Constitution Gardens; www.humanesocietywalk.org.

**National Christmas Tree Lighting: December.** Holiday cheer your hound can walk around (but no dogs at the opening ceremony). December; The Ellipse; 202/208-1631; www.nps.gov/whho/national_christmas_tree_program.htm.

**Enid A. Haupt Garden,** with its brick paths and hanging baskets. The National Mall is located between Constitution and Independence Aves.; 202/426-6841; www.nps.gov/nama.

## 2 Washington Monument

🐾🐾 🐾 (See the Downtown map on page 26)

At over 555 feet tall, the Washington Monument is one of the city's most prominent sights. When we lived in California we navigated by the ocean, in Colorado by the mountains; here in the District of Columbia, this white Egyptian-style obelisk is the best drive-by-landmark point-of-reference. Thanks to DC building height restrictions, it's visible in more places in the metro region than you might initially surmise.

Because dogs are not allowed inside the monument, you don't have to feel guilty for not spending half the morning lined up waiting for tickets at the kiosk on 15th Street NW. Instead, walk up the hill to the monument's American flag–encircled base and survey the sights: Jefferson Memorial to the south,

Lincoln Memorial to the west, White House to the north, and U.S. Capitol building to the east. Even on the most stagnant dog days of summer, you can usually pick up a hint of a breeze at this crossroads, and on blustery days it can feel like a wind tunnel. Denali loves to raise her nose in the air, sniffing with her nostrils tilting sideways as only dogs can do.

It pleased her very much to learn America's first president kept the company of many hounds. George Washington so loved dogs he once called for a cease-fire during the Revolutionary War to return the British commanding officer's terrier, who had somehow wandered across enemy lines at the Battle of Germantown. Some historians argue this genuinely touched the British General William Howe and won his respect, so that he never pursued Washington's troops with quite the same zeal again, perhaps contributing to the British's ultimate defeat.

As you continue your dog walk down the paved pathway of wide grass grounds, take one last look over your shoulder. If you look carefully, you will see a subtle line about one-third of the way up the Washington Monument. Due to a lack of funds, the monument's construction was forced into a 20-year hiatus starting in 1856; when it resumed, the marble's color did not quite match. The Washington Monument is bounded by Constitution and Independence Avenues and 15th and 17th Streets NW. 202/426-6841; www.nps.gov/wamo.

### 3 National World War II Memorial

(See the Downtown map on page 26)

Before visiting this memorial, Denali's only connection with the Greatest Generation it honors were her human great-grandparents, whom she had only met as a small puppy. Controversial for its location between the sight-lines of the Washington Monument and the Lincoln Memorial, as well as for its old-fashioned format, the WWII Memorial's traditional expression honors the 16 million who served in the U.S. armed forces during the war in straightforward, symbolic ways: 56 pillars, one for each state and territory from that period; two triumphal arches to represent the Atlantic and Pacific theaters of war; a wall of 4,000 gold stars, each signifying 100 Americans who died during World War II.

Despite the somber engraving, "Here We Mark the Price of Freedom," the mood at the National World War II Memorial tends to be more lighthearted than at the Vietnam Veterans Memorial. The fountains spray, kids splash their hands in the edge of the Rainbow Pool and squeal, and dogs and owners sniff out the pillar representing their home state to pose for a photo. Located at 17th St. and Independence Ave. NW; 202/619-7222; www.wwiimemorial.com.

## 4 Constitution Gardens

 (See the Downtown map on page 26)

These oft-overlooked gardens offer 50 restful acres to sit by a small lake and watch the birds and squirrels (or, as Denali prefers, salivate over them). Constitution Gardens were originally beneath the Potomac River until the U.S. Army Corps of Engineers dredged the site around the turn of the 20th century, creating the land that is now East and West Potomac Parks. Beginning in World War I, the Navy established "temporary" office buildings that would remain until President Richard Nixon ordered their removal in the 1970s. The paw-destrian-friendly gardens we see today didn't come to be until 1976, just in time for the American Revolution Bicentennial tribute. Under Reagan's administration, a memorial to the 56 signers of the Declaration of Independence was dedicated on an island in the Constitution Gardens Lake near 19th Street and Constitution Avenue NW. Try to find parallel parking on the street. 202/426-6841; www.nps.gov/coga.

## DIVERSION

While the Metro might be off-limits for most pooches, another form of environmentally friendly transit will leave Rover raving. Bicycle taxis, also known as pedicabs, offer your dog and you a fresh way to travel around the National Mall. Denali caught a ride with **Capitol Pedicabs** and sat in the open cab with the regality of a beauty queen on parade, much to the delight of pointing pedestrians. Call 24–36 hours in advance to make arrangements, or hail a pedicabber circling the Mall. At press time, this was a fairly new operation with less than a dozen pedicab drivers. Fare varies by driver, but expect about $15 for a 20-minute ride. 202/232-6086; www.capitolpedicabs.com.

## 5 Reflecting Pool

😾😾😾 🐾 (See the Downtown map on page 26)

Despite what you've seen in *Forrest Gump*, no wading is allowed in the Reflecting Pool. As one ranger put it, "No dogs and no humans either. These aren't swimming pools." The same rule goes for the Tidal Basin and Constitution Gardens. Mallards clearly aren't held to the same standards, as ducks blissfully paddle and waddle through the rectangular pool—garnering Denali's full attention. Approaching the steps of the Lincoln Memorial, it's easy to imagine the powerful echo of Martin Luther King Jr.'s "I Have a Dream" speech reverberating over crowds that lined the Reflecting Pool during the 1963 March on Washington. If you, too, get lost in thought imagining the civil rights and political protests that have unfolded here, all it takes is an insistent tug from the other end of the leash to spin you back into the present. Denali, for her part, was perfectly content to observe the Reflecting Pool—and its urban wildlife— in the here and now. Located between the World War II Memorial and the Lincoln Memorial. 202/426-6841; www.nps.gov/nacc.

## 6 Vietnam Veterans Memorial

😾 🐾 (See the Downtown map on page 26)

While it makes for a sobering walk in the park, Denali appreciated her visit to the Vietnam Veterans Memorial, where more than 58,000 names etched in polished black granite pay tribute to the men and women who died in the Vietnam War. Understated and powerful in its presentation built into a grassy rise, the memorial's inscribed names appear in the chronological order that soldiers

## THINK GLOBALLY, BARK LOCALLY

Some military analysts estimate as many as 10,000 allied and U.S. lives were saved during the Vietnam War alone by dogs working as sentries, scouts, and bomb-sniffers. Despite the fact that dogs have served in the U.S. military during every modern war, no national monument exists to honor these unsung canine heroes—an oversight the National War Dogs Monument, Inc. is aiming to fix. After being denied space on the National Mall by the National Park Service in 2005, NWDM won federal approval in 2008 for a plan to construct the monument at Fort Belvoir in Fairfax County, Virginia. Draft plans depict the **National War Dogs Monument** as a bronze statue of a soldier accompanied by a German shepherd, Labrador retriever, and Doberman pinscher, the primary breeds used in battle since World War II. Learn how you can help honor a group of the military's scrappiest veterans at www.nationalwardogsmonument.org.

became casualties. The Vietnam Wall is tallest where casualties peaked in the longest war in U.S. history. The stark design was submitted by 21-year-old Yale architectural student Maya Lin to the nationwide design contest in 1981; her winning concept stirred enough controversy to later prompt the installment of two more traditional sculptures to appease detractors.

The Vietnam Wall draws thousands of visitors every year, so anticipate a crowd. Leashed dogs are permitted along the wall and can attend park ranger lectures that take place daily 9:30 A.M.–8:30 P.M., but it may be difficult to find a specific soldier's name if you're visiting with Fido. Search for curbside parking along the Mall; you'll have better luck if you come early. 21st St. and Constitution Ave. NW; 202/426-6841; www.nps.gov/vive.

## 7 Albert Einstein Memorial
🐾🐾 🐕 (See the Downtown map on page 26)

Denali couldn't decide whether she felt more intimidated by Einstein's giant intellect, or the four-ton bronze statue in his honor. A quick skulking sniff of the 12-foot-tall statue's big toe confirmed the famed German physicist meant her no harm. The Albert Einstein Memorial allows you and your dog a relatively intimate visit with the genius, tucked away in an elm and holly grove on the southwest corner of the National Academy of Sciences. It's a quick encounter, one best combined with a longer walk around the Constitution Gardens, but a favorite. Located across the street from Constitution Gardens on the corner of 22nd St. 2101 Constitution Ave. NW; 202/334-2000; www.nationalacademies.org.

## 8 Lincoln Memorial
🐾 🐕 (See the Downtown map on page 26)

Although you're not allowed inside the memorial's dome with Fido in tow, even from the marble steps the view of "The Seated Lincoln" is powerful. The Great Emancipator stares out on the National Mall with a stern gaze that can soften depending on the light and time of day. Sculptor Daniel Chester French's 19-foot-high statue is among the top five sights you must see within the nation's capital, primarily for the view inside the memorial, but also for the one behind you. The Greek pantheon is the westernmost bookend of the Memorial Parks, with the Memorial Bridge crossing the Potomac River into Virginia to the west and the Washington Monument and Capitol rising to the east. The 36 Doric columns (a sort of invisible line you're not supposed to cross with your travel companion) represent the 36 states in the Union at the time of Lincoln's death. Free interpretive ranger talks are available via cell telephone by calling 202/747-3420, so you can learn about Honest Abe as you continue your dog walk. If you're famished, there is a snack shop nearby. Independence Ave. and 23rd St. NW; 202/426-6841; www.nps.gov/linc.

### 9 Korean War Veterans Memorial

 (See the Downtown map on page 26)

Denali felt ill-at-ease around the 19 stainless steel statues of soldiers staggered in a triangle and marching perpetually after an American flag in the "Forgotten War." Many of the helmet-clad soldiers wear expressions of exhaustion, and the memorial is especially eerie and lonely at night. When Denali let out a low growl at the figures draped in ponchos and carrying rifles she perceived to be a threat, we decided it was time to leave.

The Korean War Veterans Memorial honors the 1.5 million Americans who fought in the inconclusive, bloody, armed conflict to prevent South Korea from falling to Communism. Located just south of the Reflecting Pool, at Daniel French Drive and Independence Avenue. 202/426-6841; www.nps.gov/kowa.

### 10 JFK Memorial Hockey and Soccer Fields

(See the Downtown map on page 26)

This is one feature of the National Mall you won't find written up in most guidebooks. Most tourists are less keen on pinpointing uninterrupted grass fields. In the summertime, the athletic fields named for our 35th president are cordoned off with plastic fencing, as is much of the National Mall and Memorial Parks, but in other seasons they provide a landing strip–sized rectangle of open space to play with your pooch. It's proportioned similar to the National Mall itself, but smaller and more off the beaten path. The National Park Service sometimes lets the grass grow tall so that if you visit in the early, dewy morning, your pup's wet nose might get wetter and your socks might get damp. Teams do, in fact, play field hockey and soccer games here, but we've found the fields completely empty on most occasions.

Just south of the JFK fields you'll come across one of the capital's lesser known war memorials. The **World War I Memorial** is a stone Doric temple, the white marble of which has seen better days. Rin Tin Tin, the German shepherd rescued in France at the end of WWI before becoming a Hollywood top dog, might wonder at its unpretentious display. According to the DC Preservation League, "it was the first memorial on the Mall to list all DC residents who lost their lives in the war, regardless of their race, class, or gender." The memorial is 40 feet in diameter and large enough to hold the 80-member U.S. Marine Corps Band, but it's a modest statement compared to the nearby World War II Memorial. Located south of the Reflecting Pond and north of Independence Avenue. 202/426-6841; www.nps.gov/nacc.

# Downtown and Penn Quarter

Downtown DC can be a bustling, daunting place even for the bone-a fide city dog. In Downtown you'll find the financial district as well as Federal Triangle, a city wedge filled with many of the most recognizable three-letter govern-

## DOG-EAR YOUR CALENDAR

Lassie can pose for the paw-parazzi at these red carpet Washington Humane Society events.

**Sugar and Champagne Affair:** A dessert reception and silent auction featuring the crème de la crème of DC's pastry chefs, sparkling wines, champagne… and dogs! Tickets cost $85 per person to benefit the WHS's humane law enforcement and humane education programs. January; 202/723-5730, ext. 204; www.washhumane.org/events.asp.

**Bark Ball:** Washington's only black-tie gala for the four-to-the-floor crowd. Tickets cost $225 per person, and the fundraiser soiree occurs at a different upscale Downtown DC hotel every year. June; 202/723-5730 ext. 204; www.washhumane .org/barkball.asp.

ment acronyms. Even the power suits of Washington DC enjoy bringing Fido to Take Your Dog to Work Day (it's in June), but good luck without a proper badge and a trip through the metal detector. At least one corporate office, the Humane Society of the United States National Headquarters on L Street, has made a point to walk, or rather, wag, its talk and allows staff members to bring their dogs to work every day; of the 300 Humane Society employees, about one-third do.

As the business and tourism heart of Washington, Downtown and Penn Quarter also boast the majority of paw-friendly accommodations—some with five stars! Downtown is the closest Washington DC ever comes to feeling like a big city, but even here Pierre L'Enfant's carefully orchestrated squares and rotary circles bring green pockets into the densest parts of the District. Unlike New York City, here your pooch can avoid the indignity of squatting over a tiny sidewalk tree planter—a wider patch of grass is always only a short walk away. The section includes the city blocks east of 17th Street NW, south of M Street NW and Massachusetts Avenue NW, west of 1st Street NW, and north of Constitution Avenue NW.

## PARKS, BEACHES, AND RECREATION AREAS

### 11 Lafayette Square

🐾🐾 🐾 (See the Downtown map on page 26)

This manicured seven-acre park sits immediately in front of the most famous address in the country—1600 Pennsylvania Avenue—so it's no surprise the flower beds, grassy squares, and shade trees are tended with extra care and scrutiny. (Be sure to bring an extra plastic bag or two; we're not sure what Homeland Security might dream up if your dog poops this close to the White House's front stoop.) Downtown DC has other squares—Farragut, McPherson, Franklin—but they just don't measure up to Lafayette.

Lafayette Square affords a closer, more intimate view of the White House than from the iron fence on the South Lawn, where security measures bottleneck sightseers into a tightly packed crowd that's unforgiving to paws underfoot. Here in "President's Park," as it used to be called, White House staffers and tourists fill the pleasant benches during lunchtime—and you can do the same. If your pup is antsy and prefers to sniff around, head to center-square to admire the prominent statue of Andrew Jackson on a horse. At the time of its unveiling in 1853, it was the first equestrian statue in the country. A tribute to the park's namesake Lafayette, a French nobleman who helped champion the American Revolution, is located in the southeast corner of the park.

Note that Lafayette Square is typically calm, but not necessarily quiet. At the edge of the square you'll find anti-nuclear-war picketers-in-residence William Thomas or Concepción Picciotto, who have kept an ongoing "Truth and Peace Vigil" every day since 1981—that's more than a century in dog years. Located on H Street between 15th and 17th Streets NW.

## 12 The Ellipse
😺😺 (See the Downtown map on page 26)

Eleven months out of the year, the Ellipse is a grassy circle eclipsed by the White House immediately to its north. That's fine by Denali since it means most sightseers cluster at the South Lawn fence, leaving her more elbowroom. The Boy Scout Memorial is located nearby, as is the even lesser known Zero Milestone, a hip-high monument dating from the 1920s to honor the Army's first attempt to send a convoy of military vehicles cross-country. Denali likes to think of it as the Road Trip Memorial.

In December, the roles reverse and the Ellipse becomes the star attraction once the President flips the switch to light the National Christmas Tree, a tradition on the north side of the Ellipse since 1923. Bounded by Constitution Avenue and E, 15th, and 17th Streets.

### PLACES TO EAT

**Austin Grill:** This local chain Tex-Mex eatery is right around the corner from the furr-tabulous Hotel Monaco and within close range of the National Portrait Gallery, Spy Museum, and the Verizon Center (all three venues, unfortunately, not fur-friendly). In addition to accommodating doggies on the roped-off patio, Austin Grill is also very accommodating to people with gluten/wheat allergies (the perks of corn tortillas). Just ask the hostess for a gluten-free menu. 750 E St. NW; 202/393-3776; www.austingrill.com.

**Busboys and Poets:** The third and newest location of this poetry-slam-meets-comfort-food café has 15 dog-friendly outdoor tables. Like the original Busboys and Poets on 14th and V, it seeks to be "a restaurant, bookstore, and gathering place where people can discuss issues of social justice and peace," and the menu, like the clientele, is progressive and includes vegetarian and vegan options. For dinner, sample the catfish with corn cakes and collard greens, or try the rustic pizza. Weekend brunch is served until 3 P.M., and both the buckwheat waffles and French toast hit the spot. Busboys and Poets' name is a nod to African American poet Langston Hughes, who worked as a busboy at the Wardman Park Hotel in the 1930s before gaining recognition as a poet. The Mount Vernon Triangle location paws the somewhat arbitrary line between where Downtown DC ends and Northwest DC begins, but if you're in Chinatown, it's only a few more blocks over. Located at 5th and K Street NW. 1025 5th St. NW; 202/789-2227; www.busboysandpoets.com.

**Equinox:** Freshness of ingredients and concern for animal welfare pair like peas and carrots at one of DC's finer restaurants. Chef Todd Gray uses fresh, organic ingredients grown within 100 miles of the restaurant whenever possible, giving his food a distinctly Mid-Atlantic flavor, and the menu identifies dishes made from animals raised in accordance with Humane Farm Animal Care guidelines. "Locavore" diners and their dogs are invited to sup at the eight or nine tables outside, and servers will usually bring refreshments for all. In fact, co-owners and dog lovers Todd and Ellen Gray host the Washington Humane Society's "Sugar and Champagne Affair," a fundraiser they created. It bears mentioning that Denali, on her writer's assistant budget, can only afford to eat at Equinox on the summer and winter solstices. Dinner for two will easily top $100. 818 Connecticut Ave. NW; 202/331-8118; www.equinoxrestaurant.com.

**Gordon Biersch:** Gordon Biersch is known for its authentic-style German lager beers that follow the strict specifications of the Rinheitsgebot, a 1516 law that says beer can be brewed with only four ingredients: barley, hops, yeast, and water. After settling on a hefeweizen, we never got past the appetizer page of the menu, so distractingly tasty were the gorgonzola pear salad, crispy artichoke hearts, and signature garlic fries. The hostess recommended the Italian sausage and ground beef meat loaf as her favorite entrée. Denali hopes for a doggy bag next time. Centrally located in Penn Quarter, the restaurant resides in the restored 1891 Riggs Bank, with 12 dog-friendly tables on the seasonal patio. *Prost,* puppies! 900 F St. NW; 202/783-5454; www.gordonbiersch.com.

**Park Place Gourmet:** This cafeteria-style eatery caters to the corporate lunch crowd (open 6 A.M.–4:30 P.M. Mon.–Fri.) but welcomes friendly pups at the awning-covered metal picnic tables fastened to the sidewalk out front. Most eaters are in a rush to grab their food and go, so we've rarely seen the outdoor seating crowded. If it is, simply walk across the street to a park bench in Farragut Square. Located on the corner of 17th and I Sts. 1634 I St. NW; 202/783-4496.

**Penn Quarter Sports Tavern:** The covered patio might be a tight squeeze for big breeds, but smaller Redskins-rootin' Rovers will feel right at home. The menu sticks to the playbook with classic American sports bar fare, such as beer-battered fish sandwiches and quesadillas. Stop by for casual dining and the latest score. Located near 7th and D Sts. NW. 639 Indiana Ave. NW; 202/347-6666; www.shelfdc.com.

**Poste:** Is Hotel Monaco's modern brasserie dog-friendly? "Oh, definitely," came a server's emphatic reply. Canine patrons can cozy up under the 15 or 16 outdoor tables in Poste's garden-style courtyard, and the wait staff usually brings water for doggy diners. The handmade goat cheese ravioli stuffed with organic beets, crispy shallots, and pine nuts comes highly recommended, though not cheap; most Poste entrées range $20–30. The upscale restaurant is accessed through a historic carriageway portal, which we had always assumed led indoors, and is named for the 1841 General Post Office sorting room where it now resides. 555 8th St. NW; 202/783-6060; www.postebrasserie.com.

**Teaism:** If you're looking for light, Asian-inspired fare, Teaism is your best bet within reasonable walking distance of the Mall. Tie up your pooch, order takeout, and head to the nearby U.S. Navy Memorial Plaza with its sprawling map of the globe to sip and sup. Also check out Teaism's Lafayette Square location (800 Connecticut Ave. NW; 202/835-2233), which has fur-friendly patio seating. 400 8th St. NW; 202/638-6010; www.teaism.com.

## PLACES TO STAY

**Hamilton Crowne Plaza:** Medium-size dogs may stay at the elegant, restored 1920s boutique hotel—but it's a gamble. Your $250 deposit could be docked due to noise disturbance. Fortunately, each of the Hamilton's 318 rooms features a way to counteract the yap: a CD player to play FiFi's most soothing musical selection. Human guests enjoy plush accommodations including royal blue robes and a seven-layer bed. Pets are permitted only in third-floor rooms. Rates range $99–650. Located on 14th and K Sts. NW. 1001 14th St. NW; 202/682-0111; www.hamiltonhoteldc.com.

**The Hay-Adams:** Small, *refined* dogs are welcome at this historic hotel. "Dogs must be trained, not running around like a Tasmanian devil," the woman at the front desk explained in an upper-crust European accent. For pups weighing 25 pounds or less, the Hay-Adams offers lavish accommodations in one of Washington's finest luxury hotels. Dogs stay free of charge in the hotel's 145 rooms; however, owners must sign a waiver accepting liability for damages should your Pomeranian, say, shred the custom Italian bed linens. Rates range $700–1,000, with lower weekend rates available. Valet parking is $35 overnight plus tax. Located across Lafayette Square from the White House. 16th and H St. NW; 202/638-6600; www.hayadams.com.

**Hotel Monaco:** The bellman didn't blink an eye as Denali trotted up the narrow, canopied entrance. This Kimpton hotel continues to live up to its

## DIVERSIONS

The best way to learn about Washington's past is to hear it from the experts. These walking tours allow Lassie to participate in the learning.

**Anecdotal History Tours:** Although journalist-turned-tour-guide Anthony S. Pitch is only offering private group tours these days, he says, "All my tours are dog-friendly" (assuming dog-friendly transportation can be arranged). 301/294-9514; www.dcsightseeing.com.

**Spies of Washington Tours:** Learn all about Washington espionage in a special two-hour walking tour arranged for DC-area dogs and their humans. colleen@prosinthecity.com; www.spiesofwashingtontour.com.

**Tourmobile Sightseeing:** Dogs small enough to be scooped up and comfortably carried on your lap may ride the Tourmobile tram. 202/554-5100 or 888/868-7707; www.tourmobile.com.

**Washington Walk Tours:** These dog-friendly, reasonably priced walking tours require no reservations and take place rain or shine. 202/484-1565; www.washingtonwalks.com.

reputation for guest hospitality for pets and people alike. Every evening 5:30–6:30 P.M. guest dogs and their humans are invited to the hotel lobby for a complimentary wine and beer hour. Denali, a firm teetotaler, preferred the bottled water and biscuit provided by the hotel. Besides a dose of canine conviviality, the Hotel Monaco brings to your room water and food bowls, free of charge. Dog food is even on the room service menu. Located kitty-corner to the National Portrait Gallery and the Spy Museum. Rates range $250–1,000. 700 F St. NW; 202/628-7177; www.monaco-dc.com.

**The Madison, a Loews Hotel:** Per the concierge: "We'll do whatever needs to be done to make your dog happy." Dogs 100 pounds or less are permitted at the Madison for a $25 one-time cleaning fee. Upon check-in you'll receive a goody bag with dog dish, place mat, and walking map, each imprinted with "Loews Loves Dogs." One caveat: if your darling Doberman makes a ruckus while you're out museum-hopping and neighboring guests complain, hotel staff will escort your pooch to a back room behind the front reception. News hounds will be keen to know *The Washington Post* building is one block down the street. Rates range $189–599. 1177 15th St. NW; 202/862-1600; www.loewshotels.com/madison.

**The Quincy:** This unpresuming hotel, tucked next to the popular James Mackey Irish pub, has some of the best rates Downtown. Small dogs (40 pounds and under) are allowed for a less-cheap $150 fee. Dogs may be left unattended in the hotel, contingent on good behavior. Each room comes equipped with a coffeemaker, microwave, refrigerator, and free Wi-Fi. In high season, the 99-room hotel reaches full occupancy so it's best to reserve well in advance. Rates range $119–209. Guest parking is available for $28 per night. 1823 L St. NW; 202/223-4320; www.thequincy.com.

**Red Roof Inn Downtown Washington DC:** At the northeast edge of Chinatown you'll find this reasonably priced hotel. One dog weighing 20 pounds or less is permitted per room for no additional charge. If you leave him or her in the room alone, be sure to let the front desk know so housekeeping doesn't stray into your room while you're away. Hotel amenities include an exercise facility with sauna and a coin-operated laundry. Depending on events Downtown, the hotel can book up. It's best to make arrangements in advance. Rates range $119–309. 500 H St. NW; 202/289-5959; www.redroof-washington-dc-downtown.com.

**Renaissance Mayflower Hotel:** Washington's largest luxury hotel has hosted an inaugural ball for nearly every president since Calvin Coolidge, as well as harbored a political affair or two (most notably Clinton and Lewinsky and former New York Governor Eliot Spitzer). Small dogs (30 pounds or smaller) may check into any of the 583 rooms or 74 suites for a $200 fee. Should your pint-sized pooch feel dwarfed inside the bustling, block-long lobby, perhaps set him at ease with FDR's famous quote: "The only thing we have to fear is fear itself." The president-elect penned these words in rooms 776 and 781 while he and his family waited to move into the White House, four blocks away. Rates range $199–509. Valet parking is $35 overnight. 1127 Connecticut Ave. NW; 202/347-3000; www.marriott.com.

**Residence Inn by Marriott, Vermont Ave:** Designed for longer-stay visitors, including dogs of any size, the Residence Inn includes kitchens in each room and complimentary breakfast for guests on the go. Pets stay for a $100 fee plus an additional $8 per day cleaning fee. Valet parking is available for $20 a day with in/out privileges (though no vehicles taller than 6 feet). Rates range $209–389. Located near Thomas Circle. 1199 Vermont Ave. NW; 202/898-1100; www.marriott.com.

**Sofitel Lafayette Square Washington:** Dogs are tame fare for the Sofitel Lafayette Square—this swanky spot once accommodated a cheetah. There are no size restrictions and no fees, but housekeeping won't clean your room if your dog is left alone inside. Dogs are permitted on the popular patio of Le Bar, where cozy outdoor seating goes nicely with some of the best martinis in town. Rates range $330–600. 806 15th St, NW; 202/730-8800; www.sofitel.com.

**The St. Regis, Washington DC:** Renovated in 2007, the 1927 St. Regis reigns on in updated opulence, fairly dripping with crystal chandeliers, ornate ceilings, rich upholstery—and butlers! Small canines in accoutrement (25 pounds or less) may check in for a $100 fee plus an additional $25 per day charge, with one pet per room. To set tails wagging, the executive chef personally designed martini-shaped and "pseudo cannoli" dog biscuits, which room service delivers in a silver bowl. Dogs cannot be left in the room unattended; however, hotel staff—or this book—can recommend nearby doggy daycare facilities. Rates range $495–3,200. 16th and K St. NW; 202/638-2626; www.stregis.com/washingtondc.

# Foggy Bottom

Sounds like "Froggy Bottom," thinks Denali, licking her chops. In fact, Foggy Bottom earned its name from the fog rising off the Potomac River and the industrial smog that would hang thick in the air in the 1800s; it is one of the oldest neighborhoods in Washington. Today Foggy Bottom, sometimes called the West End, is a delightfully walkable neighborhood of tree-lined streets with an understated collegiate atmosphere thanks to George Washington University. (Actually, *The* George Washington University; with so many "George" schools in the DC metro area, GW makes a point to distinguish itself.) This section includes the city blocks east of the Potomac River, south of M Street, west of 17 Street NW, and north of Constitution Avenue NW.

### PLACES TO EAT

**Blue Duck Tavern:** Named number 12 on *Washingtonian Magazine's* list of the 100 Best Restaurants 2008, this pricey West End neighborhood tavern will treat you to wholesome American fare. Inside the tavern, patrons can watch the culinary action in the open staff pantry and wood-burning-stove kitchen. Where you'll be dining alfresco with your pupster on the patio, it's easy to appreciate the umbrella shade and splashing fountain in the background. Located in the Park Hyatt Hotel. 24th and M Sts. NW; 202/419-6755; www.blueducktavern.com.

**Potbelly Sandwich Works:** This sandwich shop is located on the street level of George Washington University's aptly named Ivory Tower residence hall. Potbelly has one of the largest street-side fenced patios in the neighborhood and tastier eats than you'll find at Subway or Quiznos. There is a bow-wow-ntiful selection of sandwiches, and the price is right (less than $6 for a sandwich). Had Denali the gift of speech (and quoting movies), she might drop this infamous *Austin Powers* one-liner: "Get in my belly!" 616 23rd St. NW; 202/242-8700; www.potbelly.com.

**Sizzling Express:** With dozens of fresh salad, pasta, sushi, hot entrée, and sandwich choices inside, and at least two dozen umbrella-covered tables in the courtyard outside, Sizzling Express is an easy go-to for lunch with your doggy. The quality of service is predictable—you serve yourself. Sizzling Express is a pay-by-the-ounce buffet, which can quickly get a smidge pricey if your eyes

are bigger than your stomach. Your pooch will have to wait outside while you tackle the buffet line. Located in the Columbia Plaza. 538 23rd St. NW; 202/659-1234; www.sizzlingexpress.com.

**Tonic at Quigley's Pharmacy:** Billing itself as "American comfort food with a twist," Tonic at Quigley's Pharmacy offers pleasant patio dining. In 1891, its brick building originally opened as a pharmacy owned by a GW alumnus (can you guess his name?), then operated as an administrative building for the university, and now serves barbecue wings, mac and cheese, and beer on tap to undergrads. Best of all: "Of course you can bring your pooch!" says the general manager. The restaurant doesn't reserve the 10 outdoor tables due to the unpredictable weather in DC, but there's rarely a long wait. 2036 G St. NW; 202/296-0211; www.tonicrestaurant.com.

## PLACES TO STAY

**Doubletree Guest Suites:** Since the Doubletree is within easy walking distance of the John F. Kennedy Center for the Performing Arts, this is a great place to stay if you plan to see a show or concert (and hotel policy says it's OK to leave Lassie in the room). Should your dog like to howl *a cappella* with ambulance sirens, however, be forewarned that George Washington University Hospital is just up the street. The Doubletree has no size restrictions but also no pet amenities; dogs can occupy the hotel's lower level only for a $20 per day per dog fee. Rates range $149–379. 801 New Hampshire Ave. NW; 202/785-2000; www.doubletree.com.

**The Fairmont:** Whenever you stay with your canine companion, the Fairmont donates 5 percent of the bill to the Washington Animal Rescue League—reason enough to check in. Add to that complimentary dog biscuits baked by the hotel's pastry chef, a peaceful garden courtyard, and service noted by one reviewer as "on par with the nearby Ritz-Carlton," and most pooches are on board with this "do good, feel good" experience. The Fairmont welcomes all breeds ("We've had Great Danes stay here before") and the concierge genuinely seemed delighted to greet four-legged guests. Dogs stay for free, but owners must sign a damage waiver and pups cannot be left unattended in rooms. Rates range $279–1,350. Located just east of Georgetown on M Street. 2401 M St. NW; 202/429-2400; www.fairmont.com/washington.

**The Melrose Hotel, Washington DC:** While the 240-room Melrose Hotel officially draws the line at 50-pound dogs for a $100 fee, no one complained when 62-pound Denali crossed the marble foyer. In fact, one of the clerks noted her spots and chatted about his two Dalmatians and Labrador at home. Rates range $289–409. 2430 Pennsylvania Ave. NW; 202/955-6400; www.melrosehoteldc.com.

**Park Hyatt Washington DC:** Denali wished she'd had a bath before stepping paw in this sleek, glass-faced hotel. Fortunately, the front desk was still willing to check her into one of the 215 generously sized rooms for a $150 fee, which goes for all dogs, stinky or clean. Unlike the Fairmont across the street, Park Hyatt permits pups to be left in the room alone, and dogs are also allowed on the classy Blue Duck Tavern's patio. Weekday rates start at $549, with lower weekend rates available. 1201 24th Ave. NW; 202/789-1234; www.parkwashington.hyatt.com.

**Ritz Carlton, Washington DC:** From the first step inside this 300-room luxury hotel, the interior has the warm glow of burnished wood you would expect from a Ritz. It's the kind of ambience that leaves your dog thinking, *There must be filet mignon around here somewhere.* Well-behaved dogs weighing 25 pounds or less can stay for a $125 fee, but no more than two per room. Canine guests are permitted in their guest room, hallways, the lobby, and the *porte-cochère* (that would be "coach door" or "carriage door"—don't worry, Denali had to look it up too). As a sign of the Ritz's famous attention to detail, size-appropriate dog pillows are provided so your Chihuahua need not feel overwhelmed in a bed built for a corgi. Rates range $299–5,800. 1150 22nd St. NW; 202/835-0500; www.ritzcarlton.com/washingtondc.

**The River Inn:** Situated on a quiet street of attractive brownstones, though not quite the Potomac River, this 125-suite hotel accepts all sizes of dogs for a $150 fee. The River Inn does not offer special pet amenities, but the hotel lounge and on-site restaurant have framed prints of William Wegman's famed weimaraners on the walls—which Denali took as a good omen. The spacious rooms include full kitchens and free wireless Internet and Nintendo, not that it does critters lacking opposable thumbs much good. Rates range $99–399. 924 25th St. NW; 202/337-7600; www.theriverinn.com.

**The Westin Grand:** Completing the trio of pet-friendly hotels together with the Park Hyatt and the Fairmont in the trendy West End, the Westin Grand invites dogs 40 pounds or less to stay (though not without a $50 deposit and signed damage waiver). Dog bed, toy, and plastic cleanup bags are provided. Located just east of Georgetown on M Street, adjacent to the Fairmont. Rates are $229–1,200. 2350 M St. NW; 202/429-0100; www.westin.com/washingtondc.

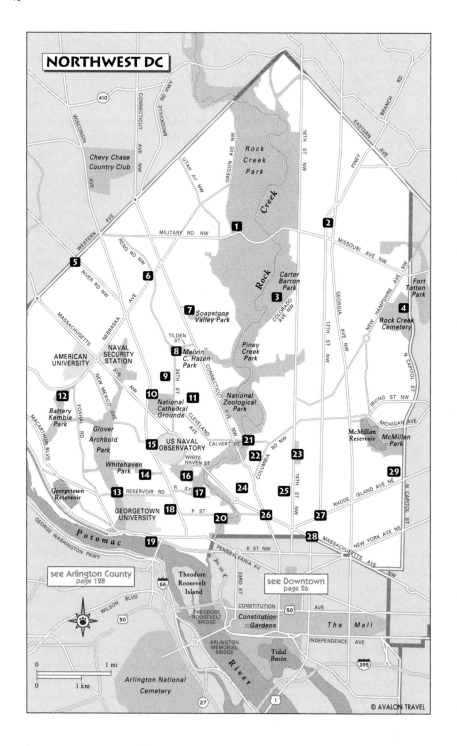

# CHAPTER 2

# Northwest DC

Without question, Northwest DC is the doggiest territory in the District. If you're new to the neighborhood or new to puppies, rest assured that you're soon to make many new friends. With the wagging bundle of fluff at the end of your leash, you will break the code into one of DC's best secret societies. No, not Skull and Bones, we mean the Dog People. Neighbors in your apartment building who formerly coughed to ignore you in the elevator will be falling over themselves to set up playdates between your puppies. Perfect strangers will walk up to you and strike up a conversation about clicker training. Within two weeks you'll have a half dozen new acquaintances known not by their first names but as "Gracie's mom" or "Napoleon's dad."

Not to say the sweet life has always been served on a silver kibble bowl for DC dogs. Historically, the city's dogs, the majority of whom live in Northwest DC, have found themselves somewhat marginalized citizens in the District. Unlike New York, Boston, San Francisco, Los Angeles, Seattle, or Chicago, dog

## PICK OF THE LITTER—NORTHWEST DC

BEST PARKS
**Rock Creek Park,** throughout Northwest DC (page 49)
**Soapstone Valley Park,** Cleveland Park (page 59)
**Dumbarton Oaks Park,** Georgetown (page 68)
**Montrose Park,** Georgetown (page 69)

BEST PLACES TO EAT
**Amsterdam Falafelshop,** Adams Morgan (page 78)
**Commissary,** Logan Circle (page 88)

BEST PLACE TO STAY
**Hotel Palomar,** Dupont Circle (page 84)

BEST PLACE TO GET HIGH (UP)
**Fort Reno Park,** Tenleytown (page 56)

BEST PLACE TO SHOP
**U Street and 14th Street,** Logan Circle, Shaw, and U Street
(pages 86–87)

BEST HOTEL YAPPY HOUR
**Hotel Helix,** Logan Circle (page 89)

parks are not a common feature in the cityscape. At the outset of research-ing this book, not a single official city-owned, fenced, off-leash dog park had opened. It has been a contentious dogfight for years, not least of which when the District initially said the Health Department would have to certify a pro-posed dog park site was rat-free. For a five-block radius. In a city.

But all that is changing. A new era for Washington paws has finally arrived, largely driven by dogged efforts—for a decade or more—of dog lovers in Northwest DC and elsewhere in the city. In 2008, the DC Department of Parks and Recreation began approving the creation of a handful of official dog parks, and Mayor Adrian Fenty earmarked $1.2 million to go toward their construc-tion, setting into motion legislation passed three years earlier. Those proposed sites are noted throughout this chapter and elsewhere in the book. As a sign that times really are changing, the DC DPR opened a temporary dog park at Shaw Junior High School to tide over the pent-up pets until the other official off-leash parks open.

Northwest DC includes a huge swath of the city—about 40 percent of all the land in the District and much of its parkland. There's much to see and even more to explore. This chapter includes the northwest quadrant of Washington DC from its northern border with Montgomery County, Maryland, to the Potomac River and M Street to the south, and N. Capitol Street to the east.

# Chevy Chase

National Lampoon jokes aside, yes, there's actually a community (and a bank) named Chevy Chase. And no, they're not named after the actor. Most of Chevy Chase lies in Maryland, but it straddles Western Avenue with one foot in Washington DC. In this well-to-do DC village and its neighbors Hawthorne and Barnaby Woods, there's a better chance dogs will have a backyard of their own in what was developed in the early 1900s as a planned "streetcar suburb." Chevy Chase has the telltale signs of a suburb—front lawns, Subarus, and single-family homes—only in the city instead. With Rock Creek Park beckoning conveniently to the east, Chevy Chase dogs are a lucky bunch. This section includes the area east of Reno Road, south of Western Avenue, west of Rock Creek Park's east border, and north of Broad Branch Road and Military Road.

## PARKS, BEACHES, AND RECREATION AREAS

### 1 Rock Creek Park
🐾🐾🐾🐾 🦴 (See the Northwest DC map on page 46)

Inside the wooded hollows of 1,754-acre Rock Creek Park, you will hardly believe you are inside a major city of more than half a million people. Rock Creek Park winds through DC's Northwest quadrant like a forested backbone, connecting different neighborhoods to its streambeds. For water dogs and retriever types, the creek offers a refreshing reprieve from the sweltering summer humidity, and for landlubber pups, there remains an extensive network of trails to explore. Put simply, Rock Creek Park is the cornerstone of doggy playgrounds in Washington DC.

Because Rock Creek Park bisects Northwest DC, nearly every neighborhood in this chapter has at least one point of access to the park. We include several favorite places below, not all of which are necessarily close to Chevy Chase or Hawthorne; we also note numerous spurs and side trails to Rock Creek Park in the sections to come.

Each weekend, sections of Beach Drive, the main road that runs the length of the park, are closed to traffic. Cyclists, rollerbladers, and joggers quickly replace the cars. Sometimes you'll see leashed dogs walking in their midst, but Denali asks, why dodge the weekend warriors on pavement when there are trails to explore? Just the word trails is enough to set her whining excitedly.

The northern reaches of Rock Creek Park stretch beyond the Montgomery County-DC line, but here at Boundary Bridge is where the green-blazed

## DETOURS

Do your errands around town where you can bring your hound.

**C & C Custom Cleaners:** Dog sheds on suit. Suit goes to dry cleaner. Dog joins you to pick up suit. Repeat. 5511 Connecticut Ave. NW; 202/364-2227.

**Happy Paws:** Pet food and supplies, grooming, and cage-free daycare and boarding. 4904 Wisconsin Ave. NW; 202/363-7297; www.happypawsdc.net.

**Hudson Trail Outfitters:** Backpacking in West Virginia? Make Fluffy carry in her own food. She can select a dog backpack at Hudson Trail Outfitters. 4530 Wisconsin Ave. NW; 202/363-9810; www.hudsontrail.com.

**Monarch Paint:** What shade should you paint the den? Bring along your canine color consultant. 5608 Connecticut Ave. NW; 202/686-5550; www.monarchpaintdc.com.

**Politics and Prose:** Find a new title in animal rights activism together. 5015 Connecticut Ave. NW; 202/364-1919; www.politics-prose.com.

**PetMAC:** Quality, natural pet foods with a portion of proceeds benefiting Homeward Trails, a dog rescue organization. 4220 Fessenden St. NW; 202/966-PETS; www.petmac.org.

**Tenleytown Ace Hardware:** Dogs are welcome at the "subterranean" hardware store. You'll find it in the parking garage level of the Cityline building beneath The Container Store. 4500 Wisconsin Ave. NW; 202/364-1902; www.acehardwaredc.com/tenleytown.html.

Western Ridge Trail and the flat Valley Trail begin. These are the two primary footpaths that run north–south through Rock Creek Park. Be warned that even the best trail hounds can get lost on the frequently unmarked trails that diverge from these main two, so allow yourself enough daylight to find your way back to the car or apartment. Or consider buying a detailed trail map if you plan to explore in earnest (the Potomac Appalachian Trail Club sells a good one; www.potomacappalachian.org).

A great launch pad into Rock Creek Park if you're arriving by car is the **Pierce Mill Art Barn** at the corner of Tilden Street (same as Park Road) and Beach Drive. The parking lot typically has open spaces, and the grassy picnic area is popular with the pups and a pleasant place to spend a free morning or afternoon. Plus the Western Ridge, Valley, and Melvin Hazen Trails all converge near here.

Another go-to spot is **Military Road** at the parking lot not far from Picnic Area 22 and the Park Police Rock Creek Station. There is a really stunning, secluded trail on the west bank of Rock Creek south of Military Road that passes Rapids Bridge and Pulpit Rock, with lovely scenery along the way. Dogs howl with delight for the shade and creek and sandy trail. When Beach Drive is closed, you can access this parking lot from the west side of the park (driving east on Military Road from Chevy Chase).

Denali's all-time-favorite Rock Creek haunt is a tucked-away dirt trail that we've yet to learn the name of, so we'll dub it the **Woodley Park-Dumbarton Oaks Shortcut,** since that's the route. We typically pick up the trail at Dumbarton Oaks Park in Georgetown, but you can just as easily start in Woodley Park. Parallel park as close to 24th Street as you can, and then descend the steep sidewalk past a grassy area with exercise equipment toward Rock Creek. When you come to the pedestrian footbridge, don't cross it but veer right onto the dirt trail instead. You're bound to meet doggy friends along the way, especially at the swimming hole about a mile down.

An interesting bit of trivia: Rock Creek Park has the largest density of raccoons in the United States. We've never seen one, but that's probably because we don't venture into Rock Creek Park after dusk—generally a good rule of thumb. 202/895-6000; www.nps.gov/rocr.

## PLACES TO EAT

**Parthenon:** Just a few doors down from the Avalon Theater, the oldest surviving movie house in Washington, you'll find the Parthenon, a house of Greek eats that's nearly as venerable. You can dine on reasonably priced, authentic Greek cuisine alongside the front patio's baby blue canopy with your dog at your feet. 5510 Connecticut Ave. NW; 202/966-7600; www.parthenon-restaurant.com.

**Señor Pepper:** With her birthplace in Southern California, Denali's standards for Mexican food might be higher than some. She was pleased to find

Señor Pepper hits closer to the mark than most in DC. The free chips and salsa are nice, too. *Perros* are permitted on the patio. 5507 Connecticut Ave. NW; 202/244-7774.

# Petworth and 16th Street Heights

When Denali learned that a neighborhood on the other side of Rock Creek Park was named Petworth, she thought she must have found Washington's Mutt Mecca. She was only partly right. Located northeast of the Petworth neighborhood, you'll find one of the brightest spots for homeless animals in the entire country: the Washington Animal Rescue League. In fact, WARL attracts experts from around the world who come to tour the enlightened facility, which was built for creature comfort from the ground up.

In other parts of Petworth, 16th Street Heights, and surrounding neighborhoods, scratching out dog-friendly spots is more difficult. When the *Washington City Paper* nicknamed the neighborhood "Notyetworth" it created a furor in the blogosphere, but there is a bit of truth to the epithet, at least from a doggy's perspective. Petworth boasts a few novel canine diversions with room to grow. Often your best bet is to wander westward into the sea of green that is Rock Creek Park, but we've sniffed out some other highlights for you to enjoy: A hauntingly beautiful cemetery. An indoor doggy playground. A pet-friendly Slavic kitchen. So head up straight-as-an-arrow 16th Street, or Georgia Avenue, or N. Capitol Street, and decide for yourselves. This section includes the area east of Rock Creek Park, south of Eastern Avenue, west of N. Capitol Street, and north of Upshur Street.

## DIVERSION

Raining cats and dogs outside? **Little Rascals Indoor Off-Leash Dog Park** can shelter you from the downpour. What once was an old car warehouse has been converted to 7,000 square feet of heated doggie play space. Your little rascal can chase tennis balls across the epoxy-coated cement floor, balance on agility equipment, or tussle with a buddy as early as 6:30 A.M. daily. Think utilitarian when you visit: your seating choices include the back seat of a van and a few benches. But Little Rascals earns three solid "Arfs!" from Petworth pets. Daily passes cost $5 on weekdays and $7 on weekends, with monthly packages available, including reduced rates for multi-dog families. Little Rascals also offers daycare, boarding, grooming, and training services. And did we mention the free wireless Internet? 5917 Georgia Ave. NW; 202/669-0170; www.littlerascalsdogpark.com.

## PARKS, BEACHES, AND RECREATION AREAS

### 2 Fort Stevens Park

(See the Northwest DC map on page 46)

Yes, there were some empty Budweiser cans and broken glass marring the only Washington fort to see enemy fire during the Civil War, but Denali appreciated the novelty of crawling through the trenches of the lumpy landscape. Unlike most of the Fort Circle Parks where little remains of the Civil War strongholds, Fort Stevens has been partially restored to resemble its wartime heyday. Cleverly molded cement "logs" mimic the wooden walls that were once built into the hillside, and earthen parapets give you a sense of what it must have been like to peer around them and exchange gunfire with Confederate troops. Two cannons and a waving American flag complete the site. We wouldn't recommend planning your weekend around a visit, but if you're in the neighborhood it's worth stopping by. Located at 13th and Quackenbos St. NW; 202/895-6000; www.nps.gov/cwdw.

### 3 Carter Barron Park

(See the Northwest DC map on page 46)

*... And dog will have his day.*

Hamlet, Prince of Denmark, Act 5, Scene 1

Best known for the outdoor Carter Barron Amphitheater, where you can listen to music under the stars (they're up there somewhere) or watch a free community performance from the Shakespeare Theatre Company, this corner of Rock Creek Park should be on every Washingtonian's "try it at least once" list. Sadly, dogs are not allowed in the amphitheater, so even Shakespeare-loving curs are barred from seeing the Bard performed in the 3,750-seat venue. From a canine perspective, the reason to come to Carter Barron Park are the large grass athletic fields near the park entrance or the parking lot's easy access to the Rock Creek trails. Time your visit strategically: Morning is the best time to visit the fields since soccer leagues usually take to the grass after work. If looking for a hike, the connector trail begins at picnic site number 24, which is to the right as you enter the park. This side trail descends to meet the Valley Trail, one of the two main footpaths through Rock Creek Park. Walk south (or to the left) on Valley Trail and you'll be rewarded with lovely scenery past Rapids Bridge. Continue for a little less than a mile and you'll reach the swimming hole by Pulpit Rock, a favorite for dog paddling and fetch. 16th St. and Colorado Ave. NW; 202/895-6000; www.nps.gov/rocr.

## ⁴ Rock Creek Cemetery

🐾🐾 (See the Northwest DC map on page 46)

The Gothic beauty of this silent city beckons as you drive past on North Capitol Street. St. Paul's Episcopal Church, established in 1712, is the only surviving colonial church in Washington DC and it maintains the cemetery, which is nearly as old, dating back to 1719. As long as your leashed companion doesn't pee on the historic headstones, you're more than welcome to take a contemplative dog walk through 86-acre Rock Creek Cemetery. While an afternoon jaunt through a graveyard might seem kooky these days, the cemetery was designed as part of the rural cemetery movement to function both as a final resting place and as a public park. And indeed this is one of the largest green patches in Petworth outside of Rock Creek Park proper. While Congressional Cemetery in Capitol Hill South wins as the all-time doggy favorite for its off-leash privileges, the tranquility of Rock Creek Cemetery is part of the draw. In fact, besides the security guard driving laps around the sizable cemetery, you'll probably have the place to yourselves.

The most famous statue in the cemetery sits in the Adams Memorial, located in section E near the church (maps are available at the cemetery office). Commonly called *Grief*, the cloaked, bronze figure bears no inscription, no title, and no dates. Henry Adams commissioned the memorial in 1886, after his wife committed suicide. The cemetery gates open at 7:30 A.M. and close at dusk. Rock Creek Church Rd.; 202/829-0585; www.rockcreekparish.org/cemetery.

### PLACES TO EAT

**Domku:** Unless your pet name for your pup is "my little pierogi," Domku

## DOG-EAR YOUR CALENDAR

The **Washington Animal Rescue League's PawFest** is an annual open house showcasing the shelter's animal rehabilitation and adoption center. And what a facility! The oldest animal shelter in Washington DC underwent a dramatic remodel in 2005 and 2006, transforming it into a therapeutic haven to soothe the frazzled nerves of its animal inhabitants. Gone are the steel-bar cages and cold cement floors, the kennel cough, and dogs barking themselves hoarse. Instead you'll find individual "dog dens" built with glass brick, radiant heating, individual airflow vents, Murphy beds with Posturepedic mattresses, and the constant, calming sound of running water. The open house features reunions for pet alumni and refreshments and entertainment for both people and animals. PawFest usually takes place in late October. 71 Oglethorpe St. NW; 202/726-2556; www.warl.org.

might be the first place you'll hear of these stuffed dumplings. Other Slavic and Scandinavian specialties on the menu are equally tricky to pronounce and just as delicious: gravlax (salt- and herb-cured salmon), *nalesniki* (Polish crepes), kielbasa (Polish sausage), and if your tongue fails you on all of these, just point to the Swedish meatballs. Domku invites dogs to its outside seating: four small tables arranged behind white planters of sunflowers and herbs. *"Witamy w domku"* means "Welcome to the little house" in Polish. Denali wonders how to say, "Welcome to the little patio." 821 Upshur St. NW; 202/722-7475 www.domkucafe.com.

## PLACES TO STAY

**Motel 6—Washington:** One small dog is permitted per room at this reasonably priced 72-room motel. Besides free parking, free coffee each morning, and wireless Internet in all rooms, this Motel 6 has expanded cable and a seasonal outdoor pool. Rates range $80–90. 6711 Georgia Ave.; 202/722-1600; www.motel6.com.

# Tenleytown and Friendship Heights

In some respects Tenallytown, as it was known back in the day, is not so different now than when it was founded. Eighteenth-century locals frequented John Tenally's roadside tavern, which stood near where Wisconsin Avenue meets River Road. After throwing back a few pints, someone must have shouted to the bartender, "Tenally, we should name the town after you!" And so they did. Tenleytown is still a social place with American University in its midst, and it's a paw-friendly part of town, too, with two specialty pet stores and numerous sidewalk cafés where dogs can hang with the family during dinner. American University is also home to DC's NPR radio station, WAMU 88.5, which airs the pet-centric radio show *Calling All Pets* at 7 A.M. Saturday.

This section encompasses several neighborhoods, including Tenleytown, Friendship Heights, American University Park, Forest Hills (or Van Ness, as it's often called), and Spring Valley. It includes the area north of Loughboro, Nebraska, and Van Ness Streets, east of Western Avenue, south of Military Road and Broad Branch Road, and west of Rock Creek Park.

## PARKS, BEACHES, AND RECREATION AREAS

### 🖪 Fort Bayard Park

🐾 (See the Northwest DC map on page 46)

What today is a quiet neighborhood park once served as a strategic military site for the nation's capital during the Civil War. The capital's only defense was Fort Washington, a relic from the War of 1812 located 12 miles down the Potomac River. The industrious Army Corps of Engineers promptly beefed it up to help protect President Lincoln and his military advisers. According to the

## DOG-EAR YOUR CALENDAR

Lace up your training shoes and head to the Washington Animal Rescue League's **Mutts Strut,** a two-mile dog walk or 5K (3.1-mile) run that raises money for the no-kill shelter located on Oglethorpe Road NW. The run is for humans only, but dogs are welcome on the two-mile walk. The event usually takes place at American University in the first weekend of June. As many as 700 people and 350 dogs have strutted their stuff in previous years. 202/726-2556; www.warl.org.

National Parks Service, "by spring 1865, the defense system totaled 68 forts and 93 batteries with 807 cannons and 98 mortars in place... Washington had become the most heavily fortified city in the world."

Your dog can enjoy the fruits of these engineers' labor by visiting Fort Bayard Park or one of the other Civil War forts preserved as the Fort Circle Parks. Of the Fort Circle Parks, Fort Bayard is one of the nicer ones. Unfenced and hilly, there are picnic benches tucked strategically into shaded groves, a baseball diamond, and a fenced playground. Fort Bayard Park is bounded by Western Avenue, River Road, and Fessenden, 46th, and 47th Streets NW. Parking on Fessenden is conveniently close to a drinking fountain. 202/895-6000; www.nps.gov/cwdw.

## 6 Fort Reno Park

🐾🐾🐾 (See the Northwest DC map on page 46)

Mountain mutts pay attention: Fort Reno Park is the closest to an alpine summit you'll find in Washington DC. At 429 feet, this truncated grass hill is the highest point in the District.

After her initial sniff of disdain—she *is* named after a 20,320-foot mountain—Denali happily discovered Fort Reno is the best place in all of Washington DC to watch the sunset. If you park on Belt Road, you can march up a steep hillside and sit with your back against a chain-link fence to watch the show. This modest perch next to the fenced-off reservoir gives you a sense of height and perspective that's hard to find in this city except from the top of the National Cathedral or the Washington Monument, where dogs are not permitted.

Chances are good you'll have company here. This side of Fort Reno Park is so popular with Tenleytown tail-waggers that it has earned the moniker "Dog Hill," and you'll see why if you visit after work. Locals sometimes use the grassy slope as a *de facto* dog park, but leash laws still apply in this 33-acre federal park. After an arsenic scare in 2008 (that's a whole other story), the spot has been under more careful scrutiny by the National Parks Service and DC police, and both agencies have been ticketing with much more frequency, so be aware.

## DIVERSION

The summertime **Fort Reno Concert Series** welcomes dogs. Perhaps that's because if your rottweiler howls during the performance, frankly, no one will hear him. You won't find the Jonas Brothers performing here. Sandwiched between Woodrow Wilson Senior High School and Deal Middle School, and close to American University, this concert venue tends to be a younger scene. It's a place where the underage crowd can listen to DC's underground rock groups without having to borrow a fake I.D. to get into a club or bar. But you'll also find families with young kids here and even a die-hard music fan in her eighties who has coming since the series began in the late 1960s. The number of rock hounds in the audience has been growing steadily, too. The free concerts take place 7:15 P.M.–9:30 P.M. Monday and Thursday evenings mid-June through mid-August. Look for concert organizer Amanda MacKaye and her beagle Miller greeting newcomers to the show. 202/355-6356; www.fortreno.com; amanda@fortreno.com.

Dog Hill and a DC sunset are reason enough to visit, but there's more to see. As you round the park's midsection to explore more grass and sniffs—look, it's a castle! In fact, it's the Fort Reno Pumping Station, but the turreted towers would make King Arthur proud. Denali cocked her head as we continued past medieval times to the wider grassy area and wooden platform that is home to the dog-friendly Fort Reno Summer Concert Series.

Parking at Fort Reno is usually easy in the evenings, less so during the day. Parallel-park along Nebraska Avenue, Fessenden Street, Belt Road, or

## DOG-EAR YOUR CALENDAR

Any parent with a child at St. Ann's Academy can tell you that springtime means two things: Spring Carnival and Wagfest! Your leashed little one (no, not your three-year-old) doesn't have to be enrolled in the private Roman Catholic school to join in the fun. Every May, **St. Ann's Academy Wagfest** hosts doggy competitions with categories such as Most International, where pets compete for the most exotic pedigree, and Best Rescue. The competition entrance fee is $10, benefiting a scholarship fund for the school's students. Don't miss the pet parade around the school grounds. St. Ann's Academy is easy to find, just look for the St. Bernard–sized stone church of the same name on Tenley Circle. 4404 Wisconsin Ave. NW; www.stannsacademy.org.

Chesapeake Street NW, the four roads that bound the park; 202/895-6000; www.nps.gov/cwdw.

### PLACES TO EAT

**Café Ole:** Mosey up to the Café Ole for fresh Mediterranean cuisine and great tapas. With your chowhound in tow you will be seated under the green umbrellas on the patio. If dining on a Sunday, take advantage of the half-price bottles of wine with brunch or dinner. Café Ole is located on Wisconsin Avenue just past the estate-like (and, since the 2008 financial crisis, somewhat infamous) Fannie Mae Headquarters. 4000 Wisconsin Ave. NW; 202/244-1330; www.cafeoledc.com.

**Chef Geoff's:** Unlike the Downtown location, the original Chef Geoff's near Tenleytown is very paw-friendly. Dogs can lounge beneath your table on the patio, and restaurant owner and namesake Chef Geoff Tracy has been to known to host Yappy Hours for nonprofits such as PAL: People Animals Love (www.peopleanimalslove.com). The menu changes seasonally, but a co-worker who moonlights as a waitress there says you can't go wrong with the fresh tuna, no matter how it's plated. Other favorites among the contemporary American fare include the crab cakes and madras curry chicken. For appetizers, don't miss the tuna sashimi and duck spring rolls. 3201 New Mexico Ave. NW; 202/237-7800; www.chefgeoff.com.

# Woodley Park and Cleveland Park

Cleveland Park acquired its name after President Glover Cleveland bought property in the neighborhood hoping to find a secluded summer home. As one historian put it, so much for anonymity. Immediately to the south of Cleveland Park, Woodley Park has acquired famous residents of a different species altogether: Mei Xiang, Tian Tian, and their cub, Tai Shan, the National Zoo's family of giant pandas. No pets are allowed in the National Zoo, which is probably a good decision ("Ma, look! A poodle is in the lion den!"), but at least one species has escaped from the zoo to greet your pets. Every black squirrel in DC traces its lineage back to 18 Canadian jailbirds who made a run for it from the National Zoo during the presidency of Teddy Roosevelt. Denali hears they're extra tasty. This section includes the area east of Wisconsin Avenue, south of Van Ness Street, west of Rock Creek Park, and north of Calvert Street.

## PARKS, BEACHES, AND RECREATION AREAS

### 7 Soapstone Valley Park

🐾🐾🐾🐾 🐾 (See the Northwest DC map on page 46)

One of the loveliest corners of Rock Creek Park is cloistered away near Van Ness, not but a block away from Connecticut Avenue. While you won't find any soapstone left, the valley part of the name still holds true. A dirt trail maintained by the Potomac Appalachian Trail Club leads you through an intimate stream valley that grows closer in, greener, and more deeply set the farther you walk, until you reemerge into the sunlight on the shoulder of Broad Branch Road in Rock Creek Park. Your pup had best be up for getting her paws wet, and you should ready yourself for rock hopping, because there are many stream crossings along the way. After a downpour, you might want to reschedule your hike. Denali met an exuberant Jack Russell terrier who charged down the trail, showing her the way. If you don't come across such an enthusiastic guide, simply follow the direction the stream flows and the yellow blazes to Rock Creek Park proper, slightly less than a mile away. Make a careful dogleg across lanes of traffic and you can hook up with the Western Ridge Trail. Take this south and you can complete a loop with the Melvin C. Hazen Trail. Parallel-park on Albemarle Street. Open dawn to dusk. The trailhead is located at Albemarle and 32nd Street NW. 202/895-6000; www.nps.gov/rocr.

### 8 Melvin C. Hazen Park

🐾🐾 (See the Northwest DC map on page 46)

Another quiet offshoot of Rock Creek Park, Melvin C. Hazen Park provides a short, mostly shaded dog walk by itself or as a 1.5-mile passage to reach the grassy area next to the Art Barn. You can pick up the Melvin C. Hazen Trail in Cleveland Park from two places along Reno Road: at Rodman Road and at Tilden Street. Although the two entrances are just a block away from each other, your pooch will probably have a preference for the Tilden trailhead, which leads past a small lagoon pooled underneath a stormwater outtake—retriever heaven, if you're not too squeamish. (Do be careful though; at least one dog has fallen ill swimming in Broad Branch after someone dumped turpentine down a storm drain—grrrr.)

The yellow-blazed Melvin Hazen Trail is broken into two segments by Connecticut Avenue. The first half mile of the trail is flatter and feels slightly more urban, with the occasional tree trunk tagged by graffiti. Keep to the left when the trail splits and cross the wooden footbridge over the—dirty dog alert—very messy mud flats. If somehow your leash has slipped off your fellow hiker's neck along the way, be sure to reattach it now. You'll emerge in a parking lot behind an apartment complex, and busy Connecticut Avenue is straight ahead.

If traffic is brisk, which it usually is, head left to the crosswalk at Sedgwick Street less than a block uphill before doubling back on the other side. The second half of the Melvin C. Hazen Trail, from Connecticut Avenue to Rock Creek Park, is lovelier than the first. Creek water runs clearer here and sunlight filters softly into the narrow stream valley. Along the initial, steep switchbacks a surprising number of trees have fallen and stacked haphazardly in the gulley like pickup sticks, but the trail gets nicer as you go and then, once again, there you are—in the heart of Rock Creek Park! 202/895-6000; www.nps.gov/rocr.

## ⑨ Rosedale Conservancy

🐾🐾🐾 (See the Northwest DC map on page 46)

One of the best-manicured lawns in Cleveland Park belongs to one of DC's oldest houses; during certain hours of the day, it also belongs to local dogs. The 18th-century farmhouse Rosedale has perched on its grassy hill in Cleveland Park since Revolutionary War hero General Uriah Forrest purchased the land in the late 1700s. The Rosedale Conservancy, Cleveland Park's "village green," came about in 2002 through an impressive showing of neighborly preservation and fundraising.

In recent decades, Rosedale had been occupied first by the Washington Cathedral School, and then by the nonprofit Youth for Understanding (YFU), which both allowed neighbors to stroll on the grounds. (A doggy aside: The family of refugee Elian Gonzalez stayed in the farmhouse during the long legal dispute regarding the boy from Cuba. Rumor has it that President Clinton lent his dog Buddy to the family for good cheer, and Buddy proceeded to chew up the edging of the farmhouse front windows.) When YFU faced bankruptcy and the property hit the market, neighbors rallied to raise an eye-popping $12 million to purchase the property and put it into a land trust, becoming a public park. Through the agreement reached, although the distinguished yellow farmhouse is a private residence, the three acres of open space on the south lawn are open to the public.

Cleveland Park's village green also serves as a private dog park during designated hours, although membership strongly favors Cleveland Park residents. More information is available on the conservancy website. The cost is $125 for one dog and $150 for two dogs, pooches must wear their Rosedale tags anytime they're on the property, and canine and human visitors are requested to stay off the grass after it rains. The Rosedale Conservancy is open for off-leash play 7 A.M.–2 P.M. on weekdays and 8–11 A.M. on weekends, and 4:30–6:30 P.M. every day. There is two-hour parking available on the street. 3518 Newark St.; www.rosedaleconservancy.org.

## 10 National Cathedral Grounds

(See the Northwest DC map on page 46)

DC's take on an Old World cathedral has a distinct American flair. Take the moon rock in the stained glass Space Window. Or the gargoyle of Darth Vader on the eaves. We doubt you'll find that in Koln, Germany. (You'll most likely need binoculars to spot Darth; see www.cathedral.org for more detailed instructions.) Although it's hard to imagine the Washington skyline without the National Cathedral's soaring towers, the structure was only fully completed in 1990, 83 years after the foundation stone was laid. Whenever we visit the cathedral Denali wonders what flying buttress smells like, but she tries—really she tries—to stay on her best behavior. Her favorite part of the immaculate grounds is the Bishop's Garden to the south of the cathedral with its herbs, rose bushes, and koi pond, but Cathedral Heights dogs on leash can be seen sniffing all around the well-trimmed lawn. Every October 4, in celebration of the Feast of St. Francis, the patron saint of animals, dozens of pets and their handlers gather on the cathedral steps to be sprinkled with holy water and blessed by clergy at the Blessing of the Animals. It's at once a heartwarming and humorous sight to behold. Located on Massachusetts and Wisconsin Avenues. 202/537-6200; www.nationalcathedral.org.

## 11 Klingle Road

(See the Northwest DC map on page 46)

*I love a dog. He does nothing for political reasons.*

Will Rogers

One of the nastiest, most drawn-out snarlfests in local DC politics revolves around this dilapidated strip of asphalt. For the most part, DC hounds have managed to stay above the fray, content to enjoy a jaunt through this surprisingly quiet, wooded enclave, but there are others who can't say the same. In one end of the ring, Repair Klingle Road, a pro-road advocacy group insisted that DC needs the east-west connector through Rock Creek Park repaired. On the other end, the Save Klingle Valley group insisted the road should stay closed to preserve the urban oasis.

The saga traces back to 1990, when a major washout rendered Klingle Road impassable. District authorities put up chain-link fences, closed the road, and, slowly, nature began to regain the corridor. Klingle Road has become a favorite haunt for dog walkers, runners, and other pedestrians in the neighborhood, especially on weekends. Even on a weekday evening, Denali encountered four dogs roving off-leash.

At the writing of this book, Klingle Road still had a post-Apocalyptic feel with felled trees, graffitied Jersey barriers, and crumbling roadway, with the yellow median line still visible in spots along the steep, winding road that runs less than 0.7 mile—all beneath the canopy of the stream valley forest. But it seems the debate is drawing to a close. District plans are moving forward to turn the former road into a hiker-biker trail. In case construction of the trail closes Klingle Road temporarily, you and your pooch can instead visit the small network of walking and bridle trails at the adjacent **Tregaron Conservancy** (www.tregaronconservancy.org), a nonprofit dedicated to protecting and restoring the 23-acre Tregaron Estate built in 1912. To access Klingle Road and the Tregaron Conservancy, park near Woodley Avenue and 32nd Street NW and walk down Klingle Road. The estate is located just before the chain-link fence, and Klingle Road is located just beyond the fence.

## PLACES TO EAT

**Café Deluxe:** Think upscale diner food: fancy meat loaf, deluxe hamburgers, and upscale chicken pot pie. On pleasant evenings the patio can get quite packed. There's a fence, and your dog has to be tied to the outside. 3228 Wisconsin Ave. NW; 202/686-2233; www.cafedeluxe.com.

**Lebanese Taverna:** The Woodley Park location of the family-owned Lebanese Taverna has a lively, dog-friendly patio where well-mannered Lassies can bat their eyelashes and hope for a bite of chicken *shawarma*. Wide green umbrellas help beat back the summertime heat, as do the refreshing mezza plates. For vegetarians, or anyone interested in new tastes, the *fatteh bel bathenjan* is a flavorful dish of eggplant and chickpeas topped with toasted Lebanese bread, warm yogurt, pine nuts, and pomegranate seeds. While it sounds like a carnival of fiber on a plate, trust me—it's delicious. Another unexpected favorite is the Lebanese-style pizza. 2641 Connecticut Ave. NW; 202/265-8681; www.lebanesetaverna.com.

**Open City:** Owned by the same folks who bring you Tryst and The Diner in Adams Morgan, Open City follows the same winning recipe: a coffeehouse, diner, and bar neatly rolled into one. Breakfast is served all day so you can order a Western omelette or brioche french toast at 11:30 P.M. if you choose. Open City also makes a mean burger; try it topped with apple-smoked bacon and aged white cheddar. Unfortunately, dogs have to be checked at the patio fence (or tied to the hooks outside the benches/waiting area), but if you score a corner table you'll be sitting close to each other. The wait staff is friendly and will bring puppy refreshments at your request. 2331 Calvert St. NW; 202/332-2331; www.opencitydc.com.

**Sake Club:** At first glance, this upscale Japanese restaurant looks as though there is not a hound's shot in Hades that it will allow dogs in the outside seating. But no sooner had we dismissed the sleek entrance and long, narrow patio, that we heard an "Arf!" Low and behold, Sake Club is dog-friendly. True to its name, Sake Club serves more than 50 varieties of the traditional Japanese rice alcohol. Some argue this is the best sushi in DC. It's not cheap. 2635 Connecticut Ave. NW; 202/332-2711; www.sakeclub.net.

## PLACES TO STAY

**Marriott Wardman Park Hotel:** This enormous hotel has hosted the entire U.S. Olympic team on several occasions when the world-class athletes have flown to Washington to shake hands with the President. Indeed, it's an Olympic-size place—the largest hotel in DC—with more than 1,300 rooms and 195,000 square feet of meeting space for conferences and other functions. Dogs 25 pounds or less can stay here for a one-time $50 fee. No more than two dogs are permitted per room. Two-legged guests will enjoy unwinding at the outdoor heated swimming pool and sundeck, open seasonally. Four-leggers will enjoy sniffing around the hotel's 16 acres of landscaping. The labyrinthine complex includes a Starbucks, two restaurants, a bar, and a deli. Rates range $279–409, but could be as much as $3,200 for suites. On-site parking is available for $31.36 daily, or $36.96 for valet (sheesh, down to the penny). 2660 Woodley Rd. NW; 202/328-2000; www.marriott.com.

**Omni Shoreham Hotel:** Since 1930, the four-diamond Omni Shoreham has catered to Washington's elites and its visitors. The grand hotel has no fewer than seven ballrooms and 834 luxury rooms, many with lovely views of Rock Creek Park. Any size dog may check in for a $50 fee, although the hotel has a policy that, and we quote, "Extreme or Wild Animals not allowed (i.e., snakes, pit bulls, etc.)." Denali doubts her pit bull brethren appreciate being compared to an anaconda. Still, the Omni Shoreham means well. For the past few years, the luxury hotel has hosted an annual yappy hour fundraiser for the Guiding Eyes for the Blind, a nonprofit organization that provides visually impaired individuals with professionally trained guide dogs (the hotel also donates the $50 pet fee to this organization). The yappy hour usually takes place on May 1 in the hotel gardens and typically costs $30. RSVP as the date draws near (202/756-5111; cltaylor@omnihotels.com). Rates range $149–559. Parking costs $24 per day. 2500 Calvert St. NW; 202/234-0700; www.omnishoreham.com/washingtondc.

# Glover Park and Foxhall

Whether pronounced Gloh-ver Park or Gluh-ver Park, in Denali's opinion, Glover Park might as well be renamed Rover Park. The largely residential neighborhood north of Georgetown is known for its friendly population of graduate students, young families, and more dogs than you can shake a stick at—not that you'd want to. This section also includes Cathedral Heights and

Mclean Gardens in the shadow of the National Cathedral, and to the west, the secluded estates on Foxhall Road with the grandest mansions you'll see in DC without diplomat license plates on the cars in the driveway, though there are some of those, too. Denali hasn't seen so many Sotheby's realty signs since she left Malibu, California.

Glover Park Rovers and Foxhall Fidos have the superb luck of landing near both Battery Kemble Park and Glover Archbold Park, narrow greenbelts with winding trails, cool streambeds, and dappled shade. Despite the number of dogs you'll see roaming off leash on these trails, Northwest DC is still in need of an official off-leash dog park, but that call might be answered soon. In 2008, the DC Department of Parks and Recreation officially approved the construction of an off-leash dog park near the Newark Community Gardens, and at the writing of this book, all plans were moving forward in that direction, but not without the gnashing of teeth from organic gardeners in the neighborhood who have long fought the project.

This section includes the territory south and east of Loughboro Road and Nebraska Avenue, west of Wisconsin Avenue and 37th Street to Whitehaven Park, and north of the Potomac River. It includes the Glover Park, Foxhall, Wesley Heights, and Palisades neighborhoods.

## PARKS, BEACHES, AND RECREATION AREAS

### 12 Battery Kemble Park
🐾🐾🐾🐾 (See the Northwest DC map on page 46)
In DC, as with most places, there are two types of parks: the patch of grass around the corner, and then the destination park where both you and your pup

really want to go when you have the time. For all but the lucky few who live in this well-to-do neighborhood, Battery Kemble Park falls firmly in the second category. You'll be driving here, but it's worth it.

On a map, Battery Kemble Park looks like a green inchworm wriggling between the Foxhall and Palisades neighborhoods. The rutted dirt entrance on Chain Bridge Road is about as close to off-road driving as you'll see in the city (if you haven't traded in your gas-guzzling SUV for a Prius yet, here's one time you'll be grateful). Drive slowly as you round the corner because you're entering Bowser Country, and, DC leash laws aside, its denizens tend to be running free. In fact, on Wikimapia.com this spot is identified simply as "Dog Park."

If you visit in the early evening, a posse of dogs from Northwest DC will probably be gathered at the bottom of the steep, perfect sledding hill in the basin of the park, ready to trot over to smell the newcomers. Their owners will likely be chatting amiably beneath trees on the edge of the small gravel parking lot, often seated at the picnic tables. A dual drinking fountain is located over there, one spigot for you and one for your dog.

If you visit in the morning or midday, Battery Kemble is a popular walkabout spot for owners and professional dog walkers. Beagles, basset hounds, and other low-to-the-ground hunting dogs will love to rustle through the underbrush, while Labradors muck through the mud "spas" in the creek (bring a towel). If you're lucky, you might even find some wild raspberries—just don't go for the low-lying ones! A 1.3-mile trail runs the narrow length of the park from MacArthur Boulevard to Nebraska Avenue, but you can while away an afternoon exploring all the side trails, especially if you link up with Glover Archbold Park via the Wesley Heights Trail to the east.

Poop is the one thing that spoils bucolic Battery Kemble. For whatever reason, it hasn't customarily been part of the Battery Kemble culture to clean up after your pet. Consider changing this trend, and if you're feeling extra conscientious, clean up after someone else's dog. You'll add new meaning to the term "brownie points."

To reach Battery Kemble Park from MacArthur Boulevard, take a sharp right turn onto Chain Bridge Road. The park entrance will be on your right. 202/895-6000; www.nps.gov/cwdw.

## 13 Glover Archbold Park

🐾🐾🐾 (See the Northwest DC map on page 46)

This 183-acre offshoot of Rock Creek Park is a treat—maybe not a smoked marrowbone–caliber treat, but certainly as good as a rawhide. Denali stumbled across the park where the trail picks up across from Georgetown University Hospital, but the 3.1-mile hiking trail starts at the C&O Canal and hopscotches over several roads all the way up to Van Ness Street near Johnson's Flower and Garden Center. If your pooch is a running breed and you don't mind trotting along, here's the place for you. Besides the C&O Canal towpath to the south,

Glover Archbold links up to Battery Kemble Park to the west and is within a quick jaunt to Rock Creek Park on the north end. The slender park also makes for a fine walk in the woods. Since Glover-Archbold Trail follows the Foundry Branch Creek, it stays fairly cool even in the jungle-sticky summers. In winter, be sure to watch your footing on icy spots by the streambed. If entering the park on the north end, park along or near Upton Street. The grassy area inset forming the corner of Upton and Van Ness Streets is a popular, albeit illegal, place to play fetch. If accessing the park on the south end, it's easiest to park on Reservoir Road and walk to the trailhead at 44th Street—don't blink or you'll miss it. 202/895-6000; www.nps.gov/rocr.

### 14 Whitehaven Park

🐾🐾🐾 (See the Northwest DC map on page 46)

When people talk about the Glover Park Dog Park, that obscure field tucked away over the wooden stairs where 39th Street ends—this is where they mean. It's no wonder no one calls it Whitehaven Park, because there are no signs. Only on a map will you see the name of the forested arm between Burleith (the neighborhood behind Georgetown University) and Glover Park. The field feels more isolated than it really is and has two main entry points: one where 39th Street dead-ends a block south of W Street, and another west of 37th near U Street where you'll see a narrow, tan-dirt ribbon of a trail beeline for the woods. Your curiosity—and your companion's keen sense of smell—will lead you through a heavily shaded trail until you emerge on a grass field worn bald in patches by happy dog feet. It's a peaceful paddock if you ever have the place to yourselves, when the only sounds to hear are the birds, the wind in the trees, the bounce of the tennis ball, and four paws hurtling after it.

It's important to note that park police do occasionally venture back here to ticket leash violators. For dogs more interested in walking the woods than playing in a field or owners not interested in risking a ticket, there is also a cross-town trail called Whitehaven Trail, accessible from the 39th Street entrance to the park (walk right, or west, on the trail as you enter from the street). There is a doggy-accessible drinking fountain inside the park; remember to bring poop bags. Parking is available in the neighborhoods. 202/895-6000; www.nps.gov/rocr.

### 15 Guy Mason Dog Run

🐾 🐕 (See the Northwest DC map on page 46)

Though Washington DC opened its first legal public dog park at the writing of this book, there have been some gray areas. Guy Mason Dog Run is one of those. On the DC Department of Parks and Recreation website it's described as an "informal" dog park. It's fenced, dogs run it, there's even a very official-looking sign informing you that only three dogs are allowed per person, a reasonable request considering the size of the dog run. Is it totally legal? Next question...

The Guy Mason Dog Run might not be glamorous or expansive, but it is functional. Besides having a double-gate, a bark-chip interior, and poop bags, it's located on the corner of the Mason Recreation Center, making it a good spot to wait for a Little League or corporate softball league game to wrap up. In the summertime, do visit early in the morning, however. The tiny park has no shade to speak of, so your dog can overheat when the mercury climbs. Parking is easy at the recreation center and you can even wave hello to the Vice President's Mansion on the Naval Observatory grounds. The dog run is located on Calvert Street off Wisconsin Avenue. 3600 Calvert St. NW; 202/282-2180; www.dpr.dc.gov.

## PLACES TO EAT

**Einstein Bagels:** For a different kind of schmear campaign in DC, swing by Einstein Bagels for a toasted sesame bagel with cream cheese. Order a doggy bagel for $0.99, too. 1815 Wisconsin Ave. NW; 202/333-4436; www.einsteinbros.com.

**Jetties:** Do you like delicious specialty sandwiches in generous portions? Do you lament that Thanksgiving happens only once a year? Has your dog stolen the holiday turkey so many times that you simply cook a bird just for her? Jetties, a sandwich shop off Foxhall Road, has an easier solution. Jetties' crown jewel is the Nobadeer, a masterpiece of fresh-carved turkey, house-made stuffing, and cranberry sauce on sourdough. Denali, whose favorite holiday is unquestionably Thanksgiving (so many extra dishes to lick clean!), is thankful this is on the menu. All of Jetties' sandwiches are named after Nantucket beaches, and the list is extensive and includes vegetarian options, too. To help satisfy your sweet tooth, Jetties also serves Gifford's ice cream and cookies that are truly worth the calories. Dining is very casual at the picnic tables out front. This is possibly the family- and fur-friendliest eatery you'll find near Georgetown. 1609 Foxhall Rd. NW; 202/965-3663; www.jettiesdc.com.

# Georgetown

In upscale Georgetown, Denali inevitably feels underdressed. Her perky Dalmatian spots, normally so dapper on her chest, seem somehow unrefined when walking down M Street next to the high-fashion toy breeds that frequent Georgetown's shopping district and give new meaning to the term "fashion hounds." Even so, Denali must admit this wealthy enclave of Washington DC is delightfully indulgent of its pets. In addition to two pet boutiques, one animal rescue league, and some of the finer paw-friendly sidewalk cafés in Washington, Georgetown has a few canine celebrities. The most famous is Jack, Georgetown University's 55-pound English bulldog mascot-in-residence. Although Jack belongs to Jesuit priest and religion professor Father Christopher Steck, each year co-eds compete for a slot on the 20-student

## DOG-EAR YOUR CALENDAR

A challenge to aspiring yogis: If you think tree pose is difficult, try it with a pug tugging on a leash around your ankle at **Doga in the Park.** Yoga instructor Kimberly Wilson of Tranquil Space Studio in Dupont Circle and her pug Louis will show you how at Rose Park's annual doga, or dog-yoga, event. Since 2005, Kimberly's fundraiser for the Washington Humane Society has drawn rave reviews from Downward Facing Dogs across the District. The outdoor yoga class usually occurs in mid-May on a Saturday afternoon. For a $10 donation, you can center your *chakras* while your dog indiscreetly sniffs the person in front of you—for a good cause, of course. To learn more, contact Kimberly (202/328-9642; kimberly@tranquilspace.com) or the Washington Humane Society (202/723-5730 ext. 204; www.washhumane.org).

Bring Bowser to **Bonnets and Bones,** an Easter bone hunt for dogs. What more could you want? Perhaps photos with the Easter Bunny and a competition for the best doggie Easter Bonnet? Done. The fundraiser benefits the Washington Humane Society. Discounted advance tickets can be purchased from The Dog Shop. To learn more, contact The Dog Shop (202/337-3647; www.dogshopdc.com) or the Washington Humane Society (202/723-5730 ext. 204; www.washhumane.org).

On top of Book Hill near the Georgetown Library, come participate in the patriotic **Fourth of July Doggie Parade,** including a contest and ice cream social. The event usually takes place the weekend before the Fourth. To learn more, contact The Dog Shop (202/337-3647; www.dogshopdc.com).

---

team of "Jack's Crew" to have the privilege of coaxing the stubbornly spirited smushnose on walks across campus three times per day. Denali hardly needs so much convincing to explore Georgetown's parks and overgrown spaces, especially now that the waterfront has been re-landscaped. In addition, both Dumbarton Oaks Park and Montrose Park, located on R Street near 31st Street, offer plenty of room to roam. Georgetown includes the area east of Glover-Archbold Park, south of Whitehaven Park and Parkway, west of Rock Creek, and north of the Potomac River.

## PARKS, BEACHES, AND RECREATION AREAS

### 16 Dumbarton Oaks Park

🐾🐾🐾 (See the Northwest DC map on page 46)

Dumbarton Oaks is a 19th-century Federal-style mansion famous for its role in the early formation of the United Nations. Today the stately brick home and the 10 acres of formal gardens surrounding it are a Harvard-owned center for scholarly research on Byzantine, pre-Columbian, and gardens and landscape studies. To this, all Denali has to say is "Yawn." History isn't her thing. So she wasn't too disappointed to learn that dogs cannot tour the Dumbarton Oaks estate. The real place of interest from her perspective lies beyond the estate's walls. Behind the famous mansion and its manicured grounds, you'll find woods—all 27 acres of the Dumbarton Oaks themselves. And here is a doggy's dream: a creek and several trails knit through Dumbarton Oaks Park. In summer, the far side of the park becomes junglelike as kudzu vines and English ivy swallow oaks whole. This deep pocket of greenbelt is a serenely peaceful place to stroll. You can access Dumbarton Oaks Park in the north end at Whitehaven Street, or more commonly from R Street near 31st Street in Georgetown. Follow the signs down steep Lover's Lane. 202/895-6000; www.nps.gov/rocr.

## 🐾 Montrose Park

🐾🐾🐾🐾 (See the Northwest DC map on page 46)

"Montrose Park is paradise for dogs!" is the refrain you'll hear. What's so special about this shaded corner of Georgetown? Well, there's the number of wagging friends you'll meet on the lawn. There's the free agility and holiday events hosted by The Dog Shop (1625 Wisconsin Ave. NW; 202/337-3647; www.dogshopdc.com). But really the draw to Montrose Park is its easy access to the swimming hole at the bottom of Lover's Lane, the paved drive between Montrose and Dumbarton Oaks Parks that is closed to traffic. For dog paddlers, that's reason enough. To reach the best swimming hole in the District, follow these instructions: after parking along R Street or nearby 31st Street (two-hour parking from Monday–Saturday), walk to Lover's Lane, where you'll see a sign for Dumbarton Oaks Park. Trot down the steep paved drive. Your dog's ears are probably perked forward now, tail arched. At the bottom of the steep hill you will come to a three-way branch. Dumbarton Oaks Park will be to your left, a graded gravel trail into Rock Creek Park is straight ahead, and there is a third trail to your right. Take this third option. After a short distance the path will split again. Keep to the left this time and cross the bridge over the stream. By this point your dog will undoubtedly be frothing at the mouth in excitement. You'll most likely hear dogs before you see them retrieving tennis balls from the creek on your right side. Montrose Park is located on R Street between Dumbarton Oaks (the estate) and Oak Hill Cemetery, roughly between 31st and 30 Streets. 3099 R St. NW; 202/282-1063.

## 🐾 Volta Park

🐾 (See the Northwest DC map on page 46)

This mostly fenced community recreational center is busiest in summer, when the popular outdoor swimming pool is bopping with Georgetown and Glover Park sun worshippers and water babies, though sadly, Denali notes, no dog

## DIVERSIONS

While some dog owners would argue the saying should go, "Like a dog to water" instead of "Like a duck...," Denali had (until later in the research of this book!) a catlike abhorrence for water. But even she will occasionally tolerate a pleasure cruise aboard a small boat. Unless you keep the company of a teacup Yorkie, kayaks are nearly impossible to paddle with a dog on your lap so we recommend sticking with a canoe or rowboat. One final warning if you've never paddled a canoe before: you'll need two people to navigate in a straight line unless you can figure out the J-stroke in a hurry. Here are some places you and your furry friend can find ways to hit the water.

**Capitol River Cruises:** Well-behaved and leashed dogs can join in these 45-minute narrative sightseeing tours of DC by riverboat. Tickets costs $13 for adults and $6 for kids; dogs are free. The cruise operates April through October and is located in Washington Harbor at very end of 31st Street. 800/405-5511; www.capitolrivercruises.com.

**C&O Canal Boat Rides:** Dogs are allowed to join handlers on a historic cruise on a mule-pulled canal boat ride. Open seasonally. Tickets cost $5 per person. Dogs are free. Georgetown Visitor Center, 1057 Thomas Jefferson St. NW; 202/653-5190; www.nps .gov/choh/planyourvisit/publicboatrides.htm.

**Fletcher's Boat House:** Prefer to paddle the river or the C&O Canal instead? Fletcher's rents canoes, rowboats, and kayaks. Rates range $8–11 per hour or $20–24 per day. Located at the intersection of Reservoir and Canal Roads; 4940 Canal Rd. NW; 202/244-0461; www.fletcherscove.com.

paddlers. Even for the non-swimmers, it has a little something for everyone: basketball courts, tennis courts, and a kiddie playground. Dogs usually run the bases of the baseball diamond or across the pint-sized soccer field. Be sure to clean up poop to keep the peace with Little Leaguers. The city park is located one block west of Wisconsin Ave., and is bounded by Q St., 33rd and 34th Sts., and Volta Pl. 3300 Q St. NW; 202/282-0380; www.dpr.dc.gov.

## 19 C&O Canal

🐾🐾🐾🐾 🐾 (See the Northwest DC map on page 46)

While not the successful business enterprise originally conceived in 1828 when construction began, the Chesapeake & Ohio Canal has become a dearly loved destination for dogs throughout the greater Washington area, and the owners who dry them off. Better known as the C&O Canal, the waterway was supposed to stretch from Georgetown to Pittsburgh, Pennsylvania, connecting the tidal flats of the Chesapeake Bay to the Ohio River and establishing a

**Jack's Boathouse:** Jack's has rented boats since World War II. Rates are $10 hourly and $35 daily. Located beneath Key Bridge at 3500 K St. NW; 202/337-9642; www.jacksboathouse.com.

**Thompson Boat Center:** A major hub for crew, Thompson Boat Center also rents canoes, kayaks, and sailboats. Rates range $8–10 per hour and $24–30 per day. Located on the south end of Washington Harbor at the mouth of Rock Creek at 2900 Virginia Ave. NW; 202/333-9543; www.thompsonboatcenter.com.

passage for goods and supplies, such as coal. However, construction for the Baltimore and Ohio Railroad began the same day. By the time the C&O Canal reached Cumberland, Maryland—not even halfway to its end-goal—the railroad was nearly to the Ohio River. Despite falling short of its vision, the canal's 184.5-mile expanse has become a permanent fixture in recreation along the Potomac River. Denali loves jogging down the graded clay-and-gravel towpath. If she were less fussy about getting her feet wet, she would probably dive into the canal to chase ducks, too. Some days you'll see so many dogs promenading down the towpath it looks like a parade.

The Georgetown Visitor Center is located at 1057 Thomas Jefferson Street NW, but most folks head directly to K Street NW (also shown as Water Street on some maps), beneath the Whitehurst Freeway. Parking is notoriously difficult here—and the meter maids don't mess around—so if push comes to shove there is a parking garage next to the AMC Loews Georgetown Movie Theater at Wisconsin Ave. 202/653-5190; www.nps.gov/choh.

## DETOURS

Most of the stores in Georgetown are pet-friendly, so don't be surprised to see glossy little eyes staring up at you from the shoe section. Here are two stores just for dogs. **The Dog Shop** has supplies, training, and a dog wash. 1625 Wisconsin Ave. NW; 202/337-3647; www.dogshopdc.com. **Georgetown Pet Boutique** focuses on puppy clothing and accessories. 2910 M St. NW; 866/434-8609; www.georgetownpetboutique.com.

## 20 Rose Park

 (See the Northwest DC map on page 46)

This grassy tract between P Street and Rock Creek Parkway is stretched out like a boomerang. Tennis courts lie at its southern end, a baseball field is in the middle, and an open field—where you'll find the dogs—is at the northern end. It's important to keep your dog on leash here, with the on-ramp to busy Rock Creek Parkway only too close (and it's the law). Rose Park is located between P and M Streets NW, bounded on the west side by 26th and 27th Streets and on the east side by Rock Creek Parkway; 202/282-2208; www.dpr.dc.gov or www.roseparkdc.org.

### PLACES TO EAT

**Bangkok Bistro:** Here's a reliable standby for tasty Thai food. Its location on Prospect Street is conveniently close to Wisconsin and M Streets, but much quieter and with patio seating on a sidewalk wide enough to accommodate your whole family, dog included. If you and Gus don't want to leave the couch, Bangkok Bistro also offers free delivery anywhere in Georgetown on orders of $12 or more. For spicy food lovers, try Drunken Noodles or Kapow—you'll experience a similar sensation on your taste buds. An extra perk about Bangkok Bistro is that you eat free on your birthday (bring your I.D.). No word yet on whether you can eat free on your dog's birthday. 3251 Prospect St. NW; 202/337-2424; www.bangkokbistrodc.com.

**Leopold's Kafe:** Tucked away in Cady's Alley, this Austrian café is one of those very chic places that you would never expect to be dog-friendly. Desserts are the real reason to visit Leopold's, but the watermelon salad called *frische wassermelone salat* (amazing how it sounds like English phonetically) and an olive tart called *olivenpissaladiere* are both fresh starters. Don't come here too hungry or too broke, because you'll leave in much the same way. But if you want a quick trip over the Atlantic to savor light flavors in European style, right down to your dog sitting politely at your patio table, then Leopold's is worth the splurge. 3318 M St. NW; 202/965-6005; www.kafeleopolds.com.

**Martin's Tavern:** Martin's bills itself as the "Heart of Old Georgetown;" for once, here is truth in advertising. Four generations of Martins have owned and operated the tavern since it first opened, the day after the Prohibition ended in 1933. Gussied-up Georgetown mutts like Martin's in hopes they might get a cut of sirloin. Traditional American fare of great steaks, chops, seafood, and fresh pasta are all hallmark dishes for the tavern. A visit to Martin's Tavern is an encounter with history, too. Every president since Harry Truman has dined here. In fact, John F. Kennedy proposed to then Jackie Bouvier in booth number 3. Located on Wisconsin Avenue between N and Prospect Streets. Outdoor tables cannot be reserved, so there could be a wait. 1264 Wisconsin Ave. NW; 202/333-7370; www.martins-tavern.com.

**The Bean Counter:** This narrowest of cafés has a small patio out back where you can grab a quick breakfast with your dog. Besides brewing a good cup of coffee, The Bean Counter also makes a mean Cuban sandwich at lunchtime. 1665 Wisconsin Ave.; 202/625-1665.

## PLACES TO STAY

**The Four Seasons, Georgetown:** This premier 211-room Washington hotel accepts very small dogs weighing less than 15 or 20 pounds for no additional fee. The Four Seasons only requests that you do not leave your dog unattended in the room. Said the front desk, "We love pets, and if you let us know when you're making your reservation, we'll have a special treat ready." While these luxurious, five-diamond accommodations range from a top spa to a fitness center with yoga instruction to 24-hour room service, what has hotel staff most excited is Bourbon Steak, a brand-new restaurant by famed L.A. chef Michael Mina (www.michaelmina.net). Rates range $395–3,500. Valet parking costs $42. 2800 Pennsylvania Ave. NW; 202/342-0444; www.fourseasons.com/washington.

**Ritz-Carlton, Georgetown:** Situated on Wisconsin Avenue and K Street in Georgetown, this 86-room Ritz exudes the posh luxury you would expect for this address—and it also has the five-diamond AAA rating to prove it. Dogs up to 50 pounds may check in for a $125 one-time fee. Valet parking costs $35 for all day and overnight, $20 for day-parkers only. Rates range $599–5,000. 3100 South St. NW; 202/912-4100; www.ritzcarlton.com/georgetown.

**Washington Suites Georgetown:** Any size dog can check into this 124-room hotel for a $20 fee—the caveat is that they are only permitted in the smoking rooms on the first floor. Complimentary amenities include continental breakfast each morning, fully equipped kitchens, and high-speed Internet in every suite, an on-site exercise room, *The Washington Post* delivered Mon.–Fri., and—this was the kicker for us—fresh-baked cookies at check-in. Call for rates. 2500 Pennsylvania Ave. NW; 202/333-8060; www.washington suitesgeorgetown.com

# Columbia Heights and Mount Pleasant

It's a bit of a hike to get Rover to Rock Creek Park from Columbia Heights (less so from Mount Pleasant), but fortunately dog-friendly cafés are close at hand. Besides a wealth of quick Salvadorean eateries, try one of these furr-tastic establishments (in the outdoor seating, of course).

## PLACES TO EAT

**Columbia Heights Coffee:** Often dubbed a diamond in the rough, Columbia Heights Coffee has a couple of small metal tables out front for you to sip a cappuccino and read a newspaper with your best friend. Located between N. Monroe Street and N. Park Road. 3416 11th St. NW; 202/986-0079.

**Logan @ The Heights:** Dogs are a common feature on the 80-seat patio of The Heights, another restaurant from EatWell DC, the company that cooked up Logan Tavern and Commissary in Logan Circle and Grillfish in Dupont Circle. If fried chicken, meat loaf, and other home-style favorites transport you to a happy place, then you'll be flying high at The Heights. 3115 14th St. NW; 202/797-7227; www.theheightsdc.com.

**RedRocks:** The pizza magic happens in the brick oven for which this pizzeria is named. The pies come out in classic Neapolitan style, thin-crusted and chewy. RedRocks' outdoor patio is very Fido-friendly. Chimay beer is always on tap. 1036 Park Rd. NW; 202/506-1402; www.firebrickpizza.com.

**Sticky Fingers Bakery:** Denali wholeheartedly agrees with this vegan bakery's tagline: "Vegan sweets so irresistible you can't keep your paws off 'em." From raspberry chocolate cheesecake to sticky cinnamon buns, all of  the desserts and baked goods are 100 percent vegan, meaning they contain no animal-derived ingredients such as dairy and eggs. And they taste good (well, almost as good as if they had butter, Paula Deen reminds us). Denali mostly likes feeling warm-fuzzy inside about being kind to the rest of the animal kingdom. 1370 Park Rd. NW; 202/299-9700; www.sticky fingersbakery.com.

**The Wonderland Ballroom:** Opened in 2007, this sports bar has an uncanny feel of having been around the neighborhood for much longer than it has. Dogs are often seen hanging out under the picnic benches of the outdoor, fenced-in "Bohemian Beer Garden," which is an excellent place to sample the Wonderland's frequently revolving beer selection. Wonderland has even been known to allow dogs to wander into the bar. 1101 Kenyon St. NW; 202/232-5263; www.thewonderlandballroom.com.

# Adams Morgan

To outsiders, Adams Morgan is better known for boozehounds than for hound dogs, but as it turns out, this nightlife hot spot has appealing options for Spot, too. From a first glance at the Madam's Organ mural on 18th Street, her 13-foot breasts covered just so by the blues club's name, you know you're entering a lively part of town. As Arianne Bennett, co-owner of the Amsterdam Falafelshop and two Italian mastiffs named Saxon and Duce, put it, "Adams Morgan's tolerance for stimulants is higher than in most places." You're more likely to find dog-friendly individuals around here for that very reason.

Adams Morgan's name is a nod to the neighborhood's racial and ethnic diversity. In the 1950s, after the U.S. Supreme Court decreed segregation in schools to be unconstitutional, the all-white John Quincy Adams School and all-black Thomas Morgan School were two of the first to integrate peacefully. The city renamed the region after the two schools to mark this new chapter. Adams Morgan is a gateway community for immigrants, as you'll recognize by the assortment of ethnic restaurants on the strip. This section includes the area east of Connecticut Ave. and Rock Creek Park, south of Harvard Street, west of 15th Street, and north of U Street and Florida Avenue.

## DOG-EAR YOUR CALENDAR

Adams Morgan need never be boring for your bulldog. In September, avenge your dog and get some free stuff, too, at DC's **Crafty Bastard Arts and Crafts Fair.** Georgetown's The Dog Shop usually hosts a dunk tank to benefit the Washington Humane Society. Sink your dog's most hated humans: trainer, groomer, vet, and dogcatcher. Located at the Marie Reed Learning Center. 18th St. at Wyoming Ave.; www.dogshopdc.com or www.washingtoncity paper.com/craftybastards.

April offers a little ruckus for Rover: a full day of demonstrations, workshops, adoptions, contests, first aid, and pet care just for the fun of it. The canine community event **BowWow PowWow** is hosted by the AdamsMorgan MainStreet Group. Located at the Marie Reed Learning Center. 18th St. at Wyoming Ave.; 202/232-1960; www.ammainstreet.org.

## PARKS, BEACHES, AND RECREATION AREAS

### 21 Walter Pierce Dog Park

🐾🐾 🐕 (See the Northwest DC map on page 46)

Described to us as the first quasi-official DC dog park, Walter Pierce is an experiment launched in 2005. A community group named Adams Morgan Dogs maintains the fenced park and DC police generally respect the space as a dogs' off-leash zone, even though it's not 100 percent official yet. It sure looks like the real deal, though, with a double-gate entryway, three picnic benches, dog bowls, and trees for shade. Clark Ray, director of the DC Department of Parks and Recreation, explained that Walter Pierce Park is situated on something of an archeological smorgasbord: the largest post-Civil War cemetery for African Americans in DC; earlier it had been the city's first Quaker burial ground; and earlier still Native Americans used the land. So how did a historical cemetery become the dusty soccer field and off-leash dog area you see today?

Knowledge of the cemetery had all but faded from public memory until the DC Department of Parks and Recreation started a soil erosion project to shore up a wall in Walter Pierce Park in summer 2005. Artifacts kept turning up in the project's preliminary stages—a red flag that numerous surveys and analyses would need to take place before improvements could be made or the dog park could get DC DPR's official blessing. Progress is moving forward slowly.

In the meantime, the off-leash area wags on in its semi-official, slightly ramshackle state. Walter Pierce Dog Park tends to attract big lugs who play rough, so owners of toy breeds might want to look elsewhere, or at least exercise caution when visiting during peak hours after work on weekdays. Located north of Calvert Street, just before the Duke Ellington Bridge. 202/673-7025; www.dpr.dc.gov or www.amdogs.org.

### 22 Kalorama Park

🐾🐾 (See the Northwest DC map on page 46)

While Kalorama Park is close to the Kalorama neighborhood, it's in fact closer to Adams Morgan, located only two blocks away from Madam's Organ Blues Bar. Kalorama Park bridges the two neighborhoods. You're bound to meet dogs most any time of day in this three-acre triangular park, which also houses a playground, community garden, and basketball court. Conscientious dog owners keep a stash of plastic grocery sacks tied to the signs that warn you about the $50 fine for failing to clean up dog poop. As a result, Kalorama Park is a tidy slice of urban greenery. Located at the intersection of Columbia Road, Kalorama Road, and 19th Street. 1875 Columbia Rd. NW; 202/673-7606; www.dpr.dc.gov.

## DETOURS

Adams Morgan's international flair makes for fun shopping. These pet-friendly shops and services mean you're not stuck window-shopping with your pooch.

**BB&T Bank:** Make a deposit with your dog. No, not that kind of deposit. 1801 Adams Mill Rd.; 202/332-3891; www.bbt.com.

**The Brass Knob:** Salvaged architectural bits and pieces to let your imagination run wild. Dogs can join in the hunt. 2311 18th St. NW; 202/332-3370; www.thebrassknob.com.

**Toro Mata:** Despite the store's name, this is not a place for bulls in a china shop. The gallery sells handmade Peruvian ceramics, furniture, and folk art ranging from $14 to $2,000. Even so, dogs are welcome. Just ask Angel, or Angelito, the shop dog. Co-owners James Nixon and Hector Zarate travel to Peru every six to eight weeks to purchase the shop's inventory directly from artisans. 2410 18th St. NW; 202/232-3890; www.toromata.com.

## 23 Meridian Hill/Malcolm X Park

🐾🐾🐾 🐾 (See the Northwest DC map on page 46)

This 12-acre park is an ornate, neoclassical affair, modeled after an Italian villa with grand symmetrical stairs ascending next to a 13-tiered cascading fountain. On warm-weather Sunday afternoons, an informal drum circle gathers on the top terrace, instilling a vital, earthy rhythm into the air. Denali tends to get all riled up listening to the African, Latin American, and Caribbean beats, so we hang lower in the open grass flanking the symmetrical staircases. In fact, this is where you'll find most dogs—hemmed in by the park's tall outer walls and out of the way of yogis on the lawn below and soccer players on the fields above. Meridian Hill Park is unofficially known as Malcolm X Park for its role as a gathering place for political protests and rallies.

If you loop around Meridian Hill/Malcolm X Park, as many neighborhood dogs do on their daily constitutionals, you'll see several sculptures of note,

including images of James Buchanan, Dante, and Joan of Arc. Denali, for her part, is more interested in the park's wildlife than its sculpture—the squirrels, the sparrows, the fat, gray rat scurrying past! Even DC rodents like to get some culture, it seems.

Meridian Hill/Malcolm X Park is bounded by 15th, 16th, and Euclid Streets and Florida Avenue NW; 202/282-1063; www.nps.gov/mehi.

## PLACES TO EAT

**Adams Mill Bar and Grill:** If you visit before the nighttime crowd gets rowdy, dogs can relax inside the casual atmosphere of Adams Mill Bar and Grill's generously sized patio. Beneath the fluttering Miller Lite flags, dogs are not only allowed inside the patio's fence, but we once witnessed a German shepherd sprawled out on top of the picnic table. 1813 Adams Mill Rd. NW; 202/332-9577.

**Amsterdam Falafelshop:** Did you see the enormous water bowl out front? Falafelshop owners Scott and Arianne Bennett live above the restaurant with their two Italian mastiffs, Duce and Saxon, who weigh an intimidating 98 and 150 pounds, respectively. Night manager Ian Walker often keeps his giant schnauzer Greta at work. All three lucky dogs at one point or another get to hoover the stray fries and bits of falafel that land on the patio—and so can yours, if you pay them a visit. In 2009, Zagat rated Amsterdam Falafelshop a best buy in Washington DC. The menu is straightforward and satisfying: top-it-yourself falafels in pitas, twice-fried Dutch-style fries, and virgin brownies. The falafels are fried right in front of you while you contemplate the 18 different sauces, salads, and pickles for toppings, ranging from excruciatingly spicy to creamy and garlicky. Amsterdam Falafelshop is open 11 A.M.–4 A.M. on Friday and Saturday, not quite so late other nights. Cash only. 2425 18th St. NW; 202/234-1969; www.falafelshop.com.

**Chief Ike's Mambo Room:** Chief Ike's has hosted numerous yappy hours for Adams Morgan Dogs, the community group that maintains the Walter Pierce Dog Park. And your canine is welcome on the patio every day of the week 4–8 P.M., the regular happy hour for humans. There's a water bowl for pup refreshment. It's best to clear out of here before the bar and dance crowd show up. 1725 Columbia Rd. NW; 202/327-1036; www.chiefikes.com.

## DIVERSION

The **Doggie Style Happy Hour,** sponsored by Doggie Style Bakery, kicks off at Adams Mill Bar and Grill 6–8 P.M. every Friday from mid-May until the weather gets too cold. Bowsers get to snack on samples from the bakery while their humans sip discounted beer. For more information, contact Adams Mill (1813 Adams Mill Rd. NW; 202/332-9577) or Doggie Style (1825 18th St NW; 202/667-0595; www.doggiestylebakery.com).

**Rita's Water Ice:** Two of our former roommates who grew up in southern New Jersey, not far from the franchise's Bensalem, Pennsylvania, birthplace, always rave about Rita's Water Ice. Denali never had a chance to try the much-hyped frozen treats until Rita's recently opened a handful of DC locations. After she received a complimentary sample of vanilla garnished with a dog biscuit, Denali, too, caught the water ice fever. 1781 Florida Ave. NW; 202/332-7482; www.ritasice.com.

# Dupont Circle, Kalorama, and Embassy Row

Dupont Circle is a bohemian, slightly leftist pocket in the traditionally buttoned-up fabric of Washington. Best-known for its proud LGBQT community, Dupont has become a diverse neighborhood of well-heeled residents of all backgrounds and preferences. Some of Washington's most doted-upon, and well-dressed, dogs hang out in these digs. North of Dupont Circle is Kalorama, which in Greek means "beautiful view." As you walk your dog here and up and down Embassy Row, you'll discover why real estate in this part of town is consistently followed by six zeroes.

While sniffing around Embassy Row, be sure to pay homage to the bespectacled and sandaled statue of Mahatma Ghandi across Massachusetts Avenue from the Embassy of India. Denali likes to meditate on one of his many wise social commentaries: "The greatness of a nation and its moral progress can be judged by the way its animals are treated."

## PARKS, BEACHES, AND RECREATION AREAS

### 24 Mitchell Park

🐾🐾 (See the Northwest DC map on page 46)

The debate wages on: Did Elizabeth Mitchell bequeath her property to the District to create a park in *honor* of her dog or to create a *dog park*? As the story goes, Mrs. Mitchell deeded the prime real estate to DC in 1918 under the condition that the grave of her beloved French poodle, Bock, remained undisturbed. As of 2009, dog owners were still actively petitioning the DC Department of Parks and Recreation to establish an official off-leash dog park inside Mitchell Park and to give Bock a legacy to really make his fellow dogs proud. In the meantime, Mitchell Park operates much like other unofficial dog parks in the District. Doggies play gleefully off-leash on the well-kept grassy field. Angry neighbors call the police. Doggies move elsewhere. After a few months, the whole cycle repeats itself. It's a conflict over open space that has escalated to fisticuffs before. When we visited we noted a park sign with

## DETOURS

A few misbehaving mutts spoiled the Dupont Circle FreshFarm Market for the rest of Dupont's dogs in 2006. These scoundrels of hounds stole fruit samples, peed on produce, and—the breaking point—picked fights until finally the FreshFarm Market organizers intervened and said no more dogs. Fortunately, there are still some nearby DC farmers markets where pups haven't worn out their welcome.

**Adams Morgan Farmers Market:** Open 8 A.M.–1 P.M. Saturday, May 6–Dec. 23. Located on Columbia Rd. and 18th St. NW; 301/587-2248.

**Bloomingdale Farmers Market:** Open 10 A.M.–2 P.M. on Sunday, May–November. Located on 1st and R Sts. NW; 202/234-0559; www.marketsandmore.info.

**Chevy Chase Farmers Market:** Open 9 A.M.–1 P.M. Saturday, Apr. 29–Nov. 25. Located at 5701 Broad Branch Rd. (Lafayette School Parking Lot); 304/229-7222.

**Eastern Market Outdoor Farmers Market:** Open 7 A.M.–4 P.M. Saturday and Sunday year-round. Located at 225 7th St. SE; 202/544-0083; www.easternmarketdc.com.

**Foggy Bottom FreshFarm Market:** Open 3–7 P.M. Wednesday Apr. 19–Nov. 15. Located on I St. near New Hampshire Ave. and 24th St. NW; 202/362-8889; www.freshfarmmarkets.org.

**H Street FreshFarm Market:** Open 9 A.M.–noon Saturday May 6–Oct. 28. Located at 600 block of H St. NE; 202/362-8889; www.freshfarmmarkets.org.

**Penn Quarter FreshFarm Market:** Open 3–7 P.M. Thursday April–November. Located on Eighth and D Sts. NW; 202/362-8889; www.freshfarmmarkets.org.

**USDA Farmers Market:** Open 10 A.M.–2 P.M. Friday June–October. Located on 12th St. and Independence Ave. SW; 202/720-8317; www.ams.usda.gov/farmersmarkets.

**14th and U Farmers Market:** Open 9 A.M.–1 P.M. on Saturday May–Nov. Located in front of Reed Center. 202/234-0559; www.14andufarmersmarket.com.

No Dogs Allowed scribbled in permanent marker block letters. "Oh that. Pay that no mind," said a dog owner as she tossed a ball for her poodle across the grass. A telephone call to the DC Department of Parks and Recreation, however, confirmed that dogs are technically not supposed to be on athletic fields in the District of Columbia (though we hardly saw how this patch of lawn qualified as a regulation-size soccer or football field).

To play it safe, it's probably best to follow the rules and keep a leash firmly attached until your pet can legally romp off-leash. If you follow the letter of the law, there is also a small landscaped path where you can walk your dog without stepping foot on the field.

And as long as leashes are required, you might need to walk your pooch a bit more to tire him out. While you're in the neighborhood, a quick trip to Washington's version of Rome's **Spanish Steps** is in order. They're just kitty-corner from the south side of Mitchell Park, at 22nd and S Streets. Mitchell Park is located across from the Lao Embassy in the 2200 block of S Street. From Connecticut Avenue, turn onto California Avenue and then left on 23rd Street NW and then another left on S Street NW. 23rd and S St. NW; 202/673-6871; www.dpr.dc.gov.

## 25 S Street Triangle Park

(See the Northwest DC map on page 46)

Everyone loves a happy ending. Dupont Circle dogs hope that theirs is almost written. In 2008, the DC Department of Parks and Recreation officially approved a fenced, off-leash dog park in the median between New Hampshire Avenue and S and 17th Streets. The triangle park is 5,600 square-feet, which sounds much larger than it is, but Circle Dogs are tickled pink at the prospect of having a place in the city to call their own. The park is tentatively slated to open in summer 2009. www.dpr.dc.gov.

## 26 Dupont Circle

(See the Northwest DC map on page 46)

Denali agrees that Washington DC's most famous traffic circle has the best people-watching in the city. It's a place that is at once at rest and on the go. Bike messengers and commuters use the circle as a shortcut. When the weather is fine you'll often see dogs sunbathing on blankets with their humans or lounging in the shade of elm trees. Chess players match wits on the permanent

## DOG-EAR YOUR CALENDAR

After the Capital Pride Parade and the High Heel Race, arguably the best-attended event in Dupont Circle is the annual **Pride of Pets Dog Show.** Every June since 1993, the drama has unfolded with characteristic oohs and aahs as Dupont dogs vie for a place on the Astroturf-covered podium. Best Vocal Performance, Most Mysterious Heritage, Least Obedient, and Most Butch are just a few of the prize categories. The charity dog show benefits Pets-DC, a nonprofit that helps HIV/AIDs patients and victims of other debilitating ailments care for their companion pets. 202/234-7387; www.petsdc.org.

## DETOURS

**Adams National Bank:** A woman-owned bank that welcomes dogs. 1604 17th St. NW; 202/772-3650; www.adamsbank.com.

**Best Cellars:** With this vintner's novel wine classification system and in-the-wall storage, most bottles are out of tail's way. Even better, all the wines cost less than $15. 1643 Connecticut Ave. NW; 202/387-3146; www.bestcellars.com.

**Biagio Fine Chocolate:** One of several dog-friendly, upscale chocolate stores in the area. 1904 18th St. NW; 202/328-1506; www.biagiochocolate.com.

**Blue Mercury:** High quality makeup for you. Treats for the dog. 1619 Connecticut Ave. NW; 202/462-1300; www.bluemercury.com.

**Books-A-Million:** Track down a copy of *Where the Red Fern Grows* together. 11 Dupont Circle NW; 202/319-1374; www.booksamillion.com.

**Comfort One Shoes:** How all three stores stay in business a bone's throw away from each other, we don't know. Dogs are welcome. 1607, 1621, and 1630 Connecticut Ave. NW; 202/667-5300, 202/232-2480, and 202/328-3141; www.comfortoneshoes.com.

**Commerce Bank:** This bank hired a photographer to take photos of owners and dogs when it opened. 1753 Connecticut Ave. NW; 202/232-4837; www.commerceonline.com.

**Doggie Style Bakery:** How does an all-natural, ecoconscious, humane-ingredients birthday cake for dogs sound? Good?

---

chessboards at the circle's north side, vendors sell handmade jewelry, and bongo players' rhythms add to the bohemian ambience. Couples, gay and straight, lounge on the steps of the white marble fountain and the benches that surround it. On rare occasion you might even see a dog splashing in its center. The fountain centerpiece is the handiwork of sculptor Daniel Chester French, more famous for his iconic statue of the Seated Lincoln at the Lincoln Memorial. Located at the intersections of Massachusetts, Connecticut, and New Hampshire Aves. and P St.; 202/673-7665 www.dpr.dc.gov.

## PLACES TO EAT

**17th Street Café:** The co-owners, Chris Stone and David Liedman, also own City Dogs, a dog walking service, so it goes without saying that the patio is open to Dupont Circle dogs. The menu is limited but has appetizing salads, soups, and sandwiches, of which the blue cheese burger is a fave. 1513 17th St. NW; 202/234-2470; www.cafe17.net.

**Java House:** With plenty of outdoor seating and a barista, Haydee, who

Top it off with one of 10 flavors of doggie ice cream. Also a pet store and groomer. 1825 18th St., NW; 202/667-0595; www.doggiestylebakery.com.

**Human Rights Campaign:** The tagline is: Working for lesbian, gay, bisexual, and transgender equal rights. Supporters, including canine ones, can visit. 1633 Connecticut Ave. NW; 202/232-8621; www.hrc.org.

**Kim's Cleaners:** Dog-friendly dry cleaning with a smile. 1422 21st St. NW; 202/466-5225.

**Lambda Rising:** The website says you'll find "more rainbow-themed gifts than you've ever seen in one place!" The staff at Lambda Rising, one of the nation's best-known gay bookstores since 1974, loves dogs. 1625 Connecticut Ave. NW; 202/462-6969; www.lambdarising.com.

**Locolat:** The signature dark chocolate truffles cost $18 per half-pound, which is good for your waistline and bad for your wallet. Pups can sniff but not sample (for obvious reasons). 1781 Florida Ave. NW; 202/518-2570; www.belgiumlocolat.com.

**Melody Records:** An independent music store since 1977, and fur-friendly to boot. 1623 Connecticut Ave. NW; 202/232-4002; www.melodyrecords.com.

**Salon Charisma:** For a change of pace, bring your pooch along for *your* grooming session. 1365 Connecticut Ave. NW; 202/331-9807; www.saloncharisma.com.

dotes on Dupont dogs, Java House is an old standby for coffee and a snack. 1645 Q St. NW; 202/387-6622; www.javahousedc.com.

**Lauriol Plaza:** After mom buys a dog treat at Doggie Style Bakery, more than one Dupont Circle canine usually ends up tied outside the fence of this Spanish and Tex-Mex restaurant. It can get very hot for the hounds when it's sunny, so see if you can score a table in the back of the patio where the building sometimes provides more shade. 1835 18th St. NW; 202/387-0035; www.lauriolplaza.com.

**Pasha Bistro:** All you need to know can be summed up in two words: delicious kabobs. Your dog may join you on the patio of this Mediterranean eatery, which tends to serve meals that are a good value. 1523 17th St. NW; 202/588-7477.

**Steam Café:** With comfortable outdoor seating, tasty chai, and some argue the best croissants in the neighborhood, it's easy to post up at Steam Café with the pooch for a slow-moving morning. There is also free wireless Internet. 1700 17th St NW; 202/483-5296; steamcafe.wordpress.com.

## PLACES TO STAY

**Carlyle Suites Hotel:** Here is one of the best bargains in the city. The art deco Carlyle Suites Hotel includes 170 rooms with fully equipped kitchenettes and complimentary use of the Washington Sports Club, located five blocks away. Other small but crucial perks: a coin-operated laundry and free, limited on-site parking. Pets can stay for no extra fee, but please call ahead to alert hotel staff. Rates range $129–359. 1731 New Hampshire Ave. NW; 202/234-3200; www.carlylesuites.com.

**Hotel Madera:** When we walked in the door, a sign read Welcome, Isis! with a paw print. Denali was quite taken with this red carpet treatment. If you call ahead, the Hotel Madera will set out a welcome sign special for your dog, too. Positioning itself as a *pied-à-terre,* this boutique hotel seeks to serve as your second home: a pet bed, bowls, and treat are all complimentary, as is a pet sitter and dog walker who can be called on request. Guest rooms are large (measuring an average 430 square feet) since the Hotel Madera, like many Kimpton Hotels, used to be an apartment building. Room service is available from the delicious Firefly Bistro, although if you have a moment *sans* puppy, take a gander inside the restaurant. The floor-to-ceiling "firefly tree" is worth a look. Overnight parking is available for $35, but ecofriendly hybrids park for free. Low season rates start at $129 during holidays and summertime; rooms from $149 the rest of the year. Dogs stay free. 1310 New Hampshire Ave. NW; 202/296-7600; www.hotelmadera.com.

**Hotel Palomar:** As concierge Philip Biggerstaff put it, the chocolate-brown dog-beds at the Hotel Palomar come in three sizes: super huge, not-so-super-huge, and the least super huge. Even your Irish wolfhound can get a good night's sleep. In line with the luxury hotel's themed pet package "It's Reigning Cats and Dogs," as many as 30 dogs have been known to stay at the 335-room Palomar at one time. Bring your pooch to the Bark Bar, the three-tiered water bowl outside this Kimpton Hotel, before venturing inside to your own watering hole. Besides a dog bed, complimentary pet amenities include food bowls and treats (neighborhood dogs know to beeline for the self-serve jar of biscuits near the dramatic glass entrance). For a fee, the pet concierge can also coordinate dog walking, daycare, grooming, massage, and yesterday's newspaper. With an eye on safety, the hotel provides tags with local contact information should you own a Houdini-inclined pup. Rooms range from $149 to as much as $600, depending on availability. Pets stay for free but need to be crated if left unattended. 2121 P Street NW; 202/448-1800; www.hotelpalomar-dc.com.

**Residence Inn by Marriott—Dupont Circle:** If your pet is on a special diet that requires cooking, consider checking into the 10-floor Residence Inn by Marriott. Each of the 107 suites comes equipped with a full-size refrigerator, conventional and microwave oven, dishwasher, and pans, silverware, and dishes. Two pets are permitted per room for a $100 one-time fee plus a $10 per day cleaning fee. The hotel provides food and water bowls and a dog bed, and

## DIVERSION

In the summertime, the Fairfax at Embassy Row hosts a **Doggie Happy Hour** 5–7 P.M. Thursday in its circular driveway, which it blocks off to traffic. You don't have to be a guest to join in the fun or nibble the lavish display of dog treats. Happy hour drinks and spirits are on hand for humans, too. 2100 Massachusetts Ave NW; 202/293-2100; www.starwoodhotels.com.

its policy allows mild-mannered pups to stay alone in the room, although don't expect housekeeping to come knocking. Rates range $135–600. On-site parking is available for $28. 2120 P St. NW; 202/466-6800; www.marriott.com.

**Topaz Hotel:** Zen in the city is a good way to describe the 99-room Topaz Hotel. The Eastern-inspired boutique Kimpton hotel is a health-conscious retreat for humans and dogs. If you request a Yoga or Energy Room, your lodging will come equipped with an alcove dedicated to the exercise of your choice: a recumbent or spinning bike, elliptical machine, or yoga mat and equipment, plus a sound system and workout DVDs. In past years, the Topaz Hotel has offered a "Doga for Dogs" package that includes a tongue-in-cheek photographic guide for "dogis" by Jennifer Brilliant. It's very cute. Rates start at $169 during holidays and summertime and at $369 the rest of the year. Overnight parking costs $30. Hybrid cars park free, and dogs stay free. 1733 N St. NW; 202/393-3000; www.topazhotel.com.

**The Fairfax at Embassy Row:** What a location. Besides eyeing the remarkable mansions on Embassy Row, you and your roving dog can amble over to Mitchell Park, Rock Creek Park, Dupont Circle, and Georgetown with relative ease. The Fairfax, formerly the Westin, admits dogs weighing under 40 pounds for no additional fee. Amenities include a luxurious signature bed for you and a dog bed for your furry friend. Sporty sorts will be pleased to know there is a 24-hour exercise facility. Dogs may not be left unattended in rooms. Rooms range $169–459. Overnight parking costs $20; valet costs $30. 2100 Massachusetts Ave NW; 202/293-2100; www.starwoodhotels.com.

# Logan Circle, Shaw, and U Street

Thanks to an influx of young professionals and a number of new pet-friendly lofts, the Greater Shaw area is experiencing one of the most burgeoning dog populations in all of Washington DC. It seems this part of town better known for jazz, Duke Ellington, and the Black Cat concert venue is developing something of a reputation for dog owners as well. A community group called Dog Owners of Greater Shaw led the charge to convert a portion of the Shaw Field area at 11th Street NW and Rhode Island Avenue into a fenced field for dog

## DETOURS

While U Street, Shaw, and Logan Circle might be short on green space, they're chockablock with enlightened shopping. MidCity Dog Days—the area's annual sidewalk sale in August—is actually a nod to the dog days of summer, not its clientele, but with the number of dog-friendly stores in this neighborhood it might as well be. The MidCity Business Association is actually in the process of designing window decals to identify dog-friendly stores. Until then, simply look for the universal Fido Welcome sign: a full water bowl.

**ACKC:** A bacon chocolate bar? The cruelty of it all. Theobromine poisoning notwithstanding, dogs can visit Artfully Chocolate Kingsbury Confections. 1529-C 14th St. NW; 202/387-2626; www.thecocoagallery.com.

**Barrel House Liquor:** Amazingly, we failed to notice the front door is built into an enormous wooden barrel the first time we visited. And no, we hadn't been drinking yet. Mutts can join you to pick up martini fixings. There is free parking behind the store (off Rhode Island Avenue). 1341 14th St. NW; 202/332-5999.

**Garden District:** Grow your own basil and get friendly advice on how to do it. Gardeners at both locations will coo over your wagging companion. Inside shop for houseplants: 1520 14th St. NW. Outside shop for gardens: 1801 14th St. NW; 202/797-9005; www.gardendistrict-dc.com.

**Go Mamma Go:** Italian glassware, Dutch art, Pennsylvania tableware, Czech crystal, you name it. Small dogs, or breeds that tread lightly, are welcome. 1809 14th St. NW; 202/299-0850; www.gomamago.com.

**Greater Goods:** Want to install solar panels? Or a tankless water heater? Or maybe just looking for biodegradable poop bags? Here is your one-spot shop for saving the planet—and Sparky can help. 1626 U St. NW; 202/449-6070; www.greatergoods.com.

**Green Pets:** If you subscribe to the mantra "healthy food, healthy pets," you've found the right place. It's affiliated with Dogs by Day,

owners to walk and play with their unleashed pets—and they succeeded! The "leash-cutting" ceremony for DC's first, albeit temporary, dog park garnered a chorus of happy, approving yaps (www.shawdogs.org).

## PARKS, BEACHES, AND RECREATION AREAS

### 27 Logan Circle

🐾🐾 (See the Northwest DC map on page 46)

On weekdays before and after work an uncanny ritual unfolds. Big, leashed Labradors pull with extra horsepower down the sidewalk and Boston terriers the boarding and daycare facility next door. 1722 14th St. NW; 202/986-7907; www.greenpets.com.

**Home Rule:** Like a very mini department store, stocked with your home necessities—stylish, too. 1807 14th St. NW; 202/797-5544; www.homerule.com.

**Lee's Flower and Card Shop:** Say hello to Lily the cat, the feline member of the family who has owned the store for three generations. Cute dog cards, too. 1026 U St. NW; 202/265-4965; www.leesflowerandcard.com.

**Logan's Hardware:** The store has treats! It's a clever sales ploy: Your dog drags you inside. You buy yet another extension cord. The friendly folks at Logan Hardware also sell pet food and supplies. 1416 P St. NW; 202/265-8900; www.loganhardware.com.

**Mitchell Gold + Bob Williams:** The upscale furniture store has a resident greeter, a Welsh terrier named Mensch. 1526 14th St. NW; 202/332-3433; www.mgandbw.com.

**PNC:** Bank and bark. 1405 P St. NW; 202/835-7900; www.pnc.com.

**Pulp:** Best offbeat greeting card selection in town. As the sign on the door says, Dogs Are Always Welcome (Owners Too). 1803 14th St. NW; 202/462-7857; www.pulpdc.com.

**RCKNDY:** Sweet home décor with modern lines—also friendly for calm dogs. 1515 U St. NW; 202/332-5639; www.rckndy.com.

**Shoe Fly:** Satisfy your shoe fetish. Dogs without a hankering for leather may join you. 1520 U St. NW; 202/332-1077; www.shoeflyonline.com.

**Sun Cleaners:** Say hi to Packoo and Yeppy, a Korean Jindo and shih tzu, respectively, who hang out behind the counter. 1408 14th St. NW; 202/462-2502.

**U Street Organic Cleaners:** Leashed dogs welcome. 1513 U St. NW; 202/745-5722.

snort in anticipation at the crosswalk as their furry pals come streaming into Logan Circle. You would think the Pied Piper sat at its center instead of the bronze statue of Civil War General-Senator John Alexander Logan atop his horse. Tails wag and leashes tangle as the Circle Dogs touch noses and sniff around the wide, shaded grass rotary. Logan Circle is known as the heart of Washington's premiere neighborhood for Victorian architecture—there's even a Christmas tour of the late-19th-century beauties—and it's quickly becoming the heart of a burgeoning community of "dog people," too. Circle-goers occasionally use the low-fenced area around the equestrian statue for off-leash doggy play, but it usually ends with a ticket from DC police. Another warning: Watch out for chicken bones, especially near the benches. Logan Circle is located at the junction of Vermont and Rhode Island Avenues, and 13th and P Streets NW.

## 28 Thomas Circle

(See the Northwest DC map on page 46)

Surrounded by busy, honking traffic, Thomas Circle is a pit stop, not a destination. But given the aforementioned scarcity of grass here near Downtown, we decided to include it. There is just enough lawn to snuffle about and tip your hat (or, ahem, lift your leg) to the statue of Union General George Henry Thomas. Conveniently close to two paw-friendly hotels, the Residence Inn and the Westin, Thomas Circle is located at the junction of Massachusetts and Vermont Avenues, and 14th and M Streets NW.

### PLACES TO EAT

**Ben's Chili Bowl:** The home to the most famous dog in Washington DC—the chili half-smoke. Ben's celebrated a half century of serving the Shaw neighborhood in 2008, with Bill Cosby emceeing. Ordering at Ben's Chili Bowl is really a two-person affair, since you can't bring your dog inside and U Street is not an ideal place to tie up and leave your dog. 1213 U St. NW; 202/667-0909; www.benschilibowl.com.

**Café Saint-Ex:** The aeronautical theme inside this contemporary French-American bistro is a tribute to French aviator-author Antoine de Saint-Exupéry, who wrote *The Little Prince*. From the patio—that's where you'll be sitting—it's a pleasant sidewalk café. Dogs are allowed on the periphery of the flower boxes (or tucked in between them), although it's a little tricky figuring out where to tie the leash. The leg of your chair is a good option. Waiters will bring water if you ask. 1847 14th St. NW; 202/265-7839; www.saint-ex.com.

**Caribou Coffee:** At least six people directed us to this a hound-happy haven. The Minnesota-based coffee company brews a less-burned roast than you'll find at Starbucks, and the staff at this location is unflappably friendly. There is a spacious pet-friendly patio and also free wireless Internet. 1400 14th St. NW; 202/232-4552; ww.cariboucoffee.com.

**Commissary:** Not only does Commissary have pet-friendly outdoor seating, it even has a few items for dogs on the menu! These app-PAW-tizers include sweet potato bars and carob bears. Human diners can look forward to tasty sandwiches, salads, pizza, and other casual dining favorites. Commissary opened in 2008 in the space formerly occupied by Merkado and is under the same ownership. 1443 P St. NW; 202/299-0018; www.commissarydc.com.

**Logan Tavern:** This neighborhood restaurant and bar serves up dependable burgers and hand-cut French fries, plus other American comfort food favorites with a hint of Asian flair. The weekend brunch, complete with mimosas or

Bloody Marys, is especially good. Circle Dogs frequent the tavern's patio. 1423 P St. NW; 202/332-3710; www.logantavern.com.

## PLACES TO STAY

**Hotel Helix:** The 178-room boutique Kimpton hotel makes every effort to be shagadelic, right down to welcoming guests who are actually shaggy. The fun starts when you walk through the gold curtain entrance inspired by Hollywood; at check-in your pooch receives amenities such as a bed, bowl, mat, and treats. Leashes, toys, and food are also available for purchase in case you left home without them. Be sure to return to the lobby for the daily "bubbly hour" so you can toast to your 15 minutes of fame. Cheers! Rates start at $149 during holidays and summertime; they start at $329 the rest of the year. 1430 Rhode Island Ave. NW; 202/462-9001; www.hotelhelix.com.

**Hotel Rouge:** The vampish, loungy 137-room Kimpton boutique hotel sets the mood with low lighting and deep, sexy red hues accented by Venus statues. Rooms are reasonably priced, clean, and spacious, and include extra perks such as Aveda bath amenities and delivery of *The New York Times* each morning. Your sassy sidekick stays free of charge and enjoys Hotel Rouge's "No Need to Beg" pet program. The complimentary package includes a copy of *Fido Friendly* magazine, treats, a walking map for the neighborhood, and poop bags. Hotel Rouge welcomes pets of all breeds, species, and sizes—in fact, a traveling Sea World show once stayed here. So trust us, hotel staff won't bat an eye if you check in with your Tibetan mastiff. Located on 16th Street, just north of Scott Circle. Rates start at $149 during holidays and summertime; they start at $329 the rest of the year. 1315 16th St. NW; 202/232-8000; www.rougehotel.com.

## DIVERSION

The Hotel Helix opens its festively lit brick patio 5–8 P.M. Wednesday mid-June through September for a **Frisky Business Happy Hour.** Hotel Helix jointly hosts the yappy hour with the Washington Humane Society and AnimalAttraction.com, an online community targeting pet-loving singles. Choose themed drinks and eats off the "Bark Bites" menu while your social schnauzer enjoys tasty nibbles, and a portion of the proceeds will benefit the Washington Humane Society. Likewise, AnimalAttraction.com will donate $1 for every guest who joins its interactive website. But that's not the best part: Every week, the Washington Humane Society will bring an adoptable dog to make friends and hopefully find a home. Should you find yourself expanding your family of fur-balls, the Hotel Helix will donate a complimentary overnight stay. 1430 Rhode Island Ave. NW; 202/462-9001; www.hotelhelix.com.

# Bloomingdale and LeDroit Park

LeDroit Park and Bloomingdale are rapidly gentrifying neighborhoods that are still very much in transition, with some of its brownstone homes lovingly tended and some sitting in neglect. A newcomer to the neighborhood told us a story about walking Pixie, his rescue Pomeranian-Papillon mix, past a bunch of police cars outside an apartment complex on Florida Avenue. In their curiosity, they failed to notice the arrested man, cuffed on the curb. Even in that hour the cuffed man couldn't help but comment, "Man, your dog is adorable!" In its own way Bloomingdale is becoming a very dog-friendly place. A dog park application has even been submitted for part of the grounds at the recently closed Gage-Eckington School. "It's in the middle of nowhere but close to a lot," said Pixie's owner. Word to the wise: watch for loose, unfriendly guard dogs on First Avenue south of Florida Street.

## PARKS, BEACHES, AND RECREATION AREAS

### 2.9 Crispus Attucks Park

(See the Northwest DC map on page 46)

Affectionately called an "urban oasis" by the gardeners who tend it, Crispus Attucks Park is a landscaped courtyard behind a single city block of row houses in DC's Bloomingdale neighborhood, tucked out of view from the street. The 1.36-acre community park might not turn heads in upper Northwest DC, but here the grass and gardens are a rare find and a relief to pavement-trodden paws.

Crispus Attucks Park, on the former site of a burned building and hotbed of illegal activity, is now a patchwork of neighborhood devotion, each landscaped corner weeded or mowed by someone who lives nearby. We're talking about a tear-the-decrepit-concrete-up-with-your-bare-hands-and-plant-daisies kind of devotion. Aided by organizations such as Casey Trees, the Embassy of Australia, and to a lesser degree, DC Government, Bloomingdale residents slowly cultivated what used to be nicknamed the "Cave Yard" into Crispus Attucks Park, named after the first man, a former slave, to die in the Revolutionary War.

The park is privately owned for public use, which, as you can imagine, is complicated. As of 2008, the park board of directors had cordoned off much of the park with green temporary fencing to distinguish the "dog-free" area from the "dog-friendly" zone. Sadly, Bloomingdale dogs got the short end of the stick in this community tug-of-war; neighbors whose property borders the lot had tired of stepping in dog doodoo. To keep the remaining portion of the park open to frisky visitors, please respect the rules: stay in the designated pet-friendly zone, keep your dog out of the planters, and use the complimentary poop bags provided by Tails of the City (202/261-6615; www.tailsofthecitydc.com). If you find yourself a regular at the park, consider signing up for some weeding.

The park is bounded by the alleys of the 2000 blocks of North Capitol, First

## DETOURS

**Timor Bodega:** You won't find this anywhere else in Washington DC: a place to grocery shop with your dog. Denali, who waits patiently in front of Safeway several times per week (sometimes per day), is unspeakably envious. The small organic market is the pet project of owner Kim Wee, who opened up shop in 2007. Since Wee does not have his own dogs, he loves on yours instead. Think of Timor Bodega as Whole Foods in a sardine can—stocked with wholesome organic groceries and farm-fresh produce. Wee bought the market after becoming interested in coffee roasting. He sells limited amounts of coffee he roasts himself on weekends, and he also plans to host dog-friendly wine-tastings. 200 Rhode Island Ave. NW; 202/588-5612; www.timordc.com; 4:30–8:30 P.M. Mon.–Fri., 8:30 A.M.–7:30 P.M. Sat.–Sun.

**The Brass Knob Backdoors Warehouse:** If architectural scavenging pushes your buttons, then head to the Brass Knob Backdoors Warehouse to sniff out the gems. There is one very important caveat: the warehouse is also home to kitties. One frequent scavenger warned that an assertive dog combined with an inattentive owner could lead to disaster "on the scale of a Tom and Jerry cartoon." 57 N. St. NW; 202/265-0587; www.thebrassknob.com/backdoors.

Streets NW and the unit blocks of V and U Streets NW. Again, you won't see it from the road. Park on the street, and follow the sign for Crispus Attucks Court. www.crispusattuckspark.org.

## PLACES TO EAT

**Big Bear Coffee Shop:** "A bug light for the yupster crowd," is one patron's apt description for Big Bear Coffee. Your parched pup will find not one, but three or four water bowls on the stone pavers out front and at least one barista keeps the company of a dog. These guys are serious about their beans. As a purveyor of Counter Culture coffee (the puritanical roaster based in Durham, North Carolina), Big Bear brews a mean cup o' Joe and serves cappuccinos and lattes with an artful flourish. On the food menu, the salads and sandwiches are simple, satisfying morsels, of which the grilled cheese reigns king. Big Bear's ecofriendly, compostable cornstarch cups and free wireless Internet score extra points, too. On Sunday afternoon, there is no better spot in the neighborhood than sitting under the coffee shop's umbrellas. The petite Bloomingdale Farmer's Market sets up on R Street 10 A.M.–2 P.M. on Sunday May through November. A narrow triangle park lines the opposing side of R Street, a handy pit stop en route to Big Bear Coffee Shop. Located at First Street and R Street NW. 1700 First St NW; www.bigbearcafe-dc.com.

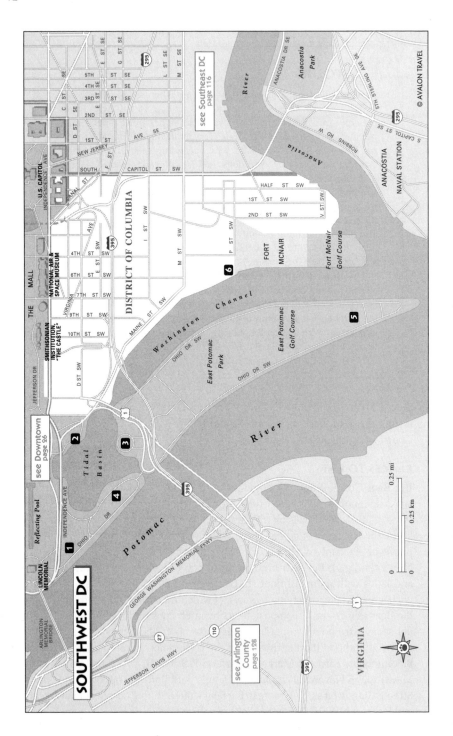

**CHAPTER 3**

# Southwest DC

Although it's the smallest of the District's quadrants, Southwest DC is nearly one-third paw-friendly parkland. We calculated this ratio through a highly technical and scientific method of measuring the extra Denali drool on the car window. We won't go into the details. Our findings, we assure you, are trustworthy: Dogs like Southwest DC.

In large part thanks to the sizeable East Potomac Park, better known as Hains Point to many, tiny Southwest has some wide expanses to explore. It's a perfect place to spread a blanket, have a picnic, and watch the sunset—that is, after chasing the geese first. During DC's annual National Cherry Blossom Festival, thousands of people fly in from around the world just to visit the Tidal Basin in Southwest DC and witness the delicate pink blossoms throw off winter's stronghold.

This quadrant includes the Thomas Jefferson Memorial and the Franklin Delano Roosevelt Memorial (complete with a larger-than-life statue of

## PICK OF THE LITTER—SOUTHWEST DC

BEST PARK
**East Potomac Park,** Tidal Basin and Washington Channel
(page 96)

BEST MEMORIAL
**Franklin Delano Roosevelt Memorial,** Tidal Basin and
Washington Channel (page 96)

BEST PLACE TO EAT
**Cantina Marina,** Waterfront (page 98)

BEST PLACE TO STAY
**L'Enfant Plaza Hotel,** Waterfront (page 99)

Fala, the 32nd president's Scottish terrier), and also lesser known statues and memorials such as the Women's Titanic Memorial and the Maine Lobsterman. In fact, I-395 bisects Southwest and separates the out-of-towners from the locals in an uncanny way. Walk east of the Interstate for a more local flavor.

If you're hungry, look no farther than the small waterfront lined with seafood restaurants on the Potomac River. Whatever you do, don't miss the Cantina Marina's doggie happy hour 5–8 P.M. on Mondays. Although really, Denali says anytime is a good time to visit the Cantina. With the new Nationals Park stadium completed in nearby Southeast DC, Cantina's manager says, "81 days a year Southwest is the safest part in town." Southwest DC includes the area south of Independence Avenue, inland of the Potomac River, and west of South Capitol Street.

# Tidal Basin and Washington Channel
## PARKS, BEACHES, AND RECREATION AREAS

### 🐾 Polo Fields
😊 (See the Southwest DC map on page 92)

No, the Polo Fields are not a new fragrance Denali is wearing. It's a real place. The grassy expanse is located between Independence Avenue, Ohio Drive, and the Tidal Basin. DC dog owners often traipse over to these waterfront athletic fields to take advantage of the fenced-in grass fields for off-leash play, a risky move on National Park Service land. Polo is in fact played here occasionally, but more often you'll see heated Ultimate Frisbee and softball games unfolding. A walk on the riverfront just south of the Polo Fields in the direction of Hains Point is another favorite activity. From DC, take Constitution Avenue toward the Potomac to a left on 17th Street (away from the White House). Turn right on Independence Avenue. Take your second left at the light onto Ohio Avenue. Park wherever you can. 202/426-6841; www.nps.gov/nama.

## 2 Tidal Basin

🐾🐾🐾 🐾 (See the Southwest DC map on page 92)

During cherry blossom season, Denali likes nothing more than to walk the 1.8-mile loop around the Tidal Basin—that is except during the actual National Cherry Blossom Festival, when sidewalk space is as hard to find as an English bulldog without sleep apnea. The trick is to tour this quintessential Washington rite of spring just prior to the two-week festival, which occurs in late March and early April, or else visit early in the morning. Time it right and you'll be able to set fresh tracks through the feathery light-pink Akebono and white Yoshino cherry blossoms that float from the branches with the softness and delicacy of a springtime snowfall.

The 1,300 blossoming trees around the Tidal Basin date back to 1912, when the city of Tokyo, Japan, gifted 3,000 cherry trees of 12 different varieties as a token of friendship. More than 3,700 trees now grow in East and West Potomac Parks and on the Washington Monument grounds.

The Tidal Basin is a worthwhile dog-walk or dog-jog during the other 50 weeks of the year, too—just note that it's not a good dog-swim. A few individuals have braved jumping into the Tidal Basin, but these waters aren't meant for dog-paddling, so be sure to keep Lucy on leash. Limited parking is available near the Tidal Basin paddleboat house on Maine Avenue SW, but your best bet is to park at East Potomac Park and backtrack on foot. 202/426-6841; www.nps.gov/nama or www.nps.gov/cherry.

## 3 Thomas Jefferson Memorial

🐾🐾 🐾 (See the Southwest DC map on page 92)

We're lucky Thomas Jefferson was the primary author of the Declaration of Independence, and not one of his two Briards, a breed of French sheepdog. Just imagine what inalienable rights might have been penned instead—perhaps the right to "Life, Liberty, and the pursuit of...Cats!" At the Jefferson Memorial, as with the Lincoln Memorial, dogs are not allowed inside the dome. Even so, a walk up these white marble stairs is well worth the trip, especially at night. Not only will you be rewarded with a glimpse of the 19-foot bronze statue of our third president through the memorial's stately Ionic columns, but if you spin 180 degrees, to the left of the Washington Monument you'll see one of the best views of the White House in the city. Located on the southeast side of the Tidal Basin; 202/426-6841; www.nps.gov/thje.

## 4 Franklin Delano Roosevelt Memorial

🐾🐾🐾 🐾 (See the Southwest DC map on page 92)

Franklin D. Roosevelt is the only U.S. president to have served four terms in office, and his famously loyal Scottie, Fala, is the only presidential pet to be immortalized in a national memorial. The Franklin Delano Roosevelt Memorial is picturesquely situated on the west side of the Tidal Basin with vistas of the Washington Monument framed by cherry trees. A visit to the memorial is a sensory experience for dogs, with a rushing waterfall fountain and Great Depression-era sculpted figures whose bronze overcoats they can walk right up and sniff. The memorial's location near the Tidal Basin and Polo Fields allows for convenient add-ons to lengthen your dog walk, too.

The memorial is divided into four outdoor "rooms," one for each of the 32nd president's tumultuous terms. While Denali is no history buff, she took special note of the third room, where a bronze statue of Fala sits at the president's feet. Officially named "Murray the Outlaw of Falahill" after one of Roosevelt's Scottish ancestors, Fala witnessed history as few dogs have: As representatives of 26 nations signed a Declaration by the United Nations endorsing the Atlantic Charter in the president's study, laying the foundation for the UN's ultimate formation three years later, one witness recalled, "the only sound came from Fala who was stretched out sleeping heavily—oblivious of the momentous happenings." Located between the Tidal Basin and the Potomac River off Ohio Drive, where limited parking is available. For additional parking, continue on to Hains Point; 202/426-6841; www.nps.gov/fdrm.

## 5 East Potomac Park

🐾🐾🐾 🐾 (See the Southwest DC map on page 92)

Better known as Hains Point, this narrow 328-acre peninsula juts into the Potomac River, helping to create Washington Channel and the protected harbor of the Southwest Waterfront. During its busiest hours, East Potomac Park is an active training circuit, with runners, cyclists, in-line skaters, and triathletes jockeying for space on the smooth, one-way, 3.2-mile road around the peninsula. More often, however, this pancake-flat point is nearly empty save for a few anglers at the river's edge and a handful of federal workers playing hooky at the 18-hole public golf course in the spit's middle. This is the loneliest stretch of the annual Marine Corps Marathon in late October.

Denali, if given half a chance, beelines for the tip of Hains Point, a wide grassy area ideal for romping and sniffing Canada geese poop. She likes to approach the point after a long walk on the slanted sidewalk that circumscribes the entire park, affording views of airplanes taking off and landing at Ronald Reagan Washington National Airport to the southwest, and small sailing boats and yachts bobbing at the docks to the northeast. Just watch for fishing hooks under-paw. To drive to East Potomac Park, take the Potomac Park exit off I-395. Located southeast of the Tidal Basin on Ohio Avenue. Hains

Point is closed to traffic 3 P.M.–6 A.M. on summer weekends and holidays. 202/426-6841; www.nps.gov/nama.

# Waterfront

That fishy smell means you're getting closer. The Southwest Waterfront is one of those places that many people catch a whiff of but never visit, and you owe it to your four-pawed companion to change that. Every DC dog should visit the waterfront at least once. It can be raucously noisy in some places, such as in the Maine Avenue Fish Market, and astonishingly peaceful in others, such as at the foot of the Women's Titanic Memorial. Just mosey along the strand until you find the area that best suits you and your dog's sensibilities.

Even though the Tidal Basin is just a stick's throw away, you'll find few tourists at the waterfront. In fact, you'll find far more tour bus drivers, since this is a convenient place to park while their passengers flock to the National Mall and Memorial Parks. A notable exception is during the National Cherry Blossom Festival, when this is a prime place to view the fireworks.

One of Denali's favorite waterfront activities is to ogle the Washington Channel marinas, whining at the lucky dogs hopping in and out of the sailboats, yachts, and party barges that push off into the Potomac from here. Oddly, you'll find a handful of boats from very landlocked places in these slips (West Virginia? Arizona?). But then this river harbor is hardly the open sea, even if it does have that potent fishy perfume. While focused on the waterfront proper, this section includes the entire area south of Independence Avenue, east of the Tidal Basin and Washington Channel, and west of South Capitol Street.

## PARKS, BEACHES, AND RECREATION AREAS

### 6 Titanic Memorial
🐾 🐾 ⬤ (See the Southwest DC map on page 92)

At first glance, Denali thought the sculptor of the Women's Titanic Memorial had taken a cue from film director James Cameron. As it turns out, it's the other way around. The memorial was erected in 1931, as the inscription reads, to honor "the brave men who perished in the wreck of the *Titanic,* April 15, 1912. They gave their lives that women and children might be saved." Often overlooked unless you happen to be chugging out of Washington Channel by boat, the 13-foot granite sculpture's image of a man with outstretched arms has achieved cinematic superstardom through Leonardo DiCaprio and Kate Winslet's bow scene in the 1997 blockbuster *Titanic.*

More than 1,500 people perished when the unsinkable *HMS Titanic* sank. Twelve dogs were known to be aboard, and of those, only three survived: two Pomeranians and a Pekingese. One Titanic passenger named Ann Isham is reputed to have refused to board a lifeboat without her Great Dane—sadly, though not surprisingly, neither lived. The memorial is a short walk south from the Cantina Marina, near where the sidewalk ends across from Fort Lesley J. McNair. You'll also find a nice grassy patch that is popular with local dogs in front of some nearby waterfront apartments. The closest intersection is 4th and P Street SW.

## PLACES TO EAT

**Cantina Marina:** At the far end of the Southwest waterfront you'll spy the blue-and-yellow tin-roofed shack on the river, your portal to the Gulf Coast. On an evening with the breeze in your face and Tom Petty tunes piped overhead, the Cantina Marina can't be beat. The cuisine is both Tex-Mex and Cajun-Bayou, the drinks are mostly margaritas and beer, and the atmosphere is about as laid-back as you can find inside District lines. Denali comes here for the bar food that inevitably lands on the blue pool deck floors. The outdoor deck is open from April through October. As an outdoor restaurant, and thus not bound to the same DC health code restrictions as regular restaurants, the Cantina is dog-friendly every day of the week. Dogs are only turned away if the Cantina is at capacity. 600 Water St. SW; 202/554-8396; www.cantina marina.com.

**Maine Avenue Fish Market:** This open-air fish market proved to be too overwhelming for Denali, who tucked tail shortly after setting paw in the parking lot on a busy Sunday afternoon, but hardier mutts might fare better. For one of the cheapest waterfront meals in DC, order from the selection of fried fish and shellfish at one of these floating fishmonger stalls. Then amble less than a mile along the Southwest waterfront to the benches of the Titanic

## DIVERSION

From Memorial Day to Labor Day—once summer is officially under way—the Cantina Marina hosts a **Doggie Happy Hour** 5–8 P.M. on Monday evenings. The deal includes free pigs' ears, rawhide chews, or other snacks for your mutt, and discounted corn dogs and "Cadillac Margaritas" for you. Mmm... junk food. Water St. SW; 202/554-8396; www.cantina marina.com.

Memorial to nibble your catch. Be discriminating when you buy fresh seafood here during the dog days of summer. A safe and tasty bet is the fried "crab balls," mini crab cakes from Jimmy's Grill. Open 7 A.M.–9 P.M. daily. Located at 1100 Maine Avenue SW, just east of the I-395 overpass. You'll find more than 10 stalls in the market, but a few of the larger names are **Pruitt Seafood,** 202/554-2669; **Jessie Taylor Seafood,** 202/554-4173; and **Captain White Seafood City,** 202/484-2722.

## PLACES TO STAY

**L'Enfant Plaza Hotel:** This 370-room hotel is wedged into cement building federal-land. Thank goodness the Southwest waterfront and the National Mall are within easy walking distance. The hotel's namesake L'Enfant Plaza provides manicured grass and a Louvre-like glass pyramid for your dog's more urgent visits (of course, it's best to pee on the lawn, not the pyramid). Pups are allowed on the 12th floor only, with no more than two pets per room. There is a $250 deposit plus a $25 per-pet-per-night fee. For human guests, L'Enfant Plaza Hotel has a year-round rooftop swimming pool and free wireless Internet. The hotel is situated directly over the L'Enfant Plaza Metro Station. Should you descend into the station, one of DC's busiest, take a close look at the NASA-sponsored artwork above either exit. You might be surprised by who the astronauts inside the spacesuits are. Rates range $109–409. 480 L'Enfant Plaza SW; 202/484-1000; www.lenfantplazahotel.com.

**Residence Inn by Marriott, Capitol:** Designed for extended stays, all 233 suites of this Residence Inn include fully equipped kitchens with cookware, dishes, and cutlery. If you and your pup are staying for the long haul, take advantage of the hotel's complimentary grocery shopping service to fill your refrigerator. Dogs are allowed for a $200 nonrefundable fee plus a $10 per day cleaning fee. Rates range $159–509. Located very close to the National Mall at 333 E St. SW; 202/484-8280; www.capitolmarriott.com.

**The Mandarin Oriental:** This is top dog of lavish (read: pricey!) accommodations in Southwest DC, with 400 rooms of four-star decadence. The Mandarin Oriental's grand scale is apparent even from I-395 as you drive past. One friend lucky enough to stay here said the marble showers are bigger than our entire bathroom at home. While at the Mandarin Oriental you will find a top-rated spa and CityZen, the District's second best restaurant according to *Washingtonian Magazine,* but what you won't find is big dogs. Only pooches 40 pounds or less may check in for a $100 fee on the first day and a $50-per-pet-per-night fee thereafter. One dog is permitted per room, and dogs may not be left unattended. The Mandarin Oriental provides water and food bowls and a dog bed. Rates range $300–10,000. 1330 Maryland Ave. SW; 202/554-8588; www.mandarinoriental.com/washington.

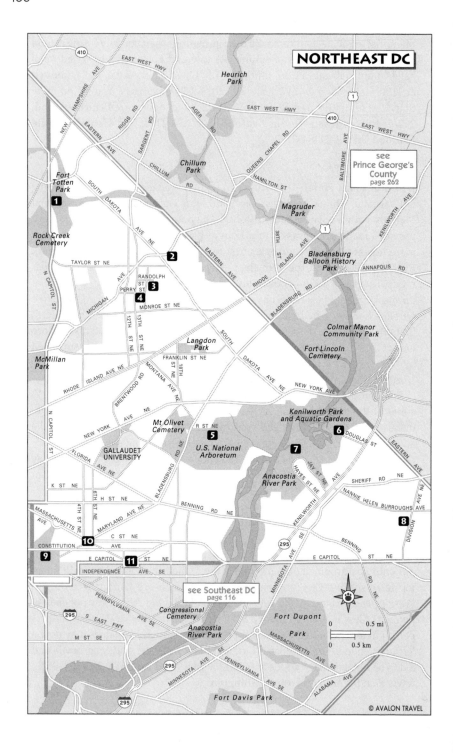

NORTHEAST DC

**CHAPTER 4**

# Northeast DC

Of Washington's four quadrants, Northeast DC is the most like a quiet middle child. For the most part it is steady and unassuming—and a bit overlooked. If you live outside of largely residential Northeast, chances are good you don't dedicate much brainpower to the place. Which is exactly what gets Denali wiggling: A new place? A new place to explore?

While Northeast DC makes less fuss over wagging tails than its Northwest counterpart, here you'll find three of Washington's most unexpected gems: the Mount St. Sepulchre Franciscan Monastery, the U.S. National Arboretum, and the Kenilworth Aquatic Gardens. These parks must be explored on leash, but they offer a refreshingly different take on being a tourist in your own city than the marble pomp and circumstance downtown. Each has its own intrigue and new smells for those closer to the ground. True, there are pockets of Northeast that are best walked only in broad daylight, and a few we wouldn't step paw inside, but the general mantra is to use your common sense.

## PICK OF THE LITTER—NORTHEAST DC

BEST PARKS

**U.S. National Arboretum,** New York Avenue (page 108)
**Kenilworth Aquatic Gardens,** Kenilworth (page 110)
**Lincoln Park,** Capitol Hill North (page 113)

BEST PLACE TO EAT
**Union Pub,** Capitol Hill North (page 114)

BEST PLACE TO STAY
**Hotel George,** Capitol Hill North (page 115)

Excluding Capitol Hill, most of Northeast resides beyond the scope of Pierre L'Enfant's original vision for the federal city. Middle and working class neighborhoods began to build up between 1900 and 1940 in particular, aided by the developing railways and streetcars, and many remain commuters' towns. As you move back toward the city's center, Capitol Hill quickly comes into focus. L'Enfant said it was clear where the U.S. Capitol belonged, as Jenkins Hill was "standing ready as a pedestal." Northeast DC includes the area east of North Capitol Street, south and west of Eastern Avenue, and north of East Capitol Street.

# Fort Totten

Best known as a commuter's hub for the Red, Green, and Yellow Metro lines, Fort Totten has a trash transfer station, reasonably priced housing, and the Civil War–era fort the Metro station is named for. That might change in coming years: Already work is under way on a $300 million 9.5-acre development project, The Dakotas, that will add 900 condos and apartments, a grocery store, restaurant, and other commercial real estate across the street from the Fort Totten Metro Station. The new complex, likened to Ballston in Arlington, Virginia, will be located on Riggs Road and South Dakota Avenue NE. No word yet on whether the new complex will include a pet store.

While not the worst part of town, Fort Totten is not immune to muggings in the early morning and late evening so stay vigilant, or swap Buster's Burberry collar for the studded leather one. This section includes the area east of North Capitol Street, south and west of Eastern Avenue, and north of Taylor Street NE.

## PARKS, BEACHES, AND RECREATION AREAS

### 🔟 Fort Totten Park

🐾 (See the Northeast DC map on page 100)

When you say it quickly, Fort Totten almost sounds like "forgotten," which is the feeling of this earthen fortification from the Civil War. Fort Totten is another in the chain of 68 forts and 93 batteries constructed to protect the Capitol from secessionist Virginia and trigger-happy Southern sympathizers in Maryland. What's left of these Civil War defenses has been preserved as the Fort Circle Parks.

Today you'll find a grassy hillside and a few picnic benches where barracks, officers' quarters, and a mess hall once stood. Denali's nose isn't as keen as some hounds', so she wasn't much help in sniffing out the low dirt walls located about 50 feet into the woods from the highest point on the U-shaped gravel road that cuts through the park. According to the National Parks Services, this is what's left of Fort Totten's "abattis [sharpened branches pointing outward], powder magazines, and rifle trenches, as well as the gun openings on the parapets." From Denali's point of view, this is a quiet park with a lot of grass to mark, but she wouldn't come here after dark.

The park is located on Fort Totten Road, just south of Riggs Road. Park on the street, and walk, don't drive, the gravel loop. 202/895-6000; www.nps .gov/cwdw.

# Brookland

Home to more than 60 Catholic institutions, Brookland is sometimes called "Little Rome." From most vantage points you can see a great dome dominating the hillside above the neighborhood. That's the Basilica of the National Shrine of the Immaculate Conception, a Catholic church whose edifice is as big as its name—in fact among the 10 largest church buildings in the world. With Catholic University and the Pope John Paul II Cultural Center just a few rosary beads down the road, the nickname quickly begins to make sense. Even with a strong Catholic presence, Brookland is hardly a place of homogeneity; you'll find it a racially and demographically diverse neighborhood. Dogs will be excited to visit Brookland for its off-the-beaten-path dog-walk destinations.

## DOG-EAR YOUR CALENDAR

In honor of St. Francis of Assisi, the patron saint of animals, the Franciscan Monastery welcomes pets of all sizes and persuasions to the annual **Blessing of the Animals.** The ceremony typically takes place in the church square around October 4, the feast day of St. Francis. While traditionally a Catholic celebration, many denominations in and around DC participate, including those listed here.

### WASHINGTON DC
**All Souls Memorial Episcopal Church,** Woodley Park
**Church of the Epiphany,** Downtown
**Mount St. Sepulchre Franciscan Monastery,** Brookland
**National City Christian Church,** Thomas Circle
**St. Luke's United Methodist Church,** Glover Park
**St. Thomas' Parish Episcopal Church,** Dupont Circle
**St. Timothy's Episcopal Church,** Hillcrest
**Washington National Cathedral,** Cathedral Heights

### VIRGINIA
**All Saints Episcopal Church-Sharon Chapel,** Alexandria
**Arlington Presbyterian Church,** Arlington
**Cherrydale Methodist Church,** Arlington
**Christ Church,** Alexandria
**Holy Trinity Lutheran Church,** Falls Church
**Silverbrook United Methodist Church,** Lorton
**St. Andrew's Episcopal Church,** Burke
**St. Mary's Episcopal Church,** Arlington

This section includes the area bounded by New York Avenue NE to the south, North Capitol Street NE to the west, Taylor Street NE and Michigan Street NE to the north, and Eastern Avenue to the east.

## PARKS, BEACHES, AND RECREATION AREAS

### 2 Triangle Park
🐾 (See the Northeast DC map on page 100)
Despite a contentious community debate on whether an official off-leash dog park was to be established here—and some finger-pointing about gentrification—this 60,000-square-foot wedge of grass remains one of the few

MARYLAND

**Grace Episcopal Church,** Silver Spring

**Holy Trinity Episcopal Church,** Bowie

**Little Flower Parish,** Bethesda

**Potomac United Methodist Church,** Potomac

**St. Dunstan's Church,** Bethesda

**St. James' Episcopal Church,** Potomac

**St. John's Episcopal Church,** Chevy Chase

**Unitarian Universalist Church,** Silver Spring

open spaces for pups in this part of Ward 5. This is even truer now that the Turkey Thicket Recreation Center and Howard University School of Divinity grounds are off-limits to Bowser. Large elm trees shade portions of the lawn, and sunshine washes over the rest of the flatland park. This is a good spot to pull up a lawn chair on the weekend if your dog enjoys sitting with you and watching the world drive by.

Brookland dog owners' bid to turn this wedge into a District-sanctioned dog park failed, and so it remains unfenced, adding a reason beyond DC laws to keep dogs on leash next to busy Michigan Avenue. Locals will sometimes still use the triangle park for off-leash romps. History buffs might be interested to know the park's south corner borders one of the oldest intersections in

## DOG-EAR YOUR CALENDAR

The Brookland Area Writers and Artists (BAWA) congregate to read poetry on a different theme each month—but in June the event adopts a special wag. BAWA has held the **Dog Day Poetry Reading** on the second Wednesday in June every year since 2004. Don't expect personal poetry. This is not an open mike but rather local writers reading famous odes to dogs. The four-to-the-floor crowd is sadly not invited to this literary opus in their honor, but dog lovers can still enjoy the free verse (yes, literally—no entry fee!).

Denali double-dog-dares you to keep a straight face during cartoonist-turned-poet Lynda Barry's "I love my master I love my master," a crowd favorite that is read every year. (A teaser: canine stream of consciousness meets "special brownies.") Located in the Brookland Visitor's Center on 9th Street across from Colonel Brooks' Tavern. 3420 9th St. NE; www.bawadc.com.

Northeast, dating back to the 1800s. Park on the street and remember to bring your own drinking water. Located between Michigan Ave. NE, Bunker Hill Rd. NE, and 18th St. NE; 202/673-7647; www.dpr.dc.gov.

## 🐾 Mount Saint Sepulchre Franciscan Monastery

🐾🐾🐾 (See the Northeast DC map on page 100)

Though not a devout Catholic, or any type of Catholic, Denali felt right at home in the rose gardens of this beautiful Franciscan monastery. Perhaps that is because St. Francis of Assisi, founder of the Franciscan monk order, is the patron saint of animals. Leashed dogs may sniff throughout the 44 acres of meticulously landscaped grounds and explore the Rosary Portico, an open-air hallway that wraps around the front lawn, church, and visitors center. The monastery also includes a rosary walk that winds through replicas of famous shrines and catacombs.

Throughout the contemplative lower gardens, the Stations of the Cross are tucked into fern-covered niches. One statue, however, resonated with Denali more than all those of the Virgin Mary: an alabaster figure with a distinct likeness to her own mother, a German shepherd, resting at the feet of Saint Francis. You'll find the dog statue near the Ascension Chapel, the gazebo-like stone structure close to 14th Street. The gate to the rosary walk is located midway down the Rosary Portico on the right side and closes at 4:45 P.M. Free parking is available in the lot on the corner of 14th and Quincy Streets. 1400 Quincy St. NE; 202/526-6800; www.myfranciscan.org.

## 4 Fort Bunker Hill Park

😽 (See the Northeast DC map on page 100)

While this wooded patch of military history doesn't merit the gas money for a trip on its own, it is a nice add-on to a loop around the grottos and gardens of the monastery. The overgrown park is crisscrossed with several trails once trod by Civil War soldiers and, like Fort Totten, is one of the Fort Circle Parks.

For those a little rusty on American history, this isn't *the* Bunker Hill of "Battle of Bunker Hill" distinction. That Revolutionary War fort is in Massachusetts and is the more famous site after which this Civil War fortification in DC was named. Nonetheless, Fort Bunker Hill at one point wielded 13 guns and mortars in the capital's defense. Denali, for her part, just likes getting a little dirt between her toes (do watch for glass, however). Located between 13th and 14th Streets NE and Otis and Perry Streets NE. The most convenient entrance from the monastery is on Perry Street. 202/895-6000; www.nps.gov/cwdw.

### PLACES TO EAT

**Colonel Brooks Tavern:** Named after the neighborhood's founder Col. Jehiel Brooks, this tavern can cook you a burger for carryout while you wait with your pooch outside. (The tavern has outdoor seating, but unfortunately it's only accessible by walking through the restaurant.) If you're lucky, you might catch the Dixie tunes that play here on Tuesday evenings. 901 Monroe St. NE; 202/529-4002.

**Yes! Organic Market:** Closer than the Whole Foods Markets in Northwest, this small natural foods market sells similar groceries and produce. You can usually find organic pet food, too. 3809 12th St. NE; 202/832-7715.

# New York Avenue and the Atlas District

We had the hardest time pinning down in what neighborhood the U.S. National Arboretum is located. It's flanked by Kingman Park, better-known Trinidad, Ivy City, and Gateway, a small industrial and residential 'hood across New York Avenue where *The Washington Times* is printed, but really the arboretum is an island unto itself in Northeast.

Denali packed her sun hat upon embarking toward Trinidad. Needless to say, she was sorely disappointed. A blog dedicated to the area, *Frozen Tropics*, says it all. The name of this predominantly working-class, African American neighborhood northeast of Capitol Hill likely traces back to the original landowner, rumored to have died in Trinidad before he could move to his new home. Hard hit by the crack epidemic in the 1990s, the streets of Trinidad are not a doggy destination—in fact, after a rash of homicides in summer 2008 and the military-style police checkpoints that followed, we recommend you steer clear of Trinidad entirely. The nearby U.S. National Arboretum, on the other paw, is absolutely worth a visit.

If you're looking for urban revival, head to the Atlas District just north of Capitol Hill, so named for the Atlas Performing Arts Center, a refurbished 1930s art deco cinema with multiple theaters and dance spaces for neighborhood performances. Rioting after the 1968 assassination of Martin Luther King Jr. decimated the popular shopping district along H Street, and a pulse of nightlife, restaurants, and entertainment is only now returning to the corridor. One eatery in particular, the Argonaut, makes a point to keep dogs in the mix.

This section includes the territory south of New York Avenue NE, west of the Anacostia River, north of H Street NE, and east of North Capitol Street NE.

## PARKS, BEACHES, AND RECREATION AREAS

### 5 U.S. National Arboretum

🐾🐾🐾 (See the Northeast DC map on page 100)

Odds are good you have driven past the arboretum before… and kept driving. From the highway it appears to be a dated USDA research facility, forgotten between New York Avenue's seedy nightclubs and tightly barred gas stations. But like C.S. Lewis' Narnia, step through the wardrobe and you'll find an adventure—and acreage—worth exploring on the other side.

The 446 acres of botanical research and cultivation are ideal for dog lovers itching to stretch their legs. Nine miles of roads and nearly as many trails

connect the numerous themed gardens, splendid in any season. You can hike up Mount Hamilton in late April amidst a blaze of blooming azaleas or return later in the year to admire the fall foliage of your home state's tree in the National Grove of State Trees.

Did we mention the sniffs? This is Denali's favorite part. The 2.5-acre herb garden is filled with 800 types of herbs from around the world. It was all she could do not to nibble the fresh mint. Which brings us to a few ground rules in the arboretum: In addition to remaining on leash, dogs cannot harm any plants, so that means no sampling the sweet bay, no peeing on the peonies, and no rolling in the rosemary. And of course, clean up after your pet.

In the entire park, only one garden is off-limits for dogs: the National Bonsai and Penjing Museum, where a vigorous tail wag could damage the collection of precious trees, valued at roughly $5 million. One bonsai, the Japanese White Pine, dates back to 1626—150 years before the United States of America even existed! If your pet is comfortable tied up outside the museum, it's absolutely worth a trip inside.

Despite these few no-paws zones, the National Arboretum's rolling expanse has far more places where dogs are allowed than where they are not. Open 8 A.M.–5 P.M. daily, except for December 25. Admission is free, as is the ample parking. The main entrance is on 24th and R Streets NE, off Bladensburg Road, but you can also enter at 3501 New York Avenue NE. 3501 New York Ave. NE; 202/245-2726; www.usna.usda.gov.

## PLACES TO EAT

**The Argonaut Tavern:** Does the Argonaut allow dogs? Yarrrr, she does, but only the salty dogs. Or was it the scurvy dogs? Denali can never keep it straight. This neighborhood bar is named after the Greek seafarers of the ship *Argo*, and as a result is whimsically themed with all things nautical (and pirate).

The Argonaut strives to serve seasonally inspired, local food with rustic sensibilities and always has a few good beers on tap. Rovers are invited inside the patio fence during the bar's doggy happy hours on Saturday afternoons before 5 P.M., but otherwise dogs must park it on the sidewalk. Incidentally, the Argonaut endorsed the proposed Kingman Field dog park, yet one more reason (besides the sweet potato fries) to patronize this friendly spot. If you can't remember the exact address of the Argonaut, just look for the garishly green building on H Street, a stark contrast to the wooden accents and soft light inside.

On weeknights, the Argonaut opens at 5 P.M. and stays open till the wee hours of the morning. You can also catch a late Saturday lunch there and brunch on Sunday. Metered street parking is free after 6:30 P.M. and all day Sunday. 1433 H St. NE; 202/397-1416; www.argonautdc.com.

# Kenilworth

## PARKS, BEACHES, AND RECREATION AREAS

### 6 Kenilworth Aquatic Gardens

🐾🐾🐾 🖐 (See the Northeast DC map on page 100)

In the eastern reaches of Washington, this 12-acre sanctuary is a blend of natural marshland and cultivated water lily gardens unlike anywhere else in the city. Kenilworth Aquatic Gardens feature more than 35 ponds filled with a wide range of tropical and hardy water lilies, lotus, and other aquatic plants. The lotus blooms peak in mid-July and are best viewed in the morning. If you plan to picnic, don't make it dinner: the gated park is open 7:30 A.M.–4 P.M.

Denali is not much of a water dog—but bogs, now that's a different story. One sniff of that fishy, muddy muck and she's ready to jump in paws-first. You have to wonder if it's the doggy equivalent of a Dead Sea beauty treatment. To her dismay, and the interior of the car's relief, the park requires dogs to stay on leash. It's best to follow one ranger's advice: "Keep her out of the mud unless you want her smelling like frogs."

The 1.4-mile round-trip detour along the River Trail is highly recommended; you can pick up the trail to the right of the lily ponds as you enter the park. Turtles, white egrets, blue herons, and Canada geese all call this swampland home, as do an unfortunate number of aluminum cans, plastic bottles, and other urban detritus—but the Anacostia is getting cleaner, if slowly.

Located across the Anacostia from the National Arboretum, the gardens can be hard to locate. Drive north on the Baltimore-Washington Parkway (US-295), and take the Eastern Avenue exit. At the light, make a U-turn to the left onto a southbound service road. After the U-turn, US-295 should be on your left. Drive two blocks and turn right on Douglas Street, then right again on Anacostia Avenue. The park will be in about 1.5 blocks on the left. 1550 Anacostia Ave. NE; 202/426-6905; www.nps.gov/keaq.

### 7 Kenilworth Park

🐾🐾 (See the Northeast DC map on page 100)

We visited Kenilworth Park on a misty Saturday morning and, aside from a pee-wee football game taking place at the neighboring Kenilworth-Parkside Recreation Center, we had the grassy floodplains to ourselves. Considerably quieter than the already quiet Kenilworth Aquatic Gardens just upriver, the advantages to Kenilworth Park are in some respects its disadvantages, too. You feel somewhat isolated walking through the mowed fields along U-shaped Deane Avenue and the marshy banks near the Anacostia River. That made for unhampered doggy playtime—Denali found plenty of Canada geese to greet— but we also felt compelled to keep one watchful eye on the park entrance. The parkland is flat and open, so it's fairly easy to see when another person or car is joining you. Had we brought a buddy it would have been easier to drop our guard. It's that funny fact that you usually feel safer in a crowd than alone with a single stranger. From the Baltimore-Washington Parkway (US-295), exit at Minnesota Avenue and turn left onto Deane Avenue NE and look for the park sign. 202/426-6905; www.nps.gov/keaq.

## 8 Marvin Gaye Park

(See the Northeast DC map on page 100)

In 2006, DC renamed the longest municipal park in its jurisdiction for legendary soul singer Marvin Gaye. Formerly named Watts Branch Park for the creek that drains into the Anacostia, the 1.6-mile-long park cuts directly through Ward 7 from the famed musician's boyhood home. (Gaye spent his teenage years on 60th Street NE in a low-rise DC public housing project in the easternmost corner of the District.) The name is not all that has changed in this long-neglected park in recent years. A revitalization effort spearheaded by nonprofit Washington Parks & People has cleaned up 2.7 million pounds of bulk trash and debris from the stream valley over five years—a fitting tribute to the environmental justice message in Gaye's songs "Mercy, Mercy Me (The Ecology)" and "What's Goin' On?" Where once stood the infamous Needle Park, a former open-air drug market, you'll now see a mosaic sign announcing Marvin Gaye Park and a Saturday farmers market. We saw several leashed dogs and owners ambling along the paved path that runs the park's length. That said, if this isn't your turf you might not feel totally comfortable here. Park activists hope Marvin Gaye Park will soon be the east-of-the-river equivalent of Rock Creek Park, but it's not there quite yet. Located near Division Avenue and Foote Street NE. Park on the street. 202/673-7647; www.dpr.dc.gov or www.washingtonparks.net/marvingaye.html.

# Capitol Hill North

In many ways Capitol Hill is its own microcosm, a world where everything you need is within 10 blocks of your front door and as a result, more than a few Hill hounds quite happily stay put. One owner confessed, "I hardly ever get off the Hill." Some local dog owners do neat rounds between Lincoln Park, Union Pub, and the Union Veterinary Clinic, and then back to the pub.

This is a neighborhood where politicians have handlers just like dogs, and every four to eight years there are new alphas to mark the territory. In few places will you witness such vigorous multitasking as on Capitol Hill: Residents walk the family golden retriever while balancing checkbooks, talking on the phone, and checking their BlackBerries. Trailing a few paces behind, their dogs catch up on "pee-mail."

Perhaps the best part about Capitol Hill is that sidewalk cafés are plentiful, as is the people-watching, and most restaurants allow well-behaved pets to join you if they are tied up outside the patio's fence nearest to your table. Capitol Hill will soon become a better place for dogs to play, too. In 2008, the DC Department of Parks and Recreation approved plans for an official dog park at Kingsman Field (1375 E St. NW). "Hill Hounds" (www.groups.yahoo. com/group/hillhounds), the community group that had doggedly lobbied for the park, count this as cause for jubilation. This section includes the area north of East Capitol Street, east of North Capitol Street, south of H Street NE, and west of 14th Street NE.

## PARKS, BEACHES, AND RECREATION AREAS

### 🐾 U.S. Capitol Grounds

🐾🐾🐾 (See the Northeast DC map on page 100)

> [My dog] can bark like a congressman, fetch like an aide, beg like a press secretary, and play dead like a receptionist when the phone rings.
>
> Gerald B. H. Solomon, U.S. Congressman

A friend once said if you ever look at the U.S. Capitol and don't feel impressed by its weighty, neoclassical heights, it's time to leave Washington. Rising 285 feet above the ground and weighing 4,500 tons, the twin-shell white dome is a marvel of 19th-century engineering that still inspires. Non-service dogs cannot enter the Capitol, but with nearly 59 acres of landscaping immediately surrounding the bastion of "Yankee democracy" and approximately 274 acres under Capitol jurisdiction in total, your pup won't miss the tour of the inner chambers.

Although post-9/11 security measures have fenced off and detracted from some of the grounds' simple beauty (note: look for the approximately 40 trained German shepherds who help the U.S. Capitol Police patrol the perimeter), there are still lovely corners of the Capitol grounds to sniff out, a few we previously had not known existed. If the summer heat is insufferable, consider walking over to the **Summer House**, a brick hexagonal structure on the sloping hillside on the northwest corner of the grounds. The shaded structure contains benches and three drinking fountains, as well as an ornamental fountain to cool DC's stickiest afternoons. A much larger fountain can be found in the distance between the Capitol and stately Union Station, where the **Senate Garage Fountain,** with its lion head sculptures, sprays water. If you hear a musical chiming, turn to face the nearby 100-foot-tall **Robert A. Taft Memorial and Carillon** and its 27 French-cast bells. The U.S. Capitol is located between Independence Avenue on the south, Constitution Avenue on the north, 1st Street NE/SE on the east, and 1st Street NW/SW on the west. 202/225-6827; www.aoc.gov.

## 🔟 Stanton Park

🐾 (See the Northeast DC map on page 100)

With its central location on the Hill, Stanton Park comes alive during "the dog hour," that window after work and before dinner when ties get loosened, pantyhose come off, and—wheeeeee! Out the door you both go for some fresh air at last.

While Stanton Park regulars are known to treat the square as a de facto dog park, they have to be quick on the leash draw—this is one corner of the city where police will issue warnings and occasionally ticket. With four acres, Stanton Park has just enough room to avoid tangling leashes and contains all the critical ingredients: grass, shade, and a drinking fountain (just bring a bowl). The main hitch is that pets are not allowed in the fenced-in playground, a conundrum for parents who arrive with both dogs and kidlets.

In the poetic way that city geography sometimes echoes history, Stanton Park is connected by Massachusetts Avenue to another popular Capitol Hill spot: Lincoln Park. When President Abraham Lincoln died, Secretary of War Edwin Stanton is reported to have issued his famous remark, "Now he belongs to the ages." Located at C Street NE between 4th and 6th Streets NE; 202/619-7225; www.nps.gov/cahi.

## 1️⃣1️⃣ Lincoln Park

🐾🐾 (See the Northeast DC map on page 100)

As Capitol Hill's largest green space with seven acres, Lincoln Park attracts equal crowds of frolicking children and frisky pets. On a midday stroll, both young mothers and dog-walkers can be seen with their charges. At least one doggy-deprived couple has been known to miss canine companionship so much that they sit in Lincoln Park with a full water bowl at their feet—a clever ploy to spend time with neighborhood dogs.

Lincoln Park is exactly one mile due east of the Capitol building; Pierre L'Enfant intended it to be the mile by which all other distances were measured. The long rectangle is like a sandwich: grass and trees on the outside and a sidewalk linking two statues heavy in symbolic importance in the middle. On Lincoln Park's west side, *Emancipation* depicts President Lincoln standing above an African American man as he breaks free of chains. Significantly, freed slaves paid for the statue's commission.

On the park's east end, well-known African American educator and government advisor Mary McLeod Bethune stands between two fenced-in playgrounds with drinking fountains (no dogs allowed). Hers was the first monument to honor a black woman in a public park in the District of Columbia, and only the second monument to honor an African American. The first was Alexander Archer, the model for the freedman in Lincoln's statue and the last person captured under the Fugitive Slave Act. Lincoln Park is located on East Capitol Street, between 11th and 13th Streets NE. Metered parking is available on the street. 202/619-7225; www.nps.gov/cahi.

## PLACES TO EAT

*A door is what a dog is perpetually on the wrong side of.*

Ogden Nash

**Armand's Pizza:** Deep dish Chicago-style pizza is what Armand's Pizza does best. Denali always wants to order the same toppings ("Meatzza! Meatzza!"), but less carnivorous folks will also find the white pizza scrumptious. It bears mentioning that Armand's doesn't cater to dogs like Union Pub across the street, but with pizza this good, be grateful your little fella is allowed under the green-roofed patio at all. 226 Massachusetts Ave. NE; 202/547-6600; www.armandspizza.com.

**Ebenezer's Coffeehouse** Here's a testimony to changing times around Union Station: As recently as 2002, this coffeehouse was a crackhouse. Now instead you'll find iced mochas, *café au laits,* free wireless Internet, and a lovely, wide brick patio for you and your dog to read the Sunday newspaper. Thirsty mutts will be pleased to find a water bowl out front.

Ebenezer's is independently owned and operated by National Community Church. The church holds services in the basement of the coffee shop on Saturday evenings—that's the worship band rumbling beneath your feet as you order your drink. 201 F St. NE; 202/558-6900; www.ebenezerscoffeehouse.com.

**Union Pub:** In Capitol Hill you could argue it's a fence. All that changes at the Union Pub, where dogs are allowed *inside* the patio during the seasonal Pooches on the Patio happy hours. On Saturday noon–4 P.M. May through September, a small gate in the wrought iron fence opens, and in no time at all one of the neighborhood's largest patios goes to the dogs.

Union Pub has several attractions: fully shaded seating with ceiling fans to make the summer heat more sufferable, more than two dozen tables to accommodate pups and their humans, and reasonable drink specials, including Flying Dog Tire Bite Golden Ale and Dogtail Vineyard wines. If you're lucky, a decent breeze even blows up Massachusetts Avenue. "It's just a nice leisurely thing for the neighbors here," explained owner Matt Weiss, especially as the city empties out on muggy August weekends.

On a quiet Saturday afternoon, a beagle, a greyhound, a golden retriever, a Great Dane, and a Portuguese water dog happily noshed on biscuits and water courtesy of nearby pet boutique Chateau Animaux and dog training experts at Anytime K9. Waiters say it's not uncommon for there to be four times as many dogs, so shy mutts are probably best left at home. 201 Massachusetts Ave. NE; 202/546-7200; www.unionpubdc.com.

**White Tiger Restaurant:** If you have a couple of spare hours and a hankering for lamb vindaloo, head to the White Tiger. Though not known for speedy service, it is known for reasonably priced and delicious Indian cuisine. Dogs can dine, but only if tied outside the wooden fence surrounding the patio. White Tiger's fence has more heft than some other Capitol Hill eateries, so this isn't an ideal setup for dogs struggling with separation anxiety—of course, Denali hears that is nothing a little chicken tikka masala can't fix. 301 Massachusetts Ave. NE; 202/546-5900; www.whitetigerdc.com.

## PLACES TO STAY

**Hotel George:** Our first president George Washington took his dogs very seriously, and so does this Kimpton hotel that shares his name. Conveniently located near Union Station and the U.S. Capitol, technically in Northwest DC, the hotel resides in a rarely mentioned Capitol Hill neighborhood called Swampoodle. (Denali asks if this is the doggy version of the Creature from the Black Lagoon.)

Hotel George is the quintessential paw-friendly accommodation on Capitol Hill. Pet packages change from year to year, but invariably Hotel George finds a way to give your pooch the presidential treatment. The 139-room boutique hotel offers a host of amenities, including complimentary dog walking and complimentary shoe shining (for you, not the dog). Other people perks include a 24-hour fitness center, men's and women's steam rooms, and Aveda bath products. The French-inspired Bistro Bis next door is not dog-friendly, but for breakfast see if you can order the cinnamony granola with berries to go—it's divine (15 E St. NW; 202/661-2700; www.bistrobis.com).

Some presidential trivia: George Washington, credited with breeding the American Foxhound, owned almost 40 hunting hounds with names such as Taster, Tipsy, Tippler, and Drunkard. As it turns out, Hotel George isn't a half-bad place to get a drink either. The hotel hosts a wine hour for dogs and guests on Monday through Friday evenings. Rates start at $169 in the low season, $309 in the high season. 15 E St. NW; 202/347-4200; www .hotelgeorge.com.

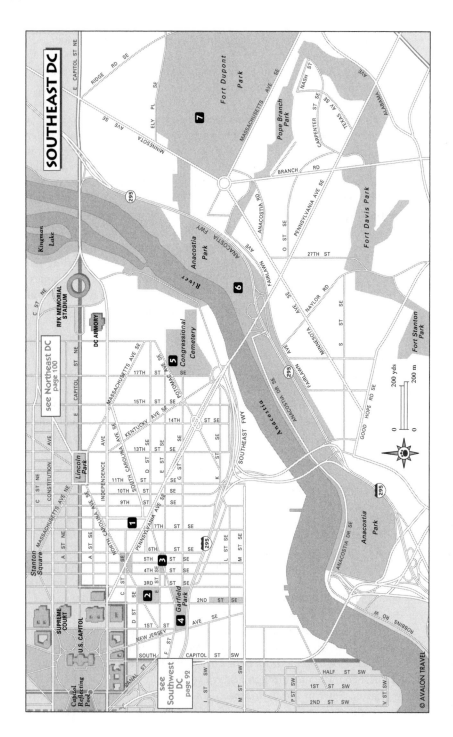

SOUTHEAST DC

see Northeast DC
page 100

see
Southwest
DC
page 92

Kingman
Lake

RFK MEMORIAL
STADIUM

DC ARMORY

Fort Dupont
Park

Pope Branch
Park

Fort Davis Park

Fort Stanton
Park

Anacostia
Park

Anacostia
River

Congressional
Cemetery

Lincoln
Park

Stanton
Square

SUPREME
COURT

U.S. CAPITOL

Capitol
Reflecting
Pool

Garfield
Park

Anacostia
Park

200 yds

200 m

© AVALON TRAVEL

# CHAPTER 5

# Southeast DC

Southeast DC is at once a cultural institution and the poorest DC quadrant. The cityscape changes dramatically as you drive east on Pennsylvania Avenue and cross the Anacostia River. Ironically, the president of the United States lives on the same street as some of the most poverty-stricken, crime-ridden neighborhoods. Even so, Southeast has a bad rap it only partially deserves and there are many, many places worth exploring here—yes, even in Anacostia.

On Capitol Hill you'll find a curious number of lawyers-turned-dog-trainers, or pet-store owners, or other dog-related occupation that makes them happier than being a Cujo in court. Capitol Hill–based trainer Nancy Kellner (202/543-8468; www.whatagooddog.net) and the owners of both Barracks Row pet stores Chateau Animaux and Pawticulars are among those. Capitol Hill's Eastern Market is a local favorite, with its flea and farmers market full of sights and smells, while Congressional Cemetery is a tail-friendly spot with a twist and a redeeming tale of canine community activism.

## PICK OF THE LITTER—SOUTHEAST DC

BEST DOG PARK
**Congressional Cemetery,** Capitol Hill South (page 121)

BEST CITY PARK
**Garfield Park,** Capitol Hill South (page 121)

BEST TRAIL RUN
**Fort Dupont Park,** Anacostia (page 126)

BEST PLACE TO EAT
**Belga Café,** Capitol Hill South (page 123)

BEST PLACE TO PICK YOUR BONES
**Union Meat Company,** Capitol Hill South (page 119)

Southeast DC also boasts the shining-new Nationals Park, home of the Washington Nationals Major League Baseball team (catch a fly ball for Fido!). As of yet, however, the only dog allowed in the stadium is the half-smoke of local institution Ben's Chili Bowl fame. (For a doggy stadium day you'll have to head to Maryland for Bark in the Park Day with the double-A Bowie Baysox.) On the other side of the Anacostia River, you'll find restful Anacostia Park, which lines the river with fields and open spaces and Fort Dupont Park, a historic Civil War defense with some worthwhile single-track. This chapter includes the area south of the Capitol and East Capitol Street, east of the Potomac River, and north and west of Southern Avenue.

# Capitol Hill South

Your impression of Capitol Hill's dog-friendliness likely has a lot to do with your frame of reference. One woman, recently returned from the Netherlands with her handsome blue-eyed Border collie mix, lamented all the District rules. No dogs on the Metro. No dogs in bars. No off-leash dogs in parks. Another Capitol Hill dog owner counted the neighborhood's praises. Denali sides with the latter camp. The woof scene might not rival Europe's tolerance for tail-waggers, but by DC standards, Capitol Hill is definitely a hot spot for Spot. Sidewalk cafés abound here, and you're hard-pressed to find a place that *doesn't* allow dogs in the outdoor seating (or at least close by, if the patio is fenced). The restaurants on the 600 block of Pennsylvania Avenue, on 7th

Street as you approach Eastern Market, and along historic Barracks Row on 8th Street are filled with good options. Add to that not one but two pet specialty boutiques and you've got a fur-friendly neighborhood. This section includes the area south of East Capitol Street and the Capitol building, west and north of the Anacostia River, and east of North Capitol Street.

## PARKS, BEACHES, AND RECREATION AREAS

### 1 Eastern Market

🐾🐾 🐾 (See the Southeast DC map on page 116)

Even a serious fire in April 2007 couldn't stamp out this Capitol Hill treasure. Open since 1873, this is DC's oldest continually operated fresh food public market. Meats, produce, seafood, pasta, baked goods, cheeses—if you need a wholesome ingredient, you'll find it at Eastern Market. Best of all, your foodie-inclined Fido can help you select farm-fresh produce grown throughout the Mid-Atlantic in the "farmer's line" along 7th Street on Saturday and Sunday, or help you fawn over vintage posters and handmade pottery (watch the tail!) from more than 175 weekend exhibitors. If your pup needs to get out some ya-yas before shopping, there is a very small fenced dog run near the flea market entrance at 8th and C Street.

Eastern Market's historic redbrick South Hall is located at 306 7th St. SE, but as the roof and interior undergo a $20 million renovation to repair extensive fire damages, vendors are housed in stalls inside the new, temporary East Hall, a white tent across the street. While your dog can't shop inside with you—a pity since farm kitchen restaurant Market Lunch is also located in here— you'll find, in Denali's opinion, the reason we came to Eastern Market in the first place: **Union Meat Company** (202/547-2626; unionmeat@comcast.net) sells beef bones ($0.89 per pound) and lamb bones ($1.29 per pound) for your

dog's gnawing pleasure. Eastern Market's indoor merchants are open Tues.–Sun.; the popular open-air farmers and flea markets are open on Saturday and Sunday. You'll need to drive the neighborhoods to find street parking. 202/544-0083; www.easternmarketdc.com.

## ❷ Folger Park and Providence Park
 (See the Southeast DC map on page 116)

While there are more popular dog hangouts on south Capitol Hill, these back-to-back parks merit a mention. Of the two parks, Providence is larger and has more turf, making it the better doggy destination. You'll sometimes hear locals call it "X Park" for the two pathways that crisscross the grassy city block.

Fifty years ago there wasn't a park here at all, but instead Providence Hospital, the oldest continuously operating hospital in the District. When Providence Hospital moved to Northeast DC and the original building was demolished in the 1970s, Congress purchased the empty lot to build a dormitory for the congressional page program. In the decades that followed the empty lot became a fixture for Capitol Hill dogs and Little League teams, and everyone keeps hoping Congress will postpone constructions plans indefinitely.

After letting your dog mark the spot in X Park, head to Folger Park to rest on the long, shaded benches in the memorial to 19th-century secretary of the treasury Charles J. Folger. The two blocks of parks are located between 2nd and 3rd Streets SE and D and E Street SE; 202/619-7225; www.nps.gov/cahi.

## ❸ Marion Park
 (See the Southeast DC map on page 116)

This 1.5-acre city park is in front of the DC Metropolitan Police First District Substation. To the benefit of the neighborhood, a symbiotic relationship has developed between local dog owners and the officers of Police Service Area 105. Capitol Hill pooches socialize on the grass between the short cast-iron fence that partially borders the park, and police officers benefit from these canine patrollers, whose presence on the streets during their morning and

## DOG-EAR YOUR CALENDAR

Since 2003, once a year Capitol Hill officers have organized a police lineup of a different breed: the **Annual Police Service Area 105 Dog Show.** With the aid of a regulation police bullhorn, the DC Metropolitan Police oversees this friendly competition between neighborhood dogs. Award categories include Waggiest Tail, Celebrity Look-Alike, Smallest Dog, and crowd favorite Owner/Dog Look-Alike. The dog show typically takes place in Marion Park the morning of the last Saturday in July. 500 E St. SE; 202/698-0068; www.mpdc.dc.gov.

evening constitutionals helps keep the Hill a little safer. The fully fenced playground on the park's west side is off-limits for Bowser, though you'll sometimes see dogs there late in the evening when kids are tucked into bed. Bring poop bags and a bowl to fill up at the water fountain. Located between 4th and 6th Streets SE and at the intersection of E Street and South Carolina Avenue SE; 202/690-5185; www.nps.gov/cahi.

## 4 Garfield Park

 (See the Southeast DC map on page 116)

Nearly hidden in the shadow of I-295, Garfield Park can be easily overlooked—but what a shame! This is arguably the favorite public park among south Capitol Hill dogs and their humans. (Congressional Cemetery wins as the all-time favorite—but dog-walking privileges cost a pretty penny there.) Due to its irregular shape, Garfield Park is larger than it looks at first glance. It is rarely crowded on the weekend; on weekdays, it's a mainstay for Capitol Hill dog walkers. You'll see these strong-armed men and women wrangling four or five pups at a time through the lawn and sidewalks.

Park users gravitate to different corners of the green space depending on their interests. Jocks head for the tennis, bocce, basketball, and volleyball courts in the park's east end. Kids and their caretakers carve out the middle of the park with its two playgrounds. The dog crowd tends to congregate on the west end of the park, where you'll find a communal plastic water bowl near one of the drinking fountains and poop bag dispensers provided by the Friends of Garfield Park. But that's not to say this is a segregated park. In fact, one young mother says Garfield Park is her favorite because it's one of the rare places on the Hill where her tots and separation-anxiety-prone Prince Charles spaniel can amuse themselves together in the unfenced playground. Garfield Park is located between I-295, 3rd St., F St., and South Carolina Ave. SE; 202/673-7647; www.dpr.dc.gov.

## 5 Congressional Cemetery

 (See the Southeast DC map on page 116)

There was a time in the not-so-distant past when historic Congressional Cemetery was a junkie hideout, and unmowed grass obscured the headstones, including the likes of J. Edgar Hoover, first director of the FBI; Mathew Brady, widely considered the father of photojournalism; or John Philip Sousa, patriotic conductor and composer of The Stars and Stripes Forever.

The dog walkers changed all that. In the mid-1990s, the K-9 Corps began under the unofficial leadership of the late Saint Bernard Greta and her human Patrick Crowley, the vice chairman of the Association for the Preservation of Historic Congressional Cemetery (APHCC). At first 100 dogs, and then double—triple—that came to frolic inside the fully fenced, 33-acre cemetery without fear of ticketing because the cemetery is private property. Besides

## DETOURS

Besides Eastern Market, more than a few Capitol Hill shops let you bring your furry best friend shopping. What a capital idea.

**Blue Iris Flowers:** "All family members are welcome" at this family-owned flower shop. You can also often find owner Angela Brunson selling flowers in the market near North Carolina Avenue, where she lets thirsty dogs drink from the flower vases. Although the address is on Pennsylvania Avenue, the entrance is on 7th Street, two doors up from Bread & Chocolate. 660 Pennsylvania Ave. SE; 202/547-5777; www.blueirisbouquet.com.

**Chateau Animaux:** Behind the fancy name, this 5,000-square-foot boutique has the largest selection of dog food on the Hill and is in fact the largest independently owned pet store in the District. Six do-it-yourself dog washes are in back ($15 per visit), plus regular grooming services are offered (best booked in advance). 524 8th St. SE; 202/544-8710; www.chateau-animaux.com.

**Frager's Hardware:** If accustomed to shopping at Home Depot, you'll be amazed how everything you need fits in this neighborhood hardware shop, paint store, equipment rental, and garden center. Still can't sniff out the right screwdriver? Just ask the knowledgeable staff. Of note: the aisles are narrow, so claustrophobic Bernese mountain dogs and other large breeds might want to skip this errand. 1115 Pennsylvania Ave. SE; 202/543-6157; www.fragersdc.com.

**MotoPhoto:** Pooches can help you pick up reprints, or pose for a pet portrait ($20 per session; additional fee for prints). 660 Pennsylvania Ave. SE; 202/547-2100; www.motophotocapitolhill.com.

**Pawticulars:** This petite pet boutique is also an active hub of dog walkers for hire. The owner and shop dog trainer co-hosts a radio show, The Pet Pros, at 8:30 A.M. Sunday on 106.7 FM (or listen online at www.wjfk.com). 407 8th St. SE; 202/546-7387; www.pawticulars.com.

essentially supplying 16-hour-per-day surveillance, K-9 Corps volunteers provided maintenance for the cemetery, throwing away hypodermic needles in the early days and planting hundreds of trees.

Since those initial years, the dog-walking program has begun to feel the strain of its own success. With the cemetery again safe, families have returned to visit gravestones of relatives … and are aghast to see dogs playing king of the mountain on top of the crypts. In an effort to strike a balance between the doggies and what is first and foremost a historic and active cemetery, Congressional Cemetery is a members-only affair with dues and a waiting list to join.

The fees aren't cheap: $200 must be "donated" annually to APHCC, plus an additional annual $50 per dog for walking privileges.

For many District dogs and their owners, however, the opportunity for peaceful walks in this rolling landscape where the sidewalk ends and the crumbling corners of history emerge between the off-kilter headstones and monuments is more than worth it. APHCC requests that dogs and their owners visit before 10 A.M. or after 3 P.M. on weekends and leave dog toys at home. New dog walkers must attend an orientation and present proof of canine vaccination. 1801 E St. SE; 202/543-0539; www.cemeterydogs.org.

## PLACES TO EAT

**Belga Café:** Waffles, beer, chocolate—how could the tiny country of Belgium claim so many epicurean delights? Washington is lucky enough to have its own "Brussels on the Hill." Denali likes the Belga Café because, in true European style, she can sit politely under the table since the café's six outdoor tables are unfenced. For weekend brunch, which starts at 10 A.M., don't miss the *roer eitjes*, or green eggs (fresh herbs mixed into scrambled eggs), and of course the Belgian waffles. For dinner, try the mussels, scrumptious with bacon, asparagus, red ale, and onions, or other combinations, paired with *pommes frites* and one of Belgium's famous drafts on tap. If your pup is also thirsty, servers will bring her a bowl of water. 514 8th St. SE; 202/544-0100; www.belgacafe.com.

**Bread & Chocolate:** You'll need to wait for a table on the edge of the patio (the usual drill: dogs outside the fence). But really, when the main dishes on the menu are bread and chocolate, how can you go wrong? Unless, of course, you can only order off half the menu—sorry Denali. At least the patio is fairly well shaded, a must on hot days. 666 Pennsylvania Ave. SE; 202/547-2875.

**Marty's:** This casual American pub is the place to go for reasonably priced sandwiches and burgers served with potato chips on Barracks Row. Both kid and dog friendly, the patio seating is roped off, but so long as your pup sits with derriere on the sidewalk you're in the clear. Be advised that eating the nine-ounce Marty Burger—which your pup surely hopes you'll order—is a two-handed operation. We recall a pair of bulldogs watching the meal unfold, it seemed silently chanting, "Doggy bag, doggy bag." 527 8th St. SE; 202/546-4952; www.martysamericanrestaurant.com.

**Marvelous Market:** The Capitol Hill location of this upscale market franchise not only keeps water bowls out front but also stocks a few items to raise your dog's eyebrows. Exhibit A: a six-pack of nonalcoholic Bowser Beer, a loving concoction of filtered water, pure malt barley, and beef extract. Exhibit B: peanut butter pretzel dog treats, also made by the 3 Busy Dogs company. At $15 per six-pack and $2 per package, these aren't inexpensive treats, but then, neither was your artichoke chèvre omelette croissant. No one ever said gourmet was cheap. Your dog will be thrilled to discover she is permitted *inside* the partially fenced patio. 303 7th St. SE; 202/544-7127; www.marvelousmarket.com.

**Mr. Henry's:** If Mr. Henry's were a dog, it would be a golden retriever—that's the kind of friendly and earnest service you're going to find at this eatery. Mr. Henry's has been on the menu since 1966 with a winning recipe of tasty pub fare and live music. Soul and R&B singer Roberta Flack got her start here in 1968, singing to sold-out crowds on the second floor. The younger set will recognize one of Roberta's most famous songs, "Killing Me Softly With His Song," thanks to the Fugees remake with Lauryn Hill on lead vocals. Live music still plays at Mr. Henry's 8–10 P.M. Thursday. Due to DC health code, mutts must stay outside the fenced patio but waiters will bring them a water bowl and anything else you order: hamburger meat, diced chicken breast, you name it. Mr. Henry's is also one of the first gay- and lesbian-friendly bars in the District. 601 Pennsylvania Ave. SE; 202/546-8412; www.mrhenrysrestaurant.com.

**Tortilla Café:** Southern California–born Denali laments how difficult it is to find decent Mexican food in the DC metro area. The Tortilla Café is several big *pasos* in the right direction. This hole in the wall across from Eastern Market serves up inexpensive Mexican-Salvadorean dishes such as fried tilapia fish tacos and sweet corn tamales. The same family that operates Canales Delicatessen and Canales Quality Meats at Eastern Market owns the café. Seat yourself at one of the small tables out front with your wagging *perrito.* 210 7th St. SE; 202/547-5700.

**Tunnicliff's Tavern:** Another no-frills neighborhood staple, Tunnicliff's Tavern has a dog-friendly patio that is open year-round thanks to heating lamps. Open for a late breakfast and lunch and dinner, Tunnicliff's serves up classic all-American fare. The bartender warns that Saturday and Sunday brunch on the patio can get rather packed with Tunnicliff's doggy patrons. "Babies, too," she added. Servers will bring your dog water in a carryout container. 222 7th St. SE; 202/544-5680; www.tunnicliffstaverndc.com.

# Anacostia

The word Anacostia is derived from the name of the Nacochtank tribe, who lived at the confluence of the Potomac and Anacostia Rivers. Today, sadly, the word Anacostia has come to be synonymous with crime and urban blight. While this part of the District does have a 34 percent poverty rate and violence does happen here, Anacostia has its own charms. The intrepid dog and owner can find acreage of Southeast parkland to explore during daylight hours. The two large parks described in this section are where Denali felt safest and most adventurous. This section is larger than the Anacostia neighborhood proper and includes the area south of the Anacostia River and East Capitol Street, east of the Potomac River, and north of Southern Avenue.

## PARKS, BEACHES, AND RECREATION AREAS

### 6 Anacostia Park

😺 😺 (See the Southeast DC map on page 116)

There are more than 1,200 acres stretched out in the narrow, winding, river-front ribbon that is Anacostia Park, making it one of the larger recreational spaces in the District. Leashed dogs are invited to stroll along the Anacostia River or observe one of the hard-fought games of Ultimate Frisbee unfolding on the athletic fields. If you have a Frisbee hound, be sure to keep him tightly tethered—even the pickup games aren't usually looking for four-legged players. A pity, sniffs Denali. Anacostia Park actually encompasses Kenil-worth Aquatic Gardens and Kenilworth Park of Northeast DC, as well as the Langston Golf Course, three marinas, four boat clubs, a public boat ramp, plenty of picnic tables, and, possibly by the publication of this book, the completed Anacostia Riverwalk, which will connect with a network of multiuse trails that stretch well into Prince George's County.

The one activity *not* encouraged here is swimming—for dogs or humans. Notorious for its unsavory water quality, the 8.4-mile Anacostia River is subjected to 1.5 billion gallons of untreated wastewater annually. But hope might be on the horizon for this forgotten river. The DC Department of the Environment has stated its goal to restore the Anacostia to a fishable and swimmable river by the year 2032, aiming to undo in two

Phil Frank

decades the harm of at least a century of neglect. Let's hear an "Arf! Arf!" and a little "Amen" for that.

To drive to Anacostia Park, head eastbound on Pennsylvania Avenue across the Anacostia River. Take the first right onto Fairlawn Avenue. Go to the stop sign and turn right again on Nicholson Street to enter the park. Parking, drinking fountains, and restrooms are all available near the Anacostia Park Pavilion, that oddly Soviet-looking skate park. 202/472-3884; www.nps.gov/anac.

## 7 Fort Dupont Park

🐾🐾 (See the Southeast DC map on page 116)

Fort Dupont is another Civil War fort that never saw any action. Now preserved as one of the Fort Circle Parks, the fort remains a quiet place. Forest covers most of the 376 undulating acres, much of it untrodden. Trail hound that she is, Denali insisted we sniff out the scene.

Fort Dupont Park is part of a larger, 8.5-mile, gravel and single-track trail system that slices through Southeast DC, connecting three of the Civil War forts. Known as the Fort Circle Hiker-Biker Trail, it starts at the parking lot of the Smithsonian Museum of African American History and Culture and ends in Fort Mahan Park at Benning Road and 41st Street SE. You're not going to find pristine nature. The creek water is suspiciously orange. Even so, this is pretty darn decent single-track. Denali could run on leash without the two of us falling over each other, and there were enough dips and turns to keep us both interested. Do watch for mountain bikers, however; this is the only single-track trail in DC where mountain biking is permitted.

As far as safety goes, trust your gut. Without question, this is not a place to be stuck after dark. In daylight, it might be best to bring a buddy (besides your best friend on the leash) or come in a small group. Part of the trail's appeal is also what makes Denali hesitant—it's surprisingly isolated.

Where the forest fades away in Fort Dupont Park you'll find gathering places in the Anacostia community: the largest pea patch Denali has ever seen in the District, a popular picnicking area, an indoor ice hockey rink reputed to have awesome views of the Capitol, and the Summer Theater Stage. On Saturday evenings from mid-July through late August, free outdoor jazz concerts serenade visitors as they sit on the grassy hillside surrounding this stage. Musically inclined mutts are invited to listen but are not allowed in the concert seating.

To drive to Fort Dupont Park, go east on Pennsylvania Avenue SE and cross the Anacostia River. At the next stoplight, turn left onto Minnesota Avenue. After about a half mile, turn right onto Randle Circle, then leave the circle on Fort Dupont Drive. Turn left into the parking area after 0.2 miles. On foot, descend to the stage; you'll find the narrow path just to its right. As of 2008, you could find more detailed trail descriptions on www.singletracks.com or www.rundc.com. 202/690-5169; www.nps.gov/fodu.

# VIRGINIA

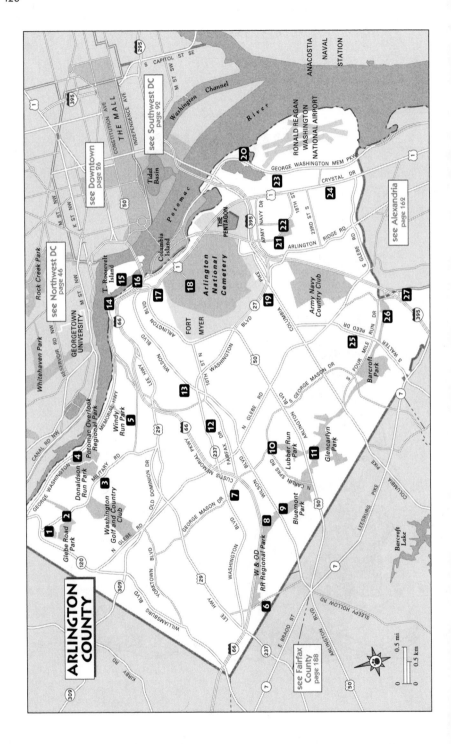

**CHAPTER 6**

# Arlington County

At 25.7 square miles, Arlington is the smallest self-governing county in the United States. Despite its diminutive size, or perhaps because of it, Arlington County's different neighborhoods boast a strong sense of community, especially for dog owners. Grab the leash and explore the county's worthwhile regional parks along the banks and bluffs of the Potomac, or the stream valleys (often called "runs") that feed the river. Or ditch the leash and head to one of the eight off-leash dog parks—aptly named "community canine areas" by the county. In fact, plenty of DC dogs venture into the Old Dominion while waiting for the District of Columbia to catch up with official off-leash areas, more often than not taking a weekly pilgrimage to the ever-popular Shirlington Dog Park.

Arlington dog lovers even have their own advocacy group, **Arlington Dog Owners Group,** an all-volunteer organization with more than 500 members that petitions for responsible dog guardianship (www.arlingtondogowners .org). And if there is ever a bone to pick between dog owners, neighborhoods

## PICK OF THE LITTER—ARLINGTON COUNTY

BEST DOG PARKS
**Glencarlyn Park,** Glencarlyn (page 139)
**Shirlington Park,** Shirlington (page 158)

BEST PARKS
**Potomac Overlook Regional Park,** Palisades (page 133)
**Potomac Heritage Trail,** Rosslyn (page 147)
**Theodore Roosevelt Island,** Rosslyn (page 148)

BEST PLACE TO PICK UP A PIZZA AND
SUPPORT ANIMAL RESCUE
**Lost Dog Café,** Westover (page 136)

BEST DIVE BAR
**Jay's Saloon & Grille,** Clarendon (page 144)

BEST PLACE TO STAY
**Hotel Palomar Arlington,** Rosslyn (page 151)

like Clarendon and Shirlington have numerous eateries where you can yap it out over a beer and a good meal with your respective hounds under the patio table.

What Denali likes best is the casual ease with which this Northern Virginia locality has accepted dogs as family. It's not without restrictions—no more than three dogs per family without a special license—but for the most part Arlington County gets two dewclaws up for dog friendliness. You might even say Virginia is for *dog* lovers.

# Cherrydale and the Palisades

Cherrydale and the Palisades have a distinctly small-town feel. In 1904, the railroad arrived and rapidly transformed the cherry orchards into the predominantly residential community you see today. We like to take walks and admire the wide-ranging personalities of cozy houses in the neighborhood, as described by the Cherrydale Citizens Association website, the "typical two-story 'farm' houses favored by the early commuters, 1920s Sears houses, 1930s bungalows, 1940s 'war boxes,' and the currently popular neo-Victorian and colonial style in-fill homes." Some locals refer to "the Cherrydale Vortex," the boomerang quality of their comfortable hometown, like an old, well-constructed shoe that just fits. For our purposes, this section includes a few neighboring communities, too, such as Maywood and Woodmont. And Denali likes the Palisades region even better. She knows all the side streets and parks along Military Road where she can step off the sidewalk and onto trails overlooking or approaching the Potomac River: Windy Run, Potomac Overlook Regional Park, Donaldson Run. Shhh… it's hound heaven, and some afternoons you nearly have it to yourself.

## PARKS, BEACHES, AND RECREATION AREAS

### 1 Fort Ethan Allen Park

🐾🐾🐕 (See the Arlington County map on page 128)

This community canine area is tucked behind the Madison Community Center and Senior Center, and the emphasis truly is on "community." Calm, caring, fully vaccinated hounds have the opportunity to participate in pet therapy for the elderly on the third Wednesday of every month. The pet parade takes place 2–3 P.M. through the Madison Community Center gym for adult day healthcare participants. You and your pooch are invited to stay for as long or little as you like. Contact the program coordinator, Rita Bloom (703/228-5340; madisonadhc@arlingtonva.us), for more information.

In the dog park itself, wood is a recurring theme: a wooden fence and double gate, wood chips, and wooden picnic benches on a wood deck. But the company is hardly dense. The park's sponsoring group is **Madison Dogs,** which has done much to ensure the dog park stay in existence after the county relocated it from the original site inside nearby Fort Ethan Allen, another historic Civil War fort, to the space behind the community center. Lights are on until 7 P.M. and running water and poop bags are available on-site. Located off Old Glebe Road. 3829 N. Stafford St.; 703/228-6523; www.co.arlington.va.us/parks.

### 2 Gulf Branch Nature Center

🐾🐾 (See the Arlington County map on page 128)

A trip to this corner of natural parkland is a bit like a choose-your-own-adventure story. Easily bored Baxters will have a few options to keep them entertained. From the Gulf Branch Nature Center parking lot, you can cross Military Road and follow the meandering creek to the Potomac River and the Potomac Heritage Trail (it gets steep and rocky near the bottom). On the other paw, your plucky puppy can explore the dirt and paved nature trails inside 37-acre Gulf Branch Park. The nature center lives up to its purpose: Just this evening we saw a fox. Or you can beeline through to Old Glebe Road behind the park and take a short walk to Fort Ethan Allen Dog Park for a doggy duathlon (in the events of on-leash walking and off-leash romping). Dogs are

# DETOURS

**Big Wheel Bikes:** Sarge, the resident Golden retriever, can help you select a new gas-free ride to work. Specializing in triathlon bikes. 3119 Lee Hwy.; 703/522-1110; www.bigwheelbikes.com.

**Cherrydale Hardware and Garden Center:** This old-fashioned hardware store is staffed with dog lovers who insist you bring Fido inside. A salesperson usually greets you at the door, ready to lead the way to the right chicken coop wire or light switch. 3805 Lee Hwy.; 703/527-2100.

**Dogma:** This barkery and boutique's credo is simple: "In dogs we trust." Doggy treats baked fresh daily. Dogma even bakes birthday cakes! 2445 N. Harrison St.; 703/237-5070; www.dogmabakery.com.

**Dominion Pet Center:** Founded in 1981, this pet store has been feeding and outfitting Arlington dogs for longer than we've been alive. Multi-pet families can find supplies for other critters here, too. 2501 N. Harrison St.; 703/241-0100.

**PetMAC:** Homeward Trails Animal Rescue hosts cat adoption events at PetMAC every other Sunday and dog adoption events the last Sunday of every month. PetMAC has a great selection of natural foods and pet needs. There are usually several kitties up for adoption in the store, so be mindful if your dog is excessively frisky for whiskers. Located off Wilson Boulevard, next to Hurt Cleaners. 822 N. Kenmore St.; 703/908-7387; www.petmac.org.

not allowed inside the nature center, but water is available from a fountain inside. The park is open dawn until a half hour after dusk. 3608 N. Military Rd.; 703/228-3403; www.arlingtonva.us/parks.

## 🕄 Zachary Taylor Nature Area
🐾 🐾 🐾 (See the Arlington County map on page 128)

The wood-chip trails on both sides of gurgling Donaldson Run are a simple pleasure. Cruise through these forested eight acres for a leisurely post-dinner dog walk or a brisk morning sniff-and-stride. Donaldson Run, the stream running through the Zachary Taylor Nature Area, is named after the first known non-native settler in the neighborhood, Andrew Donaldson, who began farming here in the 1780s. The stream valley is one of those neighborhood finds, a greenbelt connecting quiet cul-de-sacs into a happy, communal backyard. Denali appreciates the shade of the tree canopy and gulping down creek water in the summer, and she never seems to tire of pawing at the partially frozen crust of Donaldson Run in winter. We have a regular loop we like to jog that cuts through this nature area, but our pace slackens considerably here. With Denali's exercise mantra—"Just follow your nose!"—there are too many tree trunks and fence posts to go more than a few paces at a time. Our route of choice crosses the pedestrian bridge near the park entrance and continues along the right side of Donaldson Run before it crosses another footbridge. The dirt trail exits on a residential street, but you can continue to a paved bike trail that follows a series of curvy switchbacks uphill to a grassy area near Marymount University where neighborhood dogs sometimes hang out (a little less than a mile one-way from Military Road). You'll find a drinking fountain here, though it's usually turned off in winter months. Street parking on Military Road is usually easy. Located on Military Rd. at 30th St. N.; 703/228-6525; www.co.arlington.va.us/parks.

## 4 Potomac Overlook Regional Park

🐾🐾🐾🐾 🦴 (See the Arlington County map on page 128)

One glum, self-pity-ridden afternoon shortly after moving to the East Coast, Denali discovered Potomac Overlook Regional Park. At once she knew Washington DC would be a good home after all. She trotted taller and more alert than she'd been in weeks while we explored the rolling crests and curves of the park's single-track, and she nosed through piles of leaves and sneezed. Potomac Overlook Regional Park is, in a word, peaceful. Sometimes we hear nothing but the sound of crickets and chipmunks rustling in the brush. We have even seen an eight-point buck! Which brings up an important point: the family of white-tailed deer in residence will appreciate if your dog stays on-leash. The 70-acre park is a nature preserve, after all.

Potomac Overlook is actually a bit of a misnomer these days. Trees have grown taller to block what apparently used to be a fine view of the river. Denali doesn't mind a bit—her snout is glued to the ground. Potomac Overlook Regional Park is knit with interpretative nature trails, each marked with

its own color blaze. Trail maps are available at the Nature Center (no dogs inside), but they're not necessary for a good time. If you have a couple of hours to play, follow the Donaldson Run Trail to connect with the Potomac Heritage Trail on the river's edge. Wandering under the tulip poplars, commonly used to make dugout canoes by tribes who lived in this seasonal Indian camp for nearly 1,000 years, we dare you not to catch Potomac fever.

From George Washington Parkway driving northbound only (access is more complicated southbound), exit left at Spout Run Parkway, then take your first right at the light onto Lorcom Lane. Continue straight and turn right on Nellie Custis Drive, which merges into Military Road. Turn right onto Marcey Road, and drive to the parking lot at the end. 2845 N. Marcey Rd.; 703/528-5406; www.nvrpa.org/parks/potomacoverlook.

## 🔟 Windy Run Park

🐾🐾🐾🐾 ◄● (See the Arlington County map on page 128)

In early October, 14-acre Windy Run Park transforms into a high-ceilinged autumn cathedral. Golden and red-orange leaves flutter earthward, even landing on your pup's nose like a butterfly. Denali would drag us down here every day if she could. Your canine hiking companion might like the four stream crossings along the half-mile trail through this shaded glen. While you gingerly rock-hop, she will splash across in no time and stare at you as if to say, "Silly, slow human." Even in August, Windy Run keeps cool, and after the rare snowfalls DC experiences, snow melts here last. In all seasons it's a favorite haunt for Cherrydale hounds who like to get off the beaten path. The trail leads under George Washington Parkway to a bluff above the river and a small waterfall. When the mercury drops, this waterfall freezes partially, with a beautiful falling-icicles affect. Do watch your step when it gets icy, though, especially if your dog gallops with the same glorious galumph as Denali. When the critters with four-wheel-drive start spinning their wheels, we bipeds need to take extra caution.

In 2005, a rockslide nearly destroyed the trail staircase that provides access from Windy Run to the Potomac Heritage Trail on the riverbank below. You can still pick your way downhill over the relatively stable boulders, but Denali always wonders when the rest of the hillside is going to collapse. Erosion continues to remold the landscape in several places along the trail. Mind the grit on the boulders near the bottom, and then continue straight ahead to a favorite doggy swimming hole, or sandy, muddy, clay-covered bar, depending on the river level. You can also continue to the right toward Theodore Roosevelt Island or to the left, continuing on the same trail for miles upriver. From Spout Run Parkway, take your first right at the light onto Lorcom Lane. Continue 0.4 mile and turn right on Kenmore Avenue. Park in the cul-de-sac at the end of the street. 2420 N. Kenmore St.; 703/228-6525; www.co.arlington.va.us/parks.

## PLACES TO EAT

**The Italian Store:** In truth, The Italian Store has nothing more to do with dogs than the fact it's filled with more cured sausages and meats than we previously knew existed, but ask Denali, that's reason enough. An Arlington landmark, the authentic Italian delicatessen and pizzeria often has a line winding throughout the store, and chaos reigns near the counter on Redskins game days. Oh, but it's worth it. The Bianca specialty pizza is simple, savory cheesiness, and carnivores won't want to miss the Supremo. Grab a seat in front of the Starbucks next door to hang with your dog while you wait, and admire the mint-colored scooter. *Bone appetito!* 3123 Lee Hwy.; 703/528-6266; www.italianstore.com.

**Starbucks:** The ubiquitous Seattle-based espresso chain has carved out a niche for itself in the Lyon Village shopping center. It's part of the triple threat: Italian subs, cappuccinos, and sushi all in a neat row in this strip. Dogs are often seen panting under the Starbucks patio furniture while owners sip on lattes and nosh on nibbles from all three eateries. 3125 Lee Hwy.; 703/527-6506; www.starbucks.com.

**Wasabi To Go:** Inside, the walk-up cooler has ready-made sushi boxes and rolls if you want your seaweed salad and spicy tuna and scallion roll in a hurry, or you can order at the register. Wasabi To Go also serves hot dishes such as vegetable tempura or chicken udon. There are outdoor tables when the weather is warm. Denali usually waits patiently tied to the bench in front of CVS. 3129 Lee Hwy.; 703/907-0060; www.wasabisushi.com.

# East Falls Church and Westover

Along Washington Boulevard driving west, you'll find the Arlington hamlet of Westover (Denali, perked up at the word "ham-let"), as well as the nearby community—East Falls Church—which is also the closest Metro stop. Besides having its own dog park, Westover is home to one of the coolest restaurants in all of Arlington County for a dog lover, the Lost Dog Café. Besides delicious pizza and sandwiches and a wicked microbrew selection, a portion of your bill goes to the Lost Dog & Cat Rescue Foundation.

## PARKS, BEACHES, AND RECREATION AREAS

### 6 Benjamin Banneker Park

🐾🐾🐾 (See the Arlington County map on page 128)

As with many of the community canine areas in Arlington, Benjamin Banneker Park is mostly a locals' hangout. The family dog often brings the rest of the family. The fully fenced lot has a double-fenced entry and all the other amenities you would hope to find in a dog park: a water spigot and bowls,

poop bags and trash cans, trees for shade, a couple of picnic benches, and most importantly, plenty of playmates. The wood-chipped rectangle is one of the larger Arlington dog parks, so there is easily enough room for a tail-wagging game of tag or tackle. Benjamin Banneker Park, named after the prominent African American mathematician who assisted with the 1791 survey of the Federal City, is also the starting point for the Four Mile Run bike trail so if your dog needs more exercise, you can always take to the trail. The sponsoring group **Banneker Dogs** has a parting message for you as you exit the fenced park: "Now yer dun playin' we thank you fer payin' by makin' a loop to help pick up poop!" It might be wise to bring your own cleanup bags, just in case.

As daylight gets shorter in winter months, worker bees will be pleased to know that Banneker dog park stays lit and open until 8 P.M. To reach Benjamin Banneker Park, take I-66 west to the Sycamore Street exit 69. Turn left on Sycamore, past the East Falls Church Metro Station. Turn right onto N. 16th Street, then take the first right, which dead-ends at the dog exercise area and a small parking area. 1701 N. Van Buren St.; 703/228-6523; www.co.arlington .va.us/parks.

## PLACES TO EAT

**Lost Dog Café:** Grab a slice of pizza from the Lost Dog Café on Washington Boulevard, and in doing so support the restaurant owners' ongoing efforts to rescue, sponsor, and place hundreds of abandoned and unwanted animals for more than 13 years (www.lostdogandcatrescue.org). Neither the Lost Dog, nor the Stray Cat Café a few doors down, have outdoor seating, so dining here will need to be in your pooch's honor rather than his actual presence, unless you order a pie to go. The lines here are often long, but it's worth it, and you can bide your time perusing the impressive microbrew selection. 5876 N. Washington Blvd.; 703/237-1552; www.lostdogcafe.com.

# Bluemont and Glencarlyn

These middle Arlington neighborhoods remain lesser known than the county's Metrorail-connected urban villages. Rather than be recognized by Metro stations of the same names, these neighborhoods share names with the city parks that define them—which is fine by Denali, who has no Metro access (she'd rather hang out in a park than the subway, anyway). The Bluemont and Glencarlyn neighborhoods boast more than 200 acres of parkland between the two of them.

## PARKS, BEACHES, AND RECREATION AREAS

### 7 Lacey Woods Park

😼 (See the Arlington County map on page 128)

In a petite fashion, Lacey Woods Park delivers on its name. Forest covers much of the 13-acre neighborhood park; in fact, the two largest Virginia Pines in the state grow in the landscaped area near 11th Street. Denali sniffed herself into a tizzy following the short nature trails in the park's western side, which is the most peaceful. Traffic can be noisier near the playground, basketball courts, and athletic field close to Washington Boulevard, or along the park's east side with George Mason Drive. You can walk the gravel road through the center of Lacey Woods, or follow Robert Frost's advice and take those less-traveled footpaths threading through the pocket woodland. Thirsty dogs can find a water fountain here, but bring a bowl. Lacey Woods Park has pedestrian entrances along N. Frederick Street and on George Mason Drive (thus the park's official address on George Mason Drive). It's best to parallel-park on the N. Frederick Street side. To get there, drive north on George Mason Drive from Route 50. Turn left on Washington Boulevard and turn immediately left again on N. Frederick Street. 1200 N. George Mason Dr.; 703/228-6525; www.arlingtonva.us/parks.

### 8 Bon Air Park and Memorial Rose Garden

😼😼😼 (See the Arlington County map on page 128)

Perhaps Bon Air Park smells *bon* because of the Bon Air Memorial Rose Garden, planted in honor of World War II veterans. Denali dutifully sniffed a few of the 150 varieties of prize-winning roses with names such as "Opening Night" and "Vogue," but in truth the park's wildlife interested her far more than the flowers. In a secluded lawn above the Master Gardener demonstration shade garden and azalea hill, Denali swears she found *Watership Down*—bunnies! You can see what's hopping, too, by following the trail that begins across from the bathrooms. The rose garden is actually only a small section of Bon Air Park. The 23-acre county park has shaded access to the Four Mile Run stream and the W&OD bike trail, as well as a playground and basketball, volleyball, and tennis courts. Park your car in the lot on the corner of Wilson Boulevard and N. Lexington Street. 850 N. Lexington St.; 703/228-6525; www.arlingtonva.us/parks.

## 9 Bluemont Park

😾😾 (See the Arlington County map on page 128)

Bluemont Junction was a bustling crossroads in the early 1900s. Similar to the Rosslyn Metro Station today, this stop on the Washington and Old Dominion Railway served two railroad lines. Since then bike trails have supplanted the railroad, but pedestrian and bike traffic is still brisk on a sunny weekend afternoon. When comparing the Four Mile Run, Bluemont Junction, and W&OD trails, all of which intersect here, Denali prefers the Four Mile Run Trail, which runs along the right side of the creek. It's more circuitous, better shaded, has easier access to the creek, and skirts a Frisbee golf course (Denali asks, Finders, keepers?).

In many ways Bluemont Park is a multiuse park for multitaskers and a hub of all sorts of sporty activity during daylight hours. We saw a mom on the trail exercising herself, her daughter, and her golden retriever in one fell swoop along the W&OD Trail. The 100-foot-wide, 45-mile-long W&OD trail is certainly worth a walk but tends to be busy with cyclists and in-line skaters.

You can park in the lot on the corner of Wilson Boulevard and N. Manchester Street, about one mile west of the Ballston Common Mall. There is an additional parking lot if you continue past the Bluemont Junction parking lot, turn right on 4th Road N., left on N. Montague Street, and then left back onto 4th Road N. The parking lot for Bluemont Park proper will be straight in front of you. 601 North Manchester St.; 703/228-6525; www.arlingtonva.us/parks.

## 10 Lubber Run Park

😾😾😾 (See the Arlington County map on page 128)

Shorter than we anticipated, 22-acre Lubber Run Park is still a quick, welcome escape to nature. The stream valley is boxed in between Route 50 and George Mason Drive, but beneath the hardwood forest canopy Denali was far more focused on twittering birds than the occasional sound of traffic. If you're lucky, you might hear music beyond the songbirds. In the middle of the park there is a 1,200-seat outdoor amphitheater where free concerts and the occasional movie play on summer weekends. Call Arlington Arts for more information (703/228-1850; www.arlingtonarts.org).

Open sunrise to a half hour after sunset. Park at the Lubber Run Recreation Center and walk downhill to Lubber Run Park. There is a drinking fountain at the playground near the parking lot. Located near the intersection of N. Carlin Springs Road and N. George Mason Drive (turn south on Park Drive from George Mason). 300 N. Park Dr.; 703/228-4712; www.co.arlington.va.us/parks.

## DOG-EAR YOUR CALENDAR

Join the Animal Welfare League of Arlington to raise funds for homeless animals, and the Arlington County Park Rangers to host fun for your household critters.

On two and four legs, through fair and foul weather, participants in the **AWLA Walk for the Animals** have marched annually since 1996 to benefit the Animal Welfare League of Arlington. The three-mile walk or one-mile stroll takes place in Bluemont Park in early May, drawing more than 600 dedicated animal lovers. In years past, crowds have had the opportunity to watch the Quantico Marine Base and Arlington County Sheriff's K-9 Units perform demonstrations, too. 601 North Manchester St.; 703/931-9241; www.awla.org.

Stop by to raise a pint and wag a tail at AWLA's **Barks 'n' Beer** to help celebrate "Adopt a Shelter Dog Month." The October event at the AWLA shelter offers free hot dogs and root beer for you, and a free doggy wash for your best friend. 2650 S. Arlington Mill Dr.; 703/931-9241; www.awla.org.

Despite the name, the **Catsino Night and Silent Auction** benefits Arlington cats *and* dogs. The catered event features live music and casino-style games including blackjack, Texas Hold 'em, craps, and roulette. The fall fundraiser usually takes place in Terminal A at Ronald Reagan Washington National Airport. 703/931-9241; www.awla.org.

In mid-October, Arlington County Park Rangers host **Dogtober Day,** a full day of furriendly competition and events for Fifi. Dogs must be fully vaccinated and leashed to attend or participate. Entry fees are $6 per category or $25 for unlimited categories, which include Best Kisser, Most Adorable Small Dog, and Best Tail Wagger. Lacey Woods Park, 1200 N. George Mason Dr.; 703/525-0168.

## 11 Glencarlyn Park

🐾🐾🐾🐾🐕 (See the Arlington County map on page 128)

Glencarlyn Park is a lone wolf in one respect: it has the only unfenced community canine area in Arlington. No wood chips and chain-link fence here. Visiting Glencarlyn Park means taking a short walk in the woods and most certainly a splash in Four Mile Run. The hillside next to the dog park and the stream serve as natural barriers, but if your Rover wants to go a-roving, he will find his way out. Fortunately, the off-leash area is set within the much larger 97-acre park, so the most immediate traffic danger are the bicycles on the W&OD Trail. Be sure to pack a towel in the car because tussling in the creek water—and then rolling in the flat sandbar en route to the car—is the main canine attraction. You dog is liable to look like a half-drowned, shake-and-bake chicken when the whole affair is over. But hopefully you'll both come out grinning.

An important warning about swimming in Four Mile Run: Raw sewage occasionally spills into the creek upstream. Arlington County posts signs when this happens to keep pets and kids out of the water, but you can also sign up for Arlington Alerts (www.arlingtonalert.com) to receive free email or text message notifications. Excluding these unsavory incidents, Glencarlyn Park is a place your pooch will find worth getting his paws wet.

From Route 50, head west to the Carlin Springs Road exit. From the exit, turn left at the stop sign and follow Carlin Springs Road, turn left on 4th Street, and follow it five blocks until it dead-ends at the Glencarlyn Park sign. Follow the steep, winding road into the park. Drive until you dead-end in a small parking lot. The dog park is located to the right across a pedestrian bridge. 301 South Harrison St.; 703/228-6523; www.co.arlington.va.us/parks.

### PLACES TO EAT

**Chesapeake Bagel Bakery:** The long line of Arlingtonians waiting to order an "egg'wich" or fresh bagel and coffee was a ringing endorsement. Your dog will be happier waiting on the partially fenced patio if you stop by Dogma doggy bakery first so you can both enjoy your vittles. 2453 N. Harrison St.; 703/241-1950; www.chesapeake-bagel.com.

**Crisp and Juicy:** Here you'll find fast food at its finest: a mouthwatering rotisserie chicken dinner served up in minutes. The Peruvian-style roasted bird comes with a fiery hot sauce and yucca or potato french fries. The sandwiches are also good. You can tie your dog out front while you order, or leave him in the car with the windows cracked if it's cool out—it's really that quick. There's also patio seating if you prefer to dine in. 4540 Lee Hwy.; 703/243-4222; www.crispjuicy.com.

# Virginia Square and Ballston

Moving farther down Wilson Boulevard and the Orange Metro line, you could argue the "B" in Ballston stands for "Big Box," with the four-level Ballston Common Mall defining this corner of Arlington County. But even among the apartment towers and office buildings, a discerning dog can find a few places to wag about. PetMAC Marketplace & Adoption Center and Quincy Park are two such places.

## PARKS, BEACHES, AND RECREATION AREAS

### 12 Quincy Park

🐾🐾 (See the Arlington County map on page 128)

Next to Arlington's Central Library you'll find four-acre Quincy Park, a jock's playground with softball and baseball diamonds and tennis, basketball, and volleyball courts in constant use. Offerings for doggy diversion are slightly more limited, but it's still a reasonable place to take a walk. Leashed Bowsers living in the Ballston apartment towers often circle the vicinity. After Denali nearly dragged us up a tree trunk in hot pursuit she concluded that Quincy Park squirrels are particularly sassy chatterboxes.

Twice a year the Friends of the Arlington County Library hold a mammoth book sale to make even Clifford the Big Red Dog proud. It's that big and that awesome. While dogs can't take place in the actual book-buying frenzy, you can find all sorts of dog-related literature for only a few dollars: breed reference books, how-to puppy training manuals, or maybe a gently worn copy of *Marley & Me* or *The Dogs of Babel*. The sale takes place in April and October in the Central Library parking garage (1015 N. Quincy St.; 703/228-5990), which is also a convenient place to leave your car when visiting Quincy Park. The gravel parking lot on the corner of N. Quincy Street and Washington Boulevard is reserved for teachers and staff at nearby Washington-Lee High School 9 A.M.–5 P.M. weekdays but is open on weekends and in the evenings. 1021 N. Quincy St.; 703/228-6525; www.arlingtonva.us/parks.

### PLACES TO EAT

**Café Amity:** As a sign inside this café reads, "Amity means friendship." Indeed, the waiters behind the counter are unflaggingly friendly. Café Amity's menu is split between standard American sandwiches, such as cranberry turkey or roast beef, and Turkish specialties—our preference, especially the tummy-warming lentil soup. Your dog can join at the seasonally available outdoor seating while you sip Illy espresso or Turkish coffee and surf the free Wi-Fi. 1000 N. Randolph St.; 703/243-7400; www.cafeamity.com.

### PLACES TO STAY

**The Westin Arlington Gateway:** One of the newest accommodations on the block, this 336-room, luxury hotel opened in 2006. As with all Westins, a good night's sleep awaits you and your 40-pound-or-less pooch on a Heavenly Bed and Heavenly Dog Bed, respectively. You'll need to sign a waiver, but there is no pet fee, and Westin provides a dog bowl, leash, and do not disturb sign for the room. Hotel amenities for humans include an indoor pool, gym, business center, 24-hour room service, and a full-service Starbucks in the lobby. Your dog cannot be left unattended in the room. Rates range $139–434. Valet parking is available for $22 per day. 801 North Glebe Rd.; 703/717-6200; www.westin.com/arlington.

# Clarendon

Arguably the two most popular Arlington neighborhoods for young professionals—Clarendon and Shirlington—are also the best 'hoods for hounds. Along Clarendon and Wilson Boulevards, the one-way main streets of Clarendon, you'll find a smorgasbord of paw-friendly shops and sidewalk cafés. And it doesn't take a Siberian husky to figure out that this is an active place. From the Battle of the Boulevard 10K and the high-profile CSC Invitational cycling classic, to Clarendon Day and the Mardi Gras parade, to a regular Tuesday, it's clear Clarendon is a jogging, yoga mat–toting, dog park–frequenting community. The Clarendon Alliance (www.clarendon.org), together with pet boutique **A.k.a. Spot,** deliver several doggy-dedicated events throughout the year, to the indulgence and delight of Clarendon retailers and passersby. Join in the Claren-fun.

## PARKS, BEACHES, AND RECREATION AREAS

### 13 Clarendon Dog Park

🐾 🐾 🐕 (See the Arlington County map on page 128)

What this block-wide off-leash dog park is missing in scenery, it makes up for in community. Bustling with sociability, Clarendon's small gravel-and-wood-chips lot always has tails to sniff and noses to touch. With one picnic table and a few lawn chairs for sitting, dog owners inevitably bump elbows and strike up friendly conversations, too. Arlington County is deliberating a redesign of the park that would include new landscaping, space for demonstration gardens, and a water fountain. Spearheading advocacy for the dog exercise area is **Clarendon Dogs** (703/578-0522; groups.google.com/group/clarendondogs), the active community group that currently maintains the park. Located on 13th Street, between Herndon and Hartford Streets, one block northwest of the Clarendon Metro Station. Metered street parking is available around the park, but it's a good idea to feed the meter a few extra quarters—parking tickets have left more than one visitor howling. 1299 N. Herndon St.; 703/228-6523; www.co.arlington.va.us/parks.

## PLACES TO EAT

**Boccato:** What magical ingredient makes gelato more delicious than regular ice cream? Boccato only opened its doors in 2008 but has already delighted the taste buds and widened the waistlines of a growing number of Clarendon devotees and their pets. The gelato-scooper-on-duty is usually generous with samples, which makes it easier to branch out in new culinary directions (banana biscotti? strawberry basil? mojito?). Denali appreciates the water bowl out front where you can sit at a bench and savor your dessert and she

## DOG-EAR YOUR CALENDAR

There are a number of opportunities throughout the year to dress your dog up in a fun costume and parade through the neighborhood along with pet boutique A.k.a. Spot (2509 N. Franklin Rd.; 703/248-0093; www.akaspot.com). In late February, join in the Fat Tuesday celebration by parading your pet along with the Arlington County Fire Department, the high school marching band, and if you're lucky, the DC RollerGirls, along with many others and, of course, lots of beads in the **Mardi Gras Parade.**

In June, benefit the Homeward Trails Animal Rescue by purchasing a print at **Pawcasso,** the annual cocktail-attire charity art auction. Tickets cost $35 per person or $60 per couple. www.homewardtrails .org/pawcasso.

Your last chance of the year to get out there is October's **Howl-o-ween Parade.** Participate in the costume contest, doggy parade, and trick-or-treating for bones at participating retailers.

---

can catch the drips. Boccato also serves espresso, thus, "homemade gelato and caffeinato." Located in the same building as El Chaparral Latino Market, across from Whole Foods Market. Parking is available around back. 2719 Wilson Blvd.; 703/869-6522.

**The Boulevard Woodgrill:** With cozy two-top tables that wrap around the corner of Wilson and Fillmore, this traditional American grill abides ample room for polite pups to eat out. The wood-fired oven turns out delectable smoky entrées, from Chilean sea bass to New York strip steak to molasses-and-rum baby-back ribs. The appetizers are good, too (said with confidence after three office holiday parties here), and we hear the weekend brunch is worthwhile. In the fall and spring, when DC weather is fantastically fresh, the sidewalk seating can be packed to the gills, just like other restaurants on Wilson Boulevard. Call to make reservations as soon as the thermometer hits 70°F. What's best about the Woodgrill is that it offers an upscale dining experience at moderate prices. 2901 Wilson Blvd.; 703/875-9663; www.boulevardwoodgrill.com.

**Java Shack:** Next door to A.k.a. Spot you'll find what has been billed the "Cheers Coffeehouse" of Arlington. Java Shack brewed its first cup o' Joe in 1996 and has witnessed Clarendon's somewhat dramatic renaissance from pokey Arlington neighborhood to yupster enclave. Owner Dale Roberts keeps fresh water on the patio and Bentley's Barkery dog biscuits at the counter for the pooches and supports all sorts of community causes, including two cycling

## DETOURS

Most of the stores in Clarendon, and especially in the U-shaped Market Commons mall, are very dog friendly. Here are a few favorites.

**A.k.a. Spot:** Upscale pet boutique and do-it-yourself dog wash. 2509 N. Franklin Rd.; 703/248-0093; www.akaspot.com.

**Apple:** Denali has a fetish for expensive electronics—cell phones, external computer hard drives, remote controls—she assures us they all taste delicious. Hence, Denali is never allowed in the Apple store. All other dogs are welcome. 2700 Clarendon Blvd., Suite 200; 703/875-9880; www.apple.com.

**Barnes and Noble:** Nose through the latest *Bark* magazine together. Steer clear of the café, however. 2800 Clarendon Blvd., Suite 500; 703/248-8244; www.barnesandnoble.com.

**The Container Store:** Tupperware in every shape and size imaginable to store kibble. 2800 Clarendon Blvd., Suite R750; 703/469-1560; www.containerstore.com.

**Eastern Mountain Sports:** Irked by REI's new no-dog policy? EMS is still a bastion of dog-adoring gearheads. Ask manager Harry Walters for a Milk-Bone; he usually keeps some behind the counter. 2800 Clarendon Blvd., Suite 550; 703/248-8310; www.ems.com.

**Lululemon Athletica:** For when Down Dog is a yoga position and not a command. 2847 Clarendon Blvd.; 703/807-0539; www.lululemon.com.

teams, Squadra Coppi and Lanterne Rouge. Don't be surprised if you share the patio with Spandex-clad guys and gals on Friday and Sunday mornings. Denali likes it: They're usually salty. Note the patio is sometimes a bit smoky. 2507 N. Franklin Rd.; 703/527-9556; www.javashack.com.

**Jay's Saloon & Grille:** Jay's is one of the last of a dying breed inside the Capital Beltway: dive bars. And a dog-friendly dive bar at that. The drink prices are written in felt tip marker and taped behind the bar—Domestic Bottle $3, Domestic Draft $2.50, and so on—and the patio furniture is all plastic. But the service is friendly, the beer is cheap, and the food—crab cakes, burgers, and chicken fingers—is better than expected. Ever since Jay's opened in 1993, any day of the week, any time of year, dogs are welcome on the nine-table porch. It's possible you've driven past Jay's Saloon & Grille dozens of times without knowing it was there. We took three years to find it, and we work in the neighborhood! Jay's is located next to a used car lot in a house con-

**Origins:** Natural skin products for you and your dog. Origins sells a lavender oil–based doggie shampoo. Note the ever-present water bowl out front. 2700 Clarendon Blvd., Suite 400; 703/243-5373; www.origins.com.

**Orvis:** The wooden carving of a Labrador at the entrance has befuddled Denali more than once. 2879 Clarendon Blvd.; 703/465-0004; www.orvis.com.

**The Papery:** High-quality stationary and greeting cards, including pet sympathy cards. Look for the water bowl out by the door. 2871 Clarendon Blvd.; 703/875-0391; www.thepaperyinc.com.

**Pottery Barn:** "Oh, honey, bring your dog in," one salesperson said. Just no letting your dog jump on the sofas until you buy them. 2700 Clarendon Blvd., Suite 100; 703/465-9425; www.potterybarn.com.

**Revolution Cycles:** Thanks to Revolution, Denali can now explain the difference between Ultegra and Dura-Ace shifters. 2731 Wilson Blvd.; 703/312-0007; www.revolution cycles.com.

**ShoeFly:** Like the U Street shop, the Clarendon ShoeFly invites even the furriest shoe connoisseur inside as long as they promise not to nibble the pumps. There's usually a bowl of water out front. 2727 Wilson Blvd.; 703/243-6490; www.shoeflyonline.com.

verted to a bar on 10th Street across from Hudson Street. 3114 N. 10th St.; 703/527-3093.

**Mexicali Blues:** Come cheer up at Mexicali Blues, a fiesta of Salvadoran-Mexican cuisine. Dogs are permitted on the sidewalk patio for casual, warm-weather dining, although be prepared for crowds on weekends and pleasant weekday evenings. Here you'll find a tried-and-true selection of tacos and burritos, but also more unusual fare, such as pupusas (tasty handmade corn tortilla pockets stuffed with meat, beans, and cheese). Wash down your meal with a mojito, and slip a nibble of carnitas to your friend beneath the table. Located on the corner of Wilson and Garfield, the neighborhood restaurant has been serving Clarendon dog owners for more than a decade. A live mariachi band plays 8–9 P.M. Thursday. 2933 Wilson Blvd.; 703/812-9352; www.mexicali-blues.com.

**Restaurant 3:** A Chihuahua owner turned us on to Restaurant 3, so we

## DIVERSION

Inside **Jay's Saloon & Grille,** happy hours are called "attitude adjustment hours." At Jay's gazebo-sided front porch, they're called **Doggie Happy Hours.** These yappy hours happen 1–4 P.M. one Sunday a month at owners Jay and Kathi's whim. It's best to call the saloon to find out when the next yappy hour will take place. But if you show up unannounced with Fido, you'll still find a place at the patio tables beneath the all-season Christmas lights. Dogs are always welcome. The main difference during the yappy hours is that Jay's gates off the porch entryway so patrons can let their dogs wander the Astroturf-carpeted porch without fear of the busy 10th Street traffic. 3114 N. 10th St.; 703/527-3093.

called ahead to ensure 62-pound Germations wouldn't be turned away from the patio. In response to whether Denali could sit in the outdoor seating, the host responded with a chipper, "Sure!" and noted that waiters typically seat dogs and owners on the side patio. We shouldn't have been surprised: Restaurant 3 is under the same management as dog-friendly Whitlow's on Wilson, even though it's decidedly more upscale. Restaurant 3 serves American cuisine with nuances from below the Mason-Dixon line (which, incidentally, we often forget we already are), such as grilled brie and Southern-fried catfish. 2950 Clarendon Blvd.; 703/524-4440; www.restaurantthree.com.

**Sette Bello:** Continuing in the theme of more upscale, dog-friendly restaurants that use numbers in their names, on to Sette Bello's (Beautiful Sevens), a trendy Italian kitchen just up the street. If your dog has exhausted himself at the Clarendon Dog Park and he can hardly lift a paw but you had plans to dine out, you might consider eating at Sette Bello, which is literally right around the corner from the park. The patio facing N. Highland Street is sizable and a nice place to enjoy a light antipasto and glass of chianti. 3101 Wilson Blvd.; 703/351-1004; www.settebellorestaurant.com.

**Whitlow's on Wilson:** The best brunch in Clarendon belongs to Whitlow's. From the cheesy omelettes and home fries to a breakfast buffet complete with snow crab legs and a Bloody Mary bar that will leave you stuffed just looking at it, there's a reason why Whitlow's usually has a wait on Saturday and Sunday mornings. The American diner started as a restaurant in Downtown DC on 11th and E Street NW in 1946. After changing owners 25 years later, and then changing locations 24 years after that, Whitlow's on Wilson found its way into the heart of Clarendon. Every Monday is half-price burgers. The patio seating is pleasant, as is the wait staff, who will typically bring dogs water to drink. 2854 Wilson Blvd.; 703/276-9693; www.whitlows.com.

# Rosslyn

Any skyscrapers you might have expected to find in Washington DC reside in Rosslyn, the first Metro stop in Virginia as you leave the District. A prototype for "Smart Growth" and one of Arlington County's urban villages, Rosslyn at first glance seems an unlikely spot to satisfy Spot. What attraction do high-sheen office buildings and high-rise apartments have for the canine persuasion? In a word: convenience. Rosslyn is a jumping-off point for prime-time doggy playtime. From famous National Park Service memorials to overlooked footpaths, Rosslyn is a flea-hop away from some of the best riverfront diversions this side of the Potomac.

## PARKS, BEACHES, AND RECREATION AREAS

### 14 Potomac Heritage Trail

🐾🐾🐾🐾 🐾 (See the Arlington County map on page 128)

> *Cats are the ultimate narcissists. You can tell this because of all the time they spend on personal grooming. Dogs aren't like this. A dog's idea of personal grooming is to roll in a dead fish.*
>
> James Gorman

Talk about a treasure hiding in plain sight. For as much foot and paw traffic as Teddy Roosevelt Island and the Mount Vernon trail receive, very few venture upriver on the Potomac Heritage Trail, a footpath maintained by the Potomac Appalachian Trail Club (www.potomacappalachian.org). Denali loves to race rowing shells sculling across the Potomac River parallel to the trail. Sometimes a coach will follow the rowers in a motorboat, his dog at the helm barking out orders as well as any coxswain. Denali tries to keep up, dodging through underbrush and diving over fallen logs like a champion steeplechaser.

The dirt path starts underneath the pedestrian overpass by the Roosevelt Island parking lot and hugs the river for 10 miles to the American Legion Bridge (where I-495 crosses the Potomac), with numerous points of access along the way. It's part of the larger Potomac Heritage National Scenic Trail, which when complete will stretch more than 800 miles.

We like the Potomac Heritage Trail best in the 'tweener seasons, spring and fall. In the springtime, lilies and daffodils bloom next to the trail—throwbacks to gardeners from a bygone time. In the summertime things turn fishy. Whether it's heat and hypoxia that send the fish belly up or recreational anglers who leave their catch to rot, it sure gets stinky in spots. This, to Denali's nose, is the sweetest sort of hypnotic perfume, which no amount of yelling or coaxing or pleading can persuade her from rolling in. It's still worth a visit in the summer, but if your dog's favorite scent is similarly Chinook No. 1, consider yourself warned. A few other important warnings: Portions of the Potomac Heritage Trail open up to George Washington Parkway so, Virginia leash laws aside, do *not* take your dog off-leash unless you have scoped out your route and know where it is safe to do so. Also, the trail can be rocky in places (indeed, rock quarries used to line this trail) so it's important to wear appropriate footwear. Finally, in our opinion, the trail doesn't really start to get good until about one mile upriver from Teddy Roosevelt Island, so expect to do some hiking. (Or drive to one of the trailheads farther north, such as Windy Run.) That said, enjoy! This is one of our favorite places. 703/289-2500 or 301/739-4200; www.nps.gov/pohe or www.potomactrace.org/hikingguide/nova.html.

## 15 Theodore Roosevelt Island

🐾🐾🐾🐾🐜 (See the Arlington County map on page 128)

Circling 2.5 miles on the wooden boardwalk and gravelly dirt trail around Theodore Roosevelt Island, you can quickly forget that this tiny dot of wild habitat is wedged between a busy parkway and an interstate bridge.

On the back side of Roosevelt Island, the aptly named Swamp Trail is a raised wooden boardwalk that travels the east length of the park. Keep an eye out for blue herons poised near the marsh below, as well as white-tailed deer, rabbits, squirrels, muskrats, turtles, opossums, various birds, and the occasional red and gray fox. In the center of the island is Memorial Plaza, a cement and granite space commemorating Roosevelt, with a 17-foot statue that looks every inch of his famous quote: "Speak softly and carry a big stick."

Dogs often congregate on the north end of the island—at "Dog Beach"—for an illicit off-leash dip in the Potomac River. It's a scenic spot with Key Bridge and Georgetown University in the background. But, it is strongly advised to use a leash elsewhere in the park. Teddy Roosevelt Island, as it's affectionately called, gets equal attention from families with small children and tourists from the United States and abroad, so park police are quick to ticket unleashed pets. The parking lot for Theodore Roosevelt Island is accessible only from northbound lanes of the George Washington Parkway. Turn right into the parking lot entrance, which is located just north of the Roosevelt Bridge (I-66). Cross the arched footbridge to enter the island. 703/289-2500; www.nps.gov/this.

## 16 Mount Vernon Trail

🐾🐾🐾🐾🐜 (See the Arlington County map on page 128)

Arlington County is literally crisscrossed with miles of paved bike trails. On some of these thoroughfares the saying "Do not step where angels fear to tread" comes to mind, especially if you have an excitable dog on the leash. If your Yorkie gets walloped by a bike commuter's panniers it won't be pretty for anyone. In fact, Denali learned to walk on the right side specifically to keep her from dodging in front of cyclists on the Custis Trail. While we generally steer clear of bike trails, at least when the twice-daily drama of the Tour de Arlington unfolds, there is one notable exception to this rule: The Mount Vernon Trail is not to be missed.

The Mount Vernon Trail is the pedestrian version of George Washington Parkway and it's even more scenic. In the springtime, expansive beds of daffodils trumpet the end of winter, and throughout the year Washington's monuments and bridges create a patriotic panorama across the river. The trail runs for 17 miles, from Theodore Roosevelt Island all the way to the namesake Mount Vernon estate south of Alexandria, our first President's home. Grass fills the space between the bike trail and the river in many places, which is an easy way to dodge bike traffic and, Denali vouches, discover the really good smells. We usually start from Teddy Roosevelt Island on the north end, accessed from northbound lanes of the George Washington Parkway, and hoof it south. Just listen for "On your left," or "Ding!" and keep the leash tight and to the right. You both will enjoy one of the most scenic stretches of Northern Virginia. Other access points along George Washington Parkway include Daingerfield Island (south of Ronald Reagan Washington National Airport) and Belle Haven Marina (south of Old Town Alexandria). 703/289-2500; www.nps.gov/gwmp/mtvernontrail.htm.

### 17 Iwo Jima Memorial

🐾🐾 🐾 (See the Arlington County map on page 128)

Washington DC is filled with iconic American sights, but Virginia actually claims one of the foremost: the Iwo Jima Memorial. The United States Marines Corps War Memorial, as it's also called, is much larger in real life than Denali expected. She wonders how huge it must look to a Maltese. Modeled after Joe

## DIVERSION

**At Ease, Clifford:** In the summer, the smartly rapping snare drum and trumpet of bugles signal the start of the **Marine Corps Sunset Parade** at the Iwo Jima Memorial. The concert and silent drill platoon is a free event open to the public, so it surely draws a crowd. As a result, this event isn't for every dog. Denali's beagle friend Maple, who lives near the memorial, took one look at the throng of tourists and another at the Marines swinging rifles and promptly dragged her family all the way home. The hour-long parade begins on Tuesdays at 7 P.M. in June and July and at 6:30 P.M. in August. There is no public parking at the memorial on parade evenings, so look for a spot on the street. www.mbw.usmc.mil/parade_sunsetdefault.asp.

Rosenthal's Pulitzer Prize–winning photograph of servicemen raising the flag on Mount Suribachi at the start of one of the bloodiest battles of World War II, the battle for Iwo Jima Island, the memorial (including the flag) stretches to 78 feet—it is the largest cast-bronze statue in the world. The memorial's inscription, "Uncommon Valor was a Common Virtue," is complicated to translate into canine, so after paying tribute, Denali recommends taking a short walk to somewhere very uncomplicated to enjoy: a grassy hill.

This particular grassy hill extends beneath the Netherlands Carillon (bell tower) and is one of the best places to lounge outdoors in Rosslyn. You'll often see dogs and their humans stretched out under a tree reading a newspaper. Incidentally, this is also a great place to watch the Fourth of July fireworks display—though Denali definitely stays home for that function, with classical music on high volume and doors tightly closed. Located on Marshall Drive between Route 50 and Arlington National Cemetery; 703/289-2500; www.nps.gov/gwmp/marinecorpswarmemorial.htm.

## 18 Arlington National Cemetery

🐾🐾 🐾 (See the Arlington County map on page 128)

Denali thinks it's the repetition of the straight, white headstones, not unlike rows and rows of soldiers standing at attention, that makes Arlington National Cemetery so solemn. More than 4 million people visit the cemetery annually, and an average of 28 funerals take place a day (it's projected the cemetery will be filled by 2020). Leashed dogs are permitted inside Arlington National Cemetery as long as they are properly respectful (and, trust us, veterans are watching).

With 612 acres to see, we have noted a few highlights. John F. Kennedy's gravesite, the most-visited gravesite in the country, is just west of the visitors center and is marked by an eternal flame. Next, Denali sniffed over to Arlington House, the stately Greek revival home of the Custis and Lee families, later occupied by General Robert E. Lee himself. Dogs are not allowed inside the house, or any of the buildings in the cemetery, but the Washington panorama is beautiful from outside the front door. The grave of Pierre-Charles L'Enfant, designer of the Federal City, is also only a few paw-steps away from here.

A trip to the Tomb of the Unknown Soldiers should only be attempted if your dog is preternaturally calm. Denali's spots belie her Dalmatian half, which is entirely too high-strung to watch quietly so we didn't even try. The tomb sentinels, all rigorously trained soldiers of the elite 3rd U.S. Infantry mean business. They will bark out stern orders to step back if an animal or human gets too close to the tomb. Instead we walked through Section 27, where 3,800 freed slaves are buried, all former residents of Freedman's Village, a community of ex-slaves during and after the Civil War.

Arlington National Cemetery is open 8 A.M.–7 P.M. daily Apr.–Sept.,

8 A.M.–5 P.M. daily Oct.–Mar. Located on the west end of the Memorial Bridge. Parking is inexpensive: $1.75 per hour for the first three hours, and $2 per hour thereafter. Dogs small enough to be carried are allowed on the Tourmobile trams. 703/607-8000; www.arlingtoncemetery.org.

## PLACES TO EAT

**Café Asia:** If you can't decide between Thai or Chinese, go to Café Asia, which serves dishes hailing from all over the Far East. The encyclopedic pan-Asian menu includes specialties from Thailand, Indonesia, Malaysia, Singapore, China, Japan, and Vietnam, but most patrons come for the sushi. The café's official rule is that dogs must be tied to the outside of the patio railing, but by one friend's report it seems there are exceptions, at least for smaller breeds. Regardless of which side of the railing your sushi hound sits, the wait staff will usually bring a water bowl if you request it. 1550 Wilson Blvd.; 703/741-0870; www.cafeasia.com.

## PLACES TO STAY

**Clarion Collection Arlington Residence Court Hotel:** Actually located just up the road from Rosslyn in Courthouse, this 187-room hotel offers a number of complimentary services: free breakfast buffet, dinner three nights per week, wireless Internet, a *USA Today* newspaper, access to a 24-hour fitness center, and shuttle service within a one-mile radius of the hotel. Dogs weighing less than 40 pounds can stay for a $75 fee the first night, $10 fee per night thereafter. Only one dog is allowed per room. The hotel offers both smoking and nonsmoking studio-style rooms and suites (up to three bedrooms). Daily parking costs $12. Rates range $129.95–419.95. There are government, military, AAA, and other corporate discounts. Call for more information. 1200 N. Courthouse Rd.; 703/524-4000; www.clarionhotel.com/hotel-arlington-virginia-VA058.

**Hotel Palomar Arlington:** Completed in 2007, the sleek Hotel Palomar Arlington lends a sophisticated silhouette to the Rosslyn skyline. As with all Kimpton Hotels, the Hotel Palomar invites all dogs to stay *carte blanche.* In fact, pet ambassador Sparky might be on staff to greet you. The pet packages change from year to year, but at the publication of this book, Hotel Palomar Arlington offers the Applaud the Paws Pet Package for $299 per night. It includes a generously sized pet bed, treats, bottled water, designer pet bowls, a personalized pet tag, and a souvenir toy to take home. Human guests enjoy free wireless Internet, L'Occitane bath products, and a complimentary "Wines Around the World" reception in the hotel's living room 5–6 P.M. daily. Rates at the 154-room luxury hotel start at $129 during summer and holidays, from $159 the rest of the year. Overnight parking costs $30 per day. 1121 N. 19th St.; 703/351-9170; www.hotelpalomar-arlington.com.

# Columbia Pike

Arlington living becomes more affordable along Columbia Pike. Million dollar homes give way to more modest town homes and apartments. Rush hour traffic, Goodwill stores, and strip malls are found in greater abundance along the pike, but noticeably less green space. Towers Park canine community area is a gleaming exception. If you're looking to get a bite to eat along Columbia Pike, Denali recommends ducking into one of many inexpensive Mexican restaurants and ordering something to go.

## PARKS, BEACHES, AND RECREATION AREAS

### 19 Towers Park

🐾🐾🐾🐕 (See the Arlington County map on page 128)

If your Fido is one of those tennis ball–crazed marvels who can parade around with three or four crammed into his maw at one time, have we found a park for you—oodles of tennis balls. The Towers Park canine community area is located behind a tennis court complex off Columbia Pike. For dogs less enthused with hoarding the fluorescent yellow balls, Towers Park has other reasons to recommend it. For starters, the off-leash area is divided into two sections: a larger run for more rambunctious dogs, and a smaller section for toy breeds, puppies, and special-needs dogs. At least one Chihuahua Meetup group is grateful for this mellower corner of the dog park. The Towers Park is well shaded in the summer heat and has lights that stay on until 10 P.M. in the winter—the fruits of a hard-fought battle by the **Towers Park Community Group** (www.towerscca.org; groups.yahoo.com/group/towersCCA).

A bit of insider knowledge: A regular park-goer tells us the Towers Park was built over a former dump, so keep an eye on what your dog digs up; apparently broken ceramic dishes and other oddities turn up occasionally. Located a short distance west of the junction between I-395 and Washington Blvd./VA-27 on Columbia Pike/VA-244. Turn right on Scott Street and follow

## THINK GLOBALLY, BARK LOCALLY

Arlington-based **Homeward Trails** is a dog and cat rescue organization that reaches out to rural shelters in North Carolina, Virginia, West Virginia, and Maryland, "where animal overpopulation is high and adoptions are low, resulting in the needless euthanasia of many adoptable animals." In the first half of 2008 alone, the rescue found homes for 950 pets. If you're looking to adopt or volunteer, check it out. 703/766-2647; www.homewardtrails.org.

it to the parking lot where it dead-ends. You will see tennis courts on your right, and a children's play area on your left. 801 S. Scott St.; 703/228-6523; www.co.arlington.va.us/parks.

# Pentagon City and Crystal City

Pentagon City sits in the shadow of the headquarters of the big U.S. guard dog, the Department of Defense. The Pentagon is one of the world's largest office buildings, but despite its 17.5 miles of corridors, it takes only seven minutes to walk between any two points in the building. Not that Denali has tried it. She tends to stick to the dog-friendlier shops and eateries in the Pentagon Row shopping center. Depending on your culinary persuasion, you'll likely find something to suit your taste in this paw-positive plaza.

Crystal City is a different cup of kibble. With a significant amount of the neighborhood's dining options underground in a subterranean shopping area, the pickings are slimmer for dining out with pets. City parks larger than a shoebox are also hard to locate, although Crystal City does have some nice pocket parks, which we should assume are safer thanks to Crystal City guard dog McGruff. You might know him best for his reminder to "Take a Bite Out of Crime." The National Crime Prevention Council, which runs the McGruff campaign (www.mcgruff.org), is based out of an office building on Crystal Drive.

## PARKS, BEACHES, AND RECREATION AREAS

### 20 Gravelly Point Park

🐾🐾 🐾 (See the Arlington County map on page 128)

Now here's a doggy excursion that really takes off. Gravelly Point Park is a wide grassy patch along the Mount Vernon Trail just north of Ronald Reagan Washington National Airport—really, *just* north of it. The airport's runway is hardly 400 feet away. Arlingtonians come here to dream of jet set getaways over a picnic, and more often than not, they bring the dog. The hubby and I were curious how Denali would react to the planes landing suddenly and spectacularly at such close range. Would she think, "Aaahhh! Pterodactyl!" We waited. We held our breath… to no response. Denali was so focused on our chicken shwarma carryout that she didn't even notice the airplane.

We recommend visiting at night, when the blinking lights of the aircraft and runway heighten the dramatic effect. The riverside view of the DC monuments glowing white against the black night, like an architectural tuxedo, is beautiful. The gates close at 10 P.M. so don't stay too late. Located off northbound George Washington Pkwy. There is no access from southbound; you'll need to loop around the airport to get in the correct lane. 703/289-2500.

## DETOURS

The sporty side of Pentagon City shopping has a soft spot for your furriest workout buddy.

**Gotta Run:** Fitting a running shoe can be harder than a glass slipper. This specialty running store has the expertise to please Cinderella, and your pup can supervise. Pentagon Row; 703/415-0277; www.gottarunshop.wordpress.com.

**Hudson Trail Outfitters:** Let Buddy choose his own doggy life jacket. The entrance escalator can spell treachery for tender paws so be sure to take the elevator instead (located outside the main HTO entrance near Starbucks). Pentagon Row; 703/415-4861; www.hudsontrail.com.

**Lucy:** Fantastically comfortable women's active apparel for yoga, Pilates, dance, running, fitness, and, of course—dog walking. Pentagon Row; 703/418-0608; www.lucy.com.

## 21 Grace Murray Hopper Park

 (See the Arlington County map on page 128)

Denali is hardly the first dog to traipse through this tiny pocket park named after "Amazing Grace," a pioneering computer scientist and naval officer who lived in Arlington in the latter years of her life. Denali sniffed every square inch of grass with deliberate thoroughness, a sure sign that this walkabout is a twice-daily routine for the furrier residents of the dog-friendly River House, the massive Pentagon City apartment complex that the park fronts. A couple dispensers of biodegradable dog poop bags located in the park confirmed this purpose. The park also has a small fountain and an abstract sculpture for good measure. It is located just northwest of Virginia Highlands Park, across the street from the Pentagon Row shopping center. 1400 S. Joyce St.

## 22 Virginia Highlands Park

 (See the Arlington County map on page 128)

Our apologies if these park descriptions all start to sound alike after a while. It could be worse: If Denali had her way, each entry would read, "Squirrel! Squirrel! Squirrel! CAT!!!" She argued this is what the doggy readership is really curious about, but here's hoping your pup is less singular in focus.

This 18-acre county park channels the competitive juices of Arlington's many recreation league sports with two permit-only, lighted baseball fields; soccer fields; basketball, tennis, and volleyball courts; and a pétanque court (the French version of bocce). The problem is that the sports action occasionally can crowd out your pooch, who technically isn't supposed to tread on the turf; fortunately, it's not too hard to find a route on the walking paths and practice fields. In fact, at least one Arlington County ranger laments that Pentagon City dogs find it all too easy to run all over. "It's an on-leash park that everyone thinks is off-leash," she said. So here's the dutiful reminder: Leashes are required at Virginia Highlands Park.

The perk about all the sports action is that after-work games often keep the park well lit, making this a more attractive place for evening dog walks, especially in the wintertime. Open sunrise to half an hour after sunset, except on lighted facilities. Park in the metered lot at 15th and Hayes Streets. 1600 S. Hayes St.; 703/228-6525; www.arlingtonva.us/parks.

### 23 Crystal City Water Park

 (See the Arlington County map on page 128)

Crystal City is thoroughly urban and has the hard-edged cityscape to prove it, including a subterranean passageway connecting shops and office buildings. None of these elements appealed much to Denali, but fortunately, a series of landscaped pocket parks for corporate lunchers along Crystal Drive saved the day. The Crystal City Water Park, dedicated to the city's developer Robert Smith, is one of the nicer ones. True to its name, the park displays a series of water fountains, pools, and waterfalls that Denali cocked her head to listen to more carefully (or perhaps she was focusing on the piped-in smooth jazz). Ornamental water features are certainly in greater abundance than grass here, so if doody calls, you might want to walk your doggy farther south on Crystal Drive or toward the Mount Vernon Trail, which you can access from here. Walk or jog through the pedestrian tunnel under the Virginia Railway Express commuter train, as we saw many Crystal City residents do after work during our visit. This spur trail will connect with the Mount Vernon Trail near the airport. Crystal City Water Park is located on Crystal Drive, between 15th and 18th Streets.

### 24 Eads Park

 (See the Arlington County map on page 128)

From what we saw, this is the largest patch of green in Crystal City. (Don't be fooled by its name; Crystal City's predominant architectural material is cement.) This mostly grass, not-quite-four-acre city park is built on an incline with a playground at the top and a worn-out soccer field and goal at the bottom. A walkway cuts a diagonal up the hill, but otherwise the park is all tough turf partially fenced off from Eads Street. Parallel park at the 12-hour metered street parking. Open sunrise to half an hour after sunset. 2730 S. Eads St.; 703/228-6525; www.arlingtonva.us/parks.

### PLACES TO EAT

**Chevy's:** While most of the Fashion Centre shops and restaurants in Pentagon

City are located indoors, this Tex-Mex chain borders the street and has a red-railed patio next to the wide sidewalk. If you tie the pupster to the railing, you can order up a sizzling-hot plate of fajitas and a margarita. 1201 S. Hayes St.; 703/413-8700; www.chevys.com.

**Jaleo's:** They said yes! We, too, were a tad surprised and delighted when this Crystal City outpost of one of Washington DC's better-known bastions of gastronomy agreed to let dogs sit on the patio. The menu revolves around Spanish tapas designed by star chef José Andrés, host of PBS' *Made In Spain.* 2250-A Crystal Dr.; 703/413-8181; www.jaleo.com.

**La Creperie:** If you have a sweet tooth, or a savory one, stop by this French bistro for a crepe fix for breakfast, lunch, or dinner. Dogs are allowed in the outdoor seating—a good thing, because how could it be a true French bistro experience without *mon chien, mon ami?* Pentagon Row; 703/415-0560.

**Saigon Saigon:** Big and little dogs can take a seat at one of the dozen black outdoor tables along S. Joyce Street next to this Vietnamese restaurant. The specialty is *pho,* a traditional Vietnamese beef-noodle soup pronounced like it rhymes with "huh." Other options include vermicelli, a Vietnamese-style rice noodle, and a large selection of lunch boxes to go with spring rolls on the side. Lunch and dinner specials are offered daily. Pentagon Row; 703/412-0822.

**Starbucks:** Look for the dog bowls in front of the plaza Starbucks if your hound is thirsty. At least one employee here has been known to prepare "puppacinos"—blended ice minus the coffee, milk, or sugar—for dogs in the summer. Pentagon Row; 703/415-0601; www.starbucks.com.

**Waterpark Café:** Inside the Crystal City Water Park, concession stand meets café at the Waterpark Café. The menu includes hot and cold beverages, snacks, sandwiches, and a few Greek specialties. Next to the water fountains there are quite a few outdoor tables, so this is a convenient place for a quick lunch with the pooch. Crystal Drive, between 15th and 18th Streets.

**Zen Bistro:** This trendy café and wine bar has ridden the coattails of the small plates food concept. Think Asian-style tapas for starters and pad Thai or orange peel chicken for entrées. The outdoor seating is primely situated under a garden trellis. There is live music every Wednesday and Thursday night. Pentagon Row, 1301 S. Joyce St.; 703/413-8887; www.zen-bistro.com.

## PLACES TO STAY

**Residence Inn Pentagon City:** If you really intend to take up residence at the Residence Inn, the pet fees end up being more reasonable, but if you're only staying at this 299-room hotel for a night or two it probably isn't worth your while. Any size dog can check in for a $200 one-time fee plus an additional $8 per day cleaning fee. Pet amenities include the occasional handout from the front desk. Human amenities include an indoor pool and pool table, washing machines, fitness center, complimentary breakfast every morning, and a complimentary light dinner with beer and wine three nights midweek.

Rooms range $139–349. Underground parking costs $18 per day. 550 Army Navy Dr.; 703/413-6630; www.marriott.com/hotels/travel/waspt-residence-inn-arlington-pentagon-city.

**The Ritz Carlton, Pentagon City:** The 18-story Ritz complex accepts small dogs weighing 25 pounds or less for a one-time fee of $125. While this Ritz Carlton does not have any special pet packages, the front desk said you can always make any special request with your reservation. Inside each of the 336 guest rooms, you and your lap dog will be in the lap of luxury with 400-thread count Egyptian cotton linens, terry bathrobes, flat screen televisions, and wireless Internet. The tallest rooms facing the Potomac have views of the river and monuments. Housekeeping visits twice daily, so be sure to alert the front desk that your dog is staying with you. Rooms range $189–499. Located across the street from Fashion Centre. 1250 South Hayes St.; 703/415-5000; www.ritzcarlton.com/pentagoncity.

**Sheraton Crystal City:** Official policy at this 217-room hotel says dogs up to 80 pounds are permitted, but we get the impression that doesn't typically happen. The first person at the front desk we spoke with said the limit is 25 pounds. But at the writing of this book, the official answer really is 80 pounds. If the front desk questions you at check-in, you can quote the Sheraton's website and the reservation helpline. As always, however, it's a good idea to call ahead to book reservations when traveling with your pet, so this conversation might unfold over the phone. There is no fee, but dogs cannot be left unattended in the room and you will be asked to sign a waiver at check-in. Sheraton provides a doggy bed, bowl, and treats. Rates range $114–499. 1800 Jefferson Davis Hwy.; 703/486-1111; www.sheraton.com/crystalcity.

# Shirlington and Fairlington

When the weather is fine, it's easy for a dog to spend the whole day outside in Arlington's southernmost neighborhood. Arguably the most popular off-leash dog park in the entire county is narrow, ambling Shirlington Park. The Village at Shirlington (www.villageatshirlington.com) is remarkably dog friendly, too. Space in this guidebook is all that kept us from listing nearly every

## THINK GLOBALLY, BARK LOCALLY

The Chantilly-based **A Forever Home Rescue Foundation** has a firm foothold among the Fairlington dog family, many of whom have volunteered to foster a dog in need of adoption. The 100-percent volunteer-run organization is always looking for more foster homes and fundraisers. 703/961-8690; www.aforeverhome.org.

Shirlington restaurant in the shopping center. Even **Capital City Brewing Company** (2700 S. Quincy St; 703/578-3888; www.capcitybrew.com), formerly one of the only restaurants in the mall that didn't allow dogs (because of two separate dog bite incidents in the summer of 2007) has changed its policy and is inviting dogs again (though preferably on the outside of the patio).

## PARKS, BEACHES, AND RECREATION AREAS

### 25 Fort Barnard Park

🐾🐾🐕 (See the Arlington County map on page 128)

Fort Barnard Park is actually perched on a hill overlooking Shirlington in the Nauck neighborhood. The fully fenced park is located along busy S. Walter Reed Drive, so it's extra important to carefully close the double-gates at both entrances and keep your dog on leash until you're inside the park (at least one dog has been hit here crossing the street off-leash). From first glance you'll notice some heavy-duty balls and squeaker toys inside Fort Barnard Dog Park. It's clear this is a place where serious play happens. The canine community area is equipped with everything needed to make it happen: refreshment (king-size double-water bowl, spigot, and tiered drinking fountain with one at dog level), space (medium-size as Arlington dog parks go), and, of course, friends. Each year the sponsoring community group **Douglas Dogs** (www.douglasdogs.org; info@douglasdogs.org) hosts a barbecue and Halloween doggy costume contest in late October. You can also thank Douglas Dogs' fundraising events and dogged advocacy for the floodlights that keep the park open until 9 P.M., a huge bonus for dog lovers who can't make it to the park until after sundown. Fort Barnard Dog Park is located next to the training grounds for the Arlington County Police Department's K-9 Unit. Between the chain-link fence you can see the agility equipment for the canine-cops-in-training. The K-9 squad has been a part of the Arlington County Police Department since 1967; the county now employs four K-9 squads. Fort Barnard is located at the corner of South Pollard Street and South Walter Reed Drive. 2060 S. Walter Reed Dr.; 703/228-6523; www.co.arlington.va.us/parks.

### 26 Shirlington Park

🐾🐾🐾🐾🐕 (See the Arlington County map on page 128)

More than one DC dog has made the pilgrimage over the 14th Street Bridge to Shirlington Dog Park only to wave to his neighbors from Logan Circle! The Shirlington community canine area is arguably the off-leash destination of choice for both Arlington mutts and their District counterparts thanks to shade, space to move, and easy access to water. The Shirlington Dog Park is a long, narrow alley, sandwiched between storage warehouses and the shallow waters of Four Mile Run, between Shirlington Road and S. Walter Reed Road.

## DIVERSION

Is your pup covered in muck after a dip in Four Mile Run at Shirlington Park? Nearby **Fur-Get Me Not** has a do-it-yourself dog bath. For $15, you can purchase 30 minutes of access to a professional tub, grooming utensils, shampoo, dryer, and towels. Frequent bathers can join the Suds Club and every 10th bath is free. Fur-Get Me Not also offers doggy daycare, boarding, pet-sitting, walking, and a boutique. 4140 S. Four Mile Run Dr.; 703/933-1935; www.furgetmenot.com.

It's mostly fenced (indeed, double-gated with portcullis-style fasteners to close the gates) with a few openings to the creek. Unlike many square-shaped, city block dog parks where owners post up at picnic tables, the skinny Shirlington run follows a paved bike path, making it a convenient place for walking, chatting, and making friends on the move. Shirlington Dog Park even has a fenced-off section for small dogs, puppies, and special-needs pooches, which can be a huge plus when the main corridor overcrowds on fine-weather weekends. As with all of the Arlington canine community areas, Shirlington has a sponsoring community group, **Shirlington Dogs** (groups.yahoo.com/group/shirlingtondogs).

The water quality in Four Mile Run can be a little iffy. From time to time, Arlington County posts signs alerting to sewage spills upstream. One woman said her two beagle-Labrador mixes would always get diarrhea after swimming in the creek, so she stopped letting them swim here. Other owners report no problems and say the creek is the reason they come to Shirlington and the highlight of their dog's weekend. You'll likely determine your dog's level of sensitivity in a hurry. Shirlington Dog Park is unmarked. To find it, drive west on S. Four Mile Run Drive and turn left on Nelson Street (if driving east on S. Four Mile Run Drive, turn right on Nelson). Go straight and park behind the storage facility. There is two-hour parking after 3 P.M. on weekdays and after 7 A.M. on weekends. 2601 S. Arlington Mill Dr.; 703/228-6523; www.co.arlington.va.us/parks.

## 27 Utah Park
🐾🐾🐾🐕 (See the Arlington County map on page 128)

The Utah Dog Park is Arlington's oldest, established way back in 1998. Not surprisingly, the dog community runs deep here. Dog lovers submit snapshots of their puppies to display on the covered bulletin board in the park, just like kids in daycare or Sunday school. Unlike most of the wood-chip dog parks in the county, gravel covers most of the Utah Dog Park. A few other small details set the Utah Park canine community area apart as slightly different, such as the kiddie pool in the corner. In inclement weather, humans will be happy to find a full, covered pavilion. To help with upkeep of these facilities, the sponsoring community group, **Fairlington Dogs** (www.fairlington.org/fairdog.htm), helps coordinate a group gravel-spreading day every year. The Utah Dog Park is fully fenced with double gates, water, and poop bags on hand (just look in the mailbox). 3191 S. Utah St.; 703/228-6523; www.co.arlington.va.us/parks.

### PLACES TO EAT

**Bungalow Billiards & Brew Company:** On a stool like a pedestal outside the entrance to Bungalow Billiards it sits: a red plastic basket filled with dog treats. Nothing fancy, nothing frilly, but it was enough to herald a return visit

from Denali. Bungalow Billiards serves up casual dining favorites such as ribs, sandwiches, wings, burgers, and salads. The half pizza and salad combo is a good standby. Denali also appreciated the two water bowls on the patio. 2766 S. Arlington Mill Dr.; 703/578-0020; www.bungalow4u.com.

**Carlyle:** Consistently voted a top restaurant by *Washingtonian Magazine*, Carlyle sometimes requires a long wait to get a table, particularly since you'll need to score a corner table on the patio (dogs have to be tied outside the patio railing). But the bistro-style cuisine at Carlyle, especially the jambalaya and the filet mignon, are a good value for the quality of food on the plate. Case in point: all the bread is oven-fresh from next-door **Best Buns Bread Co.** (4010 Campbell Ave.; 703/578-1500; www.greatamericanrestaurants.com). If you have no doggy bag to bring home from Carlyle because you've licked your plate clean, consider swinging by Best Buns after the meal to purchase a hefty, homemade dog biscuit for $0.90. 4000 Campbell Ave.; 703/931-0777; www.greatamericanrestaurants.com.

**PING by Charlie Chiang's:** We saw not one, not two, but four Labradors dining at this Chinese restaurant. In fact, when one energetic yellow Lab bounded forward to greet another dog, he pulled the railing he was tied to clean out of the sidewalk cement. Despite the collective gasp from all of PING's patio patrons, none of the waiters flinched. PING's patio can accommodate 20 guests (and at least four dogs). 4060 Campbell Ave.; 703.671-4900; www.charliechiangs.com.

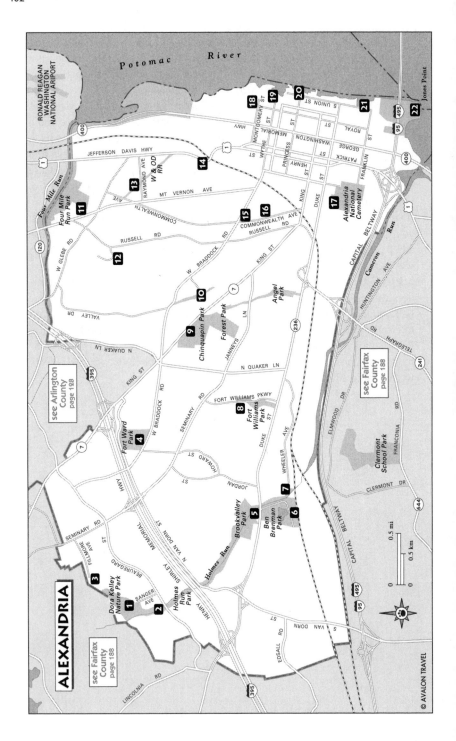

**CHAPTER 7**

# Alexandria

Alexandria is known as one of the dog-friendliest cities in the country, thanks in large part to famously puppy-whipped Old Town. "You only have *one* dog?" an Alexandria mom asked incredulously, glancing at her brood of three rescues. Here is the rare place in the DC metro area where you'll feel naked with only one wagging tail next to you. Put another way, if you were to die and be reincarnated as an Alexandria dog, life could quite possibly be looking up: Canine Cruises on the Potomac River, the original doggy happy hour, and pet parades for every season. The list of pet amenities is no less extensive, with Reiki for Rover, daycare for Daisy, acting lessons for Abby, and puppy pops and dog biscuits to feed the neighborhood.

While there have been disputes about where to draw the line in the sandbox, City of Alexandria authorities seem to recognize that the city's pet friendliness is a major part of its draw for many visitors and residents. The official

## PICK OF THE LITTER—ALEXANDRIA

BEST PARKS
**Duke Street Dog Park,** West End (page 167)
**Simpson Stadium Dog Park,** Del Ray (page 173)
**Founders Park,** Old Town (page 181)
**Windmill Hill Park,** Old Town (page 181)

BEST PLACE TO EAT
**Pat Troy's Ireland's Own,** Old Town (page 185)

BEST PLACE TO STAY
**Hotel Monaco Alexandria,** Old Town (page 186)

BEST BOAT RIDE
**Potomac Riverboat Company's Canine Cruise,** Old Town
(page 178)

BEST PLACE TO GET A SHOW DOG HAIRCUT
**Olde Towne School for Dogs,** Old Town (page 180)

Alexandria visitor's guide identifies dog-friendly establishments. And in Old Town and beyond, Alexandria has four fenced and 13 unfenced off-leash exercise areas, meaning nearly every residence in the city is within a mile of an off-leash dog spot. In fact, the city boasts Northern Virginia's very first off-leash dog park. It could be that the mayor of Alexandria has recognized this truism from Nora Ephron: "You enter a certain amount of madness when you marry a person with pets." No less so when you govern them.

# West End

More than 128,000 people live in Alexandria, and they're not all in Old Town. Alexandria's West End has a far more suburban flavor. Case in point: One of the biggest landmarks is the aptly named Landmark Mall. The West End also has many parks for puppy play; foremost among them is Cameron Station, a 164-acre Army base converted into a master-planned community with 63 of these acres reserved for parkland, including Ben Brenman Park, the Duke Street Dog Park, and a portion of the Holmes Run Trail. This section includes the area west of Russell Road, south and east of I-395, and north of the Capital Beltway (I-495/95).

## PARKS, BEACHES, AND RECREATION AREAS

### ❶ Dora Kelley Nature Park

🐾🐾🐾 (See the Alexandria map on page 162)

This is the largest park in Alexandria at 50 acres and clearly a popular choice. In the span of 30 minutes, we met half a dozen dogs and twice as many humans walking, jogging, and pushing baby strollers down the asphalt path through the hickory-oak forest that covers most of Dora Kelley Nature Park. In addition to the park's paved trails that link up with the Holmes Run Trail, there is also a series of rock-and-dirt nature trails that climb the hillside. The numbered posts along this hike correspond to a self-guided nature trail; you can pick up a brochure at the Jerome "Buddie" Ford Nature Center. If Fido digs nature observation (or consternation . . . Denali inevitably starts whining to herself while watching little furry or feathery critters), there is also a rather murky freshwater marsh that attracts wildlife. From Beauregard Street, turn north on Sanger Avenue. Park on the street near where it dead-ends into the trailhead. 5750 Sanger Ave.; 703/838-4829; www.alexandriava.gov/recreation.

### ❷ Holmes Run Park

🐾🐾🐾 (See the Alexandria map on page 162)

Connecting with Alexandria's largest park is its longest greenway, a favorite route for Alexandria hounds. Holmes Run, named for the former Chief Justice of the Supreme Court Oliver Wendell Holmes who presided at the turn of the 20th century, is fed from the dam at Lake Barcroft in Fairfax County, flowing down into the Potomac River. While the busiest section of the paved trail that follows Holmes Run is south of I-395 to Ben Brenman Park, Denali likes the woodsier stretch adjacent to the Dora Kelly Nature Park.

## DETOURS

**Old Town Doggie Wash:** This self-serve dog wash and groom costs $18 per visit, which includes shampoo and everything you need to beautify your pet. Every sixth wash is free. Closed Tuesday and Wednesday. 105 Moncure Dr.; 703/299-0587; www.oldtown doggiewash.com.

**PetSage:** One of the most comprehensive sources for holistic remedies and natural pet products in the DC metro area. Three cats—Dempsey, Ripken, and Diva—live in the shop. 2391 South Dove St.; 703/299-5044; www.petsage.com.

**Pro Feed Pet Nutrition Center:** The largest selection of premium and organic foods in the region. Located in the Bradlee Shopping Center. 3690-G King St.; 703/820-3888; www.profeedpet.com.

Sand scattered on the pavement clued us in to the creek's variable water level. Indeed, the run is wide, rocky, and reminded us of flash-flood-prone creek beds we've seen out West. At least one trail crossing submerges completely after a heavy rain. We wondered if the creek's wide profile relates to events from more than three decades ago; in 1972, Hurricane Agnes clobbered Holmes Run, destroying the Van Dorn Street overpass and piling up 29 acres of trees and debris in the stream. Fortunately, meteorology has been kinder to Holmes Run since then, although it's still a good idea to wait a few days after it's been raining cats and dogs before visiting.

The trail is accessed easily from Dora Kelley Nature Park or from Tarleton Park at Holmes Run Parkway and S. Jordan Street; 703/324-8702; www.fairfax county.gov/parks/naturelist.htm or www.alexandriava.gov/recreation.

## 🖲 Chambliss Park

👣🐕 (See the Alexandria map on page 162)

In addition to a handful of traditional, fenced dog parks, Alexandria has an assortment of unfenced "dog exercise areas." Many of them aren't worth the aggravation of tracking them down (no offense to Denali, but a bloodhound would have been a welcome addition to our research team with this task). Others are great. We've scouted these 13 unfenced sites so you won't have to share our irksome experience of finding the doggone spot, only to discover it's next to a busy road or in an unattractive alley.

Chambliss Park falls in the middle of the spectrum. It's not worth a long drive to visit, but if you live in the neighborhood, it's a decent place to let your dog run around off leash. And if you arrive and are crestfallen at this modest strip of turf, the Chambliss Street entrance to the Dora Kelley Nature Park is hardly 100 yards away. The City of Alexandria marks the exercise area boundaries with four paw-printed signposts. If your pooch doesn't respond well to voice command, you might end up feeling like you're playing four-square with your puppy. The Chambliss Park exercise area is grassy and includes the space between three posts along the sidewalk and a fence with backyards of homes that border Chambliss Street. There is a trash can on-site, but you'll need to bring your own water and cleanup bags.

From Seminary Road driving south, turn right on Fillmore Street (which turns into Chambliss Street) and continue until it dead-ends. Park next to the tennis courts. 2505 North Chambliss St.; 703/838-4340; www.alexandriava .gov/recreation.

## 🗖 Fort Ward Park

👣👣🐕◖● (See the Alexandria map on page 162)

The best preserved of the Civil War–era Fort Circle Parks, Fort Ward has much of its earthwork walls still intact and more was restored in the 1960s. A sign at the historic earthenworks reads No Games, Picnics, or Sunbathing. So put your serious face on. Fortunately, it doesn't read No Dogs, and we confirmed with park staff that leashed dogs may go anywhere humans can go, except in the Fort Ward Museum. Of interest to the pups, Fort Ward Park has a very small, unfenced off-leash area near the second parking lot. Neither the wooden stakes denoting the square nor a thin row of evergreens do much to separate the off-leash zone from a busy road, however, so be cautious.

Fort Ward's largest living history program, Civil War Camp Day, occurs each June, but smaller military reenactments are staged throughout the year. Due to mock cannon and rifle fire, for most dogs these days are best avoided. For a sweeter sound to pupster ears, visit on Thursday evenings in the summertime for a free concert series. Open 9 A.M.–sunset. 4301 W. Braddock Rd.; 703/838-4848; www.alexandriava.gov/fortward.

## 5 Duke Street Dog Park

🐾🐾🐾🐕 (See the Alexandria map on page 162)

Inside the ramp of the westbound entrance to Ben Brenman Park on Duke Street is a generously sized, circular dog park. We were rubbernecking trying to figure out where to park the car. It turns out the popular off-leash area has no parking lot of its own, so dog lovers either park at Beatley Library slightly west of the park or at the Shops of Fox Chase just east of it. Remember to bring your own water because the dog park has none. What's great about the Duke Street Dog Park is all the grass—it's amazing that how much turf has survived the daily trampling of paws and wrestling matches. There are also a handful of benches and a smattering of small trees for shade. The double-gated entrance is located on the side of the park nearest to the Shops of Fox Hall and Harris Teeter grocery store. 703/838-4340; www.alexandriava.gov/recreation.

## 6 Ben Brenman Dog Park

🐾🐾🐕 (See the Alexandria map on page 162)

Even the larger, 50-acre Ben Brenman Park, where leashes are required, is a great place to jog around the pond. The dog park inside Ben Brenman Park is hidden away across Backlick Creek behind a stand of trees. It's in a picturesque corner of the park, but with no running water, no poop bags, no grass, and no shade to speak of, we couldn't give it more than two paws. Don't let this lack of amenities deter you, though. Many dogs happily trot around this fenced square, which is noted to be a predominantly "small dog" park. (Ironically, this dog park has the most heavy-duty pooper scooper equipment of anywhere we've visited!)

After a fetch session in the park, we recommend a short side trip. When you exit the dog park with your pup on leash again, turn right and walk uphill with the picnic shelter on your right. At the crest of the hill, follow the trail through the opening in the trees toward the railroad tracks. Don't cross the tracks, but instead turn sharply to your left downhill (you should see a fainter trail through the thicket to the creek below). This sandy creek bank is a favorite among Cameron Station dogs in the know.

From I-395 South, take exit 3A to merge onto Duke Street driving east. The park entrance will be on your right side. Park in front of the baseball field. The dog park is south of the baseball field on the other side of the pedestrian bridge. 4800 Brenman Park Dr.; 703/838-4340; www.alexandriava.gov/recreation.

### 🐾 Tarleton Park

🐾🐾🐾 (See the Alexandria map on page 162)

Denali would like to make an important distinction between Tarleton Park, and the unfenced, off-leash exercise area within it. The two-paw rating has nothing to do with the exercise area, an out-of-the-way, uncomfortable space where someone had dumped a dirty diaper and it feels like you're peeping into neighbors' backyards. Few locals even know about it—with the Ben Brenman Dog Park right around the corner, why bother? But the greater six-acre Tarleton Park is a pleasant grassy wedge next to Holmes Run (the creek and the bike trail), which is a very popular dog-walking route.

From Duke Street, turn south on S. Jordan Street, which is across the street from the Shops of Foxchase shopping center, and then left on Holmes Run Parkway. Tarleton Park is located through the Western ranch-style gateway at the dead-end. If your pooch insists on scoping out the off-leash area, it's located in the point of the grassy triangle farthest away from the creek. You'll see a green Dog Exercise Area sign once you walk closer. 703/838-4340; www.alexandriava.gov/recreation.

### 🐾 Fort Williams Parkway

🐾🐾 (See the Alexandria map on page 162)

Two signs on this grassy shoulder sent us very mixed messages. One recited the rules of the official Alexandria unfenced, off-leash dog exercise area. The other officiously announced Dogs Must Be On Leash and Owner Must Clean Up. Huh. Denali agreed that's a head-scratcher, as she then demonstrated with her hind leg. Alexandria park officials confirmed the corner is still on the roster for city off-leash areas. Lift a leg, and keep walking. Located between Fort Williams Parkway and Old Fort Williams Parkway (Dearborn Place). 703/838-4340; www.alexandriava.gov/recreation.

### 🐾 Chinquapin Park

🐾🐾🐾 (See the Alexandria map on page 162)

Football practice was winding down when we visited Chinquapin Park, so we slowly drove around the minivans idling near the field and the players and cheerleaders walking back to T. C. Williams High School. Chinquapin Park is a 21-acre set of athletic facilities next door to the high school.

The reason Denali was here—the unfenced off-leash doggy exercise area—

is located behind the tennis courts near the Chinquapin Recreation Center. Look for the brown sign announcing the off-leash area rules and the modest square designated by four wooden pegs at the bottom of a small slope next to the tennis parking area. Trees hem in the back of the space. It's nothing to write home about, but this off-leash area feels more protected from traffic than some of Alexandria's other unfenced ones. Water is available in the recreation center. Bring your own cleanup bags. Open 8 A.M.–8 P.M. 3210 King St.; 703/838-4340; www.alexandriava.gov/recreation.

## 10 Timberbranch Parkway

🐾 🐾 🐕 (See the Alexandria map on page 162)

"That's it?" was our initial thought. Fortunately, first impressions proved incomplete. This unfenced off-leash area is located inside a forested culvert in a residential neighborhood. The median is very steep and not at all walkable near the entrance to Timberbranch Parkway at Braddock Road, which is where we first peered inside. The narrow ribbon of woods becomes far easier to traverse at the junction with Timberbranch Drive. To be honest, we never actually found the four paw-printed posts, but we trust they're in there somewhere. You know the drill: off-leash play is only permitted inside the wooden markers. Even without locating the official exercise area, Denali still entertained herself on a leashed walk through the abbreviated pathway through the median. We listened to the chirrup of birdies and the low whirr of lawnmowers, a sure sign that we had crossed the threshold into suburbia. It doesn't seem worth a long trek to get here, but if you live nearby it's a worthwhile dog-walk—at least for a roadside culvert. From Braddock Road, drive several blocks west of Russell

Road and turn left onto Timberbranch Drive, proceeding until you intersect E. Timberbranch Parkway. Park on the street. 703/838-4340; www.alexandriava .gov/recreation.

##  Edison Street Cul-de-sac

(See the Alexandria map on page 162)

Mount Vernon Avenue gets distinctly spicier just north of Del Ray. The tiny neighborhood of Arlandria, so named for its location on the Arlington-Alexandria border, often goes by its nickname "Little Chirilagua," a coastal village where many resident Salvadorans lived before fleeing during the country's civil war. The Edison Street Cul-de-sac off-leash area is located squarely behind this six-block section of Hispanic-owned restaurants, bakeries, and salons. When we stopped by the neighborhood it was busy: kids whizzing by on scooters to the Four Mile Run Trail that passes by the small, unfenced area, grown-ups hanging around cars with windows down and music blaring. Bring your own water and cleanup bags. A long-time Arlingtonian advised us that muggings have occurred on the W&OD and Four Mile Run Trails in south Arlington, so be alert.

From Mount Vernon Avenue driving north, turn right on W. Reed Avenue and then an immediate left on Edison Street. Park in the cul-de-sac at the end of the street. 703/838-4340; www.alexandriava.gov/recreation.

### PLACES TO EAT

**Food Matters:** The seasonally inspired menu changes monthly and most of the ingredients hail from within 150 miles of this café, a big perk for "locavores." Dogs are allowed anywhere on the patio, and usually there are quite a few. A couple of doggy water bowls can usually be found outside because "beverages matter," too. Wednesday night is Pasta Night, with salad and unlimited servings of three different pastas for $18. If you're in a hurry, Food Matters is also a quick place to grab something to go cafeteria-style (the tuna and white bean salad and grapefruit soda hit the spot). Closed Monday. 4906 Brenman Park Dr.; 703/461-3663; www.foodmattersva.com.

### PLACES TO STAY

**Hawthorn Suites Alexandria:** Each of the 185-rooms comes with a fully equipped kitchen, and guests enjoy a complimentary hot breakfast buffet that includes eggs, meats, breads, fresh fruit, cereal, and beverages (Denali asks: doggy bag?). For a $150 fee, up to two pets weighing less than 80 pounds each can check in. Extended stays require an additional $50 per month thereafter. 420 N. Van Dorn St.; 703/370-1000; www.hawthornsuitesalexandria.com.

**Washington Suites Alexandria:** Dogs can check into this 222-room hotel, which offers three configurations of rooms: studio, one-bedroom, or two-bedroom. Prepped for a long stay or a short one, each room comes with a full kitchen, flat-screen television, free high-speed Internet, and complimentary continental breakfast. Washington Suites Alexandria has both smoking and nonsmoking rooms. 100 S. Reynolds St.; 703/370-9600; www.washington suitesalexandria.com.

# Del Ray

"Del Ray... Isn't that in California? Or Florida?" Denali had never heard of this homey, paw-friendly Alexandria 'hood before we hopped in the car and drove down Mount Vernon Avenue. Originally designed as a streetcar suburb in the early 1900s, Del Ray is a front porch community and a self-described "place where Main Street still exists." Everything about the place harkens back to simpler times when all Lassie had to do was save Timmy and no one worried about pet food contaminated with rat poison. It's hard to believe you're only a half dozen Metro stops away from downtown Washington. Del Ray boasts Northern Virginia's very first off-leash dog park, thanks to the efforts of **The Del Ray Dog Owners Group** (www.ddog.org), and it's safe to say only Del Ray babies are doted on more than its dogs. The neighborhood even has an honorary canine columnist, Daisy Mae Del Ray, in the *Alexandria Gazette Packet*. This section includes the area north of Braddock Road, west of Route 1, south of East and West Glebe Road, and east of Russell Road.

## PARKS, BEACHES, AND RECREATION AREAS

### 🐾 Monticello Park

🐾🐾🐾🦮 (See the Alexandria map on page 162)

After what felt like endless circling around the block, we found Monticello Park, an antidote to our grumpiness. Denali had started losing hope for Alexandria's unfenced dog exercise areas after previously visiting several duds, but Monticello Park revived our interest. It reminds us of a scaled-down version of Glencarlyn Park in Arlington, with its leafy canopy and dirt shoulder for

## DOG-EAR YOUR CALENDAR

While Del Ray's Art on the Avenue festival draws more two-legged traffic (more than 40,000 people!), Del Ray dogs howl for a different October event: the **Del Ray Halloween Parade.** At 2 P.M. on the designated day, a crowd of pets, kids, and grown-ups line up in front of the post office—dressed in costumes that fright and delight—to march down Mount Vernon Avenue. One resident calls it "the best Halloween parade in the world." www.delraycitizen.org.

## DETOURS

The majority of businesses on Mount Vernon Avenue are still independently owned by local residents, many of whom welcome their four-legged neighbors.

**A Show of Hands:** A showcase of handmade local art. Closed on Monday. 2204 Mount Vernon Ave.; 703/683-2905; www.ashowofhands.biz.

**Aston Inc. Decorative Hardware:** Need assistance sorting through the art noveau–style doorknobs and hinges? Ask the shop's beagle, Spot Too (the original Spot retired after 16 years behind the counter). 1913 Mount Vernon Ave.; 703/548-9288.

**Barkley Square Gourmet Dog Bakery:** This all-time Old Town hounds' favorite has migrated to Del Ray. Couture leashes, fresh-baked biscuits, and custom canine birthday cakes all await you inside this perky magenta house. Also ask about pet services from Karing by Kristina. 2006 Mount Vernon Ave.; 703/628-4311; www.barkleysquarebakery.com.

**Executive Lock & Key Service, Inc.:** Besides a 24-hour emergency locksmith service, you'll find a small hardware store and—all ears perk up—treats. 2003B Mount Vernon Ave.; 703/823-2000.

**Let's Meat on the Avenue:** Butcher Stephen Gatward sells smoked marrowbones ($2 per small bone; $8 per large bone) that kept Denali occupied for nearly a whole chapter. Dogs are not allowed in the store but can sip from the water bowl while waiting out front. Closed Monday. 2403 Mount Vernon Ave.; 703/836-6328.

**Nature's Nibbles:** This got our attention: Natural and organic alternatives to commercial pet food at *reasonable prices.* Delivery for a small fee in Northern Virginia or Washington DC on orders of $30 or more. 2601 Mount Vernon Ave.; 703/931-5241; www.naturesnibbles.com.

**PetSmart:** Also has a Banfield Animal Hospital. Located in the nearby Potomac Yard shopping center. 3351 Jefferson Davis Hwy.; 703/739-4844; www.petsmart.com.

off-leash play. (Although note that dogs are only allowed to run free in the 50-by 200-foot square denoted with paw-printed wooden markers.) The stream valley park is also popular with birders.

Unlike some of Alexandria's unfenced sites, Monticello Park is set back from major traffic—a key comfort should all those weeks of obedience training suddenly fly from your dog's mind like the flutter of a robin. Open 6 A.M.–9 P.M.

Monticello Park is actually quite easy to find if you take the pesky correct turn. From Russell Road, turn north on Beverly Road. Parallel park in the neighborhood and walk across the pedestrian bridge into the woods. 703/838-4340; www.alexandriava.gov/recreation.

### 13 W&OD Railroad at Raymond Avenue

🐾 🐕 (See the Alexandria map on page 162)

W & Odd is more like it. On the south side of Del Ray, this grassy lot stands between two fenced backyards. All but one of the paw-printed wooden posts were missing, as was the standard brown sign listing the dog exercise area regulations, but the City of Alexandria Department of Parks and Recreation confirmed this is still on its registry of official off-leash spots. The partially fenced site has drainage issues, so don't visit after a heavy rain. Also, never fear, the railroad stopped running long ago and the train tracks have been removed. This grassy site interrupts the W&OD bike trail that follows the former railroad right-of-way. There is no water and no cleanup bags on-site so bring your own if you visit. Located on Raymond Avenue south of Mount Vernon, across the street from Mount Jefferson Park. 703/838-4340; www.alexandriava.gov/recreation.

### 14 Simpson Stadium Dog Park

🐾 🐾 🐾 🐕 (See the Alexandria map on page 162)

This is Northern Virginia's very first fenced dog park, and it's maintained meticulously. Enter through the large double-gated entrance and join in the fun. As with most dog parks, the Simpson Stadium Dog Park sees the most action after work, sometimes with 20 to 25 dogs at a time. The very sunny park has a generous amount of space, though it's not huge—it's comparable in size with Arlington's Benjamin Banneker Park. The current park is actually smaller than the original due to Route 1 expansion. The off-leash area is open until 10 P.M. nightly, a bonus for late-evening workers and their ready-to-play pups. Park amenities include a water fountain, a stash of spanking new tennis balls in a bag tied to the fence (at least when we visited), a few benches, and a children's play set, presumably for doggy diversion. There were quite a few plastic grocery bags on hand, but bring your own poop bags just in case. The dog park is located at Simpson Stadium Park, at the intersection of Route 1 and Monroe Avenue, next to the two baseball fields. There's free parking in the lot at Monroe and Leslie Avenues (across from the YMCA). 500 Monroe Ave.; 703/838-4340; www.alexandriava.gov/recreation.

### 15 Corner of Braddock Road and Commonwealth Avenue

🐕 🐕 (See the Alexandria map on page 162)

Busy traffic deters many dog lovers from using this unfenced off-leash dog park for its intended purpose. One ill-timed squirrel chase would be the end of Denali, so we didn't chance it. If nothing else, it's a shady, grassy corner to sniff around. Three-hour parking is available on Braddock Street. The official off-leash area is located on the southeast corner of Braddock Road and Commonwealth Avenue; 703/838-4340; www.alexandriava.gov/recreation.

## PLACES TO EAT

**Caboose Café and Bakery:** For such a homegrown name, the menu at Caboose Café is a culinary world tour: American chicken wings, Italian hero, French *salade niçoise,* Cuban sandwich, Thai chicken salad, and Ethiopian *doro watt* all served in one place. The Caboose Café and Bakery specializes in American and Ethiopian cuisine. Dogs can sit under the nine tables out front and drink from the big water bowl. 2419 Mt. Vernon Ave.; 703/566-1283; www.caboose-cafe.com.

**Cheesetique:** In 2008, Del Ray's specialty cheese store added a cheese and

## DIVERSIONS

Say "Puppieees!" Capture your best friend in a frame-worthy original. Here are local artists (or artists with local connections) who don't mind if their models drool during the shoot. If no address is listed, it means the artist will come to you or paint from photographs.

**Lee Anderson:** Crisp black-and-white studio portraits. 2409 Brentwood Pl., Alexandria; 703/765-8833; www.photolee.com.

**Simon Bland:** Oil, pastel, and graphite portraits. 540/822-3080; www.portraitsbysimonbland.com.

**Stephen Bobb:** Photojournalism-style portraits. 202/329-1670; www.fidojournalism.com.

**Gina Eppolito:** Photo portfolio includes a heart-tugging shelter series. 202/390-0169; www.fotogina.com.

**Scott S. Hunter:** Wacky and whimsical papier-mâché. 202/547-8989; www.tensecat.com.

**Amanda Jones:** This Massachusetts-based photographer does an annual shoot at A.k.a. Spot in Arlington. 877/251-2390; www.amandajones.com.

**Megan Lee:** Specializes in pet photography. 571/641-1044; www.pawsandclawsphotography.com.

**Robert McClintock:** Distinctive hybrid style of digital photography and painting. His studio is located in Baltimore. 410/814-2800; www.robertmcclintock.com.

**Mindy Mitchell:** Fur-fabulous oil portraits on linen. Supervised by the sweet Rosie, patient mutt and office mascot. 202/399-4602; www.mindymitchell.com.

wine bar. In warm weather, dogs can join you at one of the five tables out front. The cheese bar menu, like the store, offers specialty cheeses from around the world and the United States, focusing on hard-to-find artisan and small-farm producers. Denali was keener on the charcuterie (cured meat) offerings and the doggy water bowl. You might appreciate the full wine and beer menu, designed to pair with all the cheesiness. 2411 Mt. Vernon Ave.; 703/706.5300; www.cheesetique.com.

**The Dairy Godmother:** This Wisconsin-style frozen custard shop could easily have been named the "Fairy Dogmother." The Dairy Godmother sells healthy, sugar-free "Puppy Pops" for $1 each—18,000 of which were sold in 2006. Puppy Pops come in two flavors: yogurt-based banana/peanut butter or pumpkin/peanut butter. For humans, the Dairy Godmother serves a different whimsical flavor daily, in addition to vanilla and chocolate frozen custard and an assortment of sorbets on hand. The daily custard flavors are listed a month at a time on the Dairy Godmother website. Dogs are not allowed inside the shop, per Alexandria health code, but there is a bench out front where you can tie them. 2310 Mount Vernon Ave.; 703/683-7767; www.thedairygodmother.com.

**The Evening Star:** The secret is out about this neighborhood favorite that serves "sophisticated and eclectic American food." Don't come too hungry— the portions are on the smaller side—but expect delicious bites. The Evening Star is a little pricier than other Del Ray cafés, but it is not too fancy and worth a visit for a special occasion—say, a successful graduation from Olde Towne School for Dogs. Lunch, dinner, and Sunday brunch are served.

Dogs are often seen tied to the railing around the patio (management requests to the outside, please), and servers will bring a water bowl on request. You, on the other paw, have more than water to choose from. Thanks to two separate bars inside The Evening Star (one in back and another upstairs) and sister store Planet Wine next door, the wine and beer lists are extensive, featuring 19 wines by the glass, 20 beers on tap, and 10 bottled beers, plus any wine bottle you choose to purchase at Planet Wine. 2000 Mount Vernon Ave.; 703/549-5051; www.eveningstarcafe.net.

**Los Tios Grill:** Regulars rave about the freshness of the ingredients served up at this Tex-Mex and Salvadorean restaurant. The wait staff brings chips and *pico de gallo* salsa to your table right away, and the margaritas are *deliciosas,* too. When it's patio season, there's almost always at least one dog tied to the railing. 2615 Mount Vernon Ave.; 703/299-9290; www.lostiosgrill.com.

**St. Elmo's Coffee Pub:** A central watering hole in Del Ray since 1996, St. Elmo's website proclaims, and rightfully so, it's "an eclectic coffee house anchoring the Del Ray community." You can hitch your pup's leash to around the side of the coffeehouse (facing E. Del Ray Street) near the hefty trough of water while you grab a latte inside. Del Ray dogs know they get treats at St. Elmo's, so they don't mind the detour. 2300 Mount Vernon Ave.; 703/739-9268; www.stelmoscoffeepub.com.

**Taqueria Poblano:** Leashed *perros* can park it under the table at Taqueria Poblano, which usually keeps full water bowls out for its doggy patrons. The *tacos al carbon* are good here, and the Baja fish tacos reminded Denali of her So-Cal roots. (A local side note: This is the owners of Natures Nibbles' favorite restaurant—happily married Chris and Anne Gabriel met here.) 2400-B Mount Vernon Ave.; 703/548-8226; www.taqueriapoblano.com.

# Slaters Lane

Not quite in Old Town, but not quite in Arlington either, Slaters Lane is a great little corner with no fewer than three dog-friendly eateries worth checking out. It's located just north of Old Town on the west side of George Washington Parkway.

### PLACES TO EAT

**Buzz:** As the name suggests, you can choose the buzz of your choice, be it powered by sugar, alcohol, or coffee. This bakery-lounge-coffee shop caters to all three vices. Buzz cut the ribbon on its pet-friendly patio in spring 2008, and the corner has had hounds lounging there ever since. Look for water bowls outside, and homemade doggy biscuits and ice cream for purchase inside. Dog lovers will find a dangerous selection of treats for human taste buds, too. More than a few pages of this guidebook were powered by Buzz's coffee and free wireless Internet. Tip for the thrifty: coffee costs only $0.50 if you bring your own cup. Besides being pet friendly, Buzz is also very kid friendly (note the tot-sized play oven in the hallway). 901 Slaters Ln.; 703/600-2899; www.buzzonslaters.com.

**Rustico:** The wide, brick patio at Rustico is roomy enough for at least a few Labrador retrievers to squeeze in; fortunately, the restaurant management agrees. The Neighborhood Restaurant Group owns Rustico, as well as Buzz across the street. These restaurateurs also bring you Del Ray's The Evening

Star and Clarendon's Tallula—fairly dog friendly across the table. At Rustico the food is inspired by the *cucina rustica* of Southern Italy, most notably tasty pizza and more than 331 types of ales, lagers, ciders, and stouts. How's that for beer with your pizza? An abbreviated food menu is also available for carryout. 827 Slaters Ln.; 703/224-5051; www.rusticorestaurant.com.

**Tropical Smoothie Café:** The smoothie menu here presents two different schools of thought: decadent Blizzard-like, calorie-laden treats such as the Peanut Butter Cup Smoothie; and diet-conscious Splendid Smoothies, all concocted with the artificial sweetener Splenda. Sandwiches and salads are also available. If you live nearby, your dog has probably come to regard the periwinkle-colored dog bowl outside the front door as a Slaters Lane landmark. 1556 Potomac Greens Dr.; 703/299-8325; www.tropicalsmoothie.com.

# Carlyle

## PARKS, BEACHES, AND RECREATION AREAS

### 16 Hooff's Run

🐾 (See the Alexandria map on page 162)

This uneventful visit left Denali yawning. The unfenced off-leash exercise area is located on the corner of Commonwealth Avenue and Oak Street, next to the Redeemed Church of Christ. Traffic on Commonwealth is brisk here, but not as intimidating as up at Braddock Road. Even so, we both turned our noses up at the grassy corner and opted to walk the neighborhoods instead to admire the colonial-style gems within a bone's throw of George Washington Masonic National Memorial. Bring your own water and bags if you visit, and remember that your dog can only legally be off-leash within the designated four wooden posts. From Mount Vernon Avenue driving north, turn right on W. Reed Avenue and then an immediate left on Edison Street. Park in the cul-de-sac at the end of the street if there is room. 703/838-4340; www.alexandriava.gov/recreation.

### 17 African American Heritage Park

🐾🐾 (See the Alexandria map on page 162)

What a contemplative dog walk this is. The seven-acre park was designed to incorporate six leaning headstones from a 19th-century African American cemetery. These headstones are in stark contrast to the Alexandria National Cemetery across the creek, speaking to an unjustly disparate past. Bronze tree sculptures, *Truths that Rise from the Roots Remembered,* acknowledge the contributions of African Americans to the growth of Alexandria. While walking around the short cinder and boardwalk trail that loops around the park, you can read the historic headstones.

Be sure to bring your own water and poop bags. Open dawn to dusk. Look for two-hour metered parking on Jamieson Street. From Duke Street, turn south on Holland Lane. If you cross the George Washington Masonic National Memorial you've gone too far. The park is part of the mixed-use Carlyle Development. 500 Holland Ln.; 703/838-4340; www.alexandriava.gov/recreation.

# Old Town

Old Town Alexandria is a dog's dream. Decidedly upper crust, the former tobacco port is fantastically hospitable to its four-pawed companions—Old Town even has a canine mascot! Besides being home to the world-renowned Olde Towne School for Dogs, this self-consciously quaint, historic community has an Irish pub where your Irish setter can order beef stew off his own menu, a bank where tellers hand out Milk-Bones with deposit slips, and, until recently, not one but two gourmet doggy bakeries (never fear, the Old Town staple Barkley Square Dog and Cat Bakery only moved to Alexandria's nearby Del Ray neighborhood). Most of the sidewalk cafés on cobblestoned King Street permit well-behaved dogs on the patio; in fact, we only heard of one, Bugsy's Pizza Restaurant, that doesn't. Even Blockbuster and Ann Taylor allow paws inside the premises. With so much for a dog to smell and do, you might want to stop by the paw-friendly **Alexandria Visitors Center** at Ramsay Center (Open 9 A.M.–8 P.M. daily; 221 King St.; 703/838-5005; www.visitalexandria va.com) for some extra pointers and self-guided tour map.

If you're patient, you can usually find metered or free two-hour parking in Old Town; the City of Alexandria website (www.alexandriava.gov) also has a map of parking garages, which can be handy. This section includes the area south of Slaters Lane, north of Jones Point Park and the Capital Beltway, west of the Potomac River, and east of Telegraph Road and the Amtrak line.

## DIVERSION

The **Potomac Riverboat Company's Canine Cruise** leaves port every Thursday evening May–September in a double-decker charter boat. The 40-minute tour of Alexandria's seaport is such a hit that it's offered four times a night: at 6, 7, 8, and 9 P.M. Dogs must be on a six-foot flat leash (no retractable leashes). The *Admiral Tilp* holds up to 50 dogs and their humans but fills up quickly, so it's best to buy tickets in advance. The cruise departs from the Alexandria City Marina. Tickets cost $14 for humans; dogs are free (as are their treats and refreshments). "Ahoy, Arfie!" 3 Cameron St.; 703/548-9000; www.potomacriverboatco.com.

## DOG-EAR YOUR CALENDAR

**Black Tie & Tails Gala:** Alexandria's answer to DC's formal Bark Ball and a fundraiser for AWLA. February; 703/838-4774; www.alexandriaanimals.org.

**St. Patrick's Day Parade:** Bagpipers, marching bands, Irish wolfhounds, Irish setters, Irish terriers… you get the idea. Includes a dog/owner look-alike contest, among other categories, in Market Square the morning of the parade. Early March; 703/237-2199; www.ballyshaners.org.

**Doggie Bone Hunt & Easter Parade:** Denali might have preferred an Easter Bunny hunt, but an Easter bone hunt is nice, too. Proceeds benefit the Animal Rescue League of Alexandria (AWLA). March; Chinquapin Park; 3210 King St.; 703/838-4774; www.alexandriaanimals.org.

**Pet Calendar Contest:** The competition heats up as pets vie for professional photo shoots, a chance to be a Pet of the Month and the coveted calendar cover! Proceeds benefit AWLA. Summer; 703/838-4774; www.alexandriaanimals.org.

**Doggie Swim Day:** End the swim season doggy style at Alexandria's Old Town Pool the Tuesday following Labor Day 4–7 P.M. Admission costs $5 per dog, free for humans, with proceeds benefiting AWLA. Early September; 1609 Cameron St.; 703/838-4671; www.alexandriava.gov/recreation.

**Olde Towne Dogge Walke:** Join the Alexandria mayor and Scottie dog Alex, the city's mascot, for a 1.5-mile morning walk to raise money for abandoned and homeless animals in the community. The walk departs from the Olde Towne School for Dogs. Mid-September; 529 Oronoco St.; 703/836-7643; www.otsfd.com.

**Blessing of the Pets:** Dogs may join parishioners in the churchyard to be blessed at the first Episcopal church in Alexandria, completed in 1773. Early October; 118 North Washington St.; 703/549-1450; www.historicchristchurch.org.

**Howloween Costume Contest:** Hosted by the Hotel Monaco to benefit AWLA, the contest award categories include: Political Pooch, Most Glamorous Get-Up, Best Dressed Couple, and Top Dog. Late October; 480 King St.; 703/549-6080; www.doggiehappyhour.com.

**Old Town Alexandria's Scottish Christmas Walk:** More than 100 Scottish clans, Scottie dog groups, bagpipe and drum bands, Scottish Highland dancers, and Santa Claus himself parade through Old Town. Early December; 703/548-0111; www.scottishchristmaswalk.com.

**Pet Photos With Santa:** Portrait sessions with the Old Saint Nick to benefit AWLA. Located at Olde Towne School for Dogs. First weekend in December; 529 Oronoco St.; 703/836-7643; www.otsfd.com.

## PARKS, BEACHES, AND RECREATION AREAS

### 18 Montgomery Dog Park

🐾🐕 (See the Alexandria map on page 162)

Old Town has only one *fenced* off-leash dog run. The spartan dog park has one bench, a cinder and grass surface, and a single-gate entry—so watch out for puppy escape artists. There is no running water or bowls, so you'll need to bring your own. Shade is sparse, too. Montgomery Park will do in a pinch, and it's conveniently close to the Holiday Inn or Sheridan Suites Hotel in Old Town, but we far recommend a dog walk along the riverfront trail. If your pup responds well to voice commands, only seven blocks away Founders Park has a small, unfenced off-leash area. Montgomery Park is located at the corner of First and N. Fairfax Streets. 703/838-4340; www.alexandriava.gov/recreation.

### 19 Oronoco Bay Park

🐾🐾🐾 (See the Alexandria map on page 162)

For a lucky few, this Potomac shores park is their backyard. "Maybe if you sell enough guidebooks, you could move to Old Town," a gentleman remarked on his daily dog walk along the Mount Vernon Trail, which runs through Oronoco Bay Park, down to Founders Park, and beyond. He resides in one of these waterfront town homes. "Would you like that?"

Is that a rhetorical question?

## DOG-EAR YOUR CALENDAR

The Alexandria institution **Olde Towne School for Dogs** is 7,000 square feet dedicated to training, grooming, and supplying your dog. Since opening the premier facility in 1975, owners Carlos and Sandy Mejias, have trained more than 30,000 dogs and their handlers. The courses range from "Puppy Head Start" (think puppy preschool) to standard obedience lessons to advanced trainings of every distinction (show training, service dog training, therapy dog training—even theatrical training!). All trainings are individual for your dog (i.e., no group classes).

Olde Towne grooming appointments fill up faster than you can say furball, so here's a tip: From September through December, the groomers will book appointments for the following year. After that you can add your dog's name to a waiting list and hope for a cancellation among those booked-solid 25 dogs a day, six days a week. Located on the corner of St. Asaph and Oronoco Streets. 529 Oronoco St.; 703/836-7643; www.otsfd.com.

As with all of the river walks in Old Town, this is a picturesque spot framing the Potomac. Your Portuguese water dog (the "Old Town Labrador," we hear) might have a hard time sauntering next to the river rather than diving in snout-first. To give your pooch a closer on-leash encounter with the waterfront, detour to the floating dock next to the Dee Campbell Rowing Center, where cattails line the marshy edge of the bay. From Washington Street/George Washington Memorial Parkway driving south, turn left on Madison Street. 100 Madison St.; 703/838-4340; www.alexandriava.gov/recreation.

### 20 Founders Park

🐾🐾🐾 ✕ ⬤ (See the Alexandria map on page 162)

Founders Park is a pleasant destination for a leashed walk along the river, which, initially, is all we thought the park offered. But it turns out the City of Alexandria has staked out a small, unfenced off-leash area at the park's northwest corner. Again, the off-leash exercise area is completely open—it's just a corner of the grass marked with four posts—and cars and bicycles use Union Street regularly, but if your dog responds well to voice command you can enjoy an off-leash romp in the heart of Old Town Alexandria.

When the weather is fine, Founders Park has a festive, carnival feel. We recently saw two Great Danes listening to a street musician at the nearby City Marina behind the Torpedo Factory Art Center, as well as a greyhound curled up on a blanket with his owners, who had their noses in books. It's hard to imagine this landscaped waterfront park as anything other than what you see today, but this section of the riverfront, called West Point in the early 1700s, has a darker history. Besides being a major hub in the flourishing tobacco industry, Alexandria, established in 1749, was one if the South's largest slave-trading ports; African slaves were unloaded here at the docks to be auctioned off in Market Square. Founders Park stretches between the Potomac River and Union Street from Cameron Street to the south to Oronoco Street to the north. The off-leash area is located at the corner of Union and Oronoco Streets. 703/838-4340; www.alexandriava.gov/recreation.

### 21 Windmill Hill Park

🐾🐾🐾 ✕ (See the Alexandria map on page 162)

In our opinion, this is the best place for an off-leash romp in Old Town. The doggy exercise area at Founders Park, in sight of the river but not touching it, is a bit of a tease. Here, at last, your dog can splash right into the Potomac. The unfenced, waterfront lot is located at Union and Gibbon Streets, nearly at the edge

Frizbee anyone?

## DETOURS

More stores in the official Old Town visitor's guide have dog-friendly symbols than don't. Even Gap, Banana Republic, and Ann Taylor hand out biscuits.

**Burke & Herbert Bank:** Virginia's oldest bank is also kindest to its critters. Treats are always on hand here. 621 King St.; 703/684-1647; www.burkeandherbert.com.

**Enchanted Florist:** A doggy landmark in the DC metro area for more than 25 years thanks to its birdhouse full of dog bones. 139 S. Fairfax St.; 703/836-7777; www.enchantedfloristoldtown.com.

**Fetch:** This all-natural dog and cat bakery sells more than 60 kinds of healthy baked treats in flavors and shapes such as "Snicker Pooches" or "Postmen and Kitties." Look for the Wall of Fame, covered in photos of the regulars, a few of whom have been coming since the store opened in 1997. Also a small boutique. 101-A S. St. Asaph St.; 703/518-5188; www.fetch-bakery.com.

**Jake's of Old Town:** Life *is* Good. Just ask beagle Tiko who keeps shop surrounded by merchandise emblazoned with this mantra. Get treats at the register and check out the dog Frisbees, bowls, and other toys in the back of the store. Tiko might not want to say hi to your dog, so give him some space. 103 King St.; 703/299-4663; www.lifeisgood.com.

**James Wilhoit Antiques:** Upscale antique furniture, paintings, and collectibles. Say hello to Alexei, a long-haired dachshund. Closed Monday and Tuesday. 277 S. Washington St.; 703/683-6595; www.jameswilhoit.com.

**La Muse:** Nab a Milk-Bone from the stone dog statue out front, and then head inside to find an all-American-made, uplifting gift or silly card. Dogs (and well-behaved children) welcome! 108 N. Patrick St.; 703/683-1696; www.shoplamuse.net.

**Moto Photo:** Pick up photos with your pooch, or make an appointment at the Pet Portrait Studio. 711 King St.; 703/548-1145; www.motophoto.com/oldtown.

**Sugar House Day Spa:** Here's a role reversal: Your pooch can attend your grooming appointment. Dogs are allowed in the hair salon downstairs, but not elsewhere in the spa. 111 North Alfred St.; 703/549-9940; www.sugarhousedayspa.com.

of Old Town. It's not quite one mile south of Founders Park and the walk is nice, with dogs to meet along the way and lovely historic homes to admire. Across the river, the view changes for the better as the industry of Bolling Air Force Base transitions to the woods of Oxon Hill Farm, a national park in Maryland. Windmill Hill Park will be on your left across from a recreation field. You can parallel park on Union Street. 703/838-4340; www.alexandria va.gov/recreation.

## 22 Jones Point Park

🐾🐾🐾🐾 (See the Alexandria map on page 162)

"It has everything you need right here: water, woods, field," one dog lover says of the somewhat isolated, 60-acre park at the base of Woodrow Wilson Bridge. Her three vizslas punctuate her argument by chomping the sweet grass like billy goats and then rolling on their backs, their tongues lolling about in happy grins.

Jones Point has a historic lighthouse, too, a modest, whitewashed-clapboard cottage on the river's edge. From 1856 to 1926, the lighthouse's fifth-order Fresnel lens (of which light could be seen from nine miles away!) guided ships

## DIVERSION

Trot around with dog-friendly **Olde Town Horse and Carriage.** Impromptu carriage rides begin at the corner of King and Lee Streets, or call for a reservation. Hours of operation subject to weather conditions. 121 King St.; 703/765-8976.

through dangerous sandbars in the Potomac. If you sniff along the water in front of the house you'll find more history locked inside the seawall: the southern cornerstone of the original Federal City.

Even dogs disinterested in American history can find much to amuse themselves at Jones Point Park, if the telltale shredded tennis balls are any clue. There is the wide, green field hemmed in by woods and the Potomac River beckoning for a dip. A wood-chip trail leads to the tip of the point with a great view of the Wilson Bridge and the glitzy National Harbor across the river. If you come at night, bring a buddy or two besides your best friend on the leash for safety. Do watch out for dead fish and hooks.

At the writing of this book, the Jones Point Park entrance was unmarked from George Washington Parkway. Drive south on George Washington Parkway/Washington Street. Just as you leave Old Town, you will pass Church Street to your right and a cemetery to your left. Take an immediate left at the traffic light. Park in the lot and walk about a quarter mile down the paved bike trail. Jones Point Park is the grassy field that opens up to your right—you can't miss it. You can also park at S. Royal and Green Streets and then walk under the bridge. 703/838-4340; www.alexandriava.gov/recreation.

## PLACES TO EAT

**Bittersweet:** If takeout is in order, head to Bittersweet, a café, bakery, and caterer that's been around the block since 1983. The menu changes frequently

and isn't too expensive—there's even a $5 sandwich called the Recession Special (fried chicken breast topped with spicy coleslaw on a baguette). For breakfast, there is a hot cereal bar that includes oatmeal, polenta, or cheese grits. Your pup can wait and hydrate at the water bowl outside. Arrive early if you want dinner; Bittersweet closes by 6 P.M. most nights. 823 King St.; 703/549-1028; www.bittersweetcatering.com.

**Fish Market:** Denali recommends the very messy shrimp special—she gets to help clean up greasy fingers (before the wet wipes, of course). This King Street seafood institution can be busy with tourists walking up and down the cobblestone streets, but if your pooch is comfortable with a crowd she can sit tied to the outside of the railing. 105 and 107 King St.; 703/836-5676; www.fishmarketoldtown.com.

**King Street Blues:** Southern hospitality extends to Alexandria's furriest tourists and residents, as you'll see from the full bowl of water at this eatery. Dogs are welcome to sit in the outdoor seating while owners chow on jambalaya pasta, country-fried chicken, and other comfort food entrées. 112 N. St. Asaph St.; 703/836-8800; www.kingstreetblues.com.

**Pat Troy's Ireland's Own:** At Pat Troy's, dogs have their own menu: $3.95 for chopped chicken or burger, or lamb or beef stew—served with a bone. The traditional Irish restaurant and pub's wait staff brings water bowls for the pups right as you sit down on the patio. A chorus of curs agree this is the best doggy dining spot in town—no, in all of Northern Virginia. Humans can wash down shepherd's pie and corned beef and cabbage with pints of Guinness and listen to live Irish music drifting from the nightly performers inside. On Saturday nights, owner Pat Troy joins the performers in rousing renditions of the American and Irish classics, culminating with "The Unicorn Song." If you can poke your head inside while a friend watches your dog, do; it's a spectacle worth beholding. 111 N. Pitt St.; 703/549-4535; www.pattroysirishpub.com.

## DIVERSION

On Pat Troy's **It's a Doggy Dog Patio,** a dog-friendly happy hour takes place 4–7 P.M. every day. Humans enjoy half-price appetizers and drinks, while mutts peruse the usual dog menu. On **St. Patrick's Day,** if you brave the crowds early, Pat Troy's has a heated tent on the patio with reservations-required lunch and dinner seating—dogs can celebrate the luck o' the Irish, too. 111 N. Pitt St.; 703/549-4535; www.pattroysirishpub.com.

## DIVERSION

The original **Doggie Happy Hour** started years before the Hotel Monaco Alexandria came to Old Town, when the spacious redbrick courtyard belonged to the Holiday Inn. Dogs throughout the DC metro area heaved a sigh of relief when they learned Hotel Monaco would continue the tradition. Every Tuesday and Thursday 5–8 P.M. from April through October, the Hotel Monaco hosts a happy hour for social animals in the courtyard. Humans can sip cocktails from the swanky Jackson 20 restaurant and bar, and pups can choose from a heap of treats. Enter through the archway on Royal Street. 480 King St.; 703/549-6080; www.doggiehappyhour.com.

**Southside 815:** Located off most tourists' radar, Southside 815 brings Alexandria locals heartwarming and tummy-filling Southern cooking. Fried green tomatoes, blackened catfish, and chicken-fried steak are all on the menu. Restaurant policy says that dogs need to be tied outside the white rail fence, but the hostess adds that some servers are more lenient. When we visited, a toy poodle had slipped between the fence rails to sit under the table. 815 S. Washington St.; 703/836-6222; www.southside815.com.

### PLACES TO STAY

**Holiday Inn, Historic District Alexandria:** Dogs need vacations, too. Holiday Inn obliges by permitting dogs of all sizes for $25 per day per pet. It's located about five blocks away from the Montgomery Park off-leash exercise area. The 178-room hotel has amenities to make humans happy: a gym, sauna, whirlpool, and indoor and outdoor pools. Both parties will be pleased about the free newspaper delivered to your room daily. Also, kids eat free at the Holiday Inn. Parking is available for $15 per day. Rates range $149–339. 625 First St.; 703/548-6300; www.holiday-inn.com/axe-historic.

**Hotel Monaco Alexandria:** The newly renovated 241-room hotel opened its doors in January 2008 to reveal deep turquoise walls and a decor inspired by Eastern spice trade routes and North African roots. We don't know if Lawrence of Arabia traveled with a dog, but you can be certain you won't have to stash yours in a suitcase to smuggle her into the Hotel Monaco Alexandria. Doggies receive a goody bag upon check-in, and if you're lucky you'll be greeted by the Director of Pet Relations, Charlie, a distinguished bichon frise. Hotel Monaco is the only hotel located in the heart of the Old Town Historic District, so you're right in the middle of the action. Human guests will enjoy the indoor swimming pool on the 3rd floor and on-site fitness center. Dogs will love just about everything—especially the twice-weekly happy hour in the courtyard. Rates start from $159 in summer and holidays, from $279 the rest of the year. Dogs of any size stay at this Kimpton Hotel free. 480 King St.; 703/549-6080; www.monaco-alexandria.com.

**Morrison House:** If you've ever dreamed of being doted on by a butler, here's the hotel for you. The Morrison House has a 24-hour butler service for you—and your dog. The four-star, four-diamond boutique Kimpton Hotel is situated in an 18th-century-style manor house. The hotel's 45 posh rooms have two- and four-poster beds, decorative fireplaces, and Italian marble bathrooms. Rates start from $179 in summer and holidays, from $329 the rest of the year. 116 S. Alfred St.; 703/838-8000; www.morrisonhouse.com.

**Sheraton Suites Old Town Alexandria:** Bigger breeds will be pleased to learn the Sheraton allows two dogs up to 80 pounds each per room. The 247-room complex has an indoor pool and workout facility for humans. Each room comes equipped with wet bar, television, microwave, and refrigerator. A Corporate Club Floor is also available. Dogs must be registered at the time of check-in. Rates range $119–409. Overnight parking is available in an underground garage for $18 per night. 801 N. St. Asaph St.; 703/836-4700; www.sheraton.com.

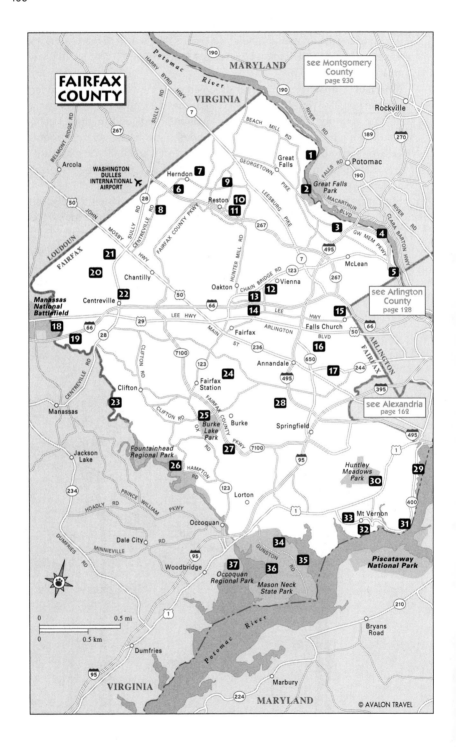

FAIRFAX COUNTY

MARYLAND
VIRGINIA

see Montgomery County
page 230

see Arlington County
page 128

see Alexandria
page 162

Rockville

Potomac

Great Falls Park

McLean

Falls Church

Annandale

Springfield

Huntley Meadows Park

Mt Vernon

Piscataway National Park

Bryans Road

WASHINGTON DULLES INTERNATIONAL AIRPORT

Arcola

Herndon

Reston

Chantilly

Oakton

Vienna

Centreville

Fairfax

Clifton

Manassas

Fairfax Station

Burke

Burke Lake Park

Fountainhead Regional Park

Jackson Lake

Lorton

Occoquan

Dale City

Woodbridge

Occoquan Regional Park

Mason Neck State Park

Dumfries

Marbury

Manassas National Battlefield

LOUDOUN
FAIRFAX

VIRGINIA
MARYLAND

0      0.5 mi
0      0.5 km

© AVALON TRAVEL

**CHAPTER 8**

# Fairfax County

Wide-open spaces still exist in Fairfax County. Though the Virginia country-side has predominantly been carved into subdivisions and mansion estates in Fairfax County, pockets of the rural Old Dominion still peek through. In Chantilly, we discovered fields of rolled hay. Along the peaceful Occoquan River, we found hardly anyone (which was a find unto itself). On the Mason Neck peninsula, where we hoped to spy the bald eagles that roost here, Denali ecstatically made her first acquaintance with a groundhog. Closer to DC, Fairfax Station and historic Clifton harbor a number of canine-friendly spots. Fairfax County in fact maintains more than 400 parks—seven of those with off-leash dog areas—on more than 24,000 acres of parkland.

If your best friend froths at the mouth for a dog paddle, this large Northern Virginia county will leave a splashy impression as well. Besides Great Falls Park and its pawrennially popular views of the Potomac River's most famous rapids, a handful of other riverfront parks bear mentioning inside Fairfax

## PICK OF THE LITTER—FAIRFAX COUNTY

BEST DOG PARKS
**Vienna Dog Park,** Vienna (page 204)
**Quinn Farm Park,** Chantilly (page 210)

BEST PARKS
**Great Falls Park,** Great Falls (page 192)
**Fountainhead Regional Park,** Fairfax Station (page 216)
**Lake Accotink Park,** Springfield (page 218)

BEST PLACES TO EAT
**Jasmine Café,** Reston (page 203)
**Clare and Don's Beach Shack,** Falls Church (page 207)
**Woody's Ice Cream,** Fairfax (page 214)

BEST PLACE TO STAY
**Best Western Tysons Westpark,** McLean (page 194)

County. Denali was equally pleased to pay a visit to lesser-known Riverbend Park and Scotts Run Nature Preserve.

Our hunt for popular, dog-friendly eateries in Fairfax County proved less successful. "This isn't Paris," said one Fairfax dog owner doubtfully. Most folks referred us to Old Town Alexandria establishments, though we did find a few hound-happy havens. You'll notice more chain restaurants listed in this chapter for this reason. Our theory is that Fairfax County residents are content to cook at home. In 2007, Fairfax County households made a median $105,241, the second highest in the entire country (neighboring Loudon County was number one), according to Census Bureau data. More than half of its adult residents have four-year college degrees, many with postgraduate degrees to boot, but it's all academic alphabet soup to Denali.

# Great Falls

When Captain John Smith and his party of 14 men set out to map the Potomac River in 1608, local tribes had been settled in the river valley for nearly 2,000 years. Although Smith and other early explorers recorded 11 different nations of American Indians living along the lower Potomac River, the Dogue Indians lived nearest to Great Falls, with a main village believed to be situated near

Theodore Roosevelt Island. According to author Ruth Baja Williams, the tribal name of the Dogue Indians was actually Tauxenent, but the British botched it: "The English corrupted the tribal name of Tauxenent first to Taux, then to Toags, Doeggs, Doegs and finally Dogue." Denali was curious to learn the tribe's name is pronounced just like "dog." So really you could argue that Dogues had roamed Great Falls for thousands of years. (Try winning over a ranger with that if your dog is caught off-leash in Great Falls Park.)

Today, river rapids aren't all that is big in Great Falls, Virginia; Denali couldn't keep her jaw closed at the sight of Great Falls' palatial real estate. This well-heeled Fairfax County community also has some of the best parks in Northern Virginia.

## PARKS, BEACHES, AND RECREATION AREAS

### 1 Riverbend Park

🐾🐾🐾🐾 (See the Fairfax County map on page 188)

Before tumbling down the rapids of Great Falls, the Potomac River takes a broad, gliding turn where the water slows to a glassy stillness. This is Riverbend Park. With more than 400 acres of forest, meadows, and ponds—and more than 10 miles of dirt trails—Fairfax County Park Authority's only riverfront park has plenty of opportunities for your leashed dog to get his paws dirty. Start by grabbing a trail map at the visitors center. One of the most popular excursions is a dog walk along the river to the better-known Great Falls Park, 1.75 miles one-way. The dirt-and-cinder path is an extension of the Potomac Heritage Trail in Arlington County, but here it is graded better and more popular with horseback riders. Keep an eye out for horse poop, always a canine culinary temptation.

In the spring, the rich soil of this floodplain forest grows one of the richest wildflower displays in Northern Virginia, with trilliums, Virginia bluebells, and bloodroot in bloom. And in all seasons the shallow water is a favorite for fishermen and fisher-birds. According to the visitors center, river otters and mink live in the park, too, though Denali has yet to befriend one.

After tuckering out your pup, return to one of the park's coolest features—the top-notch sundeck at the visitors center—to relax in an Adirondack chair overlooking the river, a great spot to read a book or rest your paws. If your pup is thirsty, there is a water bowl chained to the drinking fountain here. While Riverbend Park can be busy, it's almost always more tranquil than Great Falls Park downriver and a peaceful place Denali hopes to return to many times.

From the Capital Beltway (I-495), take exit 13 (Georgetown Pike, Route 193) west for 4.5 miles. Turn right on River Bend Road and travel two miles to a right on Jeffery Road. Proceed one mile to the visitors center entrance. 8700 Potomac Hills St.; 703/759-9018; www.fairfaxcounty.gov/parks/riverbend.

## 🄴 Great Falls Park

🐾🐾🐾🐾 🐾 (See the Fairfax County map on page 188)

The panoramic and tumultuous Great Falls cataracts attract nearly a half million people each year to this 800-acre Northern Virginia touchstone. Despite the long-standing debate of whether the Maryland or the Virginia side has better views of the waterfalls, the answer is easy when you're traveling with a dog: Virginia. On the Maryland side, dogs are not allowed on Olmsted Island or Billy Goat Trail A, which have the best views of Great Falls.

The Virginia side of the park has 15 miles of hiking trails, so it's easy to spend a day exploring the ledgy terrain and "steepest and most spectacular fall line rapids of any Eastern river," as the National Park Service asserts. Trail maps are available at the visitors center or the NPS website. Denali likes walking along the three-mile round-trip River Trail best, which skirts dramatic Mathers Gorge. You'll need to remind your four-legged hiking buddy that swimming in the Potomac River near Great Falls can be dangerous, especially upstream of the rapids. The current can be deceptively strong, and both people and pets have been swept away before. Curtailing this risk, dogs must be on a six-foot leash at all times in the park. There is a $5 per vehicle entrance fee. 9200 Old Dominion Dr.; 703/285-2965; www.nps.gov/grfa.

# McLean

Perhaps more than any other NoVA 'burb, McLean has come to be synonymous with Washington's outlying wealth. Considering that McLean fashion hounds can choose from Hermes, Tiffany's, Louis Vuitton, and the 500 stores in the massive Tysons Corner shopping complex (the largest concentration of stores on the East Coast!), its reputation is not unfounded. The community draws its name from John R. McLean, the former publisher and owner of *The Washington Post,* and McLean dogs enjoy some newsworthy benefits to living here, too. For one, the town is home to Dogtravel Company, "the world's first member-based, full service travel company for dog lovers," which offers in-cabin flights for dogs (www.dogtravelcompany.net).

## PARKS, BEACHES, AND RECREATION AREAS

## 🄴 Scotts Run Nature Preserve

🐾🐾🐾🐾 (See the Fairfax County map on page 188)

After three years of balking at the idea of getting her tail wet, lo and behold Denali finally decided to take the plunge at Scotts Run Nature Preserve. She picked a great spot to dog paddle, a deep swimming hole near the gravel River Trail that runs from the nature preserve's main parking lot on Georgetown Pike to the Potomac River. The swimming hole is just after the trail's second stream crossing, a balancing act across large cement pegs. After showing off

## DOG-EAR YOUR CALENDAR

"Now Dasher! Now Dancer! Now, Prancer and Rover!" Or so the saying goes at McLean's annual **ReinDog Parade** held at 8 A.M. the first Saturday in December at the Langley Shopping Center. The McLean Chamber of Commerce hosts the parade featuring dogs in holiday attire and antlers. 703/356-5424; www.mcleanchamber.org.

her newfound skills with clumsy gusto, Denali paddled back to the trail and we continued down to the Potomac, a comfortable, though occasionally steep, hike of less than a mile one-way. If you loop up with side trails in the bluffs above the river, you can turn the short hike into a four- or five-mile loop through slender tulip poplar and American beech forests. Leashes are required (even for dogs swimming); rangers will ticket offenders. From George Washington Parkway north, take the I-495 south exit toward Virginia, and then take exit 44 for Georgetown Pike (VA-193) west. Drive past the first Scotts Run parking area on the right and continue to the second lot 0.3 mile farther west, which has more parking spaces. 7400 Georgetown Pike; 703/759-3211; www.fairfaxcounty.gov/parks.

## 4 Turkey Run Park

🐾🐾🐾 (See the Fairfax County map on page 188)

On the way to Turkey Run, you'll pass Denali's all-time favorite sign in the metro region. There it is in all its glory shortly before your turnoff: the George Bush Center for Intelligence. It's enough to make Oliver Stone giggle with glee. (The center is actually named for the elder George H. W. Bush, who directed the CIA before becoming president.)

After regaining your composure, take stock of your surroundings at Turkey Run Park. What's wonderful about Turkey Run is how infrequently it gets used. In a dozen visits, we have yet to see the parking lot full—or even close. Most days there are only a small handful of visitors. We typically park in the first parking lot, but you can also continue to the National Park Service headquarters for the parks along George Washington Parkway. From the first lot, head down the steep switchbacks to link up with the Potomac Heritage Trail. If you head to the right, the trail narrows and you're apt to have it mostly to yourself (and a few spiders—mind the cobwebs!). Head to the left, and the trail widens, with easier access to the river. This is really the nicer direction. One time as we reached the trail's terminus at the American Legion Bridge (where I-495 crosses the Potomac River) we saw one granddaddy of a turtle. Poor terrapin must have lost his way from the University of Maryland. Fortunately, Denali was properly leashed up and observed the great turtle from a respectable distance.

The Turkey Run Loop Trails are yellow blazed, and the Potomac Heritage Trail used to be blue-blazed, and that's what all the maps will say. But in recent years the blazes have been repainted a hue better described as teal, or perhaps jungle green—an apt shade during the summer, when nonnative vines thrive in the humidity and swallow forests whole along the riverbank. And in fall, arguably the best time to visit, you're in a sea of autumn colors. Located off George Washington Pkwy.; 703/289-2500; www.nps.gov/gwmp/turkey-run-park.htm.

## 5 Fort Marcy Park

🐾🐾🐾 (See the Fairfax County map on page 188)

Like us, you may have driven past the sign for Fort Marcy on George Washington Parkway countless times. Curiosity, and this book project, finally motivated us to take the sharp right-hand exit. From Denali's perspective, the historic Civil War fort is merely an appetizer for yet another hike down the Potomac Heritage Trail. For the untrained eye, the fort today has few clues to its martial history aside from the subtly reshaped hillside, a mock field gun, and a couple of interpretative signs. We did a brief tour of duty, and then split for the trail.

This section of the Potomac Heritage Trail is a slim dirt path that joins the downhill flow of Pimmit Run toward the Potomac, approximately a half-mile journey from where trail and creek intersect. With the ever-present thrum of George Washington Parkway traffic in the background, and at one point, directly overhead, this hike is less about peacefully communing with nature than it is about finding splash-worthy doggy swimming holes in wide Pimmit Run. Our only company on the trail was a sopping wet white German shepherd and grinning golden retriever and their human mom. Which brings up a side note on safety: The trail is fairly isolated, so if your canine compadre doesn't add any intimidation factor (e.g., Dobermans tend to scare off the bad guys better than bichon frises), female hikers might want to bring a human buddy. Not to say Fort Marcy is in a bad neighborhood, it's just in an out-of-the-way portion of the Potomac bluffs.

The trail concludes at Chain Bridge, where you can alternatively park at the small lot on the Virginia side of Chain Bridge, just off N. Glebe Road, and do the somewhat steep out-and-back hike in reverse. Open dawn to dusk. Fort Marcy is accessible from northbound lanes of George Washington Parkway, just south of the Route 123 exit. 703/289-2500; www.nps.gov/gwmp/fort-marcy.htm.

### PLACES TO STAY

**Best Western Tysons Westpark:** The front desk clerk we spoke with said, "Pets are family here." And family members, at least doggy ones, stay for free. Human guests at this 301-room hotel would wish to be so lucky. While dogs

## DOG-EAR YOUR CALENDAR

For $5, your favorite dog paddler can finally have a pool day, courtesy of the Northern Virginia Regional Park Authority. The region-wide **Dog Days swim event** typically takes place noon–4 P.M. the Sunday after Labor Day. Owners must fill out a liability waiver and dogs must have a current license and rabies vaccination.

**Bull Run Water Park:** Bull Run Regional Park, 7700 Bull Run Dr., Centreville; 703/631-0550; www.nvrpa.org/parks/bullrun.

**Downpour Water Park:** Algonkian Regional Park, 47001 Fairway Dr., Sterling; 703/430-7683; www.nvrpa.org/parks/downpour.

**Great Waves:** Cameron Run Regional Park, 4001 Eisenhower Ave., Alexandria; 703/960-0767; www.nvrpa.org/parks/cameronrun.

**Pirate's Cove:** Pohick Bay Regional Park, 6501 Pohick Bay Dr., Lorton; 703/339-6102; www.nvrpa.org/parks/pohickbay.

**Upton Hill Regional Park:** 6060 Wilson Blvd., Arlington; 703/534-3437; www.nvrpa.org/parks/uptonhill.

may be left in the room alone as long as you alert the front desk, the hotel is conveniently close to **Dogtopia Daycare and Spa** in Tysons Corner (8528-F Tyco Rd.; 703/821-0700; www.dogdaycare.com). Hotel amenities include an indoor pool, exercise facility, guest laundry, game room, and daily continental breakfast. Weekend rates are $90 (as low as $60 with AAA discount); weekday rates are $200. 8401 Westpark Dr.; 703/734-2800; www.bestwestern.com.

**Crowne Plaza Tysons Corner:** Forty seems to be the magic number at this 312-room hotel. Dogs up to 40 pounds can check in for a $40 one-time fee. Pups are limited to the first-level of the hotel and need to be kenneled if left alone in the room. Amenities include a complimentary business center and fitness center (both open 24 hours), and an indoor swimming pool and whirlpool. Located directly across the street from Tysons Galleria II and the Tysons Corner Center Shopping Mall. 1960 Chain Bridge Rd.; 703/893-2100; www.cptysonscorner.com.

# Herndon

Originally a hub for dairy farming thanks to the easy transport of milk to DC on the W&OD Railroad, Herndon's commerce has transitioned to join the region's high-tech corridor. The old railroad line still bisects the town, but now as the paved W&OD bike trail. Although Herndon has received some notoriety involving the Mara Salvatrucha, or MS-13, street gang, most of the town of 23,000 retains a small-town suburban feel. Arguably, Herndon's doggy central is Bark 'N Bubbles, a premier self-service dog wash in the middle of town that keeps pups squeaky clean.

## PARKS, BEACHES, AND RECREATION AREAS

### 6 Chandon Park

🐾🐾🐾🐕 (See the Fairfax County map on page 188)

As Fairfax County dog parks go, Chandon is a bit petite, with room for 42 dogs in the main play area (to which DC dog owners guffaw . . . 42 dogs and it's *small?*). For pups weighing 25 pounds or less, there is also a triangle that can accommodate eight of these smaller breeds. Here, for once, the grass really is greener on the other side of the dog park fence; treaded by lighter paws, the smaller run has more turf still growing. The larger run has a few grassy patches and some trees for shade, but it's mostly dirt and gravel. Both areas are fully fenced and have double-gated entrances to thwart escape artists. Chandon Dog Park also has a pump hooked up to well water for thirsty dogs—although it's turned off in the winter, so bring your own during colder months—and there are a few dilapidated kiddie pools and water bowls near the dog park entrance. There's even a lone piece of agility equipment. Thank the community group **Herndon Dogs** (www.herndondogs.org) for sponsoring the park and helping to being it into existence in 2003.

It's important to note that Fairfax County is fairly aggressive about enforcing the licensing and vaccination requirements for using the park. As one Fairfax dog lover put it, "You can get a $250 ticket for not having a $5 license." Be sure your dog is properly vaccinated and registered with Fairfax County before visiting the park. More information is available on the county's website.

From the VA-267 toll road west toward Dulles Airport, take exit 10 toward Herndon. Merge onto Centreville Road and take a slight left at Elden Street. Turn right at Herndon Parkway and take another right at Palmer Drive. Park

## DIVERSION

If Fido is fur-frazzled after a doggone exhausting week of chasing ducks, it might be time for a **Spaw Day.** For $75, your pup gets the deluxe treatment: roundtrip pet taxi service provided by **Four Paws Pet Concierge** (877/727-7297; www.fourpawspetconcierge. com) within Reston, Herndon, Sterling, Ashburn, and Leesburg; a 45-minute dog walk along the W&OD bike trail; and an afternoon of doggy beautification at **Bark 'N Bubbles.** Denali, a bath-phobic, perked up at the description of the blueberry facial, a tearless blueberry and coconut oil face wash that pups can help lick off their faces. In addition, Bark 'N Bubbles is a do-it-yourself doggy wash with a boutique, coffee and smoothie bar, and free wireless Internet. Bark 'N Bubbles also hosts doggy birthday parties and monthly charity washes. 795 Center St., Ste. 1A and B; 703/437-9274; www.barknbubblesdogwash.com.

your car in the lot and walk across the pedestrian bridge near the tennis courts. (If you are approaching from the opposite direction on Herndon Parkway, note that you will see a Palmer Drive on your right. Don't turn here. Continue a few blocks farther to turn left on Palmer.) 900 Palmer Dr.; 703/324-8702; www.fairfaxcounty.gov/parks/offleash.htm.

## 7 Runnymede Park

🐾🐾 (See the Fairfax County map on page 188)

Named for Herndon's sister city of Runnymede, England, this 58-acre preserve is the town's only natural park. Accordingly, it's a great place for dogs to fill their nostrils with nature. Meandering along Sugarland Run, the park is sometimes called Sugarland Run Valley Stream Park. Naturalists have identified more than 100 species of birds, deer, fox, and other wildlife inside the park, so don't be surprised to stumble across a blue heron fishing in the creek. Runnymede meadow historically served as a cattle pasture, rather than cropland, so there exists an abundance of plant diversity, too—more than 450 plant species. To encourage public appreciation of this diverse ecological niche, the Friends of Runnymede Park (www.frpweb.org) and Herndon Parks and Recreation Department host a NatureFest celebration each September. But you and your leashed hound can appreciate it any day of the week with a dog walk here.

From the VA-267 toll road, take exit 11 to merge onto Fairfax County Parkway north. Take the Elden Street exit. Turn left at Baron Cameron Avenue westbound. Turn right at Herndon Parkway and parallel-park between Elden Street and Dranesville Road. The park borders the northeast side of Herndon Parkway. 703/435-6868; www.herndon-va.gov.

## 8 Frying Pan Park

🐾🐾 (See the Fairfax County map on page 188)

Do the kids *and* the dog have cabin fever? Then clang the triangle and rally the family: It's time for an outing to Frying Pan Park. Inside the 130-acre Fairfax County park, Kidwell Farm re-creates a family dairy farm such as those that flourished in the Virginia countryside 1920–1950. In the early spring, newly arrived calves, lambs, billy goat kids, and piglets are a delight for everyone. The barnyard smells were perfume to Denali's nose. During a visit in August, three curious, wobbly kneed calves approached her from the other side of a split-rail fence for a closer look. Denali didn't know what to make of the wide-eyed, goofy-looking… Great Danes?

Equestrian activities are popular at Frying Pan Park, too. We happened to visit during the biannual Difficult Run Horse Trials. With horses galloping and jumping obstacles in an open course throughout the park, Denali felt skittish every time we heard the approaching *clop-clop, clop-clop* and "Horse on course!" A quick escape to the no-horses-allowed nature trail in the north end of the park solved that problem. The red-blazed trail cuts a C-shape about one mile through the woods, starting at a gravel road near the upper equestrian ring and ending at the pole barns near the lower equestrian ring. You can pick up a map at the visitors center. Trail highlights include a stream cascade optimistically labeled a waterfall on the trail map, and if you detour on a yellow-blazed trail west of the "waterfall," there is a historic meetinghouse and cemetery.

From I-66 westbound, take exit 55 to Fairfax County Parkway north, proceeding for six miles. Turn left on West Ox Road, and go 1.4 miles to the park entrance on the right. Admission is free and parking is plentiful. Remember to bring poop bags and a bowl for water. 2709 West Ox Rd.; 703/437-9101; www.fairfaxcounty.gov/parks/fpp.

### PLACES TO EAT

**Chipotle:** If you're looking for a quick burrito after visiting the Chandon Dog Park, Chipotle is right around the corner. Takeout only. No outdoor seating. 1144 Elden St.; 703/435-3325; www.chipotle.com.

**The Deli:** It turns out The Italian Store in Arlington has a rival tucked away in a Herndon strip mall. The specialty sandwiches are a bit pricey ($8.95 for an 8-inch; $11.95 for a 12-inch), but they deliver on full servings of Italian deli goodness. Toppings include prosciutto, capicollo, soppressata, mortadella, genoa, provolone, and others that might leave your dog salivating on your shoe. Plan to order carryout since there is no outdoor seating. 480 Elden St.; 703/435-9085; www.thedeliherndon.com.

**Great Harvest Bread Company:** At least a few Herndon dog lovers have made a habit of swinging by this bakery after a visit to the Dominion Animal Hospital. Great Harvest fresh-grinds 100 percent whole grain wheat on the premises daily, and you can taste the wholesome deliciousness in its breads. Humans like the free samples. Pups like the fresh-baked dog treats. Closed Sunday and Monday. 785 Station St.; 703/471-4031; www.darngood bread.com.

**Rita's Water Ice:** Three words: Ice. Custard. Happiness. And Rita's serves up a dollop of vanilla frozen custard topped with a Milk-Bone for the pooches. You can sit at one of the few tables outside. In August, 6–8 P.M. Monday 10 percent of the proceeds benefit a local animal shelter in Herndon. It's located close to the Chandon Dog Park. 905-F Herndon Pkwy.; 703/657-0270; www.ritasherndon.com.

## PLACES TO STAY

**Hilton Washington Dulles:** Flying soon? This pet-friendly hotel is located only three miles from the Washington Dulles International Airport. The Hilton Washington Dulles welcomes any size dog for an $80 one-time fee, although only one pet is permitted per room. The 449-room hotel offers no special pet amenities, but humans are well cared for with a 15,000-square-foot fitness center, high-speed Internet in rooms, indoor and outdoor pool, and 24-hour room service so you can dine in with your doggy. Individuals traveling for work will be keen on the business-class rooms that can connect any digital device (computer, game console, DVD, MP3) to a 42-inch plasma HDTV. These upgraded rooms also offer walk-in rain showers. Rates start at $99 Friday–Saturday and range $249–289 Sunday–Thursday. There is plenty of free parking. 13869 Park Center Rd.; 703/478-2900; www.hilton.com.

**Hyatt Summerfield Suites:** For small-dog lovers looking for an extended stay hotel, the Hyatt Summerfield Suites might be a good fit. Hotel policy allows up to two dogs, each weighing 20 pounds or less, for a $25-per-day-per-pet fee (not to exceed $100). Human guests will appreciate the fully equipped kitchen, complimentary wireless Internet, hot breakfast buffet, and evening social hour (Mon.–Thurs.). Other perks include a 24-hour fitness center, seasonal outdoor pool, sports court, and barbecue area. Weekend rates are $89. Weekday rates are $199. Free parking is available. 467 Herndon Pkwy.; 703/437-5000; www.herndon.summerfieldsuites.hyatt.com.

# Reston

As one of the first planned communities in the nation in the 1960s, Reston is an internationally acclaimed example of how a little foresight goes a long way. Reston Rovers certainly appreciate the more than 55 miles of paved trails and dirt paths to walk. Reston was the brainchild of New York City transplant Robert E. Simon Jr. (the town's name draws from his initials: R.E.S.-ton). At the center of it all is the Reston Town Center, a popular mall with a fountain and open-air pavilion. In warmer months, an outdoor concert series plays tunes

## DETOURS

**BB&T Bank:** Note the two large water bowls outside the door. Even Great Pyrenees can greet the tellers inside this bank. 11990 Market St.; 703/437-2680; www.bbt.com.

**The Bike Lane:** Pet-friendly neighborhood bike shop. 11943 Democracy Dr.; 703/689-2671; http://thebikelane.com.

**Ecco:** Find comfortable dog-walking shoes. 11962 Market St.; 703/435-6723; www.ecco.com.

**PetSmart:** One-stop pet supply shopping. 11860 Spectrum Center; 703/796-0656; www.petsmart.com.

**Pet Valu:** Canada's largest pet supply retailer has crossed the U.S. border. 11130-D South Lakes Dr.; 703/476-7207; www.petvalu.com.

**Potomac River Running:** Athletic shoes and local running expertise help keep Denali running, too. 11911 Democracy Dr.; 703/689-0999; www.potomacriverrunning.com.

**Reston's Used Book Store:** Serving book (and dog!) lovers for three decades. 623 Washington Plaza; 703/435-9772; www.restonsusedbookshop.com.

here 7:30–10 P.M. Saturday. This pavilion is also home to the paw-fabulous Reston Pet Fiesta.

Reston has four man-made lakes—Anne, Thoreau, Audubon, and Newport—with walking trails around each. For visiting dogs, Lake Anne probably holds the most interest. It has a semicircular outdoor plaza that invokes the style of a European coastal village; it was modeled after the "new towns" concept that emerged in western England and Scandinavia in the 1960s.

My husband, a medical student, reminded us of a darker chapter in Reston. If you read *The Hot Zone*, you might recall that Reston was the site of an Ebola scare in 1989, in which laboratory monkeys from the Philippines were found to be infected with the highly infectious, hemorrhagic fever–inducing virus. In fact, Reston has a strain of the virus named after it. Denali is relieved that this scary portion of Reston's history is in the past.

## PARKS, BEACHES, AND RECREATION AREAS

### 9 Baron Cameron Park

🐾🐾🐕 (See the Fairfax County map on page 188)

Toy breeds will cheer when they see Baron Cameron Dog Park. At last, a small dog area as big as their personalities, not their statures. The Baron Cameron

Dog Park has two sections—one for dogs weighing less than 25 pounds and another for all other dogs. Both areas are fully fenced with a shared double-gated entrance. Even at lunchtime on a workday at least four dogs skedaddled around the lot, so the post-work "dog hour" must be hopping. The space can accommodate 40 dogs.

Be forewarned that hardly a blade of grass grows inside this off-leash area. The sand-and-cinder surface slips inside your shoes and between your pup's paws. The few trees standing at either end of the park provide welcome shade in the summertime. Poop bags are usually in supply, and water is available from a pump from roughly mid-March to late October. In winter months the water is turned off, so remember to bring your own.

The very active community group **RestonDogs** (www.restondogs.org) sponsors the park. Unlike other dog parks where you'll see grocery bags tied to the fence and leashes slung over the gate, RestonDogs asks that park users not hang anything on the fence and be sure to keep leashes in hand at all times (per Fairfax County Park Authority rules). From the Dulles Toll Road (VA-267) westbound, take exit 13 for Wiehle Avenue. Turn right at Wiehle Avenue, left on Baron Cameron Avenue, and right into Baron Cameron Park. The off-leash area will be on your right. 11300 Baron Cameron Ave.; 703/324-8702; www.fairfaxcounty.gov/parks/offleash.htm.

## 10 Lake Fairfax Park

🐾🐾🐾 (See the Fairfax County map on page 188)

In warmer months, this 476-acre Fairfax County park bustles with grilling parties and picnickers on weekends, and the swim-and-waterslide park Watermine is a family favorite throughout summer vacation. If your pups' paws were made for walkin', Lake Fairfax Park has several options for you. Option A: trot around the mostly dirt path that circles 18-acre Lake Fairfax, a dammed body of water that glints with sunlight. The loop will take about one hour if you walk at a moderate pace. Along the lakeshore, you will likely encounter an angler or two casting lines for the bluegills, largemouth bass, and channel catfish that swim in the lake's mossy-colored water. Unlike at Lake Accotink, dogs are not permitted on the pontoon boat or rental canoes. And no, the Watermine doesn't have a doggy swim day—we asked.

Option B: you can take a walk on the Difficult Run Stream Valley Trail, accessible in several places in Lake Fairfax Park. One convenient spot is at the end of the gravel road next to Picnic Shelter 1 (located near the cricket fields), just past the Service Vehicles Only sign. This section of the trail is marked with white-painted wooden posts with a horseshoe symbol. From the Capital Beltway, take exit 47A to Leesburg Pike west to a left on Baron Cameron Avenue, then to the second left on Lake Fairfax Drive. 1400 Lake Fairfax Dr.; 703/471-5415; www.fairfaxcounty.gov/parks/lakefairfax.

## DOG-EAR YOUR CALENDAR

As Cinco de Mayo draws near, Reston dogs begin to bark "¡Ole!" The **Reston Pet Fiesta** is almost here! The annual day of frisky antics, festivities, fundraisers, and pet adoptions takes place in the Reston Town Center Pavilion, the open-air meeting space that anchors the Reston community. Past years have drawn more than 70 booths to the Reston Pet Fiesta's expo. The fiesta also includes a "Tails on Trails Walk," canine competitions (including Best Dressed, Best Trick, and Fastest Frosty Paws Eater), and a doggie couture fashion show featuring local rescue pups on the catwalk. Speaking of cats, you might even see a few kitties on a leash at the event or a bunny in a stroller. It is the pet fiesta, after all. 1818 Discovery St.; 703/709-6300; www.petfiesta.org.

## 🔢 Difficult Run Stream Valley Trail

🐾🐾🐾🐾 (See the Fairfax County map on page 188)

Denali was thrilled to find a new trail, especially one as dynamic as this. We've yet to walk its full length, but rumor has it you can start from Tamarack Park south of the Dulles Toll Road and walk all the way to Great Falls Park to the north. Denali had first-paw experience with the middle section of the stream valley trail. We went on an adventurous jog for three miles of the trail that felt like a secret passageway through Fairfax County. Even in these short three miles, the terrain varies considerably. What starts as a wide, dirt horse trail in airy woods narrows to a winding ribbon of clay-surfaced single-track in a tunnel of low-arching branches before transitioning again to a flat gravel road through a sunny meadow and onto a paved bike trail next to a subdivision. The trail skirts close to house fences in one section, and we felt like we were mischievously sneaking through backyards (neighborhood dogs agreed and promptly sounded the alarm, *101 Dalmatians*–style). Many Fairfax dog owners clued us in to this slightly off-the-beaten-path dog walk. We hear other popular places to waggle onto the trail include near the Children's Theatre-in-the-Woods Stage at Wolf Trap National Park and at the Difficult Run parking lot near Great Falls Park (3.6 miles west of the Capital Beltway on Georgetown Pike/VA-193).

Before setting out for Difficult Run, consider the weather. While crossing a road on our run, we noticed a yellow ruler sign indicating distances 1 feet, 2 feet, on up to 5 feet above the pavement. After puzzling for a minute it dawns on us: that's to indicate the flood line! Needless to say, after heavy rains you might want to think twice about walking your dog along Difficult Run.

To traverse the trail through all of Lake Fairfax Park, start from the Skate-quest Ice Rink back parking lot. The trailhead is in the back left corner. Otherwise, catch the trail at the end of the gravel road next to Picnic Shelter 1 (near the cricket fields), just past the Service Vehicles Only sign. 1800 Michael Faraday Ct.; www.fairfaxcounty.gov/parks/cct.

## PLACES TO EAT

**Ben & Jerry's:** *The Bark* magazine named this legendary ice creamery's corporate office one of the top four dog-friendliest employers in the country in 2008. The Reston outpost for getting a scoop of Chunky Monkey and all the other deliciously rich flavors also welcomes pooches to its outdoor seating. 11928 Market St.; 703/787-9096; www.benjerry.com.

**Café Montmarte:** Situated on scenic Lake Anne, this pet-friendly French bistro features a special Vietnamese menu Wednesday through Friday. Dogs have to stay outside the patio perimeter, but with 15 to 20 umbrella-covered tables, outside seating isn't often difficult to find. The fresh fish specials are consistent winners. Located in Lake Anne Plaza. 1625 Washington Plaza; 703/904-8080; www.lakeanneplaza.com.

**Clyde's of Reston:** During the summertime Saturday evening concerts in Reston Town Center, this moderately upscale restaurant's location right next to the open-air pavilion can't be beat. Seating is first come, first served, however, so there might be a wait. Dogs can dine alfresco as long as they lie outside the roped-off patio. Inside, the mahogany-and-leather booths and antique model planes match the American-saloon menu. 11905 Market St.; 703/787-6601; www.clydes.com.

**Jasmine Café:** Though the Jasmine Café has a smaller patio than its neighbors on Lake Anne Plaza, the waiter was emphatic that "everyone who works here loves dogs." The café serves seasonal American cuisine for brunch, lunch, and dinner, with options to keep both vegetarians and carnivores happy. And what a spot overlooking a fountain near the lakefront to watch the world walk by on a lazy Sunday. You pup has to be tied outside the patio fence, but the wait staff usually will bring her water. 1633-A Washington Plaza; 703/471-9114; www.jasminecafe.com.

**Potbelly Sandwich Works:** Not only will thirsty, four-pawed shoppers find a water bowl in front of this ever-spreading sandwich shop, but Potbelly's staff at this location will even come outside to take your order so you don't have to tie up your dog. Your pooch can sit with you at one of the few outside tables. 11919-A Freedom Dr.; 703/481-5080; www.potbelly.com.

**Tavern on the Lake:** This lakefront restaurant is both an American grill and a tapas bar (side note: enunciate carefully when inviting your visiting parents to a "tapas bar"). Dogs are commonly lazing near the patio in warmer months, though they have to be on the outside of the patio. Keeping with Lake Anne's international theme, the tavern serves a good Moroccan vegetable stew and a few Ethiopian-inspired tapas. The shrimp Creole is also tasty. On Monday,

all bottles of wine are half-price. 1617 Washington Plaza; 703/471-0121; www
.tavernonthelake.com

## PLACES TO STAY

**Sheraton Reston Hotel:** Assuming your pup is on his best behavior, dogs stay
free at the Sheraton. Just sign on the dotted line of the pet waiver. Your furry
friend will be pleased to finally have pet amenities at his disposal: a doggy bed,
food bowl, and of course, poop bags. The Sheraton also provides a door hanger
that says, "My friend is with me," to warn housekeeping not to enter while
you're away from the room. Unfortunately, the suite and club levels are off-
limits to Fido. This 301-room hotel allows dogs up to 80 pounds to check in, but
only one dog per room (exceptions are sometimes made for two smaller dogs).
If you're looking for a place to walk in the morning, the W&OD Bicycle Trail
is located about a half mile away from the hotel. Parking is complimentary for
stays less than 10 days. Rates start at $89 on weekends, $154–289 on weekdays.
There are AAA and government discounts, and online offers through Price-
line and other discount travel websites generally are cheaper. 11810 Sunrise
Valley Dr.; 703/620-9000; www.sheraton.com/reston.

**Lake Fairfax Park Campgrounds:** This well-shaded campground is open
year-round, with 136 campsites for tents and 70 electrical hookups (40 15-amp
and 30 30-amp) and a dump station for RVs. Dogs are allowed in the campground as long as they remain on leash and are not left unattended. You won't
be roughing it at Lake Fairfax; other amenities include a camp store, picnic
tables, and bathrooms with sinks, showers, and toilets. Plus, grill masters will
be pleased to know there is an abundance of charcoal grills. 1400 Lake Fairfax
Dr.; 703/471-5415; www.fairfaxcounty.gov/parks/campgrounds.htm.

# Vienna

In the web of Fairfax County suburbs, Vienna might be one of the few cities
that carless District of Columbia residents will recognize, because it is the
western terminus for the Orange Metro line. Others might have seen a concert
in Vienna's Wolf Trap National Park for the Performing Arts. Dogs in the know
will tell you that the Vienna Dog Park is the softest on the paws of all the off-
leash areas in Fairfax County.

## PARKS, BEACHES, AND RECREATION AREAS

### 12 Vienna Dog Park

🐾🐾🐾🐕 (See the Fairfax County map on page 188)

Tired of dirt, rock, or cinder-surfaced dog parks? Head to Vienna Dog Park,
which has a nice wood-chip finish that is easier on the pads. Of course, the flip
side is that the Vienna Dog Park stays mucky for days after it rains. The 90- by

150-foot area can accommodate about 18 dogs. Unlike most dog parks in the region, which are overseen by Fairfax County, this exercise area is managed by the Town of Vienna with support from the community group Vienna Dogs. The fully fenced, double-gated dog park is so well shaded that even in the heat of the day on an August weekend at least half a dozen dogs scampered about. Other dog park features include agility equipment, benches, and a cement wading pool in the back corner (a boon to some dogs, a bane to some dog owners for the muddy ride home). A seasonally functioning water fountain, doggy bowls, poop bags, and trash cans are also all on hand. 700 Courthouse Rd. SW; 703/255-6360; www.viennava.gov.

### 13 Nottoway Park

🐾🐾 (See the Fairfax County map on page 188)

Though mostly made up of athletic fields off-limits to Fido, Nottoway Park also has a leafy, 0.75-mile fitness trail that is a good loop for dogs. You can also take a spin around the stately turn-of-the-19th-century mansion called the Hunter House and a large plot of community gardens worth walking around. Nottoway Park is located a few blocks down Courthouse Road from the Vienna Dog Park, so the 84-acre park can be another option to exercise away any extra doggy ya-yas. In the summertime, the park hosts "Nottoway Nights," a series of free concerts at 7:30 P.M. Thursday. 9601 Courthouse Rd.; 703/938-7532; www.fairfaxcounty.gov/parks/omp/htm.

### PLACES TO STAY

**Residence Inn Tyson's Corner:** This hotel has no pet size restrictions—"As long as it's not a horse," joked the front desk. All dogs are allowed for a $75 one-time fee. Your traveling companion will be pleased to know the 121-room hotel keeps dog biscuits in stock. You'll appreciate the fully equipped kitchen and full-size refrigerator, as well as the heated outdoor pool, on-site fitness center, and wireless Internet. Residence Inn has a Pet in Room door hanger for you to use to alert housekeeping about your four-legged guest; your pup may be left unattended if he is comfortable with your absence and won't make a ruckus. When doody calls, the hotel has positioned cleanup bags around the property, or a small county park called Freedom Hill Park is located a couple blocks northwest on Old Courthouse Road. Rates range $89–159 on weekends, $259–329 on weekdays. Some corporate discounts are available. Free parking is available on-site. 8400 Old Courthouse Rd. 703/917-0800; www.residence inntysonscorner.com.

# Oakton

## PARKS, BEACHES, AND RECREATION AREAS

### 🐾 Blake Lane Park

🐾🐾🐕 (See the Fairfax County map on page 188)

Established in 2000, the Blake Lane Dog Park has the distinction of being both the first, and the smallest, dog park under the jurisdiction of the Fairfax County Park Authority. The very sunny lot can accommodate about 25 happy hounds. Be sure to bring your own water and steer clear of the hottest part of the day in the summer. **OaktonDogs** sponsors the park, which is fully fenced and has a double gate. It's located in an almost exclusively residential area and is most popular with dogs living within walking distance. From I-66, take exit 60 (123 north). Turn right onto Jermantown Road, which turns into Blake Lane at the Trevor House traffic light. Proceed straight through the traffic light and take the second right onto Bushman Drive. The Recycling Center Parking Area is just past Bushman Drive on the right. 10033 Blake Ln.; 703/324-8702; www.fairfaxcounty.gov/parks/offleash.htm.

# Falls Church

Falls Church is an independent town sandwiched between Arlington and Fairfax counties, with several dog-friendly eateries and a location that is conveniently close to many wag-worthy parks, even if most of them are not within the small city limits. Quaint Falls Church changes drastically as you drive southeast on Leesburg Pike into the dreaded NoVa traffic black hole, otherwise known as Seven Corners, where seven main arterials converge into a stop-and-go nightmare. Denali insists this is a necessary, though weary, journey for us to buy her kibble at **PetSmart** (6100 Arlington Blvd.; 703/536-2708; www.petsmart.com).

## PARKS, BEACHES, AND RECREATION AREAS

### 15 Cavalier Trail Park

🐾 (See the Fairfax County map on page 188)

As the name suggests, a single trail is the focus of Cavalier Trail Park. Falls Church tail-waggers frequent this paved walkway for its shade, its convenient location, and its proximity to a curiously bucolic open culvert. Your Cavalier King Charles spaniel might have a special affinity for this neighborhood park for obvious reasons. Mutts might like it for the salamanders. Cavalier Trail winds in and out of a neighborhood at least twice by following the bike trail signs and crosswalks, but this led to some confusion on the return leg of our excursion. We followed the wrong bike path signs and ended up at the W&OD Trail, 90 degrees in the wrong direction. Fortunately, downtown Falls Church is not too intimidating to navigate, so if you have a similar misstep just remember your car is parked at Maple Avenue and S. Washington Street. A drinking fountain and "Scoopy Doo" bags are available at the parking lot near the park tennis courts. 703/248-5077; www.fallschurchva.gov.

### 16 Roundtree Park

🐾🐾 (See the Fairfax County map on page 188)

Denali couldn't decide what she liked better at 73-acre Roundtree Park: the out-of-the-way soccer and baseball fields or the forested trails. When we discovered the trails link up to nearby Valleycrest Park, a smaller, grassy neighborhood park, Denali's decision was made. On the whole, we found Roundtree Park a generously proportioned park with roly-poly, woodsy terrain. Look for Pink Lady's Slipper, wild orchids, and other wildflowers if you visit in the spring.

Roundtree Park also has a picnic pavilion that groups sometimes rent. When we stopped by on a Tuesday afternoon, we puzzled over the parking lot full of Chevy Impalas with Maryland plates. In hindsight, it must have been a corporate picnic. Parking shouldn't normally be an issue. To reach Roundtree Park, take the Capital Beltway exit 50B (Route 50), continuing east about 3.5 miles to a right on Annandale Road. Follow about 2.5 miles to the park entrance on the left. 3411 Casilear Rd.; 703/324-8702; www.fairfaxcounty.gov/parks/picnics/fallnics-roundtree.htm.

## PLACES TO EAT

**Clare and Don's Beach Shack:** This super-casual seafood joint opened up next to the State Theater (no dogs in the theater, but a great live music venue) since moving from its original location in Clarendon (Clare-n-Don's Beach Shack, get it?). The grouper sandwich, fish and chips, and crab cakes all come highly recommended. The walls next to the patio are decorated with fishing nets, flip-flops, surfboards, and this sign: Good Dogs Welcome. No Barking, Biting, or Peeing. Wait staff will bring your pup water on request. There is live music on Friday in summer and tons of kids running around while their parents relax on the painted wooden picnic benches. 130 N. Washington St.; 703/532-9283; www.clareanddons.com.

**Lazy Sundae:** Besides 16 flavors of ice cream, Lazy Sundae keeps Old Dominion root beer on tap ready to serve in a frosted mug for floats. Your dog can join you in the modest outdoor seating in front. 110 N. West St.; 703/532-5299.

**Sunflower Vegetarian Restaurant:** This Asian-inspired vegetarian restaurant has found ways to cook tofu that even meat-eaters enjoy. The Falls Church location (there's also one in Vienna) has a large, dog-friendly patio. 6304 Leesburg Pike; 703/237-3888; www.crystalsunflower.com/fallschurch.

# Annandale

Jon Krakauer fans who've read (or seen) *Into the Wild* may remember that Christopher McCandless grew up in Annandale. It's every bit the Capital Beltway suburbia you would expect, but Annandale's off-leash dog park attracts a friendly bunch and is worth the short trek from Arlington, Alexandria, or maybe even DC if you need a change of scenery.

## PARKS, BEACHES, AND RECREATION AREAS

### 17 Mason District Dog Park
🐾🐾🐾🐕 (See the Fairfax County map on page 188)

With room for 62 dogs to run around and a few benches for their humans to sit and congregate, the Mason District Dog Park is quite the scene as the temperatures cool and the shadows grow long on a warm summer evening. Regulars say the park usually dries quickly after a rain (except for under the benches). The **Mason District Dog Opportunity Group** sponsors the park, which was established in 2002. Though tensions have calmed, the residents in the neighboring condos have been known to call and report dog owners who don't keep their dog on leash until inside the park—so just to be careful, follow the rules. The fully fenced and double-gated park lacks running water, so bring your own.

Take the Capital Beltway exit 52B (Little River Turnpike, Rte. 236) east three miles to a left at Robert Avenue, right on Alpine Drive, and then left into the parking lot entrance. 6621 Columbia Pike; 703/324-8702; www.fairfaxcounty.gov/parks/offleash.htm.

# Centreville

Despite its name, Centreville is more famous for having been on the way *to* somewhere than being at the center itself. Both Union and Confederate armies occupied the town during the Civil War on their way to battle in Manassas. After the major conflict of the First Battle of Bull Run, the wounded were carried back to Centreville and loaded on wagons to transport to Washington. Now Centreville sits on I-66 between Fairfax and Prince William Counties. Centreville dogs know despite all the breezing in and out of town, they have it pretty good with howl-worthy regional, county, and national parks nearby.

## PARKS, BEACHES, AND RECREATION AREAS

### 18 Manassas National Battlefield

🐾🐾🐾🐾 🦴 (See the Fairfax County map on page 188)

Neither of us paid close enough attention to Civil War history growing up, so Manassas National Battlefield was an overdue field trip. Embarrassed, I had to ask what the difference was between First and Second Manassas. To anyone else who slept through American history, First Manassas was the first Civil War battle fought in Manassas, which nearly ended in total disaster for the North. This was where Stonewall Jackson earned his famous nickname. Second Manassas occurred 13 months later and was even bloodier than the first battle. The high school student working in the visitors center recited this with unblinking, encyclopedic knowledge. Sheesh. Glad someone stayed awake.

Though Denali failed to grasp the gravity of human life lost and the shaping of American history in this wide, open landscape, she loved the acreage of rolling hills with interpretative trails mowed through the meadows. It's very important to bring lots of water, since there is virtually no shade on the grassy battlefield. Also, watch your step on the sometimes-slippery boardwalks. From the visitors center, a quick jaunt leads you around the one-mile Henry Hill Loop Trail. If you have more time, try the five-mile Matthews Hill Loop Trail. Remember that dogs must be leashed throughout your visit.

Travel west on I-66 to exit 47B to Sudley Road (Rte. 234 North). Proceed through the first traffic light. The entrance to the Henry Hill Visitors Center is on the right, just past the Northern Virginia Community College. Admission costs $3 per person. 703/361-1339; www.nps.gov/mana.

### 19 Bull Run Regional Park

🐾🐾🐾 (See the Fairfax County map on page 188)

If spring has arrived and you don't dare brave the Tidal Basin crowds with your sure-to-be-trampled pup, drive west instead. In mid-April, soon after the cherry blossoms peak, the floodplain forest floor in Bull Run Regional Park sprouts a periwinkle-budded blanket of Virginia bluebells. Bull Run's 1.5-mile

## DOG-EAR YOUR CALENDAR

Have a HART and join the **Homeless Animals Rescue Team (HART)** for its annual **Dog Walk and Homecoming,** a fundraiser for homeless dogs and cats. The one-mile walk loops around the Bull Run Regional Park Special Events Area, which can accommodate groups up to 8,000 strong, and local vendors will be selling their wares. The first 100 registered walkers with at least $25 in pledges receive a goody bag, bandanna, and T-shirt. Prizes for top three pledge-raisers. 7700 Bull Run Dr.; 703/691-4278; www.hart90.com.

loop Bluebell Trail is a lesser-known Washington-area springtime rite of passage. Besides bluebells, more than 25 other varieties of wildflowers bloom here. The Bull Run-Occoquan Trail offers spry doggies and their humans 17.5 miles of all-paw terrain over steep hillsides and along deep ravines near the Occoquan River. Less peaceful but perhaps more popular with the non-dog crowd, Bull Run Regional Park also has a large outdoor pool and miniature and Frisbee golf courses open seasonally and a public shooting center open year-round. 7700 Bull Run Dr.; 703/631-0550; www.nvrpa.org/parks/bullrun.

### PLACES TO STAY

**Bull Run Regional Park Campground:** Dogs must be on leash and cannot be left unattended in the campground, but they will most certainly enjoy the fresh air at one of the 150 sites for tents or RVs. The family campground is open year-round. Rates range $20–28. 7700 Bull Run Dr.; 703/631-0550; www.nvrpa.org/parks/bullrun.

# Chantilly

For three days a year, this western corner of Fairfax County is the center of the Mid-Atlantic doggy universe. Chantilly's Super Pet Expo features more than 200 vendors of pet services and products, attracting tens of thousands of animal lovers to attend the show, many of whom bring their pet. Chantilly also has one of the county's largest, and newest, off-leash exercise areas.

## PARKS, BEACHES, AND RECREATION AREAS

### 20 Quinn Farm Park

🐾🐾🐾🦴 (See the Fairfax County map on page 188)

If aesthetics were the only criteria for a top-dog off-leash area, Quinn Farm would earn four paws. The fully fenced park is situated on a rise overlooking an open meadow, a pastoral breath of fresh air for city mutts. There's no running water and very little shade, which docks Quinn Farm's score, but otherwise it's a lovely spot for Spot. The dirt-and-cinder surface of the main section of the dog park is large enough to accommodate 80 tussling pups, and its round shape helps to keep dogs from ever feeling cornered. There is also a separate fenced area for up to 10 small dogs (less than 25 pounds). Both fenced areas have double gates and benches for doting owners to watch the action. If your darling does a doo-doo, look no further than the mailbox filled with plastic bags. There are usually a few scattered toys and water bowls here, too.

Although the Quinn Farm Dog Park is located in Chantilly, it's sponsored by CentrevilleDogs (www.centrevilledogs.org), a community group that guided the dog park's creation in 2006. From I-66 westbound, take exit 53B for Sully Road (VA-28 N). Turn left onto Braddock Road (Rte. 620). Follow Braddock Road about three miles and turn right onto Old Lee Road. Take your first left onto a gravel road into Quinn Farm Park. The dog park is to the left, past the soccer field. 15150 Old Lee Rd.; 703/324-8702; www.fairfaxcounty.gov/parks/offleash.htm.

## 21 Cub Run Stream Valley Park

🐾🐾 (See the Fairfax County map on page 188)

Cub Run is a still, narrow tributary bordered by pillows of leafy water plants. The Cub Run Stream Valley Park is a network of 2.5 miles of paved trails, with some dirt spur paths, and fair-weather stream crossings in the floodplain. In 2008, portions of this park were still being developed. We began our dog walk at the parking lot of the Cub Run RECenter, a sizable Fairfax County sports

## DOG-EAR YOUR CALENDAR

Tens of thousands of pet owners and their leashed dogs visit the **Chantilly Super Pet Expo** in March each year in hopes of finding bargains and the latest, greatest trends among the more than 200 displays of unique pet products and services. Located in the Dulles Expo Center. 4368 Chantilly Shopping Center; 301/564-4050; www .superpetexpo.com.

Try out that new leash at **Dog's Day Out,** 9–10:30 A.M. the first Tuesday of each month. Join a naturalist and her dog on a hike designed for fellow four-leggers and their humans. Reservations are required, no retractable leashes are allowed, and kids must be at least 10 years old to join. Located in Ellanor C. Lawrence Park. 5040 Walney Rd.; 703/631-0013; www.fairfaxcounty.gov/parks/ecl.

complex that even has an indoor waterslide tunnel that winds out of the building and then back inside. If you like, request a trail map inside this facility or print one off the Fairfax County website. To find the paved pedestrian trail, walk down the service road just left of the RECenter near this waterslide. The sports fields at Westfield High School (Denali cheers, "Go Bulldogs!") will be on your left side. The trails begin left of the basketball hoop around the back of the RECenter.

For most of our dog walk it was just us and the chattering katydids. Denali appreciated the stream to cool off, and we had a pleasant jaunt of tame exploration. When we walked in the nature trails immediately behind the RECenter, however, the widespread barking and howling at the nearby Dulles Gateway Pet Resort kennels unsettled Denali, so we preferred the trails to the south away from the ruckus. 4630 Stonecroft Blvd.; 703/817-9407; www.fairfax county.gov/parks.

## 22 Ellanor C. Lawrence Park
🐾🐾🐾🐾 🐾 (See the Fairfax County map on page 188)

Right away, Denali saw this 650-acre park is ideal for pawdestrians. Lily pond and splashing streambeds? Check. Handsome, 18th-century mill and homesite? Check. Lovely fescue and bluestem grass meadow with a mowed path? Check. Walking trails shaded by Virginia pine and hickory forests? Check. The trails are among the best maintained we trod in the entire DC metro region, covered in bark that's nice and springy under-paw. Even the visitors center, located in a renovated 1780s farmhouse, is prepped for canine visitors with a full water bowl outside the front door and poop bags in a dispenser near the park entrance. It's a precious park, and one created with love. David Lawrence, founder of *U.S. News and World Report,* donated the land for the park's creation in 1971 in memory of his wife Ellanor.

Besides meandering the trails and observing history peeking into the present—a hole in the ground that used to be an icehouse, a patch of daffodils where once stood a farmhouse garden—another hound favorite is checking out Walney Pond across the street from Cabell's Mill. Here anglers hope for a bite from the stocked largemouth bass, channel catfish, and sunfish, while Denali hoped to catch a frog. On the other side of Cabell's Mill, the partially paved, partially gravel Big Rocky Run Trail is another doggy destination. The 3.4-mile trail follows Rocky Run from Ellanor C. Lawrence Park to Fairfax County Parkway. With the creek and the shade, it's a good walk in the summer heat.

Ellanor C. Lawrence Park is open dawn–dusk. From I-66, take exit 53B (Sully Road/Route 28 north). Turn right at the light onto Walney Road. The visitors center is one mile on the left. 5040 Walney Rd.; 703/631-0013; www .fairfaxcounty.gov/parks/ecl.

# Clifton

Historic Clifton has one of the most charming Main Streets around. As the town website phrases it, the town has the "feeling of a Norman Rockwell painting." Clifton is also the hub for two of the most scenic parks in all of Northern Virginia. These river hikes get us excited every time, and more often than not you'll be amazed by how few people you'll find along the trail. Denali likes watching for herons and sticking her nose in tree stumps out this way.

### 23 Hemlock Overlook Regional Park

🐾🐾🐾 (See the Fairfax County map on page 188)

Although Hemlock Overlook is better known for its ropes course and group leadership building activities operated jointly by the Northern Virginia Regional Park Authority and George Mason University, the park has some paw-ticularly excellent hiking trails, too. One young couple from Reston says this is their go-to destination for quality doggy time along a four-mile loop along the Occoquan River and back through the leadership camp. This section of the blue-blazed Bull Run-Occoquan Trail has some fun stream crossings that Denali enjoyed. To reach Hemlock Overlook, take I-66 to Route 123, drive south on 123 to Clifton Road, turn right and drive 3.7 miles, then turn left on Yates Ford Road and follow it to the park entrance. 13220 Yates Ford Rd.; 703/993-4354 www.nvrpa.org/parks/hemlockoverlook.

# Fairfax

The county seat town has a hometown pet celebrity: Border collie Leroy of CBS' *Greatest American Dog* fame. While he didn't win the title, he had plenty of Snoopies cheering him on back home. A visit to Fairfax can also score your pup a free dish of ice cream from two different establishments in the warmer months. Interestingly, while Fairfax County supports hundreds of parks, surprisingly few of them are actually located inside the City of Fairfax.

## PARKS, BEACHES, AND RECREATION AREAS

### 24 Royal Lake Park

🐾🐾🐾 (See the Fairfax County map on page 188)

Firmly within Fairfax subdivisions, Royal Lake is a local's favorite. Right on cue, the post-work pet parade begins trickling in as young-gun yappers and gray-muzzled hound dogs shuffle around the lake in an evening ritual. The 36-acre lake has a boomerang shape that makes it bigger than it first looks. At the outset, we asked a woman if she knew how long the shaded circuit around the lake would be. "1.8 miles," she recited confidently while striding past. Clearly many neighbors and their pups know every step of the cinder trail around Royal Lake. We wouldn't be surprised if a few dog owners have been circling the lake since the 1970s, when the county created it as part of a watershed management project by impounding the waters of Rabbit Branch and Crooked Creek in the Pohick Stream Valley. Your pup will be pleased to come here to whine at the ducks. Open dawn to dusk. Take Beltway exit 54A (Braddock Road) west to go left on Twinbrook Road, right on Commonwealth Boulevard, and left on Gainsborough Drive to the park entrance on the left. 5344 Gainsborough Dr.; 703/324-8702; www.fairfaxcounty.gov/parks/maps/royallake.htm.

## PLACES TO EAT

**The Sweet Life Café:** Insiders know that a scoop of free homemade vanilla ice cream awaits furry four-legged friends at this deli. 3950 Chain Bridge Rd.; 703/385-5433; www.thesweetlifecafefairfax.com.

**Woody's Ice Cream:** Fairfax ice creameries seem to be quite generous with the puppies. Not only will Woody tolerate your dog, he will serve her a free dish of ice cream. Woody sells homemade soft-serve ice cream—vanilla, chocolate, and twist—as well as milk shakes, sundaes, floats, and banana splits. Obscured behind an auto body shop, the out-of-the-way ice-cream shack is open April through October and closed on Sunday. Bring cash. 4005 Stonewall Ave.; 703/273-8977.

## PLACES TO STAY

**Comfort Inn University Center:** For out-of-town hounds visiting undergrads at George Mason University, this 205-room hotel is conveniently close to campus. Humans will appreciate the complimentary continental breakfast, wireless Internet, exercise room, game room, sundeck, and indoor/outdoor pool. There is a $25 one-time pet fee (plus an extra $10 for each additional dog). 11180 Fairfax Blvd.; 703/591-5900; www.comfortinnuniversitycenter.com.

**Homestead Studio Suites—Falls Church-Merrifield:** Dogs of all sizes can check into this extended stay hotel that features fully equipped kitchens in each room. There is a $25 pet fee for each night of your stay (not to exceed $75). Pups can be left unattended in the room if you and your pooch are comfortable with that, but be sure to coordinate with the front desk and housekeeping to avoid any unwanted run-ins. Don't expect any fancy pet pampering (or people pampering) at the Homestead Studio Suites, but do expect reasonable prices. Rates range $79–89 on weekends, $129–139 on weekdays for up to six days. The nightly rate gets cheaper the longer you stay. 8281 Willow Oaks Corporate Dr.; 703/204-0088; www.homesteadhotels.com.

**Residence Inn by Marriott at Fair Lakes:** Like all Residence Inns, this 114-room hotel includes full kitchens, convenient for longer stays. Your pup can check in for a somewhat stiff $150 one-time pet fee. The hotel includes complimentary breakfast and a fitness center, outdoor pool, and whirlpool for people. 12815 Fair Lakes Pkwy.; 703/266-4900; www.marriott.com.

# Fairfax Station

Named for a stop on the Orange & Alexandria Railroad, Fairfax Station is a nexus of well-to-do planned neighborhoods, each with a jaunty sign marking the development. Despite its suburban qualities, Fairfax Station is situated in prime trail territory and it's easy to spend a day sniffing around these top-dog parks.

### PARKS, BEACHES, AND RECREATION AREAS

### 25 Burke Lake Park

🐾🐾🐾 (See the Fairfax County map on page 188)

A dirt and paved trail winds just shy of four miles around this breezy 218-acre lake. Burke Lake Park is often busy on weekends, especially as runners preparing for the Marine Corps Marathon in October begin to train in earnest. Denali enjoys the fresh air and waterfowl that also frequent Burke Lake. Besides popular walking trails, 888-acre Burke Lake Park has outdoor volleyball courts, Frisbee and miniature golf, picnic areas, an ice-cream parlor, and a carousel, playgrounds, and miniature train to entertain the kids. Take beltway Exit 54A (Braddock Road) west to turn left on Burke Lake Road, then left on Ox Road, to the park entrance on the left. 7315 Ox Rd.; 703/323-6600; www.fairfaxcounty.gov/parks/burkelake.

## 26 Fountainhead Regional Park

☻☻☻☻ (See the Fairfax County map on page 188)

Fountainhead Regional Park is here to remind the occasionally snobbish West Coast dogs, like Denali, that Virginia can be ruggedly lovely, too. A jaunt along this deeply ravined and beautiful land-scape will brighten any active dog's day. Stay clear of the 4.5-mile mountain biking single-track and instead stick to the horse trail or the white-blazed pedestrian trail, which are often papered with fallen leaves. Fountainhead Regional Park is located at the widest point of the Occoquan Reservoir, a 1,700-acre drinking water source for Northern Virginia, and so in addition to the arboreal setting, a hike through Fountainhead also means stream crossings and placid water views.

Ankles roll easily on this terrain (speaking from experience), so be sure to wear appropriate footwear. Like at Hemlock Overlook, Denali's favorite part about visiting is the wildlife, the peaceful water reflections, and the wild rhododendrons and mountain laurel when they're in bloom.

To reach Fountainhead, take I-95 south off the Beltway, exit at Occoquan and travel north on Rte. 123 approximately five miles. Turn left onto Hampton Road and drive three miles to the entrance on the left. Open dawn to dusk from March 15 to November 8. Most of the park is closed during the winter. 10875 Hampton Rd.; 703/250-9124;www.nvrpa.org/parks/fountainhead.

### PLACES TO STAY

**Burke Lake Park Campgrounds:** The 100 wooded campsites are open mid-April to late October. Campground amenities include a bathroom with sinks, showers, and toilets, a dump station, public phones, camp store, ice, picnic tables, grills, and fire rings. There are no electric or water hookups for RVs. Dogs must be on leash and cannot be left unattended in the campground. Rates range $20–25. 7315 Ox Rd.; 703/323-6600; www.fairfaxcounty.gov/parks/campgrounds.htm.

# Springfield

When driving south on I-395 as it transitions to I-95, there is a futuristic-looking section of interweaving highway overpasses. Here is Springfield from the highway. Off the highway there's fortunately far more to look at from a canine perspective. For starters, the **Olde Towne Pet Resort** (8101 Alban Rd.; 703/455-9000; www.oldetownepetresort.com) is situated in Springfield, as is

Lake Accotink Park, arguably Fairfax's most pet-friendly county park—which even does doggy cruises on a pontoon boat!

## PARKS, BEACHES, AND RECREATION AREAS

### 27 South Run District Park

🐾🐾🐕 (See the Fairfax County map on page 188)

Situated in a wide corridor beneath high-strung power lines, the South Run Dog Park is quite large, with room to accommodate 85 frisky dogs. The park was established in 2001, with considerable help from the still-active sponsor **South Run Dogs** (www.southrundogs.com). The park's downsides are its lack of running water and the split-rock surface. One regular says her Doberman has cut her paws on the rocks before during rough play sessions. But the bonuses are relatively ample space for your dog to run around, benches, poop bags provided by *The Washington Post,* and some great community events

## DOG-EAR YOUR CALENDAR

Lake Accotink has many wag-worthy activities. Call 703/569-0285 for more information.

**Easter Bonnet Pet Parade:** The only thing cuter than the Easter Bunny is your dog dressed like the Easter Bunny. April.

**Bark in the Park Parties:** Fenced enclosure, party tent, and private dog cruise on the lake are available for parties for $75. May to mid-October.

**Dog Day Afternoon Cruises:** A pleasure cruise aboard the pet-friendly pontoon boat. $5 per person, free for dogs. Limit one dog per person. Reservations and advance payment required. May to mid-October.

**Walking for Fitness Doggy and Me:** Like the name says, it's dog walking for both of your health. Summer.

**Doggone Fun Camp:** Kids' camps that involve the family mutt. Summer.

**Howloween:** Includes a dog talent show, costume contest, and boneyard hunt. October.

**Pet Pictures with Santa:** A chilly photo session with jolly Saint Nick. December.

**Pet First Aid and CPR:** Instructional classes for humans on emergency dog situations for $45. Call 703/569-0285 to register.

**Pet Place Obedience Lessons:** Everything from puppy primers to agility instruction. Year-round.

hosted by South Run Dogs, including a St. Patty's Social and a Frosty Paws Eating Contest.

From the Capital Beltway (I-495), take exit 54A (Braddock Road) west to a left on Burke Lake Road. Take a left on Lee Chapel Road, then a left on Fairfax County Parkway (VA-7100) to the park entrance on the right. Park your car in the small lot just inside the entrance to the right and cut across the street to follow the sign to the off-leash area. 7550 Reservation Dr.; 703/324-8702; www.fairfaxcounty.gov/parks/offleash.htm.

## 28 Lake Accotink Park
🐾🐾🐾🐾 (See the Fairfax County map on page 188)

At first glance Lake Accontink Park has all the trimmings of a usual major Fairfax County park: a large lake (no surprise there), fishing, pedal boats, playgrounds, miniature golf, and the requisite carousel. What makes Lake Accotink special for Fairfax Fidos is its wealth of dog-friendly activities—of which the pet-friendly pontoon boat ride is a pawrennial favorite—and its extensive trail network that connects to Wakefield Park. The basic loop around Lake Accotink is about 3.8 miles long, mostly flat, but with a few hills, but other dirt paths diverge through the 493-acre park (although you do have to watch out for mountain bikers). From I-95, take Old Keene Mill Road west, turn right on Hanover Avenue, left on Highland Avenue, and right on Accotink Park Road to the front entrance on the left. 7500 Accotink Park Rd.; 703/569-0285; www.fairfaxcounty.gov/parks/accotink.

### PLACES TO EAT
**The Swiss Bakery:** This place had us at "Swiss" and "Bakery." Located in the Ravensworth Shopping Center, this is actually the second location of the family-owned treasure trove of Bavarian delights, with the first located in Burke. Besides strudel, tarts, and amaretti cookies, the bakery sells all-natural dog biscuits, made by the owner's sister. 5224 Port Royal Rd.; 703/321-3670; www.theswissbakery.com.

**Victor's Pizza Den:** Although this pizzeria doesn't have any outdoor seating, the Athenian pizza is definitely worth ordering to go. 8406 Old Keene Mill Rd.; 703/451-0313.

# Mount Vernon

Although it's in Fairfax County, if you mail a letter to Mount Vernon or Belle Haven the address will read "Alexandria." This section of George Washington Parkway hugs the Potomac River and Denali insisted on poking her nose out the cracked window the whole way. Only 30 minutes south of Washington DC—or even Arlington—this part of Virginia starts to feel more rural and

## DIVERSION

In the **Belle Haven Marina,** your dog can help you crew one of the 19-foot Flying Scot or 14-foot Sunfish sailboats available for rental. For the nautically inexperienced, the marina also rents sit-on-top ocean kayaks, Coleman canoes, and rowboats to explore Dyke Marsh Wildlife Preserve's waterfowl and scenery. See the website for rates. 703/768-0018; www.saildc.com.

somehow more Southern. Judging by Denali's one ear sticking up, a rarity, she likes the change.

## PARKS, BEACHES, AND RECREATION AREAS

### 29 Dyke Marsh Wildlife Preserve

🐾🐾🐾🐾 (See the Fairfax County map on page 188)

At first, when the traffic noises from George Washington Parkway start to fade, you might describe Dyke Marsh Wildlife Preserve as a quiet place. Then your ears begin registering the trilling "O-ka-leee!" of red-winged blackbirds and the thrum of crickets and katydids, and it dawns on you that these 485 acres of tidal marsh, floodplain, and swamp forest are abuzz with sound.

We had nearly left **Belle Haven Park,** a pleasant Potomac River picnic spot where Scottish tobacco merchants once lived, when we spotted the trailhead for this wildlife preserve. Fortunately, Denali insisted we throw the 4Runner in reverse and investigate. What a good dog. It turns out Dyke Marsh Wildlife Preserve is the largest freshwater tidal wetland left in the DC metro area. It's exceptionally popular among birders, and with good reason. Nearly 300 species of birds have been observed here. You can traverse the preserve on a wide, dirt-and-gravel trail nicknamed "Haul Road," perhaps after all of the camera gear and binoculars you see birders and photographers schlepping down it. For dogkind, Dyke Marsh has a snuffletude to explore: great white egrets and countless other birds to spy on, a few beaches of sediment-heavy sand that's nice between the paws, and an abundance of cattails that entranced Denali (sadly, she found no cats attached). From trailhead to the wooden viewing deck at trail's end, the walk takes about 15 to 20 minutes.

If your pup is thirsty after your walk and the Potomac's murky depths won't do—its confluence with the Anacostia River *is* just upriver—a water pump and dog bowl are outside the restrooms closest to the Belle Haven parking lot. A word to the wise: the pump is powerful. (Denali accidentally got a face-full of water.) Dyke Marsh Wildlife Preserve is located inside Belle Haven Park and Marina, about one mile south of Old Town Alexandria on the river side of George Washington Parkway. 703/289-2500; www.nps.gov/gwmp.

## ⏽ Huntley Meadows Park

🐾🐾🐾 (See the Fairfax County map on page 188)

In Alexandria's Hybla Valley in Fairfax County, 1,425-acre Huntley Meadows is a rarity. Freshwater marshes are one of the most valuable habitats there are. Acre for acre, they support more living creatures than almost any other habitat. You'll often find a host of birders and photographers with tripods in hand at Huntley Meadows, drawn to this vivid biodiversity. Denali thought the wet lowlands even smelled richer and more complex.

On a crisp fall afternoon, the pancake-flat cinder path departing from the visitors center seemed to beg for a doggy trail run, so after lacing up and leashing up, we were off. Hickory-oak forest encircles the meadows, at first obscuring the rustling reeds and brighter sunlight from view, but then we saw it: The boardwalk straight ahead. Eagerly, we sped up, reading the obligatory rules listed on the boardwalk as we approached. "No Bikes." No problem, we thought. "No Jogging." We slowed to a walk. "No Dogs." Damn.

Fortunately, your visit doesn't have to end here. If you follow the Cedar Trail, which forks south, the lollipop-shaped path curves to great views of the autumn-tinged or wildflower-speckled meadows, depending on the season. Dogs are not allowed on the half-mile boardwalk from this end either, but it's less of a disappointment because several spur trails follow the edge of the wetlands (read: muddy paws and lovely scenery). Park staff has posted signs alerting visitors that these informal trails could be "wet, uneven, or difficult to follow," which seemed silly until I twisted an ankle, mid-snicker. We finished

our tour of the meadows with a gimp, but it was to our advantage. Walking meditatively, you hear the chirrup, twitter, and woodpecking of the more than 200 bird species identified in one of Fairfax County's largest parks. We learned Huntley Meadows Park is a place best visited slowly and quietly. Open dawn to dusk. Entrance is free. Take Beltway exit 177a (Richmond Hwy., Rte. 1) south 3.5 miles. Turn right on Lockheed Boulevard. Go 0.5-mile to the park entrance on the left at Harrison Lane. 3701 Lockheed Blvd.; 703/768-2525; www.fairfaxcounty.gov/parks/huntley.

## 31 Fort Hunt Park

🐾🐾 (See the Fairfax County map on page 188)

Yogi Bear would be right at home in Fort Hunt Park. "Hey, Boo Boo! Let's get us some pic-a-nic baskets." When you enter the park, you'll see that there are picnic areas A, B, C-1, C-2, C-3, D, and E, each with its own pitch-roofed eating area. During the Spanish-American War, Fort Hunt was constructed on George Washington's Mount Vernon estate as a coastal fortification; later still it became the site of top-secret World War II operations known only as "Post Office Box 1142." (According to the National Parks Service, it was an interrogation site for German prisoners of war.) Today, groundhogs have taken up residence at the garrison. Denali nearly had us burrowing after them—of all the days to forget her collar.

Circling most of Fort Hunt are two lanes of one-way traffic: the outside lane for cars and the inside lane for walkers, joggers pushing babies in strollers, and dog walkers. We actually never got that far. Denali prefers sniffing out what she swears are the *biggest* squirrels in Virginia underneath the foundation of Battery Mount Vernon, the largest of the four armaments in Fort Hunt. Free concerts take place at Fort Hunt 7–8 P.M. Sunday during summer months. Fort Hunt Park is located approximately six miles south of Old Town Alexandria along the George Washington Memorial Parkway. 703/289-2500; www.nps .gov/gwmp/fort-hunt.htm.

## 32 Mount Vernon
🐾🐾🐾 🐾 (See the Fairfax County map on page 188)

George Washington would be pleased to know that his historic plantation is dog friendly today, just as it was when the first President busied himself seeking to breed a "perfect pack of hunting hounds." Your leashed pup can sniff out the legacy of the American foxhound by exploring the Mount Vernon grounds by your side. History lesson aside, Denali likes the 500-acre Mount Vernon estate because it smells good, thanks to barnyard animals galore. She was especially entranced by a paddock of Milking Devon cows. You'll like this American destination for its panoramic views of the Potomac. Washington said it himself: "No estate in United America is more pleasantly situated than this…"

Although the Mansion Tour is off-limits for Fido, you both can join the outdoor Slave Life Tour (10 A.M., noon, and 2 P.M.) and Garden and Landscape Tour (11 A.M., 1 P.M., and 3 P.M.), which start at the Mansion circle daily April–October. Denali also liked trotting through the lower garden (rooster!), down Tomb Road to the wharf (Canada geese!) and the demonstration farm (sheep!), and back up through the Forest Trail (squirrels!). Needless to say, we were both exhausted by the end of the visit.

If you're hungry, detour to the food court on your way back to the car. Dogs can dine with you on the open-air terrace, but not indoors. Martha Washington would have approved this policy: Her husband's favorite French hound, the hulking Vulcan, stole at least one ham dinner, to her aggravation and George's amusement. A doggy water dish is usually outside the entrance to the Donald W. Reynolds Museum and Education Center, but Denali recommends bringing a collapsible bowl and water with you. She was thirsty hours ago, and we had to beg water from a gardener. Mount Vernon is located at the southern end of George Washington Parkway. Tickets cost $13 for adults (free for dogs). 3200 Mount Vernon Memorial Hwy.; 703/780-2000; www.mountvernon.org.

## 33 Grist Mill Dog Park
🐾🐾🐾 🐕 (See the Fairfax County map on page 188)

Grist Mill Dog Park is a generously sized rectangle, fully prepped for large numbers of doggies at play—up to 64 dogs, to be precise. You won't find a mud pit here. The interior space is one acre of quick-draining bluestone dust surface. When taking a breather from an off-leash game of chase or fetch, your pup will appreciate all the necessary amenities here (water spigot, benches,

poop bags, fenced perimeter) plus a few bonuses (two wading pools!). Since its establishment in 2006, the general verdict has been that Grist Mill is a clean, dry space. Perhaps this is also because Grist Mill has a hefty number of trash cans (which, comically, like all Fairfax County Park Authority trash cans, resemble Star War's R2-D2) so that anywhere inside the dog park you are within about 10 paces of one. Clearly the Fairfax County Park Authority means business by its Scoop the Poop signs. Grist Mill Park is located two miles west of George Washington's Mount Vernon estate on Mount Vernon Memorial Highway. The dog park is situated in a forested grove next to the paved bike trail, beyond the red-roofed barn and community garden. The surrounding trees help provide shade on hot days, as do the poplars growing inside the fenced area. The Mount Vernon Dog Opportunity Group (703/360-6305; www.pollow.com/dogpark) sponsors the dog park. 4710 Mt. Vernon Memorial Hwy.; 703/324-8702; www.fairfaxcounty.gov/parks/offleash.htm.

## PLACES TO EAT

**Cedar Knoll Inn Restaurant:** The pet-friendly outside tables in front of the historic Cedar Knoll Inn Restaurant offer fine views of the Potomac River. Though frequented by tour buses on their way to Mount Vernon (just as you might be), the slightly overpriced Spanish-American menu is worth a visit just for the scenery. 9030 Lucia Ln., Alexandria; 703/799-1501; www.cedarknollinn restaurant.com.

## PLACES TO STAY

**Red Roof Inn Alexandria:** This reasonably priced, 150-room hotel serves complimentary coffee in the lobby. Rooms with microwaves and mini fridges are available by request, and the hotel has a coin-laundry facility. One well-behaved family pet per room is welcome for no additional fee. Dogs cannot be left unattended in the guest room, however. 5975 Richmond Hwy.; 703/960-5200; www.redroof.com.

# Lorton

Lorton's Mason Neck peninsula has a trifecta of parks: Pohick Bay Regional Park, Mason Neck State Park, and Mason Neck National Wildlife Refuge. Add to that the Gunston Hall historical site, and you have more than 5,600 acres dedicated to recreation and wildlife management. Dogs are permitted in all but the national wildlife refuge. Also in Lorton, across from the historic town of Occoquan, a regional park by the same name serves up scenic riverside walking.

## PARKS, BEACHES, AND RECREATION AREAS

### 34 Pohick Bay Regional Park

🐾🐾🐾 (See the Fairfax County map on page 188)

While Denali enjoyed a hilly hike in the woods here, we suspect the best way to explore Pohick Bay is by boat. If you visit on the weekend, you'll have that opportunity. Friday through Sunday, the park rents Mad River canoes and Perception Carolina ocean kayaks, as well as pedal boats, johnboats, and sailboats (see website for rates), and your dog can join you at the helm. For the really ambitious wayfarers and water dogs, consider purchasing a map of the Occoquan River Trail from the camp store to expand your paddle exploration.

If visiting on a weekday or in the company of a dog who prefers to walk, the 1,000-acre Pohick Bay Regional Park has miles of hiking trails, too. We followed the blue-blazed hiking trail from the far side of the boat ramp to a scenic bench overlooking lily pads, a quick but undulating jaunt less than a mile long. You can extend your hike by connecting with the red-blazed horse trails, which park staff says tend to be steeper and more rugged. It was a hot day so Denali preferred to stay closer to the bay, where she managed discover a few tennis balls in the flotsam and jetsam that had washed ashore. We recommend bringing water on the hike.

From I-95 southbound, take exit 163 to Lorton. Turn left onto Lorton Road, and then right onto Lorton Market Street, which will change to Gunston Road after 1.5 miles (at the junction with Rte. 1). Continue straight. The park entrance will be on your left in about four miles. 6501 Pohick Bay Dr.; 703/339-6104; www.nvrpa.org/parks/pohickbay.

## 35 Gunston Hall Plantation

🐾🐾🐾 ◀● (See the Fairfax County map on page 188)

The founding fathers sure knew how to site a house. Even after first visiting the regional and state parks, Denali's favorite trail on the Mason Neck peninsula was the one that left from the back door of George Mason's historic mansion and 550-acre estate. Lesser known than his contemporaries (in part because he was a homebody—when you see his estate you'll understand why), George Mason drafted the Virginia Declaration of Rights, which went on to be a model for the U.S. Bill of Rights. The elaborate cherry tree–lined entrance sets the tone for the entire plantation, where natural scenery enhances the beauty of the formal grounds, or maybe it's vice-versa.

The fun really kicked off when Denali upset a groundhog in the boxwood garden behind Gunston Hall. The groundhog scrambled, Denali lunged, I yelped. This excitement carried us all the way down the one-mile rustic (read: overgrown) trail to the Potomac River below. The groundhog had long since disappeared, but there were deer and squirrels to enliven the rest of the journey. Although it's only about a 30-minute hike to the riverbanks, after a few cobwebs in the face we definitely got the feeling this trail doesn't see much foot traffic. There is a great picnic spot at an overlook at the end of the trail. After Denali pawed at the riverbanks and sipped some water, we hightailed it back to Gunston Hall, taking care to avoid the corner of these woods called Deer Park at the request of my rotator cuff. There is an $8 entry fee. Dogs are not allowed inside the historic home or outbuildings, but if you bring a friend you can take turns keeping your pup company outside. Do a careful tick check at the conclusion of this walk. 10709 Gunston Rd.; Mason Neck; 703/550-9220; www.gunstonhall.org.

## 36 Mason Neck State Park

🐾🐾🐾 ◀● (See the Fairfax County map on page 188)

Mason Neck is for the birds, literally. In 1965, the Mason Neck Conservation Committee was formed after two bald eagle nests were spotted on the peninsula. In the late 1960s and early 1970s, this conservation committee successfully staved off a proposed beltway, airport, natural gas pipeline, landfill, and sewer line—all of which were planned at one point! Bald eagles, herons, and many other migrating and nonmigrating birds can continue to roost on Mason Neck as a result. Be sure to bring your binoculars.

Denali sniffed signs of feathers and bird droppings everywhere we went in the 1,814-acre park. The most popular trail in the former Nature Conservancy land is the Bay View Trail, a one-mile loop that traverses surprisingly varied terrain. In this short trek Denali dipped her paws in Belmont Bay, crossed a wooden platform over a beaver marsh, and trotted through forest. Kanes Creek Overlook is also a good place to spy eagles.

Winter is a superb time to visit Mason Neck and walk along the three miles of nature trails if your pup and you can tolerate the cold, because the bare tree branches make it easier to bird-watch and the park is even quieter then. Interpretive ranger-led nature tours take place throughout the year, and dogs are welcome to join in the education, as long as they are "not frothing at the mouth," as one ranger put it, which might be asking a lot from a bird-hunting breed. Dogs are not allowed on the Woodmarsh Trail or the Great Marsh Trail, which pass through the adjoining Mason Neck National Wildlife Refuge.

The scenery in Mason Neck State Park is worth four paws, docked one paw for the fact that bird-watchers and "passive recreation" don't always mesh well with energetic dog walking. Rangers reminded us, "Your dog must be attached to a leash, *and* the leash must be attached to a person at all times in the park." (Was Denali's scheming that transparent?) There is a $3 entry fee for county residents; out-of-county residents pay $4. To reach Mason Neck State Park, follow directions to Pohick Regional Park, but continue about one mile farther down Gunston Road. The entrance for the state park and national wildlife refuge will be on your right. 7301 High Point Rd.; 703/339-2385; www.dcr .virginia.gov/state_parks/mas.shtml.

## 37 Occoquan Regional Park

🐾🐾🐾 (See the Fairfax County map on page 188)

Occoquan comes from a Dogue Indian word meaning "at the end of the water." Fittingly, the tranquil Occoquan River is ever-present in the 400-acre regional park bearing its name, as are cross-river views of yachts docked at well-to-do homes near the town of Occoquan. Denali scowled jealously at a lucky Labrador barking at her from one such dock on the Prince William County side of the river. The canine attraction to Occoquan is the paved walking trail that runs the length of the park. On weekdays, anglers cast lines into the no-wake zone and commuters idle here while waiting for the I-95 rush hour to lessen. On weekends, picnickers take to the impressive gazebos, each named after a Fairfax County town, and sports fiends drive to the far end of the park where soccer fields, baseball, diamonds, and batting cages await. These expansive fields are large enough to have accommodated thousands of participants in the DC Breast Cancer 3-Day Walk, but they were blissfully empty when Denali visited.

On the topic of women's issues, swing by the Turning Point Plaza on your way back to the car, a memorial to the suffragists whose imprisonment at the Occoquan Workhouse in 1917 tipped the scales in the fight for women's right to vote.

Open dawn–dusk March 15–Nov. 9 and 8 A.M.–dusk Nov. 10–Mar. 14. To reach Occoquan Regional Park, exit off I-95 onto Route 123 north, and follow Route 123 north 1.5 miles to the park entrance on the right. Entrance is free. 9751 Ox Rd.; 703/690-2121; www.nvrpa.org/parks/occoquan.

## PLACES TO EAT

**Dixie Bones BBQ:** The ranger from Mason Neck State Park clued us in to this authentic Southern barbecue, originally located on Capitol Hill before it inched farther south of the Mason-Dixon line into Woodbridge (just outside of Fairfax County). The real pit barbecue uses hickory wood to smoke the meat, which ranges from pork shoulders and beef brisket to chicken and spareribs. Dixie BBQ also serves up fried catfish to order and all the Southern sides you'd hope to find: coleslaw, baked beans, macaroni and cheese, and cornbread baked in cast-iron skillets. Oh yes, and desserts. The owner of Dixie Bones hails from a long line of family-owned restaurants in the South for more than a century. There is no outdoor seating so call ahead for carryout. 13440 Occoquan Rd., Woodbridge; 703/492-2205; www.dixiebones.com.

**Glory Days Grill:** Dogs are welcome beneath any of the 10 outdoor tables at this sports-themed grill and bar that features an all American line-up of rib eye steak, chili with cornbread, and cheeseburgers. Located conveniently close to the entrance onto I-95. 9459 Lorton Market St.; 703/372-1770; www.glorydaysgrill.com.

## PLACES TO STAY

**Pohick Bay Campground:** This 1,000-acre family campground features 150 shaded sites—100 with electric 30-amp hookups and 50 tent sites. All sites are convenient for car camping and include a grill, fire ring, and picnic table.

Unfortunately, dogs are not allowed in the rustic cabins that are also for rent. A one-mile trail connects the family campground to nearby Gunston Hall Plantation (the trail exits near the stately drive to the historic site), and a smaller network of trails connects walkers to the waterfront, miniature golf, and Pirate's Cove water park. Other campground amenities include a camp store and bathrooms with hot showers, sinks, toilets, and laundry. Dogs cannot be left unattended in the campground and must be kept on leash. Rates range $20–28, depending on the site. 6501 Pohick Bay Dr.; 703/339-6104; www.nvrpa.org/parks/pohickbay.

# MARYLAND

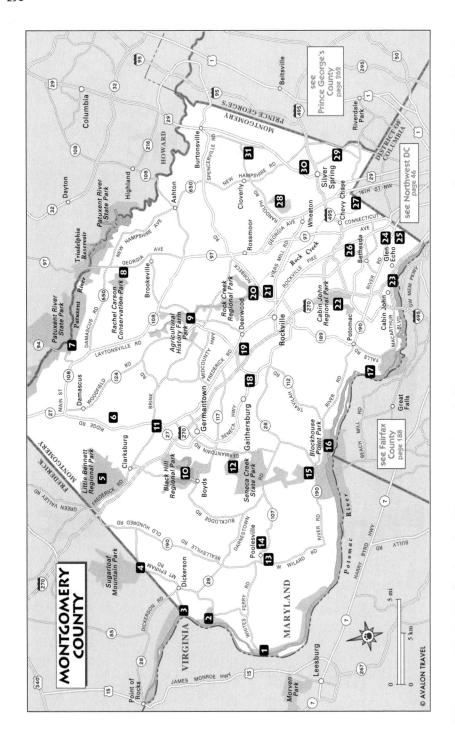

**CHAPTER 9**

# Montgomery County

Montgomery County is Maryland's wealthiest and most populous jurisdiction; it is in many ways the Old Line State's counterpart to Virginia's Fairfax County. Denali likes Montgomery County because in no time at all she gets to turn from city dog to country dog. Though for many Beltway Bandits the county invokes thoroughly urban Bethesda or commuter suburbs such as Rockville and Gaithersburg, the bumper sticker "I Love Rural Montgomery County" is nothing to scoff at. In 1980, county officials had the foresight to put nearly one-third of the county into an Agricultural Reserve. It is one of the most successful farmland preservation programs in the United States, carving out a rural crescent of more than 90,000 acres, enough to make any blue heeler or Australian shepherd let out a joyful yip. Head just 45 minutes outside Washington DC toward Poolesville and you're more likely to see a tractor on the road than a taxi. Much of Montgomery County also borders the Potomac River, providing

## PICK OF THE LITTER—MONTGOMERY COUNTY

BEST PARKS

**Sugarloaf Mountain,** Dickerson (page 234)

**Little Bennett Regional Park,** Clarksburg (page 236)

**Chesapeake and Ohio Canal National Historical Park,** Potomac (page 245)

BEST PLACE TO EAT

**Old Angler's Inn,** Potomac (page 246)

BEST PLACE TO STAY

**Little Bennett Campground,** Clarksburg (page 238)

BEST TEST YOUR DOG COULD ACE

**Off-Leash With Permission Program,** Rockville (page 251)

for some of the Mid-Atlantic's most scenic territory and a prime place for chasing—er, encountering birdlife.

For urbanite mutts, Montgomery County offers entertainment, too. Try Bethesda or Silver Spring for sidewalk dining with canine flair, or boutiques that make you say "Oo-la-la-Woof!" Even a major department store or two has taken the doggy cause to heart. For example, for several years running the Saks Fifth Avenue in Chevy Chase has hosted its "Brushes With Greatness," a fundraiser and pet spa event to benefit the Washington Humane Society. No matter what your budget or your puppy prerogative, it's not hard to make a dog's day afternoon in Montgomery County.

# Dickerson

"Downtown" Dickerson is smaller than a miniature dachshund—the Dickerson Market, the junction with Route 28, the Maryland Area Regional Commuter (or MARC) train station—and then it's gone. The countryside around Dickerson, however, is expansive enough to keep even a Great Dane entertained. Outdoors-loving doggies will find much to explore from the Potomac River to the distinctive peak, Sugarloaf Mountain, and all the farmland in between.

## PARKS, BEACHES, AND RECREATION AREAS

### 🏳 Historic White's Ferry

🐾🐾 🦴 (See the Montgomery County map on page 230)

We stumbled upon White's Ferry by accident... OK, by getting lost. It turns out White's Ferry Lane dead-ends into White's Ferry! Go figure. The 24-car barge is the last operational, cable-guided ferry on the Potomac River. White's Ferry is a novel way to reach Loudon County, Virginia, or a good place to stay on shore, as Denali did, and scan the river for interesting wildlife, which turned out to be a few men stripping to their skivvies for a swim. White's Ferry is a great place for picnicking (the charcoal grills cost $2 for the day; pay in the store), fishing, and digging into Civil War lore.

If your dog would rather captain his own boat than ride the ferry, consider renting a johnboat or canoe from the White's Ferry store. The rental fee is $7.50 per hour or $25 for the day. White's Ferry also has canoe float trips with a week's notice; inquire in the store or call. 24801 White's Ferry Rd.; 301/349-5200; www.historicwhitesferry.com.

### 🏳 Dickerson Conservation Park

🐾🐾 (See the Montgomery County map on page 230)

This place is way off the map. The 304-acre park is situated on the Potomac River nearly at the Montgomery/Frederick County border. As with all river-front from Georgetown to Cumberland, Maryland, the expansive C&O Canal towpath passes straight through Dickerson Conservation Park, affording as many miles of walking as four paws and two feet care to go. Denali was keen on the green pond scum covering the C&O Canal at Lock 26, which smelled suspiciously of horse manure, so instead we walked a short distance to the Potomac River to play fetch. A dirt path will lead you from the gravel parking lot to our favorite spot on the far right of the park's riverbank. In summer and early fall, brilliant yellow daisies grow along the trail. Judging by the fish jumping and the fly-fisher standing thigh-deep in the shallow water, it's a good fishing hole, too.

This is not untouched nature. We were sad, and a little surprised, by litter in the park, mostly around the dozen or so blackened fire rings. Still, you'll be hard-pressed to find such a tranquil and unhampered place to play fetch. Dickerson Conservation Park is a long way to drive from Washington DC, but it's a great stop to cool your paws after hiking at nearby Sugarloaf Mountain, and we thought the countryside drive was part of the fun. Bring your own drinking water; there are usually plastic bags at a dispenser in the parking lot.

Take I-270 to Darnestown Road (Rte. 28) and then left at Martinsburg Road. The park will be on your right side. Open dawn to dusk daily. 20700 Martinsburg Rd.; 301/972-9396; www.montgomeryparks.org.

## 🕄 Monocacy Aqueduct

🐾🐾◀● (See the Montgomery County map on page 230)

Considered the second-greatest engineering feat in the construction of the C&O Canal (the first being the 3,118-foot-long Paw Paw Tunnel upriver), the Monocacy Aqueduct traverses the muddy currents of the Monocacy River. It's one of 11 stone aqueducts designed to carry the canal over the major tributaries that drain into the Potomac. Your hound can take in the architectural sights while ambling on the towpath or playing fetch on the riverbanks. When we visited, two dogs happily swam in the Monocacy on the far side of the now-dry aqueduct (the banks opposite the parking lot). The C&O runs dry in this section—in fact, thick trees grow where canal boats used to float—so your pup can walk across the aqueduct bottom.

A more secluded spot for a doggy dip is a half mile down the towpath to the Indian Flats campsite. A clearing on your left will lead steeply down to the Potomac banks. Not too far away the Dickerson Power Plant rises up in stark contrast to the languid river. (Dog-owning kayakers might be interested to know the U.S. Whitewater Kayak and Canoe Team trains in a man-made slalom course in the warm water discharged from the power plant.) Pets must be on leash in national parkland, so to play fetch is to risk a ticket.

Walking on the towpath can inevitably feel anticlimactic. The junglelike tunnel of trees and the crunch of gravel underfoot and jingle of your dog's collar all start to look and sound the same. We imagine views of the Potomac River would be better in winter when the leaves are off the trees. On a warm September Saturday, we kept company with about a dozen bikers, a handful of hikers, and three dogs.

From I-270, exit at Old Hundred Road and drive south. Turn right on Barnesville Road, left on Mt. Ephraim Road, and right onto Mouth of Monocacy Road. 301/739-4200; www.nps.gov/choh/historyculture/themonocacy aqueduct.htm.

## 🕄 Sugarloaf Mountain

🐾🐾🐾🐾◀● (See the Montgomery County map on page 230)

Though the dirt does not taste of dessert as Denali had hoped, the views from Sugarloaf Mountain are certainly sweet. Sugarloaf has various well-marked trails to choose from, ranging from 0.25 to 7 miles in length, which can be combined in longer circuit hikes. At the 1,282-foot summit, check out the views of farmland unfolding below, marred only by the distant Dickerson Power Plant to the southwest. Sugarloaf Mountain is a monadnock, meaning it's an isolated mountain remaining after erosion has worn away the surrounding land. It rises distinctly above the Monocacy Valley, breaking an otherwise rolling landscape. In fact, early European explorers and settlers named the mountain for its distinctive shape like the *pain de sucre,* or sugarloaf, that were common in those days.

## DOG-EAR YOUR CALENDAR

**Doggie Easter Egg Hunt:** This Bethesda event is sponsored by the Posh Pooch to benefit the Montgomery Humane Society. March; www.theposhpooch.com.

**Paintings for Paws:** Artwork by young artists to benefit Washington Animal Rescue League. April; Discovery Galleries, 4840 Bethesda Ave.; 301/913-9199; www.discoverygalleries.com.

**Bark in the Park:** Join the city of Gaithersburg for a dog obstacle course, bone hunt, costume parade, photo booth, rabies clinic, and plenty of useful information from a variety of vendors. Located at Bohrer Park at Summit Hall Farm. Late April; 506 S. Frederick Ave.; 301/258-6350; www.gaithersburgmd.gov.

**Strut Your Mutt:** Benefits the Bethesda-Chevy Chase Rescue Squad. May; www.strutyourmuttbethesda.org.

**Paws in the Park:** Walk to raise money for homeless pets at the Montgomery County Humane Society. Located in Wheaton Regional Park, the pet walk usually includes two trails: the Yorkie Trail at 0.7 of a mile, and the Beagle Walk at 2.5 miles. May; 2000 Shorefield Rd.; 240/773-5967; www.mchumane.org/events.

**Kentlands and Lakelands Dog Swim:** September; www.kentlandsusa.com.

**Dog Day Festival:** Doggy games, contests, and activities, including a kissing booth. Slobbery. September; 395 Muddy Branch Rd.; 301/926-6005; www.bestfriendspetcare.com.

**Pet Parade at the Sugarloaf Crafts Festival:** Celebrate fall with a little canine craftiness. For a $10 donation, your pup can help benefit the Montgomery County Humane Society. No costumes are required, but why not whip up a sassy felt-and-sequins number for your pooch? Located at the Montgomery County Fairgrounds. October; 16 Chestnut St.; 240/773-5054; www.sugarloafcrafts.com.

**Halloween Parade:** Scary Fido fun at the Posh Pooch. October; www.theposhpooch.com.

**Dances With Dogs:** This annual benefit dinner and auction is black tie optional, for people and dogs, and usually takes place in a fancy Bethesda hotel. November; 240/773-5960; www.mchumane.org.

Sugarloaf Mountain is a privately owned mountain, kept open for the public to enjoy through the vision of a Chicago attorney and businessman who devoted a lifetime to its preservation. As the story goes, sometime in the 1890s Gordon Strong was riding his bicycle past Sugarloaf Mountain, and fell in love with the place. Parcel by parcel he acquired the land, then heavily deforested and pockmarked from a booming charcoal industry, until he owned 2,350 acres of the mountain. When Strong and his wife passed away, they left the mountain in care of a trust expressly designed to maintain the property and welcome nature lovers—and their leashed dogs—to visit.

Take I-495 west to I-270 north. Turn right on Route 109 (Barnesville, Hyattstown exit) and drive south three miles to the intersection of Comus Road. Turn right on Comus Road and drive west about 2.5 miles to the base of Sugarloaf. There is no fee. Download a trail map from the Sugarloaf Mountain website. 7901 Comus Rd.; 301/869-7846; www.sugarloafmd.com.

### PLACES TO EAT

**Dickerson Market:** Duck in for pizza, sandwiches, and chips. Dogs are not allowed inside, but the gas station mini-market is a quick place to grab a snack for the road. 22145 Dickerson Rd.; 301/349-5789.

**White's Ferry Café:** In the mornings, order off the greasy-spoon breakfast menu. In the afternoon and early evening, the grill dishes up hamburgers made from local, organic Angus beef, sandwiches, buffalo wings, hand-cut "ferry fries," and other all-American favorites. There are plenty of choices for seating at the dog-friendly picnic tables outside. Be sure to look for the high-water marks that top the second-floor window of the café. Open 7 A.M.–7 P.M. daily May to October (grill closes at 6 P.M.). 24801 White's Ferry Rd.; 301/349-5200; www.historicwhitesferry.com.

# Clarksburg and Damascus

Both of these villages sit right in the heart of the Agricultural Reserve. While you'll drive by some suburban subdivisions and fast-food chains, a patchwork of old barns, farmland, and rolling, forested piedmont better characterizes the region. If your dog likes to hike, head north on I-270 or Georgia Avenue to these hinterlands. Just tell her that the orange safety vest looks very flattering on her in the fall hunting season.

### PARKS, BEACHES, AND RECREATION AREAS

### 5 Little Bennett Regional Park

🐾🐾🐾 (See the Montgomery County map on page 230)

Twenty-three miles of hiking trails drew Denali north to Little Bennett Regional Park. We visited on a hot, muggy day, so the prospects of shade were high on our list. We stopped by the ranger's informational kiosk at the park campground before heading out. A helpful ranger directed us to the Kingsley parking area on Clarksburg Road (Rte. 121) since she said this is where the good swimming holes are located, even when all the others have dried up over the summer. She gave us the scoop on swimming spots in the same breath as telling us Denali needed to stay on a six-foot flat leash, but we appreciated the suggestion nonetheless. And so it was 15 minutes later we were on a pleasant walk down the 0.7-mile Kingsley Trail, a dirt-and-gravel road that comfortably follows Little Bennett Creek.

A short distance down the trail, Denali pulled us toward one of the promised great swimming holes, dubbed Bailey's Landing by a sign duct-taped to a tree. It was deep and surprisingly cool on a hot, early September afternoon; we stopped here both on the way out and back, she loved it so much. If your pup would likewise enjoy a dip, keep an eye on the side trails as you progress down the trail. This particular offshoot is located about 200 yards past the Hard Cider Trail, a few yards before a yellow reflector on a tree. According to the Montgomery County Department of Parks, Little Bennett Regional Park has some of the highest quality streams in the county.

On this walk, Denali also had her first introduction to a suspension bridge on our way to see the historic Froggy Hollow Schoolhouse, which she tackled gamely. Our route followed fairly flat terrain, but there are plenty of up-and-down routes in the Little Bennett hills. When selecting where you go, it's worth mentioning that north of Little Bennett Creek, the trails allow horses. South of Little Bennett Creek, the trails are only for hikers (and their leashed dogs). Open sunrise to sunset. 23701 Frederick Rd.; 301/972-6581; www.montgomerytrails.org.

## 6 Damascus Regional Park

🐾🐾 (See the Montgomery County map on page 230)

Walking through Damascus Regional Park might not be the blinding experience the Apostle Paul had on the Road to Damascus, but it can certainly be sunny. We visited on a hot summer day and Denali nearly overheated while cruising across the grassy fields and down the paved bike trail through the 284-acre park. Fortunately, a short distance past the busy soccer fields the Magruder Branch Hiker-Biker Trail loops into the woods, where there is plenty of shade. The paved trail continues north to follow the Magruder Branch stream valley for 4.2 miles through trees and on boardwalks over wetlands. About a mile in, the dirt path also branches to the south on a moderately rugged 3.3-mile route through open upland forest.

Turn southeast (right, if approaching from south) onto Kings Valley Road from Ridge Road (Rte. 27). Once on Kings Valley Road, you can't miss the park entrance. Look for the red, intergalactic statue inviting you to have an out-of-this-world dog walk. (The statue is actually called *Wind Harps* and creates calming sounds when the wind blows into the strings.) Open sunrise to sunset daily. 23723 Kings Valley Rd.; 301/972-6581; www.montgomeryparks.org.

## 7 Patuxent River State Park

🐾🐾 (See the Montgomery County map on page 230)

Amidst sod farms and cornfields, this 6,648-acre, undeveloped park straddles the Patuxent River on the Montgomery/Howard county line. Our visit was going swimmingly, literally—Denali found some great doggy swimming holes here—until we meandered into an area of the park marked with a small sign reading Managed Hunting Area—No Permit Required. Without a single NRA member in the family to warn us otherwise, we proceeded cautiously and came face-to-face with a hunter adjusting his neon orange cap. Needless to say, we turned tail and fled faster than you can say "Dick Cheney!" The Maryland Department of National Resources webpage should have clued us in with its sole description of the Patuxent River State Park as "5,000 acres of hunting land open for forest game, upland game, dove, and deer hunting." For a safe visit, stick to the trails that do not allow hunting (such as the Flowing Free Trail that leaves from the parking lot off Georgia Avenue), generously adorn your dog and yourself with fluorescent orange tape, and don't venture here in deer-hunting season (mid-September through January). Also be mindful of a vigorous tick population in the park.

These warnings aside, it *is* a cool park. Denali hopes to return to the creekside trail leaving from the Annapolis Rocks parking lot to practice her doggy stroke. The park has plenty of opportunities for hiking, though all but Flowing Free Trail are unmarked.

The Georgia Avenue (Rte. 97) parking lot is located about an hour north of DC immediately before the county line on your left. If you drive into Howard County, turn around—you just missed it. To reach the Annapolis Rocks parking lot, driving north on Georgia Avenue, turn left on Damascus Road (Rte. 650) and then right on Annapolis Rocks Road. The trailhead will be on your right. 301/924-2127; www.dnr.state.md.us/publiclands/central/patuxentriver.html.

### PLACES TO STAY

**Little Bennett Campground:** You can't ask for easier access to the more than 20 miles of hiking trails in Little Bennett Regional Park. The campground is open for full-time camping April through October, and only on weekends in March and November. It's closed the rest of the year. Campsite amenities include two-vehicle gravel parking areas, picnic tables, campfire rings, and lantern posts. There are 66 tent sites and 25 sites with 20- and 30-amp electrical hookups. Dogs must be on a six-foot leash at all times within the campground and cannot be left unattended. Rates range $21–29. 23705 Frederick Rd.; 301/972-9222; www.littlebennettcampground.com.

# Brookeville

President James Madison took shelter in tiny Brookeville when the British torched the White House during the War of 1812. Still tiny today (population 120!), the hamlet's claim to fame is that it served as "U.S. Capital for a Day." Urban hounds will be pleased to flee DC to the parks near Brookeville, too.

## PARKS, BEACHES, AND RECREATION AREAS

### 🐾 Rachel Carson Conservation Park
🐾🐾🐾 (See the Montgomery County map on page 230)

We had high hopes for this park, named for one of the most legendary conservationists of modern times, and we weren't disappointed. In 1962, Rachel Carson published *Silent Spring,* a landmark book that warned of ecological mayhem being caused by indiscriminate pesticide use. Conserving these 650 acres of rural Montgomery County is a fitting tribute to her legacy, and one your pup undoubtedly will appreciate more than the memorials that dot the DC landscape.

Denali loved poking her nose into the tall grasses of Fox Meadow, a portion of the park closest to the gravel parking lot. More than six miles of hiking and equestrian trails loop through the parkland, including a roundabout mowed into the meadow grass. Quaker farmers who had tilled this soil had a gentler approach with the land than many of their contemporaries, and so "you will today find rich, mature upland forest with large trees, dense patches of mountain laurel, a variety of orchids, and other uncommon and rare plants," an interpretive sign informed us. Your dog will be ready to dive after toads in the muddy black banks of Hidden Pond or snap at minnows in the Hawlings River, so bring a towel. There is no drinking water and no bathrooms at the park, so pack what you need and pee before you leave the house (dogs excluded, of course).

Rachel Carson Conservation Park is located about 40 minutes north of Washington. Driving on Georgia Avenue (Rte. 97), in Olney, Maryland, turn left on Olney-Laytonsville Road (Rte. 108), and then right on Zion Road. The park entrance will be on your right in 3.2 miles. 22201 Zion Rd.; 301/948-5053; www.montgomeryparks.org.

# Derwood
## PARKS, BEACHES, AND RECREATION AREAS

### 🐾 Agricultural History Farm Park
🐾🐾 (See the Montgomery County map on page 230)

This park reminded us of *Field of Dreams,* minus the baseball—in other words, lots and lots of corn. If your city dog wishes to be a farm dog, here's his chance. Montgomery County's Agricultural History Farm Park is a working farm

## DOG-EAR YOUR CALENDAR

Grab your fiddle, banjo, and leash, and bring your pup to the annual **Bluegrass on the Farm** festival at the Agricultural History Farm Park in mid-September. There is always space for lawn chairs, blankets, and jamming, though we suspect impromptu howling is probably discouraged. Tickets cost $15 in advance, $12 at the gate. Dogs and kids under 12 years old are free. 18400 Muncaster Rd., Derwood; 240/793-0975; www.bluegrassonthefarm.com.

preserved as it was nearly a century ago. Cornfields are the common feature of the park—fields and rolling fields of them. Denali and I walked several scenic miles on grass and dirt trails that skirt the cropland, and Denali scored at least one wind-fell corncob. While we saw fewer barnyard animals at this park than Frying Pan Park in Virginia (perhaps because of stormy weather), the 410-acre complex is also home to a flock of sheep and other farm critters. From I-270 northbound, exit to I-370 east. Proceed about 2 miles and exit onto Shady Grove Road east. Drive 1.4 miles and turn right onto Muncaster Mill Road, and then left onto Muncaster Road. The park entrance will be on the left in 1.3 miles. 18400 Muncaster Rd.; 301/948-5053; www.aghistoryfarm.org.

# Boyds

## PARKS, BEACHES, AND RECREATION AREAS

### 10 Black Hill Regional Park

🐾🐾🐾🐾 🐕 🔊 (See the Montgomery County map on page 230)

Glistening Little Seneca Lake, the DC metro area's largest lake, fills nearly one-third of this 1,800-acre regional park. The sight of it will light up the eyes of Portuguese water dogs anywhere. And the other two-thirds of Black Hill Regional Park—the dry land—merits doggy exploration, too, with more than 14 miles of trails curving around the lakefront and through in the woods. At the writing of this book, a Hiking with Dogs Meetup group organized after-work hikes at Black Hill Regional Park on a regular basis (they might still be hiking; check out www.meetup.com). If you still need convincing that a trip to Boyds, Maryland, is worth it, the popular Black Hill Dog Park should be enough for your pup to fetch the car keys for you.

The dog park is a half-acre wedge shaded by a row of leafy trees and enclosed with a six-foot chain link fence and double-gate to outsmart escap-ees. No running water is available in the off-leash area (though there are drinking fountains elsewhere in the expansive park), so it's best to bring

## DIVERSION

What better way to experience Little Seneca Lake than a **pontoon boat** ride? The naturalist-led tour aboard the *Kingfisher* can fit 30 people, and a handful of well-adjusted dogs. Children under 5 must wear a life jacket and dogs must wear a leash. Tours are available Saturday and Sunday from Memorial Day through Labor Day. First-come, first-served tickets are $4 each. Black Hill Regional Park, 20930 Lake Ridge Dr., Boyds; 301/916-0220; www.montgomeryparks.org.

your own jug. Mutt Mitts are on hand for when doody calls. The dog park is located on Picnic Lane (you'll see signs from the main park entrance on Lake Ridge Road). Dogs must display current license and rabies vaccination tags and be older than four months, and rangers requested we emphasize that dogs should only be off-leash in the official off-leash area. The park has had issues with free-wheeling dogs and has become serious about ticketing leash-law violators.

From I-270, take exit 16 toward Damascus/Rte. 27 east. Merge onto Father Hurley Boulevard, which turns into Ridge Road (Rte. 27). Turn left at Frederick Road (Rte. 355), and then left at W. Old Baltimore Road, to a final left at Lake Ridge Drive into the park. Open sunrise to sunset daily. 20930 Lake Ridge Dr.; 301/972-9396; www.montgomeryparks.org.

# Germantown

## PARKS, BEACHES, AND RECREATION AREAS

### 11 Ridge Road Recreational Park

🐾🐾🐕 (See the Montgomery County map on page 230)

Not only can your pup watch roller derby unfold at Ridge Road Recreational Park, she can play team sports of her own at the Ridge Road Dog Park. Dogs can tackle and tussle across the mostly dirt and gravel fenced area, hopefully landing on one of the few grass patches. The dog exercise area is banked on a slope in full sun, which, while not ideal during the dog days of August, is a plus after it rains. Regulars say even after a morning drizzle you can visit in the afternoon without dealing with too much mud. Thankfully this sunny spot has a shade canopy strung up over benches for onlookers and hot dogs to cool off. There are plenty of Mutt Mitts on hand for doggy cleanup, but do be sure to bring your own water. Besides the dog park, the 56-acre park has the usual recreational features—tennis courts, volleyball courts, ball fields—and the less typical, such as an in-line hockey rink. Located on Highway 355 at the junction with Ridge Road (Rte. 27). Open sunrise to sunset daily. 21155 Frederick Rd.; 301/972-6581; www.montgomeryparks.org.

### 12 South Germantown Recreational Park

🐾🐾 (See the Montgomery County map on page 230)

Holy Alpo! Denali had no idea how huge this park was before visiting. Formerly a dairy farm, the daunting 695 acres of soccer fields, baseball diamonds, miniature golf, driving range, archery, swimming pools, water parks, playgrounds, and picnic areas span both sides of Schaeffer Road. With 24 fields, the park's "SoccerPlex" is one of the premier soccer facilities in the country. But with all this human sporty activity, where is a dog to go?

Why, the duck pond, of course. Neither dogs nor people are allowed to swim in the Central Park Pond, but this rule fortunately does not apply to the waterfowl that headlined Denali's visit. South Germantown Recreational Park also has nearly seven miles of paved trails for dog walking. From Clopper Road, turn south on Schaeffer Road. Open sunrise to sunset. The behemoth recreation area straddles the Germantown-Boyds border. 18041 Central Park Circle, Boyds; 301/601-4410; www.montgomeryparks.org.

# Poolesville

Sleepy Poolesville might not be a major doggy destination unto itself, but Denali thinks of it as a gateway to the rural countryside that makes her ears perk way up. We usually approach by River Road, the scenic route, and she loves to perch shotgun, alertly watching the equestrian estates and family farms fly by. A half century ago, only 58 single-family homes stood in Poolesville. Today, there are more than 1,600 homes, still quaint by comparison to its larger neighbors nearer DC and along the I-270 corridor. Historic White's Ferry, although located in Dickerson, is very close to Poolesville.

### DOG-EAR YOUR CALENDAR

In late September, nearly everyone in Poolesville, dogs included, turn out for the annual **Poolesville Day,** a celebration of the farming community's history and sense of place. Pups don't get to star in the parade, as they often do in Old Town Alexandria pageantry, but dogs acclimated to moderate crowds will still have a hoot. Poolesville Day has all the feel-good trimmings of a small-town America festival: a classic car show (no peeing on those tires), pony rides, livestock display, pie-eating contest, 5K run/walk, and live music. Whalen Commons Park; 301/349-2123; www.poolesvilleday.com.

## DETOURS

**Hearthside Antiques:** In fact more than an antique store, you can also find plants for your garden and antiquarian books. Leashed dogs welcome. 19900 Fisher Ave.; 301/605-3900; www.hearthsideantiques.com.

**Poolesville True Value Hardware:** Free popcorn while you shop for tools with your dog. 19961 Fisher Ave.; 301/428-8925.

## PARKS, RECREATION AREAS, AND BEACHES

### 13 Whalen Commons Park

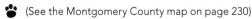
(See the Montgomery County map on page 230)

The 3.5-acre square of lawn in the middle of Poolesville isn't anything to howl home about under regular circumstances. Behind three waving flagpoles, there is grass for a doggy pit stop, hemmed in by a paved path, and a gazebo for a shady place to eat takeout. But special events liven up the scene. A free summer concert series serenades the Whalen Commons at 7 P.M. on Sunday evenings, and free outdoor movies entertain on Saturday nights. 19701 Fisher Ave.; 301/428-8927; www.ci.poolesville.md.us/recreation/parks.html.

### 14 L.M. Stevens Park

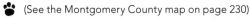
(See the Montgomery County map on page 230)

Denali was pleased to hop out of the car when we visited L. M. Stevens Park, a 7.5-acre community park with a ball field, playground, and other recreational features. It seemed to us the kind of place you would bring your dog to watch your kids play Little League. Your pooch can also progress down a paved trail past the sports fields toward the surrounding neighborhoods, with a few grassy patches to sniff out along the way. From White's Ferry Road (Rte. 109) west, turn right on Spates Hill Road in the Seneca Chase Subdivision and follow signs to the park. Open dawn to dusk daily. 301/428-8927; www.ci.poolesville.md.us/recreation/parks.html.

## PLACES TO EAT

**Austin's Café:** If you want a dog-convenient drive-through that isn't McDonald's, try Austin's Café. This coffee and tortilla wrap shop is located inside a gym. Push the buzzer at the drive-up window for service. 19942 Fisher Ave.; 301/972-8664.

**Bassett's Place:** The Bassett hound painted on this small, hospitable restaurant gave us hope it might welcome other breeds as well. Alas, Denali learned no dogs are allowed on the low-walled patio area "because that's where we serve food," but you can order a burger or *tres leches* cake to go from Poolesville's nicest restaurant. 19950 Fisher Ave.; 301/972-7443.

**The Corner Café:** This café served up a little health trivia on its menu: "Researchers found... those who drank four or more cups of coffee each day had a lower risk of developing Type 2 diabetes than those who rarely had a cup." Besides coffee, the Corner Café serves up paninis, breakfast sandwiches, and ice cream. Dogs are allowed at the four outdoor tables. There is also free wireless Internet. 19710 K Fisher Ave.; 301/349-0010.

# Potomac

Widely known as one of the wealthiest places in the entire DC metro area, you'll see why as you drive down River Road. Gazing at the palatial estates, Denali wonders what Potomac doghouses must look like. Air-conditioned with *Animal Planet* on HDTV?

## PARKS, BEACHES, AND RECREATION AREAS

### 15 Seneca Creek State Park

🐾🐾🐾 (See the Montgomery County map on page 230)

Lots of Maryland dog owners who enjoy hiking told us to go check out Seneca Creek State Park—which was befuddling when the ranger turned us back at the Clopper Day-Use Area, telling us dogs were not allowed. You see, as with most Maryland State Parks, dogs are relegated to the out-of-the-way corners. With 6,300 acres in the park, that turns out to be no problem. Where you and your energetic pup need to go instead is to the southern end of the park, along River Road not far from Potomac, Maryland. You can hike north on the sparsely marked 16.5-mile Seneca Creek Greenway Trail, which follows the creek in a lovely stream valley the whole way. While beautiful in summer, in winter you might find the isolated hike a bit spooky, tugging at some frightening memory... that nagging recall might be the film *The Blair Witch Project,* which was partly filmed inside Seneca Creek State Park. Denali is a big scary movie wimp, so we usually just visit this trail when the birds are chirping and the brook is bubbling and the leaves are still attached to the trees. The trailhead is unmarked and proceeds north from the second entrance of Seneca Road as you're driving west on River Road, just past the private Bretton Woods Golf Course. One other important note: September through January, we highly recommend only hiking here on Sundays after confirming with the Maryland Department of Natural Resources that hunting is not being allowed that Sunday. Wear blaze orange just in case.

For a less-isolated but also scenic jaunt, you can also walk along the C&O Canal on the edge of Seneca Creek State Park. Turn left on Riley's Lock Road and park near the lockhouse and pedestrian bridge over the canal to the tow-path. 301/924-2127; www.dnr.state.md.us/publiclands/central/seneca.html.

## 16 Blockhouse Point Conservation Park

🐾🐾🐾 (See the Montgomery County map on page 230)

Blockhouse Point Conservation Park gets its name from a Union defensive camp at the confluence of Muddy Branch with the Potomac River. Second to Great Falls, this 630-acre park has vistas of the Potomac River unrivaled in Montgomery County. Better yet, it's situated in the horse- and hound-happy countryside outside Potomac. Case in point: Dogs outnumbered humans four to three on our last visit to the park.

With more than five miles of forested trails to explore, Denali completely missed the river views on our first hike. We later discovered you have to walk to the end of the Blockhouse or Paw Paw trails to find the overlooks, about a four-mile hike roundtrip. (See the Montgomery County Parks website for a trail map, or study the one posted in the parking lot.) It's a good idea to bring water along for the hike. In a pinch, you can also walk down the Canyon Trail, an open, sunny downhill jaunt, to where your dog can drink from the C&O Canal. (Note that you will be opposite of the towpath side of the canal.)

From I-495, take exit 39 west on River Road (Rte. 190) toward Potomac. Proceed about 10 miles through Potomac Village to the gravel parking lot on the left (there are two parking lots, but the east one is larger). 14750 River Rd., Darnestown; 301/495-2595; www.montgomeryparks.org.

## 17 Chesapeake and Ohio Canal National Historical Park

🐾🐾🐾🐾 🐾 (See the Montgomery County map on page 230)

During Denali's first spring in DC, we made a weekly pilgrimage to the Billy Goat Trail near Potomac—one of her all-time favorite outings. The Billy Goat Trail runs parallel to the Potomac River in the C&O Canal National Historical Park and offers sweeping panoramas of Great Falls, where the riverbed narrows from 0.75 mile to 200 feet across, punching out some of the region's best white water.

Dogs are not allowed on the perennially hiker-packed section A of the Billy Goat Trail, famous for its off-kilter rock scrambling and views of the falls, but Denali is content to tour the dog-friendly lower sections B and C. These pathways shoot off from the C&O Canal towpath in respective 1.4- and 1.6-mile arches and allow more space to breathe and admire the scenery at your own dogged pace anyway. In the springtime, wildflowers such as Virginia bluebells and blue phlox sprout through winter's leafy debris in this rocky floodplain forest. Proper footwear is a good idea. Also, beware of allowing your dog to swim in the Potomac River, as the current is deceptively strong here. The C&O Canal is a safer harbor for a splash, or the calm eddy where white-water kayakers put in at the base of the Old Angler's Inn parking lot.

This stretch of the C&O Canal towpath is a must-see, too. About 0.25 mile west of Old Angler's Inn the canal broadens into Widewater, an ancient Potomac River channel that engineers incorporated into the design of their own waterway. With mirror images of bonsai-like trees balanced on rocky islands reflected in the glassy waters, Widewater is stunning. (Sadly, a sudden breach in the canal drained Widewater to Lock 5 in late 2008. The National Park Service estimates the repairs will take at least two years, maybe more.)

One last important note about visiting C&O Canal National Historical Park: dogs are not permitted on the ecologically sensitive Olmsted Island, where the Great Falls viewing deck is located. To fully view the waterfalls with your furry friend, you'll need to visit the Virginia side of Great Falls. We recommend parking in the gravel lot across the street from Old Angler's Inn (10801 MacArthur Blvd.). It's not unusual to see cars extending a half mile down MacArthur Boulevard on weekends, so arrive early to beat the crowd. You can also park inside the national park for $5 per vehicle. Great Falls Tavern Visitor Center is located at 11710 MacArthur Blvd.; 301/767-3714; www.nps.gov/choh.

### PLACES TO EAT

**Old Angler's Inn:** A Capital landmark along the Potomac, this quaint inn offers upscale dining and an outdoor terrace that can't be beat. Fireflies create ambience, and doggies who dine here rave about the cool patio flagstone on their bellies. Teddy Roosevelt, among others, would frequent this Hansel and Gretel–style cottage after fishing in the Widewater segment of what is now the C&O Canal. The inn was restored in the 1950s to continue a long tradition of entertaining in the nearby Maryland countryside. The kitchen serves contemporary American cuisine (think iceberg wedge salads and osso bucco). Reservations are highly recommended. 10801 MacArthur Blvd.; 301/299-9097; www.oldanglersinn.com.

# Gaithersburg

## PARKS, BEACHES, AND RECREATION AREAS

### 18 Green Park Dog Exercise Area

🐾🐾🐾 (See the Montgomery County map on page 230)

Gaithersburg mutts have it good. Heck, they even have statues adorning the entrance to their dog park! The Gaithersburg Dog Park, as it's also called, is a two-part, 1.5-acre fenced run. The dog run closest to the parking lot is the usual affair: chain-link fence, bluestone gravel, double-fenced entrance. It's a moderate size, 17,000 square feet, but not huge. Keep walking down the hill for the good stuff, another fenced 43,000-square-foot area with honest-to-goodness grass.

The City of Gaithersburg hasn't discovered an extraordinarily hardy variety

## DIVERSION

Music is in the air with the **Gaithersburg On Stage** outdoor concert and theater summer series. Free kid-oriented concerts take place every Monday and Thursday at 10:30 A.M. at the Concert Pavilion. Free concerts take place every Saturday; times vary. 31 South Summit Ave.; 301/258-6350; www.gaithersburgmd.gov/onstage.

of turf. The grass stays greener in this doggy pasture thanks to a clever policy of closing the grass section of the park each winter.

Gaithersburg residents with a current pet license may use the facility. Out-of-towners will have to submit a $50 annual fee and an application package that includes proof of rabies vaccination, a photo of your pup, and other paperwork. Handlers can bring a maximum of two dogs to the park. Running water and Mutt Mitts are on hand. Open 7 A.M. to sunset daily. 151 Bickerstaff Way; 301/258-6343; www.gaithersburgmd.gov.

## PLACES TO EAT

**Bruster's:** Freeeee ice cream! For dogs, that is. For humans looking for deals, visit on a Thursday and bring your own banana to get half off a banana split. 18519 N. Frederick Ave.; 240/631-1222; www.brusters.com.

**Five Guys:** How many Zagat-rated burger joints have you eaten at lately? Denali gives a look that says, "Beef is beef." Not so—at Five Guys the burgers are made with ground beef that has never been frozen. The cheeseburgers and french fries are quick and delicious. The Kentlands, 653 Center Point Way; 301/926-9200; www.fiveguys.com.

**Moby Dick's:** This local chain of kabobs and other Persian cuisine serves up spice for a reasonable price. All of the sandwiches cost between $5.99 and $6.99, and the platters cost a few dollars more. Apparently the restaurant name is a throwback to the Shah's time, when one of the most popular kabob stands in Tehran was called Moby Dick. Order takeout while your pup waits outside. The Kentlands, 105 Market St.; 301/987-7770; www.mobysonline.com.

**Starbucks:** Denali insists we should call it Starbones. Fifteen minutes and a grande coffee later, five pooches had stopped by the coffeehouse for a slurp from the water bowl in front of Starbucks during their walks. There are a handful of outdoor tables if you, too, want to sit and watch the world walk by. The Kentlands, 121 Market St.; 240/683-6931; www.starbucks.com.

**Star Diner:** That old-fashioned milk shake you have been craving is on the menu at this classic diner in the Kentlands. Star Diner has ample outdoor seating, and a litter of neighborhood dogs can usually be found here when the weather is nice. Servers will typically bring water for your hound and

**THINK GLOBALLY, BARK LOCALLY**

When you shop at **Life4Animals Thrift Shop,** not only might you find some thrift store treasures, but you are helping to fund the valuable work done by Washington Animal Rescue League. You can also donate gently used and new items to Life4Animals. See website for details on what the store accepts. Store hours are 10 A.M.–5 P.M. Monday–Friday. 15938 Luanne Dr.; 301/963-1444; www.life4animals.org.

are by most reports genuinely nice about having pups on the patio. In the summertime, the neighborhood hosts live outdoor music 7–10 P.M. on Friday and Saturday nights. The Kentlands, 705 Center Point Way; 301/921-8222; www.mystardiner.com.

**Tacos Pepito's Bakery:** Pepito's offers carryout of authentic Mexican entrées and pastries. You can order your food to go or sit with your dog at the few outdoor tables. Located in Old Town Gaithersburg. 107-B East Diamond Ave.; 301/990-1541.

**Tandoori Nights:** Chicken tikka masala and naan await you, and possibly your pup, at this Indian restaurant. The patio is very large with about 16 tables, and well-behaved dogs are allowed to sit at your elbow. The Kentlands, 106 Market St.; 301/947-4007; www.tandoorinights.com.

**Thai Tanium:** The *yum nua* (beef salad) was delicious, spicy, and limey. You can sit outside close to the summertime stage, which can be a good thing or a bad thing depending on who is playing. Dogs are allowed on the outdoor patio, even after we witnessed a bichon get in a scrabble with a passing boxer. The Kentlands, 657 Center Point Way; 301/990-3699; www.thaitanium restaurant.com.

# Rockville

## PARKS, BEACHES, AND RECREATION AREAS

### ⓭ Dog Park at King Farm

😊😊🐕 (See the Montgomery County map on page 230)

The good news first: If you live in Rockville, your pup is privy to a very nice fenced off-leash exercise area. Now for the bad news: If you don't live in Rockville, no sniffs, ands, or butts, your pup can't come. The dog run has two areas, one for small dogs and another for big ones. Other amenities include a drinking fountain for dogs and people, benches and picnic tables, and a 20- by 20-foot shade shelter. No more than two dogs are allowed per family, and Rockville residents must register with the city to use the park (see website for details). Located inside the Mattie J. T. Stepanek Park along Pleasant Drive at Piccard Drive. 240/314-8700; www.rockvillemd.gov/parks-facilities/dogpark.htm.

## 20 Rock Creek Regional Park

🐾🐾🐾🐾 🐾 (See the Montgomery County map on page 230)

Upstream of DC's beloved Rock Creek Park is its precursor, Rockville's Rock Creek Regional Park. The 1,800-acre park is just as lovely as its DC counterpart, though perhaps less of a novelty out in the suburbs. Inside it, **Lake Needwood** (15700 Needwood Lake Circle; 301/948-5053) is a sparkling 75-acre reservoir with even-graded walking paths that have top-dog lakeside views. On her first visit here, Denali encountered a suspicious sunbather near the boathouse. She was directing her uncertain growl at a bronze statue of a bear in sunglasses and flip-flops. The Lake Needwood section of the park has an archery range and a golf course (both doggy no-go zones, for obvious reasons) and is the northernmost point of the **Rock Creek Hiker-Biker Trail,** which proceeds 14 miles down to Beach Drive in DC with plenty of places to walk your dog as long as you mind the cyclists and in-line skaters.

If the Needwood Lake area of Rock Creek Regional Park is dedicated to recreation, the **Lake Frank** area (5100 Meadowside Ln.; 301/924-4141) is dedicated to nature appreciation. Besides a center for environmental studies and a nature center (no dogs allowed), the opportunities for viewing wildlife are plentiful. Your pup can have an eye-to-beady-eye encounter with birds of prey in the outdoor aviary. A turkey vulture, red-tailed and red-shouldered hawks, and a striking bald eagle named Orion reside in large birdcages here.

The route to reach 55-acre Lake Frank is surprisingly tricky to sniff out, so take the time to study the trail map near the parking lot before setting off behind the nature center. These trails are a bit more rugged and heavily wooded than those at nearby Needwood Lake but also offer gemlike lakeside views. 301/948-5053; www.montgomeryparks.org.

## DIVERSION

Bring your intrepid pet aboard the *Needwood Queen,* a pontoon boat offering 20–30 minute tours of Lake Needwood on weekends and holidays for a very reasonable $2 per person (free for dogs!). Or take paddles into your own hands and rent a kayak, canoe, pedal boat, or rowboat from **Lake Needwood Boats** for $7 per hour or $24 per day. Open May through September; closed Monday and Tuesday. 15700 Needwood Lake Circle; 301/762-9500; www.mc-mncppc.org/parks/enterprise/park_facilities/boats.

## DETOURS

**Petco:** In case you forgot the kibble at PetSmart. 1507 Rockville Pike; 301/984-9733; www.petco.com.

**PetSmart:** Pet store overstimulation for you and your pooch. 5154 Nicholson Ln., Kensington; 301/770-1343; www.petsmart.com.

**Pro Feed of Rockville:** Also well stocked with nutritious pet food choices. 5542 Randolph Rd.; 301/468-7387; www.profeedpet.com.

**Whole Pet Central:** Sort of like Whole Foods Market for your pet. 1306 East Gude Dr.; 301/217-0432; www.wholepetcentral.com.

### 21 Rockville Civic Center Park

 (See the Montgomery County map on page 230)

The crown of this 153-acre green space is the white-pillared, neoclassical Glenview Mansion, which Denali amiably ambled around. Less interested in well-to-do, 19th-century architecture, her favorite part of the park was the formal garden next to the house with its stone archways, palm fronds, and fountain. The park includes acreage of grassy fields for walking and poop bags next to the tennis courts if you need them. While Denali has never enjoyed her stints as a crag dog (Mom has no business being that high off the ground), she noted that Rockville Civic Center Park includes a modest indoor rock climbing gym inside a warehouse. 603 Edmonston Dr.; 240/314-8660; www.rockvillemd.gov/parks-facilities/civiccenter.htm.

## 22 Cabin John Regional Park

🐾🐾🐾 (See the Montgomery County map on page 230)

Not since we last passed the Smithsonian National Museum of Natural History had Denali seen so many kids. Minions of mini-people clambered over the playground, marched in matching tie-dyed T-shirts on nature hikes, and cheered gleefully on the miniature passenger train that carries visitors on a 10-minute, two-mile ride through the park. Because Denali has limited interaction with little tykes, we gave the playground a wide berth, which is easy to do within the park's 528 acres.

For dogs, the most attractive of Cabin John Regional Park's many features has got to be its four-plus miles of streamside nature trails. The paths aren't too rocky or too steep where we trod, and the dappled light filtering through the woods will put a wide grin on both of your faces. While we haven't walked the entire length ourselves, you can hike all the way to the C&O Canal on this trail. From the Tuckerman Lane parking lot, the hiking trails can be accessed next to the playground nearest the entrance, behind a green-and-yellow-painted gate and a couple dirt mounds. Additionally, the park has two miles of paved trails if your pup prefers firmer footing.

Dogs are not allowed on the replica 1863 C. P. Huntington engine—a number of No Pets on Train signs indicate this question has come up before—but there is a wooden bridge where your pooch can look down at train passengers chugging underneath. With each "Choo! Choo!" Denali would raise her head up like a meerkat and try to identify the odd call.

Also, exciting news is at the end of the leash. While construction had not begun as of 2008, the Montgomery County Department of Parks was discussing the installation of a dog park at the Cabin John Regional Park, a site to be

## DIVERSION

If your pup is well behaved, and we mean *really* well behaved, he might have a shot at becoming "off-leash certified." The Rockville City Police Department's **Off-Leash With Permission Program** gives special privileges to dogs tested and certified to have the temperament and training that allows them to be off-leash in public places. The two-part test takes place the third Saturday of the months of January, May, and September. While off-leash, your dog will be expected to sit, stay, come when called, and walk under control in the presence of numerous distractions (e.g., kids riding bikes, a stranger approaching, another dog). Pre-registration is required by calling the police department. The cost is $5 per dog. 355 Martins Ln.; 240/314-8937; www.rockvillemd.gov/residents/police/neighborserv/offleash.html.

**DOG-EAR YOUR CALENDAR**

Each year more than 400 dogs celebrate summer's end in a splashy fashion at the **Rockville Doggie Dip Day.** For $5 and proof of rabies vaccination, your mutt can join the poolside rabble at the Rockville Municipal Swim Center. The event takes place the weekend after Labor Day, and proceeds usually benefit the Montgomery County Humane Society. 355 Martins Ln., Rockville; 240/314-8750; www .rockvillemd.gov/swimcenter/dogdip.htm.

dubbed "Noah's Ark." Remember to bring a water bowl and bags. Open dawn to dusk. 7400 Tuckerman Ln.; 301/299-0024; www.montgomeryparks.org.

### PLACES TO EAT

**Addie's Restaurant:** In a converted bungalow you'll find a favorite of Rockville chowhounds. It feels like you're dining in the backyard of a chef friend. The new American cuisine is tasty, the atmosphere casual, the prices… a bit steep. Dogs are welcome on the back patio. 11120 Rockville Pike; 301/881-0081; www.addiesrestaurant.com.

**Chicken Out Rotisserie:** This eatery is the Bubba Gump Shrimp of chicken: "Chicken sandwiches, fried chicken, chicken fingers, chicken pot pie, chicken wraps . . . ." 1560 Rockville Pike; 301/230-2020; www.chickenout.com.

# Cabin John and Glen Echo

## PARKS, BEACHES, AND RECREATION AREAS

### 23 Cabin John Creek Park

🐾🐾🐾 (See the Montgomery County map on page 230)

This is one of the loveliest stream valleys Denali has set paw in around DC. Judging by the abundance of paw prints in the sandy riverbank, Cabin John dogs feel the same way. The creek runs quickly, keeping the water from turning stagnant, but not so quickly you need to worry the current will sweep away your dog. Denali, with her newfound joy for fetching sticks in the water, swam like an enthusiastic amateur; two Golden retrievers downstream showed her how to do it like a pro. The hilly 1.2 miles one-way from the park trailhead to Seven Locks Road is a great, fairly rugged doggy hike. The trail passes through a bamboo grove, along the creek's edge, and up steep narrow ridges in the hills of the stream valley. The entire trail travels 8.8 miles one-way along Cabin John Creek if you want to take an all-day excursion. (Note that you'll need to walk to the right along Seven Locks Road to pick up the trailhead on River Road.)

Although it shares the same stream valley, this is not the same park as Cabin John Regional Park, the better-known athletic facility along Democracy Boulevard where Montgomery County has plans to build an off-leash dog park.

To reach the local Cabin John Creek Park, from MacArthur Boulevard driving west, turn right into the park just after the one-way bridge. The trailhead starts behind the playground. A trail map is available on the Montgomery County Parks website (see Cabin John Stream Valley Trail in the trail directory). 7401 MacArthur Blvd.; 301/299-0024; www.montgomeryparks.org.

### PLACES TO EAT

**Bethesda Co-op:** If you need a quick snack for you and the pup, Bethesda Co-op is a grocery that sells natural foods, including dog treats. It's a good place to grab some trail mix. 6500 Seven Locks Rd.; 301/320-2530; www.bethesdacoop.org.

# Bethesda

Perhaps because it's home to the National Institute of Health, Bethesda sure has a lot of places to play outside and stay active. We wished we had more time to sniff out Bethesda Row, a section of high-falutin' restaurants and stores in Downtown Bethesda, many of them fur-friendly.

## PARKS, BEACHES, AND RECREATION AREAS

### 24 Capital Crescent Trail

🐾🐾 (See the Montgomery County map on page 230)

Pavement is a precious commodity on the most popular trail in Montgomery County. The Capital Crescent Trail is a rail-trail, built on the 11-mile Georgetown Branch of the Baltimore and Ohio Railroad. At its calmest, it is a regular route for bike commuters between Georgetown and Bethesda. At its busiest, it's a whizzing, whirring hubbub of fuel-belt equipped Team in Training

## DIVERSION

If your dog is starting to resemble a furry ottoman, it could mean you're turning into a couch potato. Here to whip you both into shape is **DogTag Boot Camp**, a canine take on Mommy and Me fitness classes. The one-hour classes usually take place at Norwood Park on Monday, Wednesday, and Friday mornings. Pre-registration is required. 4700 Norwood Rd.; 240/988-6983; www.dogtagbootcamp.com.

## DETOUR

**Lululemon Athletica:** Denali honed in on the water bowl and jar of treats outside the front door of this yoga and fitness specialty store. 4856 Bethesda Ave.; 301/652-0574; www.lululemon.com.

**J. McLaughlin:** Small dogs can shop with you in this pricey bastion of classic American fashion. 4851 Bethesda Ave.; 301/951-5272; www.jmclaughlin.com.

**PetSmart:** You know what to expect, but it might be just what you need. 6800 Wisconsin Ave.; 240/497-1350; www.petsmart.com.

**The Posh Pooch:** As you might surmise from the name, this is an upscale pet boutique to outfit dogs of all sizes. 8009 Norfolk Ave.; 301/652-1199; www.theposhpooch.com.

groups, power walkers, and kids wobbling on Huffy bikes. On days such as these, often the weekends, only bring your dog if he walks obediently on a leash and will be unruffled by the commotion. From I-495, take Old Georgetown Road (Rte. 187) southbound for 2.5 miles. Turn right onto Woodmont Avenue. Just after Bethesda Avenue, turn right into the parking lot. Parking is free on weekends but metered during weekdays. 202/234-4874; www .cctrail.org.

## 25 Little Falls Branch Stream Valley Park

 (See the Montgomery County map on page 230)

Little Falls Park, in short, has gone to the dogs. The 1.5-mile thoroughfare, like the Capital Crescent Trail it roughly parallels, is a paved hiker-biker trail, but on a weekend you're far more likely to find Bowsers than bicycles. Despite the signs indicating the leash laws, the number of "naked" dogs astonished Denali—it was like stumbling upon a doggy nudist colony! The attraction of Little Falls is no secret, however. The pathway is well shaded and follows the stream valley nearly the whole way, with a few dirt paths that hug the lazy creek more closely than the asphalt.

Parking is easiest in the gravel turnout at Massachusetts Avenue and Little Falls Parkway. You can also start at the trail's south end near Sangamore Road and MacArthur Boulevard, but parking is scant. The south end is hillier and borders Dalecarlia Reservoir. 301/299-0024; www.montgomeryparks.org.

## 26 Norwood Park

 (See the Montgomery County map on page 230)

Surprisingly larger than we had anticipated, Norwood Park is a hound-happy walkabout with a rolling mowed lawn punctuated by stately oaks. It has the regular trappings of any ol' community park—a popular playground, tennis courts, baseball and softball diamonds—but sunny Norwood Park and its leafy perimeter feel a trifle more formal, for a reason Denali can't quite put her paw on. If you're planning an outing with both the kiddos and the pup, be aware Absolutely No Dogs in Children's Play Area, per a sign at Norwood Park. We assume this explains why a vocal small dog had been tied to a tree near the playground when we visited, yap-yapping at Denali and other newcomers. Drinking water is available at the park, but bring your own bowl and cleanup bags.

It's easy to miss your turn while whizzing down Wisconsin Avenue. Look for the brown park sign in the median of Wisconsin Avenue for your turn west onto Norwood Road. 4700 Norwood Rd.; 301/299-0024; www.montgomery parks.org.

## PLACES TO EAT

**Assaggi Restaurant Mozzarella Bar:** Assaggi means "tastings" in Italian, in this case varieties of fresh mozzarella cheese from Virginia, Italy, and California. The cheeses are paired with condiments such as homemade green tomato marmalade, red onion marmalade, roasted red and yellow peppers—all the

inspiration of Italian-born chef Domenico Cornaccio. There are 30 wicker chairs at outside tables where your doggy can dine by your side. Look for the water bowl. 4838 Bethesda Ave.; 301/951-1988; www.assaggirestaurant.com.

**Black's Bar & Kitchen:** If your pup doesn't mind a bit of distance, Black's Bar & Kitchen has a row of tables at the edge of the patio where you can sit and tie your dog to the poles on the sidewalk side. Oysters and seafood in general star on the menu here. This restaurant belongs to the same culinary collection as DC's BlackSalt, Garrett Park's Black Market, and Rockville's Addie's Restaurant. 7750 Woodmont Ave.; 301/652-5525; www.blacksbarandkitchen.com.

**California Tortilla:** Order a burrito, spice it up with a hot sauce selected from the Wall of Flame, and rejoin your pup outside. Lovingly referred to as "Cal Tort" by my co-workers, this taco and burrito chain is a dependable lunch staple. 4862 Cordell Ave.; 301/654-8226; www.californiatortilla.com.

**Parker's American Bistro:** This longtime Bethesda establishment serves, not surprisingly, American cuisine. The casual bistro has outdoor seating where your pup can dine alfresco with you. The Monday night buy-one-get-one-free burger special is worth a stop. 4824 Bethesda Ave.; 301/654-6366; www.parkersbistro.com.

**Tommy Joe's:** If dogs cried tears of joy, Malibu-born Denali might have shed a few when she saw the sandy outdoor seating in the "beach" area at Tommy Joe's restaurant. Known for its drinks, karaoke, and appetizers, Tommy Joe's is often described as a frat-boy-tastic social scene, but it's a dog-friendly one at that. **DogCentric Dog Walking** (301/275-8752; www.dcpetcare.com) hosts a Canine Happy Hour here from time to time. Dog treats and water bowls are provided. 4714 Montgomery Ln.; 301/654-3801; www.tommyjoes.com.

# Chevy Chase

## PARKS, BEACHES, AND RECREATION AREAS

### 27 Meadowbrook Park

😊 😊 😊 (See the Montgomery County map on page 230)

This 16-acre park would likely merit a visit on its own, but what bumps up Meadowbrook Park's pedigree can be explained with three words: location, location, location. Rock Creek Park and the District line is less than a mile to the south and only a short dog walk away on the paved Rock Creek Hiker-Biker Trail or sandy pathways nearer the creek water. (With Meadowbrook Riding Stables right around the corner, keep an eye out for horses.)

Though rangers ticket for it, dogs often congregate in the semi-enclosed softball fields south of Rock Creek, which bisects Meadowbrook Park, for a friendly romp when games aren't in play. Between the softball diamond back-

stops, you'll also find what must be a popular doggy swimming hole, if the paw-printed beach is any indication.

Denali was a smidge disappointed that Meadowbrook Park's "Candy Cane City" is not in fact a Willy Wonka town of pepperminty, sugarcoated goodness. The name of the large playground inside the park harkens back to earlier times in Chevy Chase when the play equipment was painted in red and white stripes and visitors had to ford the creek to reach the swing sets.

While there is a small parking lot on Beach Drive at the entrance to Rock Creek Park, we appreciated having a drinking fountain and bathrooms waiting for us at the Meadowbrook parking lot. Cleanup bags are conveniently provided at a couple of points along the Rock Creek Hiker-Biker Trail. Located just south of East-West Highway (Rte. 410). 7901 Meadowbrook Ln.; 301/299-0024 or 301/650-2600; www.montgomeryparks.org.

# Wheaton

## PARKS, BEACHES, AND RECREATION AREAS

### 28 Wheaton Regional Park

🐾🐾🐾 🐕 (See the Montgomery County map on page 230)

Montgomery County's first off-leash dog park opened in Wheaton Regional Park in 2003. The cinder- and dirt-surfaced park is fully fenced with a double-gate and surrounded on two sides by woods that provide plenty of shade in the evening hours. Seating options are plentiful while your dog burns off some daily exuberance; choose from benches, a picnic table, or even a gazebo. For Labradors and boxers in the habit of pawing at their water bowls, try filling up one of the two plastic kiddie pools in the park. The watery entertainment lasts longer and might actually leave some water to drink after the fun and games. The dog park's water source is turned off in winter, so remember to bring your own. You might also bring your own poop bags, since the park's supply looked skimpy. Located next to the old ice rink in the farthest reaches of the parking lot. You must enter the park from the Orebaugh Avenue entrance, accessed by Arcola Road off Georgia Avenue.

Beyond the fence of the dog park, Wheaton Regional Park has 536 acres to explore on leash—everywhere inside the park except for the Brookside Gardens. If you hear a high-pitched call in the forest, no, that's not an owl with a falsetto hoot. It's the park's red-painted miniature train, the kid-favorite way to tour the scenery. Passengers depart the train station for a 10-minute tour of the park's forests and meadows, over a trestle bridge and past five-acre Pine Lake (which was drained when we visited). Open sunrise to sunset. 2000 Shorefield Rd.; 301/680-3803; www.montgomeryparks.org.

# Silver Spring

Thanks to the Discovery Channel's world headquarters and a publicity stunt involving a 446-foot-long inflatable Great White in 2006, downtown Silver Spring might be more closely associated with sharks than dogs. But that is changing. Denali thinks Silver Spring is taking paw steps in the right direction. The city has cut the ribbon on its pet pit stop; this small, grassy tree planter lined with a low white picket fence to the right of the Silver Spring Plaza has drinking water at dog level, a pet treat vending machine, and two mini fire hydrants. With all the outdoor eating options, Denali thinks Silver Spring is shaping up nicely. Be sure to stop by the new dog store that has helped move Silver Spring in a doggier direction, **Living Ruff** (8517 Georgia Ave.; 301/495-7833; www.livingruff.com).

## PARKS, BEACHES, AND RECREATION AREAS

### 🔟 Sligo Creek Stream Valley Park
🐾🐾🐾🐾 (See the Montgomery County map on page 230)

One of the most popular hiker-biker trails in the Capital region, and also one of the oldest, the Sligo Creek Trail stretches 10.2 miles from West Hyattsville to Wheaton Regional Park. Despite the slimy-sounding name, narrow Sligo Creek is a lovely stream valley crisscrossed with pedestrian bridges, and a favorite place to see the fall colors turn. Connected to neighborhoods up and down Sligo Creek, which is a free-flowing tributary of the Northwest Branch of the Anacostia River, it's a popular place for local dogs to stretch their legs and mark their territory. (Thus Denali's slow procession of sniffing on our walk.) Curious naturalists can learn about what is in bloom and recent wildlife sightings on the Friends of Sligo Creek website (www.fosc.org). A flock of starlings swooped and resettled on our visit.

Be wary of the water quality after a heavy rain, and think twice about letting your pup put her paws or snout into the creek. Like at Four Mile Run in Arlington, sewage overflows into Sligo Creek are not uncommon.

From the Capital Beltway (I-95), take New Hampshire Avenue south for 1.2 miles. Turn right on Piney Branch Road, proceeding 1.4 miles. Turn right on Sligo Creek Parkway and start 0.1 mile ahead on the left side of the road, from the parking lot near the tennis courts. Many other trail access points line the parkway also. Note that on Sunday a portion of the parkway is closed to traffic from Old Carroll Road to Piney Branch Road. 301/650-2600; www.montgomeryparks.org.

## 30 Northwest Branch Stream Valley Park

🐾🐾🐾 (See the Montgomery County map on page 230)

A surprisingly wilderness-like stream valley runs from Colesville Road up to Wheaton Regional Park. Twin trails flank the Northwest Branch, both great spots to take an urban hike with your dog. Climbing to the right of a steep spillway on the stream, the blue-blazed Rachel Carson Recreation Trail begins level with the placid creek but soon steepens into a vigorously hilly footpath. Only dogs and their humans are allowed to hike on this east side. Leashes are required, but we wonder how often rangers visit this off-the-beaten-path area. At least one sopping wet golden retriever was grinning from ear to floppy ear after a nice, presumably leash-free swim.

On the west side, the Northwest Branch Trail rolls more evenly across the terrain, a favorite among trail dogs and trail runners. Horses are also permitted on this side. If not for the sound of a lawn mower or picnickers in the distance, it could be easy to forget that you are barely outside the Beltway on these heavily wooded trails. Both trails continue all the way to Wheaton Regional Park and connect at a bridge. By linking the two, you can complete a 5.5-mile circuit. Many dogs, however, are perfectly happy to tromp a half mile into the woods and splash around in the creek. Park in the lot on the north side of Colesville Road (Rte. 29) about one mile past the Capital Beltway (your first left after passing Crestmoor Drive on your right). 301/625-7207; www.montgomeryparks.org.

## 31 Martin Luther King, Jr. Regional Park

🐾🐾 (See the Montgomery County map on page 230)

This 95-acre park includes lots of recreational spaces for people—outdoor and indoor swimming pools, tennis courts, ball fields, a playground—and a few that will appeal to pups, such as a small lake and access to the **Paint Branch Valley Stream Trail.** The paved trail passes by the historic Valley Mill and the former site of Snowden Mill, dating back to the 1700s. Denali was more interested in the rustling of the fallen leaves on the forest floor, usually a sure sign of some interesting critter. One gentleman who walks the trail regularly says if you visit in the evening, you almost always see deer grazing as the shadows grow long. 1120 Jackson Rd.; 301/622-1193; www.montgomeryparks.org.

## PLACES TO EAT

**Crisp & Juicy:** Like its Arlington location, this Peruvian-style chicken rotisserie is aptly named. The roasted chicken is finger-lickingly good (Denali can attest) and it's very quick. Often, you can grab takeout and be back to the car in five minutes. We prefer the yucca fries to the french fries. Silver Springs actually has two locations: 1314 East-West Hwy.; 301/563-6666; and Leisure World Plaza, 3800 International Dr.; 301/598-3333; crispjuicy.com.

**Langano Ethiopian Restaurant:** This highly regarded Ethiopian restaurant has great vegetarian platters (and lamb, for you meat eaters). Best of all, they will let you bring your small dog in to pick up carryout. 8305 Georgia Ave.; 301/563-6700; www.langanoethiopianrestaurant.com.

**Lebanese Taverna:** This location of the locally owned chain for fine Lebanese cuisine opens onto popular Silver Plaza, a great spot to sit under the green umbrellas and listen to the splashing fountain with your dog in downtown Silver Spring. 933 Ellsworth Dr.; 301/588-1192; www.lebanesetaverna.com.

**Negril Jamaican Eatery:** Finally, we could try all the dishes a Jamaican roommate had raved about to Denali for months, with a faraway, wistful look in her eyes: oxtail stew, goat curry, rice and peas (meaning rice and beans, for the non-Jamaicans). Order up authentic island specialties from this corner carryout store. Listed in the 2006 *Washingtonian's* 100 Best Cheap Eats. 965 Thayer Ave.; 301/585-3000; www.negrileats.com.

**Red Dog Café:** As the name suggests, Red Dog Café is a dog-friendly eatery, at least on its outdoor patio. Local critics have deemed the American fare tasty and reasonably priced. For breakfast, try the blueberry-corn muffins with your coffee. Lunch and dinner bring pulled-pork sandwiches and cedar-plank salmon, a nod to the Pacific Northwest that makes us smile. The "Red Dog" is Madison, a golden retriever whose human is the relaxed café's co-owner John Emanuelson. Located in the Rock Creek Shopping Center. 8301-A Grubb Rd.; 301/588-6300; www.reddogcafe.com.

# Takoma Park

Sometimes called the "Berkeley of the East," Takoma Park regularly takes a dog walk to the left of center. Besides declaring itself a nuclear-free zone, establishing an immigrant sanctuary law, and writing a 5,000-word manual

for its trash and recycling programs, in 2007 the jurisdiction adopted a resolution to impeach President George W. Bush and Vice President Richard Cheney. Home base for Takoma Park pets is **The Big Bad Woof** (117 Carroll St. NW; 202/291-2404; www.thebigbadwoof), a holistic pet supply store located just over the District line where belly rubs and ear-scratches are doled out liberally.

## PLACES TO EAT

**Middle Eastern Market:** This is a good place for reasonably priced Lebanese food to go. Small dogs are even allowed inside while you pick up take-out. 7006 Carroll Ave.; 301/270-5154.

**Savory Café:** Step into Savory for wholesome food and a healthy dose of all things activist. Here you'll find Amnesty International bumping elbows with the Animal Rights Meetup group. Be sure to try the vegan chocolate cake, which is drool-worthy even for carnivores. Your socially responsible pooch is permitted at the tables in the front driveway. Live music plays 7–11 P.M. on Saturdays; Sunday brunch is served 9 A.M.–2 P.M. 7071 Carroll Ave.; 301/270-2233; www.savorycafe.com.

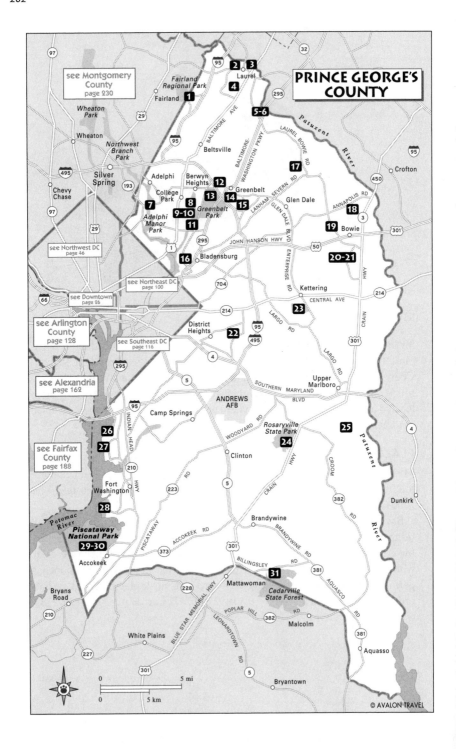

**CHAPTER 10**

# Prince George's County

America's wealthiest African American majority county is none other than Prince George's. If this fact surprises your pooch and you, so too might the canine confirmation that the sizable county indeed offers numerous places that live up to its slogan "Gorgeous Prince George's." Not far from DC, Greenbelt National Park offers a pleasant loop that is surprisingly isolated from the strip malls and highways surrounding its perimeter; about a mile east of the national park's entrance you'll find the Greenbelt Dog Park, Maryland's very first. To the north, Denali became acquainted with the Patuxent River and the surprisingly rural flavor on the outskirts of Prince George's. Farther south, she fell in love with the historic waterfront and preserved parkland near Fort Washington, from overgrown, Civil War–era Fort Foote to secluded Piscataway Park and its Native American heritage. Exploring across the Potomac River from historic Mount Vernon, Denali relished her long dog walk on land that hasn't changed all that much since George Washington's days. (For the

## PICK OF THE LITTER—
## PRINCE GEORGE'S COUNTY

BEST PARKS

**Buddy Attick Park,** Greenbelt (page 272)

**Fort Washington,** Fort Washington (page 283)

**Piscataway National Park–Accokeek Creek,** Fort Washington (page 285)

BEST PLACE TO EAT

**94th Aero Squadron Restaurant,** College Park (page 271)

BEST PLACE TO STAY

**Westin National Harbor,** Fort Washington (page 287)

record, the county's name has no relation to the first president; it was named for the 17th-century Prince George of Denmark.)

# Laurel

Two signs you must be outside the Beltway: 1. Trucks painted in full camouflage. 2. Lawnmower races. We observed both while cruising through town. Coupled with equal measures of country music and rap blaring from neighboring cars at stoplights, this paints Laurel as a novel crossroads between the countryside and the dual metropolises DC and Baltimore. Laurel Lassies are lucky enough to have two dog parks in their vicinity.

## PARKS, BEACHES, AND RECREATION AREAS

### 1 Fairland Regional Park

🐾🐾 (See the Prince George's County map on page 262)

This more-than-470-acre regional park is one of those places where there's more than first meets the eye… right down to the grass. The athletic fields were freshly carpeted with small piles of deer droppings, which Denali swears are the canine equivalent of bubble tea tapioca balls. Even so, eating them is a strict no-no. (We have had this heart-to-heart several times.) Beyond the questionable culinary delights awaiting your pooch, Fairland Regional Park also has several miles of walking trails hidden behind what first appears to be just a complex of ball fields and other humans-only sporting venues. To the contrary, a paved hiker-biker trail reaches north and south; down a steep embankment into the woods, an entertaining stretch of single-track similarly stretches in either direction, both with occasional glimpses of the nearby Fairland Golf Course. The trails are open to horseback riders and mountain bikers, too, so keep one ear to the ground.

The park sits squarely on the Montgomery/Prince George's County line. These directions will lead you to the Prince George's side. From I-95, take exit 29 toward Beltsville. At the first light, turn left onto Old Gunpowder Road and follow it for about 1.25 miles. Fairland Regional Park is on the left. 13950 Old Gunpowder Rd.; 301/699-2255; www.pgparks.com/places/parks/fairland.html.

## 🄎 Leo E. Wilson Community Park

🐾🐾🐕 (See the Prince George's County map on page 262)

We visited this off-leash area just a hair too early. The dog park was so new the padlocks had not yet been removed from the shiny double-gates. From our vantage point outside the chain-link fence, everything looked to be tip-top and ready to go, from the grass sod to the wooden benches and trash cans. The city had even planted a row of saplings to complement the handful of mature trees already growing here. The off-leash area is divided into two lots, presumably one for big dogs and one for smaller dogs. Both sides have a hilly, landscaped terrain that will undoubtedly make for great Top Dog of the Mountain duels. The park has since opened for puppy playtime.

The off-leash area is located inside a 4.6-acre community park named for a former mayor of Laurel. Take Baltimore Avenue (Route 1) north to a left on Cherry Lane, then turn right on Van Dusen Street. Leo E. Wilson Community Park will be on your right. If you pass Sandy Spring Road (Route 198), turn around—you've gone too far. The dog park is not visible from the road. Park your car and walk across the pedestrian bridge. Open dawn to dusk daily. 301/725-5300, ext. 317; www.laurel.md.us/wilson.htm.

## THINK GLOBALLY, BARK LOCALLY

Laurel, Maryland–based service and therapy dog organization **Fidos for Freedom** knows that four faithful paws can make a big difference in a person's life, from assisting individuals with mobility and hearing impairment, to cheering patients in healthcare facilities. Fidos dogs even encourage literacy in elementary school students through a one-on-one reading program; along with a Fidos human volunteer, trained dogs patiently tilt a furry, listening ear to the ABCs. To learn more about volunteering or donating, contact Fidos for Freedom. 410/880-4178; 301/570-7570 (TTY); www.fidosforfreedom.org.

## ❸ Riverfront Park

🐾🐾 (See the Prince George's County map on page 262)

The river in question at this Laurel community park is the lesser known Patuxent. Though it's not much wider than the numerous tributaries of the Potomac and Anacostia, the Patuxent River is unassumingly swift. After a steady rain, Denali was practically swimming in place while facing upstream, not unlike the endless lap pools you see inside in-flight shopping magazines. With a huge, soggy grin on her face, she looked like a smiling, oversized river otter. The 30-acre Riverfront Park and its 1.5-mile paved hiker-biker trail narrowly squeeze between Main Street and the Patuxent River, running from Route 1 to the historic dam ruins behind the Laurel Municipal Pool. Popular with Laurel doggy paddlers is an even deeper swimming hole located near the trail's westernmost end by the pool. Do be vigilant, however; a woman was murdered here in summer 2008. Also, be mindful of silt at the river's edge, which can be deeper than it looks, particularly near a large eddy. On a happier note, in September, the Laurel Municipal Pool hosts a Dog Swim Day, so in later summer also keep your eyes peeled for flyers announcing the event.

Take the Capital Beltway to I-95 north and exit at Route 216 (to Laurel). At the second traffic light, turn left onto Main Street and make another left on Avondale Street. Parking is available at the end of the road. Open dawn to dusk daily. 301/725-7800; www.laurel.md.us/riverfrontmap.htm.

## ❹ Granville Gude Park

🐾🐾 (See the Prince George's County map on page 262)

Smack-dab in shopping mall central, a dog walk around Laurel Lake might not be a bucolic experience, but it's not a bad doggy detour either. Denali couldn't complain about her nearly one-mile loop around the modest lake, and she didn't mind that the 29-acre park's scenic views included the Burlington Coat Factory. Like usual, she scanned for wildlife on our walk, excitedly spying squirrels and ducks and a jittery dachshund. What Denali didn't find was Canada geese, thanks to a novel, fur-forward approach to wildlife management that has helped to scare away the messy birds. The city of Laurel hires the Geese Police, a team of working Border collies whose intense stare prompts the birds into fearful flight. Apparently the breed can give birds quite "the eye," a look frightfully similar to the predatory stare of wolves or coyotes. As a result, you can lay out a blanket at Granville Gude Park's Movies in the Park or summer concerts with less likelihood of squashing into geese muck. Open dawn to dusk daily. 8300 Mulberry St.; 301/725-5300 ext. 317; www.laurel.md.us/gude.htm.

## ❺ Maryland City Park

🐾🐾🐕 (See the Prince George's County map on page 262)

This public off-leash park strays into Anne Arundel County but is technically still in the city of Laurel so we threw it into the chapter for good measure. After seeing all the gravel and cinder dog runs in other counties, it's refreshing to find a few adorned with grass out in the northeastern reaches of the Capital Region Maryland 'burbs.

The off-leash area at Maryland City Park is divvied up into two fenced spaces, one for big galumphs and another for daintier breeds. A water fountain is available, but only on the big dog side (and even there, the fountain is actually located outside the park fence but has been jury-rigged to pipe water into a dog bowl inside the dog run). As is often the case, the grass is patchier on the big-dog side—no doubt a result of rougher roughhousing. Keep an eye on the action from one of several aluminum benches spaced throughout both sides of the double-gated dog park, and remember to bring your own poop bags. From the Baltimore-Washington Parkway (Route 295), exit at Laurel-Bowie Road (Route 197) north. Turn right at Brock Bridge Road; the park will be on your right. The off-leash area is located north of the baseball diamonds. 565 Brock Bridge Rd.; 410/222-7313; www.aacounty.org/recparks/parks/dogparks.

## 🐾 Montpelier Mansion and Park

🐾🐾 (See the Prince George's County map on page 262)

Technically speaking, Montpelier Park is the group of soccer fields on the east side of Laurel-Bowie Road. It's a decent place to walk your dog, but if you're not there to drop your kids off at soccer practice, why not bop across the street and sniff out a bit of history instead? The stately 18th-century Montpelier Mansion sits on 70 acres of handsome parkland. (Though Denali thought it a shame to have to explore such an expansive grassy estate on a leash.) The fancy Georgian mansion originally belonged to Major Thomas Snowden and his genteel wife Anne, whose dogged hospitality welcomed such famous visitors as Abigail Adams and George Washington, who stayed several times en route to the Constitutional Convention in 1787.

From the Baltimore-Washington Parkway (Route 295), exit at Laurel-Bowie Road (Route 197) north. Drive 0.25 mile and turn left on Muirkirk Road. Take the first right into the Montpelier Mansion Grounds. 9650 Muirkirk Rd.; 301/377-7817; www.pgparks.com/places/eleganthistoric/montpelier_intro.html.

### PLACES TO EAT

**Einstein Bagels:** For $0.99, your pup can score her own doggy bagel, which Denali considers a brilliant idea from Einstein Bagels. Continuing in the dog theme, try ordering a "bagel dog," a 100 percent beef frank wrapped in a plain or Asiago bagel to go. 14402 Baltimore Ave.; 301/317-0058; www.einsteinbros.com.

**Main Street Sports Grill:** This relaxed sports bar has a handful of dog-friendly tables right on Laurel's Main Street, as well as happy hour specials every night of the week. Every Tuesday, Wednesday, and Thursday the drinks are really cheap: $1 beers 6–8 P.M. 531 Main St.; 301/490-9200.

## THINK GLOBALLY, BARK LOCALLY

Raise your awareness of **Black Dog Syndrome:** Shelter volunteers know that black dogs tend to be the last adopted, if at all. Theories on this phenomenon range from the practical (black dogs might not stand out in a poorly lit dog run) to the social (that perhaps racial prejudices play out, unconsciously, even in dog adoption). Some shelters have gone to great lengths to showcase their dark-colored mutts, even waiving adoption fees. Local photographer Pamela Black Townsend, who has owned black dogs for nearly two decades, has published *Black Is Beautiful: A Celebration of Dark Dogs* to champion the cause of these black beauties. Book proceeds benefit the SPCA of Prince George's County. www.pgspca.org.

### PLACES TO STAY

**Motel 6 Washington DC NE—Laurel:** Small dogs can check into this no-fuss motel for no additional charge. Wireless Internet is available in all rooms for a nominal fee. It's located very close to the Laurel Park horse-racing track and a short drive away from the Maryland City Dog Park. Call for rates. 3510 Old Annapolis Rd.; 301/497-1544; www.motel6.com.

# Adelphi

## PARKS, BEACHES, AND RECREATION AREAS

### 7 Adelphi Manor Park

🐾🐾 (See the Prince George's County map on page 262)

Denali, a champion bug hunter, thought the cricket field would be something very different. Once she swallowed her initial disappointment, she thought Adelphi Manor was a decent place for doggies. (It's especially important to clean up after your dog here—you wouldn't want to ruin anyone's cricket match.) This wide grass field is hemmed in on two sides by marshy meadow and mature trees along the slowly flowing Northwest Branch. The seven-mile paved Northwest Branch Trail also passes through the park en route to Montgomery County, so we took a quick walk north, noticing a lot of graffiti-tagged tree trunks along the way. But if you press on at least a half mile, you'll find the rustic, stone-and-mortar Adelphi Mill, circa 1796, the oldest and largest mill in the Washington area. To the south, the Northwest Branch Trail crosses busy University Boulevard and continues into Manor Lane Park, a larger recreational facility, water park, and picnic area. Denali preferred Adelphi Manor Park since she had it all to herself.

Adelphi Manor Park is located north of University Boulevard (Route 193) on West Park Road in Adelphi west of the University of Maryland. 7601 West Park Dr.; 301/699-2255; www.pgparks.com.

# Berwyn Heights

## PARKS, BEACHES, AND RECREATION AREAS

### 8 Lake Artemesia Natural Area

😊😊😊 (See the Prince George's County map on page 262)

Horseshoe-shaped Lake Artemesia is a hidden haven of weeping willows and gazebos circled by a wide, paved 1.35-mile trail. We say hidden because it's about the last thing you expect as you drive on a side road past the junkyards and *The Washington Post* warehouse to reach the parking lot, but Denali considered it a pleasant surprise. This strange juxtaposition has something to do with Lake Artemesia's history. The 38-acre lake came to be during construction of the Metro railway that runs adjacent to the park. The Washington Metropolitan Area Transportation Authority cut a deal: In order to construct a platform for the Green Line, construction workers could dig up dirt and gravel and, in return, would turn the hole in the ground into Lake Artemesia and develop the natural recreation area. A local resident, Ms. Artemesia N. Drefs, donated 10 lots (and her name) to the park's creation.

Lake Artemesia is stocked with trout and is popular with both anglers and birders, so bring your fishing pole and binoculars if your pooch is compatible with either activity. A yellow Labrador and coonhound happily lazed in the sunshine on a pier while their owner cast a line into the pond as we looped around the lake.

From the Capital Beltway, take exit 23 (Kenilworth Avenue) toward Bladensburg. Make a right onto Greenbelt Road (Route 193). Make a right onto Branchville Road (this road turns into 55th Avenue). The parking lot is on the left at the Berwyn Road intersection. Open 5 A.M.–11 P.M. 301/927-2163; www.pgparks.com/places/nature/artemesia.html.

## PLACES TO EAT

**Chipotle:** If you're hungry, swing by Chipotle for a tasty cilantro-lime burrito big enough to be mistaken for an aluminum foil-wrapped brick. Denali was pleased to learn Chipotle cooks with natural, humanely raised, and vegetarian-fed meats free of antibiotics and added growth hormones. There are a handful of outside tables where you can dine with your dog. Or bring your burrito to nearby Lake Artemesia or Buddy Attick Park for an impromptu picnic. 5506 Cherrywood Ln.; 301/982-6722; www.chipotle.com.

# College Park

While the University of Maryland is best known for turtles, Denali was more excited to meet a famously green amphibian on the College Park campus. Outside the Stamp Student Union on Campus Drive, Kermit the Frog sits in perpetual conversation with his maker, the late, great Muppets creator Jim Henson, a UM alumnus. A wave of nostalgia might just call you to join them on the bench. While the city of College Park is painted by the UM student body of 25,000 undergrads and nearly 10,000 graduate students, the community is also deeply rooted in American aviation history, as underscored by the College Park Aviation Museum. While walking the dog or dining on the back patio of the 94th Aero Squadron Restaurant, take a peek at the College Park Airport, which dates way back to the Wright Brothers.

## PARKS, BEACHES, AND RECREATION AREAS

### 🔟 College Park Dog Park

🐾🐾🐾🐕 (See the Prince George's County map on page 262)

Located on the edge of the University of Maryland campus inside Acredale Park, College Park Dog Park is a green, grassy, private affair. A large cable-and-combination lock cordons off the double-gated entrance to deter any would-be freeloaders enticed by the plush-between-the-dewclaws grass in this off-leash area. The dog park is open to all residents of Prince George's and Montgomery Counties for an annual registration fee of $40 per year for the first dog and $30 for other dogs in the same household, but you do have to register first. Strikingly, the park was completely empty on a pleasant Friday afternoon, leading us to wonder if the lock was a little too effective. Then we noticed plastic lawn chairs arranged in a convivial circle in one corner of the fenced park, so clearly at some point it's a social venue for dogs and their humans.

Park amenities include a doggy drinking fountain in Acredale Park near the parking lot for the dog park (shut off during the fall and winter), and plenty of Mutt Mitts for canine cleanups. The rest of Acredale Park is just as grassy with acres of soccer fields set back from busy University Boulevard. Open dawn to dusk. From University Boulevard (Route 193) eastbound, turn right on Metzerott Road. The dog park is on the right, beyond the equestrian ring. www.cpdogpark.org.

### 🔟 College Park Community Center

🐾🐾 (See the Prince George's County map on page 262)

In early autumn, we parked at the College Park Community Center and took a walk along the **Paint Branch Trail**. The hiker-biker trail passes through College Park, both the town and the campus, starting at Lake Artemesia and running north to Cherry Hill Road. The occasional student jogged or rode past as we surveyed the fall scenery. Changing leaves lent a picturesque double-entendre to the paved footpath, which is actually named for the stream it follows, a tributary of the Northeast Branch that drains into the Anacostia. At Lakeland Community Park, the next park south along the trail, we waved to a woman and her schnauzer who (albeit illegally) played a nice game of fetch inside the tennis courts. 5051 Pierce Ave.; 301/441-2647; www.pgparks.com/ places/commctr.html.

## 11 Calvert Road Park

 (See the Prince George's County map on page 262)

Frisbee golf is the main attraction at Calvert Road Park, a sport Denali does not feign to understand: Why throw a disc if it's not for her? It's one of the oldest disc golf courses in the area, dating back to the 1980s, and a well-manicured space with numerous trees growing tall across the pancake-flat parkland. Not wanting to interrupt any games, we walked a wide loop around the perimeter of the 18-hole course and promptly decided this really isn't a park for dogs. Across the street there is a grassy area with views of the College Park Airport and a couple tennis courts where at least you don't have to duck flying plastic putters.

From the Capital Beltway, take exit 23 to Kenilworth Avenue (Route 201) south. Proceed southbound approximately two miles to the second stoplight. Turn right on Paint Branch Parkway, and then take the first right onto Old Calvert Road. 5202 Calvert Rd.; 301/445-4500.

### PLACES TO EAT

**94th Aero Squadron Restaurant:** Established in 1909, the College Park Airport is the oldest continuously operating airport in the world, harkening back to Wilbur Wright's days of teaching the first American military pilots how to fly. Arguably the best way to soak in this aeronautical legacy is from the back terrace of the 94th Aero Squadron Restaurant, which overlooks the historic runway. The restaurant's exterior resembles a crumbling, war-distressed French farmhouse with WWII-replica aircraft lining the front entrance—a sight that would surely excite Snoopy's famous alter ego, the Flying Ace. Inside, more WWI and WWII artifacts and Big Band music contribute to the charming anachronism.

For a little extra romance (puppy love, anyone?), arrive between 7:30 and 8 P.M., when the twinkling lights strung above the patio are lit. You can request the fire pit or outdoor fireplace be lit, too. While in a post-9/11 world you're perhaps more likely to see deer on the runway than airplanes due to changes in flight pattern regulations, it's still an atmospheric setting to make even Lady and the Tramp swoon. Dogs may join diners on the terrace as long as they are on their best behavior (pups disrupting other patrons have been asked to leave before). The best dish on the menu? "The lobster," said the hostess without hesitation, perhaps a clue that this dining experience is best enjoyed immediately after payday. For diners on a freelance writer's salary, try the famous beer cheese soup instead. Open for lunch, dinner, and Sunday brunch. 5240 Paint Branch Pkwy.; 301/699-9400; www.the94thaerosquadron.com/collegepark/index.html.

**Pizza Boli's:** When in College Park, eat like a college student. Order up pepperoni pizza to go. 8147-G Baltimore Ave.; 301/474-1313; www.pizzabolis.com.

**Rita's:** One black cherry gelati + one vanilla custard doggy cone = sugar coma for the both of us. Denali vouches it was worth it. The left-hand turn into the parking lot of this Rita's location can be sketchy when approaching from the south, so be careful. The College Park Dog Park is right around the corner from here (down steep, steep Metzger Drive). 8900 Baltimore Ave.; 301/345-5455; www.ritascollegepark.com.

### PLACES TO STAY

**Cherry Hill Park Campground:** This 400-campsite complex has quite the setup, with two outdoor pools, hot tub and sauna, a café, playgrounds, and free wireless Internet, among other amenities. Dogs are welcome to stay at the campground, and a dog-walking service is even available. The RV hookups include electric (20-, 30-, and 50-amp), cable TV, water, and sewer, and the maximum stay for tents is seven days. Rates range $42–65. 9800 Cherry Hill Rd.; 301/937-7116; www.cherryhillpark.com.

# Greenbelt

The city of Greenbelt dates squarely from the Great Depression, at a time when millions were homeless, out of work, and, yes, Denali, too broke to buy dog food. Planned in 1935 and constructed by 1937, FDR's New Deal–era city was intended to provide affordable housing and a cooperative social model. It was, in many ways, a prototype for today's large-scale planned communities. A greenbelt of forest land really does surround Greenbelt, and city planners clumped the community's housing into "superblocks" linked by footpaths. As a result, it's still a tremendously walkable (read: dog walkable) city in the historic center.

### PARKS, BEACHES, AND RECREATION AREAS

### 12 Buddy Attick Park

🐾🐾🐾🐾 (See the Prince George's County map on page 262)

If heaven is where the squirrels are slow and Canada geese are never far away, then Denali thinks the pearly gates must lead to Buddy Attick Park. The first—

## DOG-EAR YOUR CALENDAR

**Greenbelt Labor Day Parade:** Support the SPCA/Humane Society of Prince George's County with the Black Dog Brigade, to highlight the beauty of these darker darlings and their plight as the typically last adopted. Greenbelt's Labor Day Parade has marched annually for more than half a century! Early September; Crescent Road near Buddy Attick Park; www.greenbelt.com/laborday.

**Greenbelt Annual Pooch Plunge:** Enjoy the one day when it's OK to jump in the human pool. Late September; Greenbelt Aquatic and Fitness Center, 101 Centerway; 301/397-2204; www.greenbeltmd.gov/recreational_facilities/aquatic_fitness.htm.

**Doggie Dive-In:** Another opportunity to swim with the big dogs. First weekend in October; Ellen E. Linson Swimming Pool; 5211 Paint Branch Pkwy., College Park; 301/277-3719; www.pgparks.com/places/sportsfac/swim.html.

**Blessing of the Animals:** Receive a special prayer for your pup. Close to October 4; St. George's Episcopal Church; 7010 Glenn Dale Rd., Glenn Dale; 301/262-3285; www.stgeo.org.

and as yet only—squirrel she has ever caught shook its bushy tail at just the wrong time in this picturesque park. I had absentmindedly dropped the leash while tying my shoe, and Denali sprinted after the dazed squirrel—in front of a playground full of 3-year-olds. Weakly, I waved an apology to a Baby Bjorn–outfitted mom after regaining the leash (Denali fortunately dropped her prize at this point, and it dashed out of sight).

After all the initial excitement, Denali set a brisk pace on our jog around 23-acre Greenbelt Lake, which is so naturally lovely we were surprised to learn it's man-made. More than 200 workers labored for a year to carve the reservoir where dense forest once stood.

The popular 1.25-mile cinder trail that circles the lake is a scenic circuit to walk or run your dog. Indeed, Buddy Attick Park was far busier than nearby Greenbelt National Park when we visited. A fresh breeze blew, spinning colorful windsocks and laundry line-drying in lake house backyards. On the west shore a grassy peninsula juts into Greenbelt Lake, a vantage your pup will quite like for watching the ducks and geese paddle by and where you might enjoy a contemplative moment on one of two benches. From the Capital Beltway, take Kenilworth Avenue (Route 201) north and outside the Beltway. Turn right immediately onto Crescent Road. Turn right again into Buddy Attick Park. Open 6 A.M.–11 P.M. 555 Crescent Rd.; 301/397-2200; www.greenbeltmd .gov/recreational_facilities/buddy_attick.htm.

## 13 Greenbelt National Park

🐾🐾🐾 (See the Prince George's County map on page 262)

A wooded island in an urban sea, this more-than-1,100-acre national park has become home to all sorts of wildlife crowded out by the surrounding highways and strip malls. In fact, Denali has never seen so many deer in one place. Everywhere we walked in the park, we found Bambi and his mother and uncles, great aunts, cousins, and second cousins placidly grazing, which, of course, suited Denali just fine.

With nearly 10 miles of walking trails to choose from, we thought it most appropriate to take a spin on the 1.4-mile *Dog*-wood Nature Trail, a comfortably shaded, sand-and-gravel passage through the woods. Another good place for paws is the large, grassy field at the Sweet Gum Picnic Area. If you visit Greenbelt National Park on a Wednesday evening in the summertime, your pup and you can watch aspiring Lance Armstrongs compete in a local cycling race series, which, at three decades old, is the oldest training series race in the nation. The weekly competition starts around 6 P.M. and usually draws a small crowd of families and loyal pups of the peloton. Denali used to come to cheer for her dad but ended up whining too anxiously every time he circled without stopping to pat her. (Or perhaps she was just overly concerned about whether he would bring honor to the Githens house.)

The summer we visited, the park was overrun with not only deer, but ticks and chiggers, too. The pests were so populous the National Park Service alerted visitors to the problem with a big emergency response road sign. Be sure your dog's anti-flea and -tick medication is active if you visit during summer or early fall.

From I-495, take exit 23 to Kenilworth Avenue (Route 201) south toward Bladensburg to Greenbelt Road (Route 193). The park entrance will be on the right-hand side of Greenbelt Road in 0.25 mile, across from the Golden Triangle Office Park. 6565 Greenbelt Rd.; 301/344-3948; www.nps.gov/gree.

## 14 Greenbelt Dog Park

🐾🐾🐕 (See the Prince George's County map on page 262)

Exclusive to Greenbelt residents, the Greenbelt Dog Park is a well-maintained, quarter-acre run that has the distinction of being the very first dog park in the state of Maryland. Two yellow agility tubes and a wealth of tennis balls were on hand when we peered through the chain-link fence. The grassy lot is divided into two parts that can be joined by a sliding gate, although no signs indicated whether half was designated for smaller dogs. The park came about when a developer donated land that was deemed too small a parcel for other uses. Greenbelt residents will need to remember to bring their own water, but the double-gated park had water bowls and a plentiful supply of poop bags. Only two dogs are allowed per handler, and a valid tag permit is required to use the facility (the lifetime registration fee costs $5 per dog; permits can be purchased from the city of Greenbelt).

Open 5 A.M.–11 P.M. daily. From Greenbelt Road (Route 193) eastbound, pass the Baltimore-Washington Parkway and turn right onto Hanover Parkway, which is immediately after the Greenway Park Shopping Center. Then turn right on Hanover Drive; the dog park will be on your left. 301/345-5417; www.geocities.com/greenbeltdogpark.

## 15 Schrom Hills Park

🐾🐾 (See the Prince George's County map on page 262)

This is a clean, nicely landscaped neighborhood park worth spending pawsitive time with your four-legged best friend if you live close by, but perhaps not worth the drive if you don't. A paved exercise trail runs the perimeter of the park, creating an easy place to walk (and to keep your pup's nails short!). Otherwise Schrom Hills Park has a playground, soccer field, and fenced baseball diamond—the regular accoutrements of suburban recreation. Open 6 A.M.–11 P.M. 6915 Hanover Pkwy.; 301/397-2200; www.greenbeltmd.gov/recreational_facilities/schrom_hills.htm.

### PLACES TO STAY

**Greenbelt Campground:** While it's up for debate whether the Greenbelt Campground or the private Cherry Hill Campground in College Park is closest to Washington DC, we venture to say Greenbelt is the cheapest. For $16 per night per site, you and your pup can stay within the Beltway and have access to hot showers and an RV hookup. Open year-round (though your visit is limited to 14 days per year), each of the 174 campsites includes a picnic table and charcoal grill. At least one family had caught on: A whole herd of white-tailed deer nonchalantly nibbled grass between the Winnebagos and Airstreams when we visited.

No credit card payment is available on-site; if you want to pay with a card, you'll need to use the online reservation system at www.recreation.gov.

Located inside Greenbelt National Park. 6565 Greenbelt Rd.; 888/444-6777; www.nps.gov/gree.

**Greenbelt Residence Inn:** Designed for extended stays, clearly this 120-room hotel across the street from Greenbelt National Park has been doing something right. One guest has been staying here for more than two years! Dogs of any size can check in for a one-time $100 fee, and owners will be given a door magnet to alert housekeeping to the canine occupant (your dog must be crated or you must be in the room, or housekeeping won't enter). In addition to complimentary breakfast, the hotel serves complimentary dinner Monday through Thursday. Free on-site parking. Rates range $150–269. 6320 Golden Triangle Dr.; 301/982-1600; www.marriott.com/hotels/travel/ wasgl-residence-inn-greenbelt.

# Bladensburg

## PARKS, BEACHES, AND RECREATION AREAS

### 16 Bladensburg Waterfront Park

🐾 (See the Prince George's County map on page 262)

It's hard to believe, looking at the still, murky waters of the Anacostia today, but Bladensburg was once a busy tobacco shipping port before silt slowed operations to a standstill by 1800. Bladensburg Waterfront Park interprets this historical chapter and others relevant to the riverfront, including the crucial defeat of American troops in the War of 1812 (in which, oddly, all the action seems to have unfolded in 1814). The American defeat at the Battle of Bladensburg allowed the British easy access to their march on Washington.

In our visit we didn't see any other dogs—just a few pairs of walkers, a group of students gearing up for an excursion on the water, and some drivers idling in their cars. A rust-colored pedestrian bridge crosses the sleepy Anacostia, so we decided to make like a chicken and check out the other side. On the opposite bank, the paved Anacostia River Trail continues in either direction.

From DC, take New York Avenue east and turn north on Bladensburg Road. Pass the Memorial Peace Cross on your left; you are now on Route 450. Take your first right into Bladensburg Waterfront Park. Open 7 A.M.–sunset daily. 4601 Annapolis Rd.; 301/779-0371; www.pgparks.com/places/nature/ bladensburg.html.

# Bowie

Like regular out-of-towners, we totally blew our cover. It turns out Bowie's proper pronunciation is not "Bow-wow-ie," as Denali suggested, nor "Bowwee," but "Boooey." One resident reminded helpfully, "Like the knife." Roger that.

## DOG-EAR YOUR CALENDAR

**Bark in the Park:** For any dog who has ever howled, "Take Me Out to the Ball Game," finally, now you can, with the minor league Bowie Baysox, a Double-A farm team for the Baltimore Orioles. The dog-friendly baseball games usually take place twice in the spring. Tickets cost $9–15 per person; dogs are free (but call ahead to register). Prince George's Stadium, 4101 Northeast Crain Hwy.; 301/464-4880; www.baysox.com.

## PARKS, BEACHES, AND RECREATION AREAS

### 17 Sandy Hill Neighborhood Park

 (See the Prince George's County map on page 262)

This sign caused us to raise an eyebrow: Sandy Hill—Creative Disposal Project. You see, the Sandy Hill Neighborhood Park is situated at the foot of a large grassy hill—the now-closed Sandy Hill Landfill. The landfill ceased operations in 2000, and the Maryland Department of the Environment assures everyone its perfectly safe—in fact, methane gases from the burping trash mountain help to power the NASA Goddard Space Flight Center in Greenbelt, Maryland—however, that didn't stop us from briefly channeling Erin Brockovich.

But we took a deep breath, and discovered a pleasant, out-of-the-way soccer park. Honestly, you would have no idea the park borders a former disposal site, unless your dog's nose detects scents we humans cannot. When we visited, a gentleman was chipping golf balls for his black German shepherd mix, who gleefully retrieved them. Before our entrance, they had the park to themselves. Remember to bring your own drinking water; besides the parking lot, a portable toilet is the only facility on-site. Located north of Old Town Bowie and near Bowie University on Laurel-Bowie Road. 301/445-4500.

### 18 Whitemarsh Park

(See the Prince George's County map on page 262)

Whitemarsh Park reminds Denali of everyone's favorite 1980s hairdo, the mullet: business up front, and party in the back. Lighted ball fields and picnic pavilions greet you near the entrance to the 182-acre multiuse park, all of which are well groomed and professionally maintained—and somewhat boring to a doggy on the roam. Accordingly, we pressed onward to the far side of park, where a series of nature trails depart near the Bowie Playhouse. Totaling about three miles in length, these trails are wide, wood-chipped, and well shaded by the surrounding tangle of climbing vines and hardwood forest. Drinking fountains can be found back near the athletic fields, but bring a dog bowl.

Take Route 50 east toward Annapolis and exit at Crain Highway (Route 3) north. Make a U-turn at Annapolis Road (Route 450) and backtrack south on Crain Highway to the park entrance. 100 Whitemarsh Park Dr.; 301/262-6200, ext. 3011; www.cityofbowie.org/parks/parkfacilities.asp.

### 19 Foxhill Park

 (See the Prince George's County map on page 262)

At first glance, 45-acre Foxhill Park looked like a hound-dog disappointment: Just another amalgamation of baseball fields and playground equipment where your dog must tiptoe around Little Leaguers and kindergartners to keep the peace with parents. But a playground mom reached out to us and directed us toward Woodward Pond, just down the hill. In fact, Denali received so many compliments and catcalls from kids on the jungle gym that she has rarely trotted taller. (Apparently no one had ever seen a Germatian before. Imagine that.)

The lily pond is quaint and cute, a pocket of countryside charm sized for a Pekingese. A cinder trail, half a mile at the longest, rounds the pond and crosses a handsome, old stone footbridge at the far side. We shared the path with a lady walking circuits and two boys fishing with such noisy zeal you can be sure all trout within earshot had fled the premises. To get to the pond from the parking lot, follow the paved bike path, which we initially mistook for a frontage road near Collington Road, downhill to the right. In addition to the partially shady, partially sunny loop around the lily pond, more walking paths wend in the upland forest behind the baseball fields and the neighboring middle school. Bring water and poop bags. From the Capital Beltway in Maryland, take Route 50 east. After 6.5 miles, exit onto Laurel Bowie Road (Route 197) headed north. After 0.6 miles, turn right into Foxhill Park. 301/218-7600; www.pgparks.com.

### 20 City of Bowie Dog Park

😺😺😺🐾 (See the Prince George's County map on page 262)

No dog park we visited in the entire DC metro region smelled fresher than this one. The trick? Cedar chips. The city of Bowie had recently raked a dump truck's worth across the one-acre fenced lot, which effectively counteracted the usual mutt musk. "And it makes it easier to clean up after your dog," noted a regular. Perhaps reason Number Two why the park smelled better than most.

Otherwise it's business as usual as far as off-leash areas go. The Bowie Dog Park is a long rectangle with a double-gated entrance, benches, and poop bags at your service. Chihuahuas and other smaller breeds will be pleased to learn there is a separate fenced area exclusive to them. Another pro for the park: it receives a lot of sunshine, which means it dries quickly after a rain. On the con side: it can be hot in summer and there is no water source at the park, so be sure to bring your own. Open 8 A.M.–dusk daily, although the animal control warden opens and closes the park each day, so it's closed on city of Bowie–observed holidays. Located on Northview Drive at Enfield Drive. 3600 Northview Dr.; 301/262-6200, ext. 3011; www.cityofbowie.org/parks/parkfacilities.asp.

## 21 Allen Pond Park

🐾🐾🐾 (See the Prince George's County map on page 262)

Lace up your walking shoes and grab the leash for a loop around 10-acre Allen Pond, in many respects the recreational center of Bowie. The multiuse park has something for everyone: an indoor ice-skating rink, six lit ball fields, playgrounds, a basketball court, and most recently a fancy-pants skateboard park for tiny Tony Hawks-in-training. Bowie Bowsers inevitably congregate near the waterfowl and paddleboats that bob in the stocked pond. While circling the one-mile paved trail, Denali spied a heron fishing. In the summertime, free concerts kick off in the park at 7 P.M. on Sunday. Dog-relevant park amenities include Mutt Mitts and drinking fountains (bring a bowl). 3330 Northview Dr.; 301/262-6200, ext. 3011; www.cityofbowie.org/parks/parkfacilities.asp.

### PLACES TO STAY

**TownePlace Suites Bowie Town Center:** For a $100 deposit, your pet can join you at this 119-room hotel, be it a Saint Bernard or a parakeet. The front desk usually keeps dog treats on hand, and there are cleanup-bag stations positioned on the hotel grounds. Designed for extended stays, each suite includes a full kitchen, high-speed Internet, and the ability to do small but important tasks like personalize your voicemail. Arguably the best feature of this hotel is its location within walking distance of the City of Bowie Dog Park and Allen Pond Park, as well as the numerous ready-to-go restaurants in Bowie Town Center, in case you don't feel like cooking. Rooms range $149–209; the price drops the longer

you stay. Free on-site parking. 3700 Town Center Blvd.; 301/262-8045; www.marriott.com/hotels/travel/bwibm-towneplace-suites-bowie-town-center.

# District Heights

## PARKS, BEACHES, AND RECREATION AREAS

### 22 Walker Mill Regional Park

🐾🐾 (See the Prince George's County map on page 262)

Larger than it first looks, 470-acre Walker Mill Regional Park has all the sport facilities a jock would hope to find: baseball, soccer, softball, tennis, basketball. Not being much of a ball player, Denali preferred the paved trail that cuts a narrow channel through a greenbelt running through the park.

Heading back to the car, we passed a church picnic in full swing. And slowly something processed… Church means Sunday, and Sunday means football, and football means the Washington Redskins at FedEx Field in nearby Landover. Though we tried to zip away before the game ended, our ill-timed departure landed us directly in the mass exodus from FedEx Field. If you get caught in a similar bind, pray the Redskins won so at least drivers will be in a good mood.

From the Capital Beltway, take exit 15B west to Ritchie Road. Make a left onto Ritchie Road and then a right onto Walker Mill Road. The park will be on the left. 8840 Walker Mill Rd.; 301/699-2255; www.pgparks.com/places/parks/walker.html.

# Upper Marlboro

The Prince George's county seat belongs to the incorporated town of Upper Marlboro, a jurisdiction only 0.4 square miles in size and fewer than 1,000 people, but most folks refer to greater Upper Marlboro, a much larger and more populous area. Even so, less than 10 miles east of the Capital Beltway, Upper Marlboro still manages to take on more rural feel. Denali appreciated the trip east for the abundance of large parks we found.

## PARKS, BEACHES, AND RECREATION AREAS

### 23 Watkins Regional Park

🐾🐾🐾 (See the Prince George's County map on page 262)

With a miniature train, putt-putt golf course, petting zoo, antique merry-go-round, and the largest nature center in the DC metro area, Watkins Regional Park will likely impress your two-legged li'l ones more than the furry ones on all fours. But that's not to say your dog won't have fun here, too. This regional park spans more than 850 acres, interlaced with six miles of paved and dirt trails to tucker out even a terrier. The 2.9-mile Spicebush Trail, for example,

## DOG-EAR YOUR CALENDAR

Denali always loves a car ride. Combine that with Christmas cheer, hot cider in a travel thermos, and Watkins Regional Park's **Winter Festival of Lights,** and you have a winning holiday excursion for the whole family. The animated light displays are sure to charm (and they explain the metal arches that line the park roads). Open 5–9:30 P.M. nightly Nov. 23–Jan. 1. $5 per car or van; free on Christmas Day. 301 Watkins Park Dr., Upper Marlboro; 301/699-2456.

carves a circle around the park that starts from the nature center. Deciduous forest provides ample shade, while the fairly flat terrain means you can carry on a conversation with Fido without needing to worry about your next step.

From the Capital Beltway (I-495), take exit 15A to Central Avenue (Route 214) east. Continue for approximately three miles. Turn right onto Watkins Park Drive (Route 193) and follow the park signs to the facility. 301 Watkins Park Dr.; 301/218-6700; www.pgparks.com/places/parks/watkins.html.

## 24 Rosaryville State Park
🐾🐾 (See the Prince George's County map on page 262)

"Very underutilized" is how a ranger who lives nearby and enjoys walking her dogs here describes this 982-acre day-use park. That might explain the romantic rendezvous Denali and I stumbled across on our visit—that was awkward. Apparently the ranger isn't the only one who views the park as a place where few people frequent. Besides the amorous couple, we also met a few mountain bikers packing up for the day and workers prepping for an equestrian competition, which essentially sums up the other primary park users.

Your dog will be pleased to explore the more than eight miles of woodland trails in Rosaryville State Park, including a paved path that leads to the historic Mount Airy Mansion. The mansion suffered serious fires in 1752 and 1931, so little of the original 18th-century building remains intact, but it's still a beautiful building where weddings often take place. There is also a large pond near Rosaryville Road worth checking for ducks.

Open daily sunrise to sunset. There is a $3 per vehicle charge; out-of-state residents pay $1 extra. Located just south of Osborne Road from southbound South Crain Highway (US-301). 8101 South Crain Hwy.; 301/888-1410 or 800/784-5380; www.dnr.state.md.us/publiclands/southern/rosaryville.html.

## 25 Patuxent River State Park and Jug Bay Natural Area
🐾🐾🐾 (See the Prince George's County map on page 262)

The 110-mile Patuxent River is the longest river located entirely within the state of Maryland, and a body of water deemed critically important to the health of the Chesapeake Bay. As a result, you'll find conservation has a paw up on recreation in the park (though not to say the two can't coexist). Views of the preserved marshland are stunning enough to send a bird dog into Elmer Fudd stutters. Denali, for her part, perked up considerably. After hiking a small portion of the more than eight miles of woodland trails, we concluded the best views of Jug Bay must be seen by boat. Unfortunately, the handful of canoes and kayaks for rent at the park are off-limits for Clifford ("You want to what?"), but if you have your own small watercraft, this is a field trip worth taking. Hiking trails in the park are color-coded; you can pick up a trail map at the visitors center (follow signs to the Jug Bay Natural Area).

Another route for you and your leashed canine companion is a walk along the Chesapeake Bay Critical Area Tour. This mostly paved circuit is open to cars on Sunday, but only to pedestrian and bicycle traffic the rest of the week. Although the entire tour comprises four miles, dogs are not permitted in the Merkle Wildlife Sanctuary in the lower section of the tour.

Open 8 A.M.–sunset. From the Capital Beltway, take exit 11A to Pennsylvania Avenue (Route 4) and proceed east for eight miles. Take Route 301 south for 1.7 miles. Turn left on Croom Station Road and continue for 1.6 miles. Turn left on Croom Road (Route 382) and proceed for 1.5 miles. Turn left on Croom Airport Road and continue for two miles to the park entrance. 16000 Croom Airport Rd.; 301/627-6074; www.pgparks.com/places/parks/patuxent.html.

# Camp Springs

## PLACES TO STAY

**Motel 6 Washington DC SE—Camp Springs:** Visiting Andrews Air Force Base with pooch in tow? Well, you can't get much closer to base than this Motel 6. The budget hotel permits small dogs. Rates range $50–59. 5701 Allentown Rd.; 301/702-1061; www.motel6.com.

# Fort Washington

## PARKS, BEACHES, AND RECREATION AREAS

### 26 National Harbor

😊 🐾 (See the Prince George's County map on page 262)

After weeks of gazing at then-spanking-new, 300-acre National Harbor from Alexandria's riverbanks, Denali eagerly took the trek across the Woodrow Wilson Bridge, ready to size up its dog-friendliest spots. Would the center-stage Gaylord National Resort and Convention Center, with its sky-high atrium, admit a stylish Snoopy? Nope, no dogs allowed. Would the oversized sandbox where *The Awakening* statue had resettled be as wag-worthy as the waking giant's previous abode at the tip of Hains Point? No Pets on Beach, say two signs. Harborfront McCormick & Schmick's flat-out said no to dogs on the patio. Even the water taxi that shuttles passengers across the Potomac back to furrtastic Old Town said no paws on board.

Perhaps once the varnish wears off, National Harbor will become a port for pups, too. Until then, your dog's best bet is the pathway of crushed, white shells on the riverfront, a quick ice cream cone at Ben & Jerry's, and a sniff around Jake's at National Harbor (a Life is Good store).

From Washington DC, take I-295 south for approximately 5.5 miles to exit 1B. From the Capital Beltway, take exit 2A on the Maryland side of the Woodrow Wilson Bridge. 137 National Plaza; 877/628-5427; www.nationalharbor.com.

## 27 Fort Foote

🐾🐾 🐾➤ (See the Prince George's County map on page 262)

Today tucked incongruously into a suburban Maryland neighborhood, Fort Foote was the largest and southernmost bastion in the 86-fort ring to defend the Federal City during the Civil War. Built on 100-foot bluffs abutting the Potomac, the Union camp affords peek-a-boo views of the river in winter through bare tree branches. In summer, it's an overgrown tangle of vines. During her visit, Denali was keen on the butterflies fluttering above the milkweed blossoms that sprouted from the crumbling fort's remains. Fort Foote's military history presents itself in less subtle ways than other Civil War forts around DC, with two Newfoundland-proportioned, charcoal-black war cannons still here.

The park is, in places, a wildly overgrown patch of Civil War history that even hounds disinterested in history can appreciate for its new-old terrain. Remember to bring water and consider wearing decent walking shoes to tromp across the grass and walking trail.

Open dawn to dusk daily. Admission is free. From the Capital Beltway, take exit 3, Indian Head Highway south (Route 210) and drive for approximately 3.5 miles to Old Fort Road. Turn right, go one mile to Fort Foote Rd S., and turn left. Follow the winding road through the residential area to entrance on the left for the fort. Park in the four-car gravel lot. 301/763-4600; www.nps.gov/fofo.

## 28 Fort Washington

🐾🐾🐾🐾➤ (See the Prince George's County map on page 262)

The National Harbor notwithstanding, Fort Washington remains the most imposing structure on the Maryland side of the Potomac. Though Fort Washington (or more accurately, its predecessor Fort Warburton) was meant to be a guard dog against attacks by sea, during the War of 1812 those cheeky Brits approached by the Patuxent River instead and, after a short overland hike, set fire to Washington. Facing certain defeat as British warships neared, American troops destroyed the original fort; the beefed-up Fort Washington as we see it today was not constructed until 1824.

Dogs are not allowed inside the historic fort itself, but Denali assures you it doesn't matter. She was content to cast a glance into the stronghold, eye the height of the imposing walls, and then set out exploring the park's expansive grounds. The real gem is lower on the hill. On a muggy day, we headed downhill in hopes of finding shade near the river. What a treat! The River Trail, a flat, shaded dirt path, curves along the Potomac to the left of a small, white clapboard lighthouse. It's a somewhat murky spot for a doggy swim, with "seaweed" and algae growing close to the riverbanks, but we had it all to ourselves. Follow signs for the lighthouse when you enter the park, or head to the historic fort first, and then walk downhill to check it out.

Open dawn to dusk daily. Admission costs $5 per vehicle or $3 per individual. No credit cards. From the Capital Beltway, take exit 3 to Indian Head Highway (Route 210) south. Turn right onto Fort Washington Road to the park. 13551 Fort Washington Rd.; 301/763-4600; www.nps.gov/fowa.

## 29 Piscataway National Park—National Colonial Farm

🐾🐾🐾 🦴 (See the Prince George's County map on page 262)

If you've ever visited George Washington's Mount Vernon estate, you know the first president had a mighty fine view of Maryland across the Potomac, which thanks to some congressional foresight remains nearly identical today. In 1961, Congress established Piscataway National Park, 5,000 acres that stretch about six miles from Piscataway Creek to Marshall Hall, as an easement to preserve the bucolic view from President Washington's back porch.

Inside this wooded greenery, an organization called the Accokeek Foundation has carved out the National Colonial Farm, modeled after a colonial-era

middle-class tobacco farm. Because of some *very* free-ranging chickens, dogs are not allowed inside the split-rail fence of the actual colonial farm grounds, but there are still plenty of nature trails and riverfront to keep Buster busy for at least one visit. Denali smelled something tantalizing around the 0.4-mile Persimmon Trail, which circles a pond popular with Canada geese, though the critter wisely never showed its face. Another favorite spot is the fishing pier in view of Mount Vernon, and the oceanlike waves that lap beneath it.

Open dawn to dusk daily. $2 per person. To reach Piscataway National Park from the Capital Beltway, take exit 3A onto Indian Head Highway (Route 210) and drive south for 9.2 miles. After you pass Farmington Road, take a right at the next stoplight onto Livingston Road, by B&J Carryout. Drive one block and turn right on Biddle Road. At the stop sign, turn left on Bryan Point Road and follow it 3.5 miles to the end. 3400 Bryan Point Rd.; 301/283-2113; www.nps .gov/pisc or www.accokeek.org.

## 30 Piscataway National Park—Accokeek Creek

🐾🐾🐾🐾 (See the Prince George's County map on page 262)

Piscataway National Park is in the heart of what was Piscataway Indian territory, the "first people on the Potomac." In 1609, Captain John Smith sailed up the broad river and visited the Piscataway Indian village of Moyaone, the remains of which are located in the park. We unwittingly stumbled across the Piscataway heritage on our visit, a discovery you're welcome to respectfully sniff out, too.

From Bryan Point Road before you reach the National Colonial Farm, turn right at the sign for Accokeek Creek down a gravel road to the parking lot. A paved pathway will lead you and your furry sidekick to a wobbly wooden boardwalk over protected marshland. The walk through reeds and wetland flowers, butterflies and dragonflies, smelled just fishy enough to keep Denali interested, and then suddenly and unexpectedly the boardwalk ushers you into a wide, empty meadow.

Well, not quite empty. A curious, low, igloo-shaped structure sits near the water where you first enter the meadow. This is sacred ground and the gravesite of Chief Turkey Tayac, a medicine man and renowned activist. Be sure to keep your pup on a respectfully tight leash if you approach to see the chief's framed photograph.

"You looking for somewhere to walk your dog?" a man asked me. Lo and behold, it was Tayac's son who sat at the picnic table where a small group of people had gathered in preparation for a religious ceremony. In addition to pointing out a dirt Jeep road near the riverfront that he recommended for a dog walk, Tayac's son gestured at the sacred site, inviting us to stay for the ceremony as long as we could "stay cool." The Dalmatian half of Denali is not known for keeping cool, so we opted to keep walking, and it was a marvelous dog walk—river to one side, meadow to the other, grasshoppers to snap at, and sticks to chase. We'll be going back for sure. Open dawn to dusk daily. 3400 Bryan Point Rd.; 301/283-2113; www.nps.gov/pisc.

## PLACES TO EAT

**B&J Carryout:** The long line of patrons at this red-and-white-striped roadside joint quickly enticed us to pull over. Hungry diners cue up to order greasy fries, sloppy Dixie barbecue sandwiches, and one mean BLT. An interpretative guide at the National Colonial Farm said the egg sandwiches are basically the breakfast of champions. "BJ's has been there forever," she added. You can sit with your pooch at one of the few picnic tables near the busy highway, or do as the sign says and order carryout. 15805 Livingston Rd., Accokeek; 301/292-5631.

**CakeLove:** Grab a New German Chocolate cupcake for a nibble so you have a good excuse not to share. (Sorry, Denali, but you know chocolate isn't good for you.) That's not really in the spirit of CakeLove, is it? 160 National Plaza; 301/686-0340; www.cakelove.com.

**Foster's Downeast Clambake:** A Maine tradition has migrated south to a beachside tent at the National Harbor; in fact, this is Foster's first location outside Vacationland. The messy menu will leave you stuffed and satisfied: award-winning clam chowder, corn on the cob, roasted red potatoes and onions, Maine steamer clams and cultivated mussels, and the *pièce de résistance,* Maine's famous lobsters shipped straight from the coast. Oh yes, and blueberry crumb cake for dessert. Your lucky dog will probably have a scrap or two passed under the table as you loosen your belt.

Owner Kevin Tacy said his dog is an integral part of his life and business, but he wouldn't let him wander around the dining tent. Accordingly, he requests you and your pup follow the same policy. You're welcome to post up at any of the tables on the edge of the tent and be respectful of other diners. Open to the public at 7 P.M. every Thursday from April through October. Reservations required 48 hours in advance. The restaurant recommends parking in the Fleet Street Garage. 877/404-3255; www.fostersclambakedc.com.

**Hovermale's Tastes Best:** Nothing can set the world right quite like a chocolate-and-vanilla-swirl cone. A Prince George's County institution since 1954, Hovermale's Tastes Best lives up to its name. But don't let the delicious softserve ice cream soften your grip on the leash. The roadside stand is centered on three busy roads, so keep a vice-like hold on your dog's lifeline the whole time or consider enjoying your sweet treat inside the car. 9011 Livingston Rd., Fort Washington; 301/248-2710.

## PLACES TO STAY

**Residence Inn National Harbor:** The good news first: Pets of all sizes can join you at this 162-room, seven-floor hotel. Now for the bad news: Depend-

ing on how long you're staying, you'll nearly be paying for a second room to have your furry best friend cozy up on the king-size bed with you. The pet fee is $200. Not cheap. However, if you plan to stay here for days, or weeks, on end, it could be a worthwhile investment (spending more time with your dog always is, right?). On-site parking is available for $10. Rates range $149–239. 192 Waterfront St.; 301/749-4755; www.marriott.com/wasnh.

**Westin National Harbor:** This 195-room harborfront hotel invites dogs weighing less than 40 pounds to bounce on their own Westin Heavenly Dog Bed. You'll most likely enjoy the human Heavenly Bed equivalent and the Heavenly Bath (Denali is just grateful there is no Heavenly Dog Bath), plus the 24-hour workout facility. There is no additional pet fee, assuming your darling pupster is on her best behavior and doesn't rack up any charges at the mini-bar or give the Westin any reason to make good on the damage waiver you have to sign. Valet parking is available for $30, or pay parking is available in the adjacent Mariners Garage (unfortunately you must pay every time you enter or exit so valet might make more sense). Rates range $159–424. 171 Waterfront St.; 301/567-3999; www.westin.com/nationalharbor.

# Brandywine

## PARKS, BEACHES, AND RECREATION AREAS

### 31 Cedarville State Forest

🐾🐾🐾 (See the Prince George's County map on page 262)

At Cedarville State Forest, the emphasis is on forest. Ninety-five percent of the park is blanketed with evergreens and deciduous trees, so if your dog has an obsessive-compulsive need to mark every tree he meets... this might be a long day trip. Hiking, biking, horseback riding, and, of course, leashed dog walking are permitted on 19 miles of marked trails, which are flatter and smoother than most of the rocky ankle-twisters you'll find in the Mid-Atlantic. Be advised that more than half of the state forest opens to hunting from mid-September through the end of January. If you visit during hunting season, be sure to consult park rangers about where they recommend hiking and dress yourself and your dog in copious amounts of orange clothing—undoubtedly the most important fall fashion statement you'll make. Trail guides are also sold at the office as you enter the park for $3. The state forest includes a dog-friendly family campsite, should you want to extend your visit.

Open sunrise to sunset daily. There is a $3 per vehicle charge; out-of-state residents pay $1 extra. Located about 25 miles south of DC, near the intersection of Route 5 and Route 301. The entrance is located off Cedarville Road accessible from Route 301. 10201 Bee Oak Rd.; 301/888-1410 or 800/784-5380; www.dnr.state.md.us/publiclands/southern/cedarville.html.

**CHAPTER 11**

# Beyond the Beltway

While Washington DC is a capitol place to be a canine, sometimes a dog needs a change of scenery, to go somewhere no one cares about your political stripes—or spots, Denali adds. Sometimes what *Canis familiaris* craves are new and unfamiliar smells, or perhaps an escape from all the Type Alpha personalities. What's fantastic about DC is that its middle-of-the-pack East Coast location makes weekend getaways to Virginia, Maryland, Delaware, and West Virginia enviably easy to embark on. While some popular doggy-licious locales require a husky drive (e.g., Duck and Nags Head in the Outer Banks, North Carolina, or, to a lesser degree, mountain cabins in Frostburg, Maryland, and Berkeley Springs, West Virginia), countless others are within an easy drive of the Capital Beltway. These are the destinations we describe for you in this chapter. With the exception of Assateague Island, all of these getaways are within a two-hour drive of the District. Just point the compass in the direction you want to go.

## PICK OF THE LITTER—BEYOND THE BELTWAY

BEST PLACES TO HIKE
**Catoctin Mountain Park,** Thurmont, Maryland (page 296)
**Shenandoah National Park,** Virginia (page 307)

BEST PLACES TO EAT
**Birches Restaurant,** Baltimore, Maryland (page 294)
**Rams Head Tavern,** Annapolis, Maryland (page 304)

BEST PLACES TO STAY
**Owens Creek Campground,** Catoctin Mountain Park, Thurmont, Maryland (page 301)
**Loews Annapolis Hotel,** Annapolis, Maryland (page 306)

BEST PLACES TO DOG-PADDLE
**Quiet Waters Park,** Annapolis, Maryland (page 303)
**Assateague Island National Seashore,** Maryland (page 310)

BEST PLACE TO SHOP
**Downtown Frederick,** Frederick, Maryland (page 298)

If your pup sniffs the air with wire-coiled anticipation at the hint of salt in the breeze, steer yourselves toward the Atlantic. Due east of the District, Annapolis affords a mariner-inspired mutt vacation, with dockside doggy dining in the historic capital of Maryland and the fur-famous dog beach Quiet Waters nearby. Farther to the south along the coast, the Assateague Island National Seashore protects a stretch of white sand beach untouched by development and famous for its wild ponies. While much of the island is off-limits to Lassie, the segment that is in bounds for dogs is well worth the trek. If your canine companion is a bundle of energy, head west to Shenandoah National Park in Virginia to hike it off, or veer north to Catoctin Mountain Park, not far from Frederick, Maryland. And urban hounds will delight in Baltimore's dog-friendly hospitality. So go ahead, Denali insists, scratch that travel itch behind your ear.

# Baltimore, Maryland

For some District residents and their four-legged compatriots, Baltimore never becomes anything more than the skyline of a gritty port city while driving north on I-895 into the Harbor Tunnel Thruway—and what a shame, especially since it even supports a magazine devoted to dogs called *Baltimore Dog.*

Baltimore fully lives up to its nickname of "Charm City," from paw-friendly Inner Harbor hotels to restaurants that discount the tab if you dine out with Bowser. Even the city's only official off-leash area, Canton Dog Park, strives to accommodate its guests: The park has one fenced area for larger, more rambunctious dogs, and another for smaller ones—the perfect solution for breeds tired of being trampled underfoot.

## PARKS, BEACHES, AND RECREATION AREAS

### Robert E. Lee Park

Baltimore's favorite dog park is neither in the city nor an official dog park. Robert E. Lee Park is paws-down the preferred *tour du jour* for most Baltimore Bowsers. The animal attraction is twofold. For starters, the heavily wooded park has more than 450 acres that envelop Lake Roland and surrounding streams, so on a sweltering summer day your black Labrador can swim and walk through the park, hardly having to leave the tree canopy shade. Add to that Robert E. Lee Park's somewhat overlooked location eight miles and about 15 minutes north of the Inner Harbor, and you have yourself a doggy naturist camp (a.k.a. unsanctioned leashless frolicking). According to John Woestendiek, a former blogger of all things dog for the *Baltimore Sun* (and now on www .ohmidog.com), "Lake Roland is in Baltimore County but owned by the city because it's where much of Baltimore's water used to come from. As a result of the absentee ownership, the park is a tad neglected. But also as a result, [owners] are less likely to get rousted for letting [dogs] off the leash." The Lakeside Park Loop can attract quite a crowd of tail-waggers on weekends; other sections of the park are typically very quiet. Pack a towel for muddy paws if there has been any recent rain.

Robert E. Lee Park is located in Mount Washington. Take I-83 to exit 10A for Northern Parkway. At the first intersection, turn left on Falls Road and then turn right at Lakeside Drive. Park the car and walk over the pedestrian bridge past the dam. 410/396-7931; www.baltimorecity.gov/government/recnparks.

### Patterson Park

It's nicknamed "Baltimore's Best Backyard," a sobriquet endorsed by dogs living in the row homes that border Patterson Park. The 155-acre green space is Baltimore's oldest city park, established in 1827 when the wealthy shipping merchant William Patterson donated the original six acres of land for the creation of a "public walk." Compared to DC's National Mall, Patterson Park will seem less squeaky clean, but it's large and green and great for walking dogs. Denali particularly liked the hillier western half of the park with its tulip poplars, Boat Lake, and historic pagoda.

**DETOURS**

Should you decide to break the bank for Buddy here's a list of where to start your dogcentric shopping spree in Baltimore.

**Dogma:** If the knowledgeable staff, premium food, and self-service dog wash stations don't get you in the door, maybe the **Yappy Hour** held 6–8 P.M. the first Friday of every month will. The Shops at Brewers Hill on Conkling and Boston Streets. 3600 Boston St.; 410/276-3410; www.dogmaforpets.com.

**Lucky Lucy's Canine Café:** Peanut butter crabs, chicken-flavored bones and custom doggie birthday cakes baked on the premises. Located in Federal Hill. 1126 South Charles St.; 410/837-2121; www.luckylucyscaninecafe.com.

**Pretentious Pooch:** Knitwear, ponchos, and prep school outfits for your dog, among other gifts and treats. Say hi to American bulldog Chai. 1017 Cathedral St.; 443/524-7777; www.pretentiouspooch.com.

**Robert McClintock:** View this artist's distinctive hybrid style of digital photography and painting in his Fell's Point gallery. The *Dogs That I Know* series is a Fido favorite. Closed Monday. 1809 Thames St.; 410/814-2800; www.robertmcclintock.com.

In the summer, Patterson Park becomes a hub of outdoor entertainment with free movies and concerts on a regular basis (410/276-3676; www.pattersonpark.com), and in the fall, Baltimore's Barctoberfest kicks off in its best backyard. Patterson Park is bounded by Eastern Avenue, S. Patterson Park Avenue, E. Baltimore Street, and S. Ellwood Avenue (with a wedge notched out of the northeast corner). 410/396-7900; www.baltimorecity.gov/government/recnparks or www.pattersonpark.com.

## Canton Dog Park

Balmer, as locals drawl the pronunciation of Baltimore, struggles with a paucity of paw-cities, too. At the writing of this book, Maryland's largest metropolis had only this one official off-leash dog park. It's not far from the railroad tracks on the east side of town, fenced off from an athletic field just north of Boston Street. But also like DC, plans for more dog parks seem to be moving forward at last. As of 2008, an additional dog park at Latrobe Park in Locust Point (www.locustpointdogpark.org) had received Mayor Sheila Dixon's blessing.

In the meantime, Canton Dog Park is a solid off-leash staple. It opened in 2003 thanks to the efforts of the Friends of Canton Dog Park, a group that is still active with monthly cleanups, dog park meetings, and fundraising for the approximately $2,500 it takes to maintain the park each year. The Canton Dog Park has separate areas for large and small dogs. As is often the case, the small dog side still has patchy grass while the big dog side, worn bare by heavier paws, is entirely pea gravel. Both sides are fully fenced with a few benches—if you can score a seat before lounging doggies do—and a few cherry blossom trees for shade. In addition to poop bags and a water source, the park usually has wet wipes on hand to combat that icky feeling that unfortunately coincides with responsible dog ownership.

Canton Dog Park has a couple of rules you might not see elsewhere, including that dogs must be spayed/neutered by seven months of age, owners may bring a maximum of three dogs into the park, and handlers must be at least 16 years old. Open dawn to dusk, with quiet hours before 9 A.M. and after 7 P.M. Located at the intersection of S. Bouldin and Toone Streets, just north of Boston Street; www.cantondogpark.org.

## Fort McHenry National Historic Monument
🐾🐾🐾🐾

"O say, can you see, by the dawn's early light" the biggest American flag in Baltimore? It's gallantly streaming over star-shaped Fort McHenry, and most certainly merits sniffing out before departing south back to Washington. Fort McHenry was built to protect against British invasion in the Revolutionary War, but the Brits didn't end up invading until the War of 1812. The Americans' brave defense of Fort McHenry during the Battle of Baltimore September 13–14, 1814, inspired Francis Scott Key to pen "The Star-Spangled Banner."

Dogs are not allowed inside the visitors center or the historic fort, but the Fort McHenry grounds are large enough that this posed no problem. Most dogs were hanging in the shade at family picnics facing the Inner Harbor

when we stopped by, but others walked around the point soaking in a nearly 300° view of Navy destroyers and Baltimore's port industry at work. Joggers, sunbathers, and kite flyers completed the crowd of fresh-air seekers. Don't risk an off-leash romp here; rangers will punish your impudence with a $100 ticket. Open 8 A.M.–8 P.M. Memorial Day–Labor Day; 8 A.M.–5 P.M. the rest of the year. Closed Thanksgiving, Christmas, and New Year's Day. 2400 East Fort Ave.; 410/962-4290; www.nps.gov/fomc.

## PLACES TO EAT

**Birches Restaurant:** This Canton favorite has been designated one of 12 exceptional restaurants in the Mid-Atlantic by *Gourmet Magazine,* and we couldn't agree more. Self-described as "New England style cuisine with European flair," Birches serves many delicious wonders, including a backfin crab à la vodka pasta dish and a doozy of a chocolate molten cake that requires 20 minutes' advance notice to prepare. Waiters at the cozy restaurant will bring water out to the outdoor tables for you and your dog. Birches is a bit pricey but not at all pretentious. 641 South Montford Ave.; 410/732-3000; www.birches restaurant.com.

**Pub Dog:** Still known to everyone in Baltimore as the Thirsty Dog Pub, this Federal Hill watering hole had to change its name after an Ohio brewery copyrighted the phrase, but the tasty pizza and house-brewed beers and ales remain the same. Unfortunately, you can no longer bring your dog inside the bar as you once could, so this is strictly for ordering pizza to go. Try the Thai chicken pizza. Open 5 P.M.–2 A.M. daily. 20 E. Cross St.; 410/727-6077; www.pubdog.net.

**Shuckers at Fells Point:** In warm-weather months when the outdoor patio is open, not only can you bring your dog to Shuckers' **Yappy Hour** (5 P.M.–close Wednesday), but you will get 20 percent off the bill! The sports bar serves up tried-and-true crab cakes and burgers, and your dog always gets a water bowl and biscuits. In case there is a wait to be seated, take a walk on Brown's Wharf and the waterfront, all glittery at night. The *Black-Eyed Susan* Steamer, named for the Maryland state flower, is usually docked here, too. 1629 Thames St.; 410/522-5820.

## PLACES TO STAY

**Admiral Fell Inn:** This 80-room, historic, dog-friendly hotel has been called "the cornerstone of Fells Point" by *The Washington Post.* It bears mentioning that Fells Point is best known for antique shops—and drinking, so don't be surprised if it's a bit noisy with nighttime revelers from the nearby bars. Otherwise, it's an ideal location close to all sorts of dog-friendly restaurants and places to walk along the wharf and cobblestone point.

For a $49 pet fee, your pooch will be pampered with a package that includes food and water bowls, treats, plastic toy, plastic mat, and a dog bed sized to fit small to medium breeds. Humans will like this Historic Hotel of America for its 18th-century furnishings, crackling fireplaces, hardwood floors, and maybe even a ghost story or two. There are no weight restrictions for your dog, but typically canine guests are limited to the first floor rooms. Rates range $149–269. 888 S. Broadway St.; 410/522-7377; www.harbormagic.com.

**Residence Inn Baltimore—Downtown/Inner Harbor:** Located two blocks away from the water of Baltimore's Inner Harbor, this 188-room extended-stay hotel serves a complimentary buffet breakfast daily and a social hour Monday–Thursday. Up to two dogs weighing less than 100 pounds may check in for a $100 fee. Human guests will appreciate the fitness center, open 24 hours, and the fully equipped kitchen. Rooms start at $309 (but get cheaper the longer you stay). Valet parking costs $28 per day. 17 Light St.; 410/962-1220; www.marriott.com.

# Frederick and Thurmont, Maryland

Downtown Frederick is in the midst of what can only be described as a doggy renaissance, with dozens of pet-friendly businesses in its well-preserved historic district. Rover-centric retailer Two Paws Up started championing the cause in 2004 by giving free water bowls, treats, and dog-friendly window stickers to participating downtown Frederick merchants. Now it seems the scales have certainly swung in Lassie's favor. One request from the organizers: "We love dogs, we just don't love retractable leashes," said Two Paws Up owner Allison Levitt. Apparently mayhem caused by dogs overextending their leash privileges is risking the fur-friendly headway made so far, so please stick to using old-fashioned flat leashes while in town.

 **DIVERSIONS**

Boots laced, leash secured, but not sure where to go? Try these Catoctin Mountain trails for doggie hikes. For more details, visit www.nps.gov/cato/planyourvisit/hiking-trail-descriptions.htm.

**Blue Blazes Whiskey Still Trail:** Catoctin's moonshinin' history in less than a mile.

**Hog Rock Nature Trail:** Ranger's favorite for a lovely one-mile loop to the highest point to which you can hike in the park, approximately 1,600 feet.

**Thurmont Vista:** A moderate one-mile jaunt to an overlook of town; we suspect the view is better in winter.

**Wolf Rock–Chimney Rock:** A vigorous 3.5-mile hike to two of Catoctin's best-known rock formations. Can be dangerously slippery after rain.

Outside Frederick (Maryland's second-largest city, though you wouldn't know it inside the historic district), the rolling piedmont and countryside are as appealing as they always have been. A short drive north to Thurmont, Maryland, brings you to the entrance of picturesque and surprisingly rugged Catoctin Mountain Park—and the whereabouts of secretive presidential retreat Camp David. Even Flying Dog Brewery of Aspen, Colorado, has moved its main brewing operation to an industrial park in Frederick. With a quick detour on I-270, you can pick up a six-pack of In-Heat Wheat Hefeweizen or Tire Bite Golden Ale (4607 Wedgewood Blvd., Frederick; 301/694-7899; www .flyingdogales.com) for an enjoy-at-home keepsake. We departed our day trip with a different, Denali-approved souvenir proudly displayed on the car bumper: a "My Dog's Diggin' Downtown Frederick" sticker.

## PARKS, RECREATION AREAS, AND BEACHES

### Catoctin Mountain Park
🐾🐾🐾🐾 🐾

Hiking hounds will discover more than 25 miles of trails to stretch all four legs in Catoctin Mountain Park. Denali was surprised by the steep switchbacks that had us huffing and puffing on our way to a lofty overlook at Chimney Rock, until we learned that Catoctin is inside the northernmost reaches of the Blue Ridge Mountains, a range that stretches 500 miles south to Georgia. Hikes departing from higher up on Catoctin Mountain tend to be less steep.

While today 95 percent of Catoctin Mountain Park is covered with forest—a shady reprieve your pup will appreciate—a former park superintendent said, "In 1936, there was barely a tree over the size of a fencepost" after clear-cut logging for the charcoal and tanning industries in the 18th and 19th centuries

## DIVERSION

**And... Action!:** For a modest fee, your Super Dog can leap, tunnel, and dive through a paddock of at least a dozen pieces of agility equipment at **Fido's Friends** in Thurmont, Maryland. Owners Bob and Kathryn Seelye breed vizslas, so they understand high-energy dogs. In addition to the agility course, they offer sheep herding, seasonal dock diving, a lure coursing field, go-to ground course, and training field for sporting breeds located on 275 acres of farmland. Cost is $10 per dog per day. Open dawn to dusk year-round. If no one is at the farm when you visit, Bob says there is a collection post in the field where you can insert your $10. See website for directions. 301/748-4224; www.fidosfriend.com.

had nearly picked the mountain clean. Today, a hike through Catoctin Mountain under the fall foliage is a treat fit for a president.

While it's OK to let your dog drink from Catoctin's streams, rangers request that you not allow him to splash or swim, both for environmental considerations and for his safety—Northern Water Snakes hang out in these streams. Watch for copperhead and timber rattlesnakes elsewhere in the park, though this shouldn't be a problem if your dog is on leash.

A final tip: Neighboring Cunningham Falls State Park is, with a few exceptions, *not* dog friendly. Check with National Park Service rangers for more specifics. If you do head into the state park from September through January, dress yourself and your dog in head-to-toe hunting blaze orange. No hunting is allowed in Catoctin Mountain Park. Be sure to do a thorough tick check, however. Open dawn–dusk daily. Located on Route 77, four miles west of Thurmont and US-15. 6602 Foxville Rd., Thurmont; 301/663-9388; www.nps.gov/cato.

## Gambrill State Park

Knowing ahead of time that Gambrill State Park is a mountain biking destination, we braced ourselves for diving off the trail in a hurry. As it turns out, the only mountain biker we saw was my husband who joined us, and frankly, considering how rocky and steep some of these trails are, we can't imagine how a person traverses them on wheels. If you want to make certain to dodge any mountain bike traffic, stick to the one-mile, white-blazed nature trail in the High Knob hiking area of Gambrill State Park. It's the only trail exclusively for pedestrians and pets. The pleasant, if uneventful loop toured past colonies of bright green spear ferns shooting up in the earthy underbrush of the forest, a small sampling of Gambrill's 13 miles of wooded trails. Denali certainly seemed to be enjoying herself. When excited, her Flying Nun ears perk up ready for takeoff … and her wingtips were flying on the nature trail.

We belatedly learned that the 3.3-mile Black Locust Trail and the 7.1-mile Yellow Poplar Trail both have stellar views of Frederick County from natural stone overlooks. Finally, Gambrill State Park is a trash-free park, so if your dog doodles, expect to be schlepping it to the nearest trash can in town. Park entrance costs $2 for in-state residents, $3 for out-of-state visitors. Located just outside of Frederick off Route 40 on Gambrill Park Road, uphill from the Rock Run Campground. 301/271-7574; www.dnr.state.md.us/publiclands/western/gambrill.html.

## Baker Park

You might be tempted to call it "Barker Park," considering the number of Frederick dogs who frequent this 44-acre park on their daily walks. Baker Park is

## DETOURS

Here is a new meaning of window shopping: Search for the dog bone-shaped sticker in Frederick merchants' windows to see which allow pets inside.

**Cinegraphic Studios:** As the sign says, silly things for silly people (or silly puppies). For the next time you need a bacon wallet or the world's largest underpants, this store is "One part artsy, two parts fartsy." 43A S. Market St.; 301/228-3620; www.cinegraphicstudios.com.

**Hunting Creek Outfitters:** The DogNest beds are stacked high at this full-line Orvis dealer. Ask about commissioning a pet portrait and be sure to greet Khali, the resident English setter. 29 N. Market St.; 301/668-4333; www.huntingcreekoutfitters.com.

**The Trail House:** Top-notch gear for the great outdoors for you and your dog. 17 S. Market St.; 301/694-8448; www.trailhouse.com.

**Two Paws Up:** The store that started it all. Come visit square one for Frederick's four-to-the-floor crowd, just take care not to call it an uppity "boutique." 15 S. Carroll St.; 301/668-7704; www.2pawsup.biz.

a long, rectangular green space that follows Carroll Creek on the approach to historic Frederick. Few places are better to admire the slender pointed church spires that soar above downtown Frederick. Besides surveying several miles of grass and walking trails within Baker Park, Denali zeroed in on Culler Lake to introduce herself to the locals (ducks!). An unusual feature of Baker Park is the Joseph Dill Baker Carillon, a 70-foot-tall stone tower that houses 49 bells. A professional carilloneur plays an informal half-hour concert every Sunday at noon for anyone within earshot.

In 2008, the city of Frederick put the final touches on its first official off-leash dog park along Baker Park. The Flying Dog Brewery has proposed donating money for maintenance of the park in exchange for naming rights (the Flying Dog Park has a nice ring, right?). Registration and tags are required and available at 121 N. Bentz Street. Located on the corner of N. Bentz Street and Carroll Parkway, Frederick; 301/600-1492; www.cityoffrederick.com/departments/recreation/recreation.htm.

## Carroll Creek Park

Denali suspects this handsome urban park will continue to draw out-of-town doggies back to Frederick again and again, if not for the redbrick-lined promenade and terraced greenery, then for the alfresco creekside dining. Inspired by San Antonio's 3.2-mile River Walk, the 0.75-mile canal walk through Carroll Creek Park reminded us a bit of Amsterdam, too, and even on a muggy afternoon it was a delightful departure from busy city life for both pedestrians and pawdestrians.

Carroll Creek Park is at the heart of an effort to resuscitate historic Frederick after a devastating, waist-high flood in 1976 delivered a final blow to an already dwindling downtown shopping district. City leaders have since cut the ribbon on a $65 million flood-control project that redirects most of the creek underground, and *The Washington Post* reports that the canal walk "when completed in mid-2009... will have generated more than 80 new businesses and $155 million in private investment and will draw 1.4 million visitors annually." After our visit, we can see why.

Denali in particular appreciated the Diehl Memorial Fountain, dedicated to Marie Diehl, a founder of what is now the Frederick County Humane Society. Its inscription reads "a refreshing drink to the citizens of Frederick and their beloved animal friends." Later on our walk, a squirrel left the impenetrable safety of trees to scamper over to Carroll Creek for a drink, right in front of us and the dog, and what unfolded looked like a squirrel version of *Cliffhanger*. Denali insists we return for a sequel. Located between S. Market and S. Carroll Streets; 301/600-1492; www.cityoffrederick.com/departments/recreation/recreation.htm.

## Greenbriar Veterinary Referral & Emergency Hospital
🐾🐾🐾🐕

No, this isn't a typo. This is one trip to the vet your dog won't want to miss. In the absence of any existing dog parks in the Frederick area, Greenbriar stepped in to fill the void. The pet hospital maintains a large fenced dog park that is free to the public once pet owners sign a one-time release form on their first visit and agree to abide by the park rules (e.g., no aggressive dogs or female dogs in heat). Shade cover and drinking water are available, and the grassy park is divided into a large dog corral and another for smaller breeds, which together can attract 15–20 dogs on weekends or when the weather is fine. And if there are any incidents, veterinary expertise is only feet away. Open sunrise to sunset daily. 3051 Thurston Rd., Urbana; 301/874-8880 or 800/889-9971; www.greenbriarpethospital.com.

### PLACES TO EAT

**Brewer's Alley:** Whether you're thirsty for an oatmeal stout, kolsch, IPA, or nut brown ale, you can find it in this historic building and brewpub. Servers will bring a treat and water bowl to canine diners, who must be tied outside the fence, so you'll need to score one of the half dozen tables around the patio perimeter. Besides the brick-oven pizzas, pastas, and sandwiches, we hear the iceberg wedge salads are good. 124 N. Market St.; 301/631-0089; www.brewers-alley.com.

**La Dolce Vita Café:** Microroasted espresso and coffee are on the menu, as are paninis, organic salads, sweets, fruit frappés, and other light breakfast and lunch fare. Your pooch will find a full water bowl next to the couple of outdoor tables facing Carroll Creek Park. 50 Carroll Creek Way; 240/436-6428; www .ladolcevitacafe.net.

**La Paz:** Offering Mexican favorites, specialty margaritas, and homemade sangria, La Paz has a great location at the far side of Carroll Creek Park with an umbrella-shaded outdoor seating area. The server we spoke with said dogs can join you at your table inside the fenced-in patio. 51 South Market St.; 301/694-8980; www.lapazmex.com.

## PLACES TO STAY

**Comfort Inn:** Free amenities at this 73-room hotel include continental breakfast, local calls, weekday newspaper, high-speed Internet access, and ample outdoor parking. Guests may check in with up to two dogs per room for a reasonable $10 per day per dog. Rates range $90–120. 7300 Executive Way, Frederick; 301/668-7272; www.comfortinn.com/hotel-frederick-maryland-MD160.

**Gambrill State Park Campground:** Sunnier than the campgrounds we saw at Catoctin Mountain Park, the Rock Run Campground at Gambrill State Park has nearly three dozen campsites ranging from tent sites to cabins, each with its own grill and picnic area. There is also a bathhouse, pond, and playground. Dogs are permitted but must be on leash.

Family tent camping is available late May–Aug. for $20 per night; the cabins open and close a month later (Apr.–Oct.). Campsites with electric hookups cost $25 per night; cabins costs $50 per night. There is also a $3 per vehicle day-use charge, $4 for out-of-state residents. Located just outside of Frederick off Route 40 on Gambrill Park Road. 301/271-7574 or 888/432-2267; www.dnr .state.md.us/publiclands/western/gambrill.

## DOG-EAR YOUR CALENDAR

**Walk-N-Wag:** Join hundreds of animal lovers to walk for the Frederick County Humane Society. Festivities include a flying disc championship and pet contests. Located at Baker Park. May; 301/694-8300; www.fchs.org.

**Dog Days of Summer:** A gallery walk event featuring more than 80 downtown shops, plus dog contests, dog photo booth, and a yappy hour. First Saturday in August; 301/698-8118; www.downtownfrederick.org.

**Holiday Inn—Frederick:** This pet-friendly 155-room hotel and conference center includes a recreation center with an indoor heated pool, whirlpool, miniature golf, ping pong, and other games, in addition to a 24-hour fitness room. There are no size restrictions for dogs staying at the Holiday Inn, but handlers must pay a $20 per night fee and crate their pup if they leave him alone in the room. The hotel also features complimentary parking and wireless Internet throughout the hotel. Rates range $129–164. 5400 Holiday Dr., Frederick; 301/694-7500; www.hifrederick.com.

**Owens Creek Campground:** This wooded 51-site family campground is the only one inside Catoctin Mountain Park that allows pets. Open May–Nov., it is very popular and tends to fill up on Friday nights for weekend camping. Sites are available on a first-come, first-served basis, so arrive as early as you can. We rolled through on Labor Day weekend and the campground was brimming with car-camping Fidos and friends.

Each campsite has its own picnic table and charcoal grill, organized in a somewhat secluded, woodsy arrangement. The campground has two bathrooms (or as the National Park Service euphemistically prefers, "comfort stations") with flush toilets and another with a hot shower. There are no RV hookups. Pets must stay on leash. Campsites cost $20 per night. Catoctin Mountain Park, 6602 Foxville Rd., Thurmont; 301/663-9388; www.nps.gov/cato/planyourvisit/occg.htm.

# Annapolis, Maryland

Oh, to be a salty dog. Besides being the capital of Maryland, Annapolis is often dubbed "America's Sailing Capital" for its nautical leanings. Denali gazed longingly at the stunning watercraft docked at the Annapolis City Dock and imagined skimming across the bay with the breeze catching her half-German shepherd ears aloft like puppy sails. It's nice to dream, right?

Fortunately, she doesn't have to dream about Annapolis' dog friendliness.

## DOG-EAR YOUR CALENDAR

Annapolis pet boutique Paws sponsors many wag-happy events throughout the year. If contact information isn't listed below, contact Paws for the details. 64 State Circle; 410/263-8683; www.pawspetboutique.com.

**GRREAT Happy Tails Day:** Fundraiser for Golden Retriever Rescue, Education, and Training. March; www.grreat.org.

**Canines and Cocktails for a Cause:** Yappy hour fundraisers and fun times at the Weather Rail at Loews Annapolis Hotel. April–October.

**Pirate Pet Parade:** A harrr-dy good time with the Maritime Festival at Annapolis City Dock. Dogs also compete for the Best Barkaneer (most talkative), Salty Dog (feistiest), and the Aargh, Arf Awards. Proceeds benefit Fidos for Freedom. May; www.fidosforfreedom.org.

**Crabtowne Canines March:** Join the Annapolis Fourth of July to raise money for the SPCA of Anne Arundel County. July; www.aacspca.org.

**Howl-o-ween at Quiet Waters:** A howling start to Halloween with doggy costume contests, raffles, vendors, and more. October; Quiet Waters Park; 410/222-1777; www.quietwatersdogpark.org.

**Holiday Pupparazzi Photos:** Holiday pet portraits by photographer Cameron Adams; November.

**Eastport Yacht Club Christmas Lights Parade:** Dozens of sailboats and yachts parade through Annapolis Harbor and Spa Creek, plus caroling. December; 410/263-0415; www.eastportyclightsparade.com.

It's accessible to any dog whose owner has a half-tank of gas to drive east on US-50. The historic port city is surprisingly close to DC—less than an hour if the traffic isn't awful (a big if). Many, many DC dog owners we spoke with recommended a trip to Annapolis, if only for a visit to the Quiet Waters Dog Beach and a sampling of fresh-off-the-boat Maryland blue crab.

Adding to Annapolis' seafaring tradition is the U.S. Naval Academy. Midshipmen in crisp uniforms walk about town, leading us to worry what one ill-timed puppy pounce with dirty paws would do to those summer whites.

Dogs may poke their noses into many shops along Main Street and elsewhere, most notably Paws pet boutique on State Circle. If you need additional suggestions for activities or walking routes, swing by the information booth on the City Dock, which is staffed April–October (410/280-0445) and usually has a full water bowl nearby.

## PARKS, BEACHES, AND RECREATION AREAS

### Acton Cove Park
🐾🐾

Annapolis is a place where taking a dog-walk down the sidewalk is a delight. More colonial architecture survives here than anywhere else in the country, so if your pooch has tired of drooling over the sailboats and yachts in Ego Alley, the local boaters' nickname for the City Dock downtown, instead take a walk through the neighborhoods. That's how we found Acton Cove Park, located a short walk south of Church Circle on, appropriately enough, South Street. The grass and redbrick courtyard overlooking Spa Creek is a contribution from the posh condo and town-home community called Acton's Landing. With its old-fashioned lampposts, bronze sculptured geese, black benches, and residential views of the harbor, the park is a nice spot. Located on Anna Lane and South Street.

### Quiet Waters Park
🐾🐾🐾🐾🐕

DC dog lovers wear a special, dreamy expression when they describe Quiet Waters Park in Annapolis. "Oh, and of course you know about Quiet Waters…" they'll say, and then drift off into a nostalgic happy place with seagulls calling and retrievers splashing. With such fanfare preceding it, the Quiet Waters Dog Beach was smaller than we expected—more of a shrub-covered isthmus than a full beach—but this robbed not a bit of glee from a golden's face who bobbed in the small waves. It's fantastically situated at the end of the South River Promenade, a boardwalk with views of sailboats motoring out to the Chesapeake Bay.

In addition to the dearly loved dog beach, Quiet Waters has a more traditional dog park as well. The Quiet Waters Dog Park is Anne Arundel County's first, and it's larger than average with a fully fenced perimeter, double-gated entry, running water, and grass. The dog park is divided into two sections, one for big dogs and another for the little guys. If your Energizer Doggy still craves more exercise, 340-acre Quiet Waters Park also has six miles of winding paved trails for walking. Even in a driving rain (dare we say "cats and dogs"), nearly half a dozen dogs and their doting owners were spending a Saturday afternoon at the Quiet Waters Dog Park and Dog Beach when we visited. Now that's puppy love.

A few rules govern both areas: Children under the age of six are not allowed, no more than two dogs per owner, no digging (good luck with that one), and humans aren't allowed to swim or wade. (The full list of the rules is on the park website.) There are usually poop bags in the wooden mailbox in the parking lot, and a pet-rinsing station will help you hose down your pooch, but be sure to bring towels. If your water hound really needs a good scrubbing, go to

**Muddy Paw Wash: Dog Wash and Coffee Bar** just outside of Quiet Waters Dog Park (130 Hillsmere Dr.; 410/268-7387; www.muddypawwash.com).

Follow US-50 east toward Annapolis. Take exit 22 to Route 665 (Aris T. Allen Boulevard), until it merges with Forrest Drive and continue for two miles. Turn right onto Hillsmere Drive. The park entrance is 100 yards on the right side. Follow signs to the dog park and beach. Open 7 A.M.–dusk. The dog park closes half an hour before dusk. Quiet Waters Park is closed on Tuesday. Admission costs $5 per vehicle or $30 for an annual pass. 600 Quiet Waters Park Rd.; 410/222-1777; www.aacounty.org/recparks/parks/quiet_waters_park/dogpark.cfm.

## PLACES TO EAT

**Harry Brownes Restaurant:** A bone's throw away from Paws pet boutique on State Circle, Harry Brownes offers fine dining in an elegant but not overly stuffy setting. Not surprisingly, seafood is a specialty. Your dog is allowed to sit at your feet, and waiters will usually bring a bowl of water if you ask, although the outside tables are first come, first served and fill up quickly, so arrive early to score a spot. Harry Brownes opens for dinner at 5:30 P.M. Mon.–Sat. and at 4:30 P.M. on Sunday. Lunch and Sunday brunch are also served. Free valet parking on weekends. 66 State Circle; 410/263-4332; www.harrybrownes.com.

**The Purple Tooth:** This adorable wine bar is located across the street from the Loews Annapolis Hotel. Weather permitting, dogs can join you at the handful of outdoor tables on West Street as you sample from the more than 130 hand-selected boutique wines and farmstead, artisanal cheeses. Closed on Monday. 114 West St.; 410/263-1422; www.thepurpletooth.com.

**Rams Head Tavern:** For a traditional English-style pub dining experience, walk over to the Rams Head. The Fordham Brewing Company is located inside the establishment, so you can expect good food and great beer. Dogs are only allowed at the 10 or so tables in front of the tavern, and not the larger patio around back, but it's a nice vantage point to watch passersby. The five-beer sampler for $4.95 is perfect for the indecisive. 33 West St.; 410/268-4545; www.ramsheadtavern.com/annapolis.

**Sly Fox Pub:** Your well-behaved pup can sit right under the table at this Church Circle establishment's patio. Fish and chips, shepherds' pie, bangers and mash, and other traditional English pub favorites are on the menu in this historic building. Reynolds Tavern, built in 1737, has served as a hat shop, hotel, stable, public library, and now the Sly Fox Pub and a tearoom with three rooms for lodging. 7 Church Circle; 443/482-9000; www.slyfoxpub.com.

## PLACES TO STAY

**Annapolis Royal Folly:** Like the innkeepers' own miniature poodle, Samson, non-shedding dogs weighing less than 20 pounds may stay in the downstairs suite at this top-notch bed-and-breakfast. Owners Pat and Ed Mullen also offer a Luxury Doggies Getaway package. Human guests can enjoy full gourmet breakfasts, including a Sunday champagne brunch, and an outdoor hot tub. Each of the bed-and-breakfast's 14 rooms has a private bathroom. Annapolis Royal Folly is located directly across from the beautiful St. John's College, the third oldest college in the country (after Harvard and William and Mary), perhaps best known as the birthplace of the Great Books curriculum. 65 College Ave.; 410/263-3999; www.royalfolly.com.

**Homestead Studio Suites Hotel:** Designed for longer stays, each Homestead room comes with a fully equipped kitchen, including a dishwasher. The official pet policy says only one pet is allowed per room, but from speaking

## DIVERSIONS

**Annapolis Small Boat Rentals:** Rent a power boat to cruise Spa Creek or see the U.S. Naval Academy from the water. An additional deposit may be required for bringing the pupster aboard. Located at Sarles Boatyard and Marina. 808 Boucher Ave.; 410/268-2628; www.asmallboatrental.com.

**Kayak Annapolis:** Your pup can join you in a sit-on-top kayak for a three-hour educational and easygoing guided paddle through one of America's oldest seaports. 443/949-0773; www.kayakannapolistours.com.

**Watermark:** Leashed dogs and their responsible owners are invited aboard Watermark sightseeing cruises. Be sure to take a long walk first—no reason to provide fodder for bad jokes about "poop decks." 1 Dock St.; 800/569-9622; www.watermarkcruises.com.

with the front desk, it sounds as though there might be some wiggle room regarding this rule. There is a $25 per day per pet fee up to a maximum of $150 and there are no weight restrictions. Housecleaning visits weekly. Rates range $99–169. 120 Admiral Cochrane Dr.; 410/571-6600; www.homestead hotels.com.

**Loews Annapolis Hotel:** All Loews hotels love dogs, but the Loews Annapolis Hotel has a special heart for animals. Dogs of any size (up to two per room) may check in with owners for a $25 one-time fee. Pets receive a goody bag of a pet tag, bowl, bottled water, and treat, while owners will receive a detailed brochure with local dog walking routes and pet services. Dog food is even on the room service menu!

But what makes the 217-room Loews Annapolis Hotel outshine the rest is its monthly sponsorship of **Canines and Cocktails for a Cause** events at its Weather Rail Lounge. April–October, the fundraiser series benefits animal shelters and other doggy causes, and the yappy hour usually takes place on a Friday evening with "cocktails, appetizers, mocktails, and Snoopy snacks." Contact Paws pet boutique for information (410/263-8683; www.pawspet boutique.com). All times of year, your pooch can hope to hang out with Luke, a Labrador retriever adopted from the SPCA of Anne Arundel County.

It's OK to leave your dog alone as long as you leave a cell number with the front desk, but a $10 per hour "time-out" fee is assessed if an unattended pet needs to be removed from a guest room and entertained by hotel staff to keep quiet. Amenities for human guests include a fitness room and the on-site Annapolis Day Spa. Room rates range $179–709. Valet parking is available for $22. During the Canines and Cocktails events, $2 self-parking is available at Loews. 126 West St.; 410/263-7777; www.loewshotels.com/en/hotels/annapolis-hotel/overview.aspx.

**The Westin Annapolis:** This 225-room luxury hotel accepts dogs 40 pounds or less for no additional fee, although guests must sign a damage waiver and dogs are not permitted in food and beverage areas. Your pampered pooch can expect to rest easy on his own Heavenly Dog Bed. Two-legged guests can anticipate a heated indoor pool, fitness facilities, Varuna Spa by Aveda, high-speed wireless Internet, and, of course, their own Heavenly Bed. The hotel has a Starbucks in the lobby and two restaurants on-site: Morton's Steakhouse and Azure. Rates range $199–400. Valet parking costs $22; self-parking costs $10. 100 Westgate Circle; 410/972-4300; www.westin.com/annapolis.

# Shenandoah National Park, Virginia

If it's October and the fall colors are just beginning to change, there's one thing you should do. Pack up the car, whistle for the dog, and drive to Shenandoah. The National Park Service even posts up-to-date pictures of the fall foliage progression with a Leaf Color Cam (www.nps.gov/shen/parknews/

## DIVERSIONS

Tucker out the pup with these Shenandoah hikes.

**Doyles River:** South District; 7.8-mile loop. Trailhead at Doyles River parking lot, Mile 81.1.

**Jeremy's Run:** North District; 14.7-mile loop, or shorter as an out-and-back. Trailhead at Elkwallow Picnic Area, Mile 24.1.

**Rose River Run:** Central District; 4.2-mile loop. Trailhead at Fishers Gap Overlook, Mile 49.4.

**Whiteoak Canyon–Cedar Run Loop:** Central District; 7.9-mile loop. Trailhead at Whiteoak Canyon, Mile 42.6.

fallcolors.htm), so you can see a hint of what awaits you and your puppy hiking partner. There's no better way to usher in one of DC's best seasons.

## PARKS, BEACHES, AND RECREATION AREAS

### Shenandoah National Park
🐾🐾🐾🐾🐾

As a general rule, America's national parks are hardly dog friendly. Take Yellowstone National Park, for example, where dogs are banned beyond 100 feet of a road, parking lot, or campground. So imagine Denali's wig-waggling joy when she learned that the Mid-Atlantic's preeminent national park bucks this trend. Dogs on leash are allowed on all but 20 miles of the 500 miles of trails inside Shenandoah National Park.

As you drive 70 miles west of Washington to the park entrance you might find yourself humming, or howling, "Almost heaven, West Virginia, Blue Ridge Mountains, Shenandoah River..." John Denver's "Take Me Home, Country Roads" takes on a whole new poetry after visiting this park. The most famous road through Shenandoah National Park is Skyline Drive, the 105-mile scenic byway that rides the crest of the Blue Ridge Mountains from Front Royal to Rockfish Gap, en route to the Great Smoky Mountains in North Carolina. The Appalachian Trail provides a pedestrian version of the same thoroughfare.

The most notable doggy no-go zone in Shenandoah is the approach up 3,268-foot Old Rag, which could be the most popular hike in the Mid-Atlantic. We speak from experience when we say this is for your dog's safety and your sanity. See the park website for a complete list of trails where dogs are *not* allowed (www.nps.gov/shen/planyourvisit/pets.htm).

Early in our time on the Eastern starboard, we learned firsthand Shenandoah National Park has one of the densest black bear populations documented

in the United States. We had Denali off leash (not realizing we were breaking park rules) when a black bear barreled out of a tree. The dog chased the bear. The husband chased the dog. The author sat on the ground, dazed and frantically fearing the ensuing brawl (let's just say it wasn't a shining moment of level-headedness). Fortunately, the bear outran Denali, and we all returned to the car uninjured. Denali remains firmly attached to a leash inside Shenandoah now, and we advise you follow the same policy.

Shenandoah National Park has several entrances. The closest to Washington is the North District at Front Royal, a straight shot west of DC on I-66. The entrance fee is $10 per vehicle Dec.–Feb. and $15 per vehicle Mar.–Nov. 540/999-3500; www.nps.gov/shen.

## PLACES TO EAT

**Shenandoah Waysides:** The national park concessionaire Aramark operates four snack shops or small grocers along Skyline Drive. Dogs are not allowed inside, but picnic areas are usually located outside. The numbers following Shenandoah's waysides refer to the mileposts on Skyline Drive where they are located: Elkwallow Wayside (Mile 24.1), Big Meadows Wayside (Mile 51.2), Lewis Mountain Campstore (Mile 57.6), and Loft Mountain Wayside & Campstore (Mile 79.5). The waysides close in winter. 888/896-3833; www.nps .gov/shen/planyourvisit/where-to-eat.htm.

**Soul Mountain Restaurant:** The menu blends Cajun, Caribbean, and Southern cuisine to create "Soul Fusion." Think po' boys and catfish with Bob Marley inspiration. Meals are served with sweet corn muffins. Dogs are welcome to join diners in the outdoor seating. 300 E. Main St., Front Royal; 540/636-0070.

## PLACES TO STAY

**Paws & Reflect Cabin:** On the west side of Shenandoah Valley nestled in the Massanutten Mountains is a special getaway designed with dogs in mind. Paws & Reflect is a cozy cabin that comfortably sleeps four humans and as many canines as belong in your entourage. Besides practical pet supplies such as food and water bowls and Nature's Miracle cleaning products, the cabin comes stocked with puppy perks such as pet music CDs and a doggy-size couch. It also comes equipped with a fully stocked kitchen, stone fireplace, and screened-in hot tub. Four-wheel-drive is *required* to access the cabin. Leave the Mini Cooper at home and rent an SUV if needed. Rates vary depending on the length of your stay; see website for details. Located in New Market near where Route 211 meets I-81. 866/507-7297; www.pawsandreflectva.com.

**Shenandoah National Park Campgrounds:** Shenandoah National Park has four campgrounds—Mathews Arm (Mile 22.1), Big Meadows (Mile 51.2), Lewis Mountain (the smallest; Mile 57.5), and Loft Mountain (the largest; Mile 79.5). There are no RV hookups, but most of the campgrounds have sites big enough to accommodate a large RV. Dogs are allowed in all four campgrounds and in the backcountry, as long as they are never left unattended at camp or in vehicles.

Free permits are required for backcountry camping, which can be obtained through the mail two weeks in advance or by visiting a ranger station. No fires are permitted and it's strongly advised to bring a bear-resistant food storage container. For more information about backcountry camping, visit: www.nps .gov/shen/planyourvisit/campbc.htm. Rates for car camping range $15–20 per night. The campgrounds are closed during the winter and reopen between March and May; see website for details. 877/444-6777; www.nps.gov/shen/ planyourvisit/camping.htm or www.recreation.gov.

 **DIVERSIONS**

If your pooch's paws are doggone tired, here are some alternatives to hiking.

**Front Royal Canoes/Shenandoah River Trips:** Dog-friendly canoe and kayak rentals for a float down Shenandoah River. Call for pricing. 8567 Stonewall Jackson Hwy., Front Royal; 540/635-5050 or 800/727-4371; www.shenandoah.cc/petfriendly.html.

**Luray Caverns:** Guests are permitted to carry small pets on a tour of the largest caverns in the Eastern United States. Tickets cost $19 for adults; $9 for kids; little dogs are free. 101 Cave Hill Rd., Luray; 540/743-6551 or 888/941-4531; www.luraycaverns.com.

**Shenandoah River Cabins:** Owners Brad and Donna Eames rent six dog-friendly cabins in the Shenandoah Valley. Each cabin has a fireplace and hot tub on private acreage. A maximum of two dogs can check in for an additional $10 fee per day per pet. Cabin rates range $330–395 for the first two nights. 135 Vintage Cabins Dr., Luray; 703/380-8789 or 540/743-5000; www.river-cabins.com.

**Skyland Resort:** If camping doesn't appeal to your doggy's sensibilities, Skyland Resort offers 13 dog-friendly rooms inside the national park. For a $25 cleaning fee per pet per day, you and a maximum of two dogs can cozy up in a traditional room with two double or two queen beds in the Canyon Building. Be sure to inquire about pet-friendly rooms when you make your reservations. Pets cannot be left alone in the room unless they are in a kennel and the resort should provide Mutt Mitts.

Skyland Resort is located at the highest point on Skyline Drive, 3,680 feet, and it is open late March–November. Located at Mile 41.7 on Skyline Drive. The closest entrance is Thornton Gap Entrance Station, accessible via US-211. Rates range $120–160. 888/896-3833; www.visitshenandoah.com.

# Assateague Island National Seashore, Maryland

Beaches are plentiful up and down the Atlantic coast. What makes the Maryland section of Assateague Island's shoreline special is both what you will find—wild ponies and befuddled family dogs—and what you won't—big resort developments.

## PARKS, BEACHES, AND RECREATION AREAS

### Assateague Island National Seashore
🐾🐾🐾🐾 🐾

> *I started Early—Took my Dog—*
> *And visited the Sea—*
>
> Emily Dickinson

In stark contrast to the built-up family resorts in Ocean City only eight miles north, Assateague Island is a 37-mile ribbon of undeveloped, uninterrupted sandy beach famous for its wild ponies. We had written off the barrier island as a decidedly dog-*un*-friendly place after a disappointing trip to the Virginia end. The U.S. Fish and Wildlife Service manages most of this southern half as a National Wildlife Refuge—which, we were crestfallen to learn, means dogs

## DIVERSION

Hourly and daily canoe and kayak rentals are available at Assateague Island through the **Coastal Bays Program** if you would prefer to do some puppy paddling and explore the barrier island by water. Remember: no landing in the backcountry and harassing the wildlife. Landlubbers might prefer to rent a clamshell rake instead, also available. (Denali insists her own two paws are just fine for digging, thank you.) Located on Assateague Island National Seashore at the end of Bayside Drive, second right after passing through the National Park tollbooth. Look for the brown park sign on the right that reads Canoe and Bike Rentals. Open 9 A.M.–6 P.M. daily Memorial Day to Labor Day. Limited weekend hours in April, May, September, and October. 410/726-3217; www.mdcoastalbays.org.

are strictly verboten, even inside cars. It's a long way to drive to read Marguerite Henry's classic children's story *Misty of Chincoteague* aloud to your furry best friend in a motel room rather than see the real ponies.

Fortunately, a friend clued us in to the dog-friendly loophole. As long as you drive to the beachfront campground on the Maryland side of the national seashore, your dog is invited and will usually have plenty of canine company. The idyllic white sand beach tugs at either side of your peripheral vision, stretching for miles, the perfect place to splash in the waves with your pup, read a book, or surf fish. Remember to bring sunscreen, insect repellent, and shade for the pooch, and you'll all be happy as clams. Keep in mind these are wild horses that will bite and kick if you get too close, so keep your distance and be sure your dog does the same.

The entrance fee is $3 per individual or $15 per vehicle for a seven-day pass. Located at the end of Route 611, eight miles south of Ocean City, Maryland.

Proceed past Assateague State Park (no dogs allowed) to the National Seashore. 410/641-1441 or 410/641-3030; www.nps.gov/asis.

## PLACES TO STAY

**Assateague Island National Seashore Campground:** Basic camping facilities are available at the seashore, including cold-water showers, drinking water, and toilets, but some friends who have tried staying overnight strongly advise against it. When dusk comes, hordes of man- and mutt-eating mosquitoes unleash their carnivorous fury. Still, if you're set on extending your beachside getaway there are a few steps you can take to make the evening hours more pleasant. First and foremost, bring bug spray, preferably the scary DEET variety that gets the job done. Second, remember to bring long tent stakes so in case the wind picks up at night you don't have to stumble in the dark swatting 'squiters trying to fix the tent. Four types of campsites are available: oceanside drive-in (tents, trailers, and RVs—although there are no hookups), oceanside walk-in (tents only), bayside drive-in (like oceanside, only buggier), and group campsites.

Make campground reservations well in advance for peak season camping April 15–October 15. Campsites are first come, first served the rest of the year. Sites cost $16 per night. 410/641-3030 or 877/444-6777; www.nps.gov/asis or www.recreation.gov.

# RESOURCES

# Public and Government Offices

Get in touch with your local agency to learn more about park regulations and stay up-to-date with changing operating hours and laws.

### WASHINGTON DC

**DC Department of Parks and Recreation:** 3149 16th St. NW; 202/673-7647; www.dpr.dc.gov.

**National Capital Parks—East:** 1900 Anacostia Dr. SE; 202/690-5185; www.nps.gov/nace.

**National Mall and Memorial Parks:** 900 Ohio Dr. SW; 202/426-6841; www.nps.gov/nacc.

**National Park Service—National Capital Region:** 1100 Ohio Dr. SW; 202/619-7222; www.nps.gov/ncro.

## VIRGINIA

**Alexandria Department of Recreation, Parks, and Cultural Activities:** 1108 Jefferson St., Alexandria; 703/838-4343; www.alexandriava.gov.

**Arlington Department of Parks, Recreation, and Cultural Resources:** 2100 Clarendon Blvd., Ste. 414, Arlington; 703/228-7529; www.arlingtonva.us.

**City of Falls Church Recreation and Parks Department:** 223 Little Falls St., Falls Church; 703/248-5077; www.fallschurchva.gov.

**Fairfax County Park Authority:** 12055 Government Center Pkwy., Ste. 927, Fairfax; 703/324-8702; www.fairfaxcounty.gov/parks.

**George Washington Memorial Parkway:** Turkey Run Park, McLean; 703/289-2500; www.nps.gov/gwmp.

**Herndon Parks and Recreation Department:** 814 Ferndale Ave., Herndon; 703/787-7300; www.herndon-va.gov.

**Northern Virginia Regional Park Authority:** 5400 Ox Rd., Fairfax Station; 703/352-5900; www.nvrpa.org.

**Town of Vienna Parks and Recreation Department:** 120 Cherry St. SE; 703/255-6360; www.viennava.gov.

**Virginia Department of Conservation and Recreation:** 203 Governor St., Ste. 306, Richmond; 804/786-1712; www.dcr.virginia.gov/state_parks/index.shtml.

## MARYLAND

**Anne Arundel County Department of Recreation and Parks:** 1 Harry S. Truman Pkwy., Annapolis; 410/222-7300; www.aacounty.org/recparks.

**Baltimore County Department of Recreation and Parks:** 301 Washington Ave., Towson; 410/887-3871; www.baltimorecountymd.gov/agencies/recreation.

**Baltimore Department of Recreation and Parks:** 3001 East Dr., Baltimore; 410/396-7900; www.ci.baltimore.md.us/government/recnparks.

**City of Bowie Recreation Office:** 2614 Kenhill Dr., Bowie; 301/809-3011 or 301/262-6200, ext. 3011; www.cityofbowie.org/parks/parkfacilities.asp.

**City of Gaithersburg Department of Parks, Recreation, and Culture:** 506 S. Frederick Ave., Gaithersburg; 301/258-6343; www.gaithersburgmd.gov.

**City of Greenbelt Department of Recreation:** 99 Centerway; 301/397-2200; www.greenbeltmd.gov/recreation/index.htm.

**City of Laurel Department of Parks and Recreation:** 8103 Sandy Spring Rd., Laurel; 301/725-7800; www.laurel.md.us/parks.htm.

**City of Rockville Department of Recreation and Parks:** 111 Maryland Ave., Rockville; 240/314-8700; www.rockvillemd.gov/recreation.

**Maryland Department of Natural Resources:** Tawes State Office Building, 580 Taylor Ave., Annapolis; 877/620-8DNR (8367) or 410/260-8DNR (8367); www.dnr.state.md.us.

**Montgomery County Department of Parks:** 9500 Brunett Ave., Silver Spring; 301/495-2595; www.montgomeryparks.org.

**Prince George's County Department of Parks and Recreation:** 6600 Kenilworth Ave., Riverdale; 301/699-2255; www.pgparks.com.

**Town of Poolesville Recreation:** 19721 Beall St.; 301/428-8927; www.ci.poolesville.md.us/recreation/parks.html.

# Community Groups and Resources

Life really is about community, and dog community is no different. Connect with a group who shares your love for four-legged best friends. For almost every animal rights issue or interest, there's a group ready to rally with you.

**ArlingtonDogs:** www.arlingtondogs.org.

**Cemetery Dogs:** 202/543-0539; www.cemeterydogs.org.

**DCDOGS Listserv:** Created as part of effort to establish dog parks in DC, the listserv has since broadened to wider dog issues. groups.yahoo.com/group/DCDOG.

**DC Dog Voter:** www.dcdogvoter.com.

**DC Doggie Happy Hour Meetup Group:** activedogs.meetup.com/111.

**Eastern Veterinary Blood Bank:** Dogs saving dogs' lives voluntarily. 844 Ritchie Hwy., Ste. 204, Severna Park, MD 21146; 410/384-9441 or 800/949-EVBB (3822); www.evbb.com.

**Metro DC Dogs:** pets.groups.yahoo.com/group/metrodcdogs.

**MetroPets Online:** A wealth of information for DC metro area pet owners. www.metropets.org.

**Military Pets Foster Program:** A nonprofit that finds foster homes for pets of deployed U.S. military personnel. www.netpets.org/netp/foster.php.

**People Animals Love:** 4900 Massachusetts Ave. NW, Ste. 330, Washington DC 20016; 202/966-2171; www.peopleanimalslove.com.

**PETS-DC:** To help people living with HIV/AIDS keep their dogs. P.O. Box 75125, Washington DC 20013-0125; 202/234-PETS (7387); www.petsdc.org.

**The Shiloh Project:** Teaching juvenile offenders and at-risk youth compassion, respect, and responsibility toward animals; promoting adoption of homeless animals. 703/273-4056; www.shilohproject.org.

**Virginia Voters for Animal Welfare:** www.virginiavotersforanimalwelfare.com.

# Veterinarians and Emergency Hospitals

These vets have been recommended to us by local dog owners. Listed below you'll find regular vets, specialists, and—knock on wood—emergency clinics open after-hours.

### WASHINGTON DC

**City Paws:** Two doors down from the Black Cat night club—pa-dum-pum. 1823 14th St. NW; 202/232-PAWS (7297); www.citypawsdc.com.

**Collins Memorial Hospital for Animals:** 1808 Wisconsin Ave. NW; 202/659-8830.

**Dr. Dan Teich:** 202/423-3623; www.dchomevet.com.

**Dupont Veterinary Clinic:** 2022 P St. NW; 202/466-2211; www.dupontvetclinic.com.

**Friendship Hospital for Animals:** 4105 Brandywine St. NW; 202/363-7300; www.friendshiphospital.com.

**Georgetown Veterinary Hospital:** 2916 M St. NW; 202/333-2140; www.georgetownvethosp.com.

**Union Vet:** 609 2nd St. NE; 202/544-2500; www.unionvetclinic.com.

**Veterinary Pet Insurance:** Not a local vet, but national pet insurance to help pay for any unexpected visits. www.petinsurance.com.

**Washington DC Humane Society:** Low-cost spay and neuter. 202/882-5837; www.washhumane.org/snclinic.asp.

## VIRGINIA

**Alexandria Animal Hospital:** 2660 Duke St., Alexandria; 703/751-2022 or 703/823-3601 for emergency; www.alexandriaanimalhospital.com.

**Belle Haven Animal Medical Centre:** 1221 Belle Haven Rd., Alexandria; 703/721-0088; www.bhamc.com.

**Caring Hands Animal Hospital:** 2955C S. Glebe Rd., Arlington; 703/535-3100; www.caringhandsvet.com.

**Cherrydale Veterinary Clinic:** Emphasizing wellness and geriatric care. 4038 Lee Hwy., Arlington; 703/528-9001; www.cherrydalevet.com.

**Del Ray Animal Hospital:** 524 E. Mount Ida Ave., Alexandria; 703/739-0000; www.delrayanimalhospital.com.

**Dominion Animal Hospital:** 795 Station St., Herndon; 703/437-6900; www.dominionanimalhospital.com.

**Falls Church Animal Hospital:** 1249 West Broad St., Falls Church; 703/532-6121; www.fallschurchanimalhospital.com.

**Great Falls Animal Hospital:** Holistic veterinary care. 10125 Colvin Run Rd.; 703/759-2330; www.greatfallsanimalhospital.com.

**The Hope Center for Advanced Veterinary Care:** Emergency clinic open 24 hours a day. 140 Park St. SE, Vienna; 703/281-5121; www.hopecenter.com.

**Pender Veterinary Centre:** Emergency and full-service clinic open 24 hours a day. 4001 Legato Rd., Fairfax; 703/591-3304; www.pendervet.com.

**Reston Animal Hospital:** 2403 Reston Pkwy., Reston, Virginia 20191; 703/620-2566; www.restonanimalhospital.com.

**Saratoga Animal Hospital:** 8054 Rolling Rd., Springfield; 703/455-1188; www.petmedicalcenterspringfield.com.

**Singing Stones Animal Wellness Centre:** Carol Lundquist, DVM. 2238-B Gallows Rd., Vienna; 703/206-0197.

**SouthPaws Veterinary Specialists and Emergency Center:**
8500 Arlington Blvd., Fairfax; 703/752-9100; www.southpaws.com.

**Suburban Animal Hospital:** 6879 Lee Hwy., Arlington; 703/532-4043;
www.suburbananimalhospital.net.

**Town and Country Animal Hospital:** 9836 Lee Hwy.; Fairfax;
703/273-2110; www.tnc.vetsuite.com.

**VCA Annandale Hospital:** 7405 Little River Trnpk., Annandale;
703/941-3100; www.vcaannandale.com.

**VCA Old Town Animal Hospital:** 425 N. Henry St., Alexandria;
703/549-3647; www.vcaoldtown.com.

## MARYLAND

**Alpine Veterinary Hospital:** 7732 MacArthur Blvd., Cabin John;
301/229-2400; www.alpineveterinaryhospital.com.

**Animal Medical Center of Watkins Park:** 60 Watkins Park Dr.,
Upper Marlboro; 301/249-3030.

**Animal Wellness Center:** Scott Sanderson, DVM. 8827 Center Park Dr,
Ste. E, Columbia; 410/992-7087 or 301/596-4466; www.acuvet.com.

**Belair Veterinary Hospital:** 15511 Hall Rd., Bowie; 301/249-5200;
www.belairveterinaryhospital.com.

**Bradley Hills Animal Hospital:** 7210 Bradley Blvd., Bethesda;
301/365-5448; www.bradleyhills.com.

**Canal Clinic:** 9125 River Rd., Potomac; 301/299-0880.

**Damascus Veterinary Hospital:** 24939 Ridge Rd., Damascus; 301/253-2072;
www.damascusvet.com.

**Diamond Veterinary Hospital:** 17000 Longdraft Rd., Gaithersburg;
301/869-3990.

**Fairland Animal Hospital:** 12711 Old Columbia Pike, Silver Spring;
301/622-2115; www.fairlandanimalhospital.com.

**Gaithersburg Veterinary Clinic:** 17 Firstfield Rd., Ste. 100, Gaithersburg;
301/519-3456; www.gaithersburgvet.com.

**Germantown Veterinary Clinic and Pet Resort:** 19911 Father Hurley Blvd.,
Germantown; 301/972-9730; www.germantownvet.com.

**Glenvilah Veterinary Clinic:** 12948-E Travilah Rd., Potomac;
301/963-4664.

**Kentlands Veterinary Hospital:** Acupuncture and herbal therapy
treatments available in addition to traditional veterinary care. 117 Booth St.,
Gaithersburg; 301/519-7944; www.kentlandsvet.com.

**Palmer Animal Hospital:** 9405 Baltimore Pike, Myersville; 301/293-2121; www.palmeranimalhospital.net.

**Takoma Park Animal Clinic:** 7330 Carroll Ave., Takoma Park; 301/270-4700; www.tpacvets.com.

**Veterinary Holistic Care:** Holistic medicine by Dr. Monique Maniet. 4820 Moorland Ln., Bethesda; 301/656-2882; www.vhcdoc.com.

**Wellspring Holistic Vet Care:** Dr. Julia Strum. 3900 Ten Oaks Rd., Glenelg; 443/535-0252; www.wellspringvet.com.

**Wheaton Animal Hospital:** Monica C. Maa, DVM. 2929 University Blvd. W., Kensington; 301/949-1520.

# Specialists

**Greta McVey:** Certified animal acupuncturist. 301/996-1785; www.thepointishealing.com.

**M. Susaanti Follingstad:** Certified animal acupuncturist serving Montgomery County and nearby areas. 301/251-0139; m.folling@verizon.net.

**Tellington TTouch Training:** Pam Wanveer. 8818 First Ave., Silver Spring; 301/585-5675; www.woodsidettouch.com.

# Groomers

Because clean dogs smell better, and leave less dirt on your pillow.

### WASHINGTON DC

**Bonnie's Dog and Cat Grooming:** Full-serve grooming and self-serve dog washes. 14th and E Sts. SE; 202/548-0044; www.healthydogstore.com.

**Chateau Animaux:** Professional grooming and self-serve bath stations. 524 8th St. SE; 202/544-8710; www.chateau-animaux.com.

**Chichie's Canine Design:** By appointment only. 2614 P St. NW; 202/333-3575; www.chichiescaninedesign.com.

**Doggie Style Bakery, Boutique, & Pet Spa:** 1825 18th St. NW; 202/667-0595; www.doggiestylebakery.com.

**The Dog Shop:** Self-serve dog bathing and grooming by appointment. 1625 Wisconsin Ave. NW; 202/337-3647; www.dogshopdc.com.

**GreenPets:** 1722 14th St. NW; 202/986-7907; greenpets.blogspot.com.

**PetMac Laundromutt:** 1722 Florida Ave. NW; 202/387-MUTT (6888); www.petmaclaundromutt.com.

**Wagtime Pet Spa & Boutique:** 1232 9th St. NW; 202/234-8825; www.wagtimedc.com.

## VIRGINIA

**Bark 'N Bubbles Dog Wash:** 795 Center St., Herndon; 703/437-WASH (9274); or 20604 Gordon Park Square, Ste. 170, Ashburn; 703/729-3161; www.barknbubblesdogwash.com.

**Grooming by Marcey:** More than 10 years of experience. 1610 N. Abingdon St., Arlington; 703/946-8753.

**Old Town Doggie Wash:** Self-service wash and groom. 105 Moncure Dr., Alexandria; 703/299-0587; www.oldtowndoggiewash.com.

**Olde Towne School for Dogs:** Appointments are usually booked well in advance. 529 Oronoco St.; 703/836-7643; www.otsfd.com.

## MARYLAND

**Best Friends Pet Care:** Web cams that allow you to watch from home as your dog gets groomed. 395 Muddy Branch Rd., Gaithersburg; 301/926-6005; www.bestfriendspetcare.com.

**Canine Design:** Good with older dogs. 4226 Howard Ave., Ste. 1, Kensington; 301/564-4000; www.caninedesignonline.com.

**Paws of Enchantment by Cassandra:** Highly regarded. 3415 Perry St., Mount Rainier; 301/209-0411; www.pawsofenchantment.com.

# Animal Shelters and Rescue Leagues

If you're planning to expand your furry family, contemplate bringing an adopted pet into the fold. These rescue leagues and shelters are always in need of "forever homes" for their wards. Or consider fostering an animal, volunteering, or donating much-needed funds or supplies.

## WASHINGTON DC

**City Dogs Rescue:** www.citydogsrescue.org.

**DC Animal Shelter:** 1201 New York Ave. NE; 202/576-3207; www.washhumane.org.

**Washington Animal Rescue League:** 71 Oglethorpe St. NW; 202/726-2556; www.warl.org.

**Washington Humane Society:** 7319 Georgia Ave. NW; 202/723-5730; www.washhumane.org.

## VIRGINIA

**A Forever-Home Rescue Foundation:** P. O. Box 222801, Chantilly, VA 20153; 703/961-8690; www.aforeverhome.org.

**Animal Welfare League of Alexandria:** 4101 Eisenhower Ave., Alexandria; 703/838-4774; www.alexandriaanimals.org.

**Animal Welfare League of Arlington:** 2650 S. Arlington Mill Dr., Arlington; 703/931-9241; www.awla.org.

**Fairfax County Animal Shelter:** 4500 West Ox Rd., Fairfax; 703/830-1100; www.fairfaxcounty.gov/police/animalservices.

**Friends of Homeless Animals:** P.O. Box 2575, Merrifield, VA 22116-2575; 703/385-0224; www.foha.org.

**Furry Suits Rescue:** P.O. Box 21, Herndon, VA 20172; 703/889-5335; www.furrysuitsrescue.org.

**Homeless Animal Rescue Team:** P.O. Box 7261, Fairfax Station, VA 22039-7261; 703/691-HART (4278); www.hart90.org.

**Homeward Trails Animal Rescue:** P.O. Box 100968, Arlington, VA 22210; 703/766-2647; www.homewardtrails.org.

**Humane Society of Fairfax County:** 4057 Chain Bridge Rd., Fairfax; 703/385-7387; www.hsfc.org.

**Lost Dog & Cat Rescue Foundation:** 703/295-DOGS (3647); www.lostdogandcatrescue.org.

**Ragged Mountain Dogs:** 1415 Nethers Rd., Sperryville; 540/987-9207; www.ragmtk9.org.

**SPCA of Northern Virginia:** P.O. Box 100220, Arlington, VA 22210-3220; 703/799-9390; www.spcanova.org.

**Spay, Inc.:** Low-cost spaying and neutering in Northern Virginia. P.O. Box 100220, Arlington, VA 22210-3220; 703/522-7920; www.spay.org.

## MARYLAND

**College Park Animal Control:** Office only, no shelter facility. 301/864-8877 or 240/375-3165; www.collegeparkmd.gov/animal_control.htm.

**Greenbelt Animal Control:** Adopting animals by appointment only. 15 Crescent Rd., Ste. 200, Greenbelt; 301/345-5417; www.greenbeltmd.gov/animal_control/index.htm.

**Montgomery County Animal Control and Shelter:** 2350 Research Blvd., Rockville; 240/773-5960; www.montgomerycountymd.gov.

**Montgomery County SPCA:** P.O. Box 637, Washington Grove, MD 20880; 301/948-4266; www.mcspca.org.

**The Partnership for Animal Welfare:** P.O. Box 1074, Greenbelt, MD 20768; 301/572-4729; www.paw-rescue.org.

**Prince George's Animal Shelter:** 8311 D'Arcy Rd., Forestville; 301/499-8300; www.co.pg.md.us.

**SPCA/Humane Society of Prince George's County:** P.O. Box 925, Bowie, MD 20718; 301/262-5625; www.pgspca.org.

# Transportation and Pet Taxis

In case of emergency, a trip across town, or a ride to the airport, whistle for the wheels listed below.

**Action Pet Express:** Pet transportation and domestic and international pet shipping. 525-K East Market St., Ste. 202, Leesburg, VA; 866/648-9031; www.actionpetexpress.com.

**K911 Pet Transportation:** Serving western Howard County, MD; 301/807-3463; www.barbsk911.com.

**Red Top Cab:** 703/522-3333; www.redtopcab.com.

**Vet Taxi:** 202/276-5744; www.vettaxi.com.

**Yellow Cab Company of DC:** Company allows its drivers to carry pets, but it's up to the individual drivers whether to accept fares with pets or not. Dogs must be leashed. 202/544-1212; www.dcyellowcab.com.

# Dog Walkers and Doggie Daycare

Until every workplace in the DC metro region embraces Take Your Dog to Work Day, chances are you might need a daycare or a walker. Or if you're headed out of town and Fido isn't invited, look up one of these responsible establishments or individuals.

## WASHINGTON DC

**AnytimeK9:** Dog walking or running, pet sitting, obedience lessons, and party planning in the DC metro region. 202/236-0783; www.anytimecanine.com.

**City Dogs:** 1832 18th St. NW; 202/234-9247; www.citydogs.com.

**DC Doghouse:** Hikes, trips to the dog park, and boarding. Each visit is at least an hour long. 310/592-7151; craig@dcdoghouse.com; www.dcdoghouse.com.

**Dogcentric:** Dog walkers in partnership with the Washington Animal Rescue League. 301/275-8752; www.dcpetcare.com.

**Dogs by Day (& Nite):** A supervised, cage-free daycare and boarding facility open 24 hours, 7 days a week. Located next to affiliate GreenPets. 1724 14th St. NW; 202/986-3601; www.dogsbyday.com.

**Dog-ma Inc.:** DC's first doggy daycare. The indoor/outdoor facility is cage-free. Training, bathing, and "bed and breakfast" options also available. 821 Virginia Ave. SE; 202/543-7805; www.dog-ma.com.

**Little Rascals Doggie Daycare and Boarding:** Cage-free daycare and boarding and a 7,000-square-foot heated indoor dog park open to the public for a fee (with free wireless Internet). 5917 Georgia Ave. NW; 202/669-0170; www.littlerascalsdogpark.com.

**Puppy Love Petsitters:** Dog walking and pet sitting in Northwest DC. 202/337-8456; www.puppylovepetsitters.com.

**Saving Grace Pet Care:** Dog walking and pet sitting on Capitol Hill. 224 9th St. NE; 202/544-9247; www.savinggracepets.com.

**Tails of the City:** 202/261-6615; www.tailsofthecitydc.com.

**Wagamuffin Pet Care:** A sister duo offers dog-walking and pet-sitting services in Northwest DC. Contact Carla Ferris at 202/441-9885 or Diana Suarez at 202/997-9285; www.wagamuffinpetcare.com.

**Wagtime Pet Spa & Boutique:** Boarding, cage-free daycare, grooming, and cool stuff. Pick-up and drop-off services available. 1232 9th St. NW; 202/789-0870; www.wagtimedc.com.

**Zoolatry, Inc.:** 520 10th St. SE; 202/547-9255; www.zoolatry.com.

## VIRGINIA

**Becky's Pet Care:** 6281 B Franconia Rd., Alexandria; 703/822-0933; www.beckyspetcare.com.

**Country Dogs:** Pick-up and delivery in Northern Virginia, DC, and Maryland on Monday and Thursday. Located on a 17-acre farm in Timberville, near Woodstock. 888/711-RUFF (7833); www.country-dogs.net.

**Doggy Jog LLC:** Dog jogging and power walking and pet sitting. 703/822-1632 or 703/822-3559; www.doggyjog.com.

**A Dog's Day Out:** 2800 Gallows Rd., Vienna; 703/698-3647; www.adogsdayout.com.

**Dogtopia:** Off-leash play groups organized by temperament and size. Daycare, boarding, grooming, and training available. Locations in Alexandria, Dulles, Manassas, Tysons Corner, and Woodbridge. www.dogdaycare.com.

**Donna Odmark:** 703/346-7889; donnajo24@hotmail.com.

**Fur-Get Me Not:** Daycare, training, walking, and grooming available. 4140 S. Four Mile Run Dr., Arlington; 703/933-1935; www.furgetmenot.com.

**Karing by Kristina:** By the owner of Barkley Square Dog Bakery & Boutique in Del Ray. 703/329-1043; www.karingbykristina.com.

**Olde Towne Pet Resort:** 8101 Alban Rd., Springfield; 703/455-9000; www.oldetownepetresort.com.

**Sit-A-Pet Inc.:** In business since 1980. 703/243-3311; www.sitapet.com.

**Tail Wags Pet Care:** A small, intimate dog-walking and pet-sitting service in the Alexandria and Kingstowne area. Pet taxi and doggy playgroups are also available. tailwagspetcare.blogspot.com.

**Woofs!:** Besides daycare, dog walking, and boarding, obedience and agility classes are also available. 4241-A N. Pershing Dr., Arlington; 703/536-7877; www.woofsdogtraining.com.

**Your Dog's Best Friend:** State of the "Arf" care for your best friend. Playcare, cage-free boarding, grooming, training, and pet transportation also available. 2000-A Jefferson Davis Hwy.; 703/566-1111; www.yourdogsbestfriends.com.

## MARYLAND

**All Dogs Club:** 5115 Berwyn Rd., College Park; 301/345-3647; www.alldogsclub.com.

**Clever Dog:** 2621 Garfield Ave., Silver Spring; 301/587-5820; www.cleverdog.net.

**Dogtopia:** Off-leash play groups organized by temperament and size. Daycare, boarding, grooming, and training available. Locations in Clarksville and White Flint (near Bethesda), which is also the headquarters. www.dogdaycare.com.

**Fuzzbutts and Friends:** Pet care and services by Karyn Larson. 20516 Strath Haven Dr., Montgomery Village; 301/963-7670 or 301/613-8218.

**House with a Heart:** Private boarding in a home environment with a large fenced yard. $10 of the $30 boarding fee is considered a charitable donation toward an end-of-life sanctuary for senior dogs. Located in Laytonsville. 240/631-1743; www.housewithaheart.com.

**Rivermist Kennels:** Located near Olney. 19515 New Hampshire Ave., Brinklow; 301/774-3100; www.rivermistkennels.com.

**Shady Spring Kennels:** Located in Carroll County. www.shadyspringkennels.com.

# Trainers and Behaviorists

There are some issues that even endless episodes of Cesar Millan's dog whispering can't fix. Try calling a specialist and getting professional help for you and the pooch. Some trainers offer classes at their facilities; others will come to you.

**All About Dogs Inc.:** Colleen Pelar and Robin Bennett; 14885 Persistence Dr., Woodbridge; 703/497-7878; www.allaboutdogsinc.com.

**Bark Busters:** They come to you. 877/500-BARK (2275); www.barkbusters.com.

**Bonnie King:** Capitol Hill; 866/821-9386; www.doggylama-petcoaching.com.

**C&C Co. PALS, LLC:** Carole Peeler. 7790 Willow Point Dr., Falls Church; 703/876-0284; www.positivek9training.com.

**Capital Dog Training Club:** www.cdtc.org.

**Cooperative Paws:** Veronica Sanchez. Vienna; 703/489-6452; www.cooperativepaws.com.

**Good Dog! Obedience Training:** 703/862-9079; www.gooddogobedience.com.

**Greenbelt Dog Training:** 301/345-6999; www.greenbeltdogtraining.com.

**KissAble Canine:** Lisa Colon. In-home consultation and companion pet training behavior modification. 571/312-1940; www.kissablecanine.com.

**Nature's Way K-9 Services Inc.:** John Landry, a local dog whisperer. 301/752-6401.

**Olde Towne School for Dogs:** 529 Oronoco St., Alexandria; 703/836-7643; www.otsfd.com.

**Phi Beta K-9 School for Dogs:** Penelope Brown, CPDT. Positive reinforcement training. Private sessions only. 202/986-1147; swamidogs@earthlink.net.

**Positive Dog:** Vivian Leven, CPDT. 703/628-6637; www.positivedog.net.

**School of Dogs:** 202/363-2310; www.schoolofdogs.com.

**What a Good Dog!:** Nancy Kellner specializes in rescue dogs and provides in-home training. Does not work with dog-on-dog aggression. 141 E St. SE; 202/543-8468; www.whatagooddog.net.

**WOOFS! Dog Training Center:** Erica Pytlovany. 4241A N. Pershing Dr., Arlington; 703/536-7877; www.woofsdogtraining.com.

# Dog Bakeries

For as often as you go to Starbucks, a trip to the nearest dog biscuit bakery only seems fair, right?

**Barkley Square Gourmet Dog Bakery & Boutique:** 2006 Mt. Vernon Ave., Alexandria; 703/548-3644; www.barkleysquarebakery.com.

**Doggie Style Bakery:** House-baked biscuits, doggy birthday cakes, and 10 flavors of doggy ice cream. Also sells all natural, green, and humane foods and has pet spa services available. 1825 18th St. NW, Washington DC; 202/667-0595; www.doggiestylebakery.com.

**Dogma Bakery:** 2445 N. Harrison St., Arlington; 703/237-5070; www.dogmabakery.com.

**Fetch Dog & Cat Bakery-Boutique:** 101 A South St. Asaph St., Alexandria; 703/518-5188; www.fetch-bakery.com.

# Pet Supply Stores and Boutiques

## WASHINGTON DC

**The Big Bad Woof:** Essentials for the socially conscious pet and a great community resource. 117 Carroll St. NW; 202/291-2404; www.thebigbadwoof.com.

**Chateau Animaux:** 524 8th St. SE; 202/544-8710; www.chateau-animaux.com.

**The Dog Shop:** 1625 Wisconsin Ave. NW; 202/337-3647; www.dogshopdc.com.

**GreenPets:** 1722 14th St. NW; 202/986-7907; www.greenpets.com.

**Happy Paws:** 4904 Wisconsin Ave. NW; 202/363-7297; www.happypawsdc.net.

**Pawticulars:** 407 8th St. SE; 202/546-7387; www.pawticulars.com.

**PetMAC Washington DC:** 4220 Fessenden St. NW; 202/966-7387; www.petmac.org.

**Pet Pantry:** 4455 Connecticut Ave. NW, Ste. 2; 202/363-6644.

## VIRGINIA

**A.k.a. Spot:** 2509 N. Franklin Rd., Arlington; 703/248-0093; www.akaspot.com.

**Nature's Nibbles:** Natural food for healthier pets. 2601 Mt. Vernon Ave., Alexandria; 703/931-5241; www.naturesnibbles.com.

**PetMAC Arlington:** 822 N. Kenmore St., Arlington; 703/908-7387; www.petmac.org.

**PetSage:** Holistic pet care and natural food. 2391 S. Dove Street, Alexandria; 703/299-5044; www.petsage.com.

**Pro Feed:** Vienna and Alexandria; www.profeedpet.com.

**Webers Pet Supermarket:** Closed Sundays. 11021 Lee Hwy., Fairfax; 703/385-3766.

**Wylie Wagg:** 11889 Grand Commons Ave., Fairfax; 703/830-5454; www.wyliewagg.com.

## MARYLAND

**Animal Exchange:** 605 Hungerford Dr., Rockville; 301/424-7387; www.424pets.com.

**Bark!:** 5805 Clarksville Square Dr., Clarksville; 443/535-0200; and 16822 Georgia Ave., Olney; 301/774-1944; www.barknatural.com.

**Living Ruff:** 8517 Georgia Ave., Silver Spring; 301/495-7833; www.livingruff.com.

**The Posh Pooch:** 8009 Norfolk Ave., Bethesda; 301/652-1199; www.theposhpooch.com.

# Waste Removal Services

If you can't overcome the ick factor to clean up the yard, as every responsible dog owner should, hire someone else to scoop the poop.

**DoodyCalls:** Service area includes Washington DC, Northern Virginia, Montgomery County, and Prince George's County. 800/366-3922; www.doodycalls.com.

**Your Pet's Business:** Service area focuses on Northern Virginia but serves some parts of DC and Maryland. 703/445-9911; www.yourpetsbusiness.com.

# Agility, Flyball, and Other Sports

Some active dogs, like humans, are happiest when challenged in team sports. Give these activities a whirl.

**Canine Training Association:** Agility training. 6826 and 6822 Distribution Dr., Beltsville, MD; 301/937-1431; www.caninetrainingassociation.org.

**Flyball:** www.flyballdogs.com/fursgonnafly/links.shtml.

**K9 Trailblazers:** Dog hiking group. www.k9trailblazers.org.

**Mid-Atlantic Disc Dogs:** www.mad-dogs.us.

**Performance Dogs:** 24223 Gum Springs Rd., Sterling, VA; 703/585-5765; www.performancedogs.net.

**Washington DC Dog Agility Meetup Group:** http://agility.meetup.com/69.

# Pet-Friendly Real Estate

Finding a place to live that allows a pet can be one of the biggest hurdles to city living. Below are a few real estate experts who can help you sniff out a place to live, as well as listings for apartments known to allow dogs (call for breed and size restrictions).

**Jill Barsky, Coldwell Banker:** 301/651-7785; www.jillbarsky.com.

**Trish Corvelli, RE/MAX:** 703/815-6250; www.propertiesbytrish.com.

**Denny Horner, Evers & Co. Real Estate, Inc.:** Dog-friendly residential real estate in DC and Capital Beltway suburbs. 703/629-8455; www.dennyhorner.com.

**Lindsay Reishman, Coldwell Banker:** 202/491-1275; www.lindsayreishman.com.

**Woof Real Estate:** 2613 P St. NW, Washington DC; 202/558-7019; www.woofrealestate.com.

## WASHINGTON DC

### Northwest
**1210 Mass:** 1210 Massachusetts Ave. NW; 866/420-5889.

**2400 M:** 2400 M St. NW; 866/528-1666; www.2400mapts.com.

**Andover House:** 1200 14th St. NW; 866/559-7525; www.andoverhousedc.com.

**Avalon at Foxhall:** 4100 Massachusetts Ave. NW; 866/580-3807; www.avaloncommunities.com.

**The Ellington:** 1301 U St. NW; 877/261-6542; www.ellingtonapartments.com.

**Gables Takoma Park:** 7035 Blair Rd. NW; 877/692-2109.

**Highland Park:** 14th and Irving St. NW; 888/403-6753; www.highlandparkdc.com.

**The Hudson:** 1425 P St. NW; 866/842-1989; www.pnhoffman.com/rental/hudson.asp.

**Park Crest at Glover Park:** 2324 41st St. NW; 866/702-8496.

**Post Massachusetts Avenue:** 1499 Massachusetts Ave. NW; 866/349-8111; www.postproperties.com.

**Tunlaw Gardens:** 3903 Davis Pl. NW; 888/595-6451.

**Westbrooke Place:** 2201 N St. NW; 866/626-2945; www.westbrookeplace.com.

## Southwest
**The View at Waterfront:** 1000 6th St. SW; 866/624-9032; www.myviewoverdc.com.

**Waterside Towers:** 907 6th St. SW; 888/531-1103; www.watersidetowers.com.

## Northeast
**Senate Square:** 201 I St. NE; 866/589-0745; www.senatesquaretowers.com.

**The Cloisters:** 100 Michigan Ave. NE; 888/593-2014; www.thecloistersapts.com.

## Southeast
**Axiom at Capitol Yards:** 100 I St. SE; 877/365-4973; www.capitolyardsdc.com/100 eye.asp.

**Jefferson at Capitol Yards:** 70 I St. SE; 866/720-3715; www.capitolriverfront.org/go/capitol-yards.

**Onyx on First:** 1100 1st St. SE; 877/418-7293; www.onyxapts.com.

## VIRGINIA

### Alexandria
**The Alexander:** 4390 King St.; 866/751-1126; www.the-alexander.com.

**Avalon at Cameron Court:** 2700 Williamsburg St.; 888/595-4960; www.avaloncommunities.com.

**Barton's Crossing Apartment Homes:** 205 Century Pl.; 866/212-4127.

**Bennington Crossings:** 441 N. Armistead St.; 866/878-5061.

**Carlyle Place Apartments:** 2251 Eisenhower Ave.; 866/456-1508; www.carlyleplaceapt.com.

**The Colecroft Community:** 1400 Oronoco St.; 866/807-5806; www.colecroftstationcondos.com.

**Eaton Square at Arlington Ridge:** 801 Four Mile Rd.; 866/591-0173.

**The Fields at Landmark:** 318 S. Whiting St.; 866/360-3920; www.thefieldslandmark.com.

**Foxchase Apartments:** 320 N. Jordan St.; 888/284-1996; www.foxchaseofalexandriaapts.com.

**Halstead Tower:** 4380 King St.; 866/637-3291; www.halstead-tower.com.

**Jefferson at Sullivan Place:** 5575 Vincent Gate; 866/369-5527; www.jeffersonatsullivanplace.com.

**Post Carlyle Square:** 501 Holland Ln.; 866/645-0830.

**The Reserve at Eisenhower:** 5000 Eisenhower Ave.; 866/880-4609.

**Rose Hill of Alexandria:** 6201 Rose Hill Falls Way; 888/820-9045; www.rosehill-apts.com.

**Willow Run At Mark Center:** 935 N. Van Dorn St.; 888/459-5489; www.willowrunatmarkcenter.com.

## Arlington

**Avalon at Ballston Washington Towers:** 4650 North Washington Blvd.; 866/823-0993; www.avaloncommunities.com/virginia-apartments.

**Camden Potomac Yard:** 3535 S. Ball St.; 866/521-8693; www.camdenpotomacyard.com.

**The Clarendon:** 1200 N. Herndon St.; 866/604-8320; www.clarendonapt.com.

**The Metropolitan at Pentagon Row:** 1401 S. Joyce St.; 866/692-9616.

**The Palatine:** 1301 N. Troy St.; 877/703-9257; www.monumentrealty.com/thepalatine.

**Vista on Courthouse:** 2200 12th Ct. N.; 877/566-6332; www.vistaoncourthouse.com.

**Zoso:** 1025 N. Fillmore St.; 866/490-4431; www.zosocondo.com.

## Falls Church

**The Fields of Falls Church:** 912 Ellison St.; 866/375-2263; www.thefieldsfallschurch.com

**The Fields at Westover:** 2913-A Peyton Randolph Dr.; 866/378-3448; www.thefieldswestover.com.

**The Oaks at Falls Church:** 2158 Evans Ct.; 866/397-9196.

**Oakwood Falls Church Apartments:** 501 N. Roosevelt Blvd.; 866/319-1777; www.oakwood.com.

**Pearson Square:** 410 S. Maple Ave.; 866/512-5402; www.pearsonsquare.com.

**Tysons Glen & Devonshire Square:** 2250 Mohegan Dr.; 888/301-3213; www.tysonsglenapts.com.

## MARYLAND

## Bethesda

**The Chase Apartments at Bethesda Metro:** 4903 Edgemoor Ln., Bethesda; 866/546-1245; www.chaseapts.com.

**Jefferson at Inigo's Crossing:** 5405 Tuckerman Ln., N. Bethesda; 866/282-4912; www.jeffersonatinigoscrossing.com.

**The Morgan:** 12000 Chase Crossing Cir., N. Bethesda; 866/887-2366; www.meridiangroupinc.com.

**Sumner Highlands:** 4523 Sangamore Rd., Bethesda; 866/503-0972; www.sumnerhighlands.com.

**The Fields of Bethesda:** 5079 Bradley Blvd., Chevy Chase; 866/360-3269; www.thefieldsbethesda.com.

**Upstairs at Bethesda Row:** 7131 Arlington Rd., Bethesda; 866/913-0347; www.upstairsbethesda.com.

**Wentworth House on the Green:** 5411 McGrath Blvd., N. Bethesda; 866/605-4827; www.wentworthhouseapartments.com.

**The Whitney at Bethesda Theatre:** 7707 Wisconsin Ave., Bethesda; 877/252-2429; www.whitneybethesda.com/bethesdatheater.htm.

## Silver Spring

**The Blairs:** 1401 Blair Mill Rd.; 888/783-2983; www.blairapartments.com.

**Enclave Silver Spring:** 11215 Oakleaf Dr.; 866/290-2201; www.enclavesilverspring.com.

**Falkland Chase:** 8305 16th St.; 866/260-7020; www.falklandchase.homeproperties.com.

**The Fields of Silver Spring:** 2103 Hildarose Dr.; 866/692-9590; www.kettler.com/apartments/the_fields_of_silver_spring.

**Woodleaf Apartments:** 1512 Heather Hollow Circle; 866/482-3871; www.woodleaf.homeproperties.com.

# INDEX

SNIFF!
SNIFF!

ARROOOOOOOOOOO

# Acknowledgments

Denali and I wish to say a grateful "Woof!" to the many dog lovers who took the time to share their wisdom and show us around their neighborhoods: Darren Binder, Kathy Silva, Beth McCallum, Linda Girardi, George Kassouf, Nancy Kellner, Matt Tosiello, Lisa Walthers, Pennye Jones-Napier of the Big Bad Woof, Shana Fulton, Sarah Crocker of Hotel George, and the many, many other folks who offered advice and tips. Thanks to Denny Horner for your dog-friendly real estate expertise, Kathryn Holt Springston for your historical perspective, Andrea Hatch for your spot-on portrait photography, and Jennifer Lucero for designing me some sweet business cards *pro bone-o*. And Joannah Pickett, this book would not have been possible without your endless stream of witticisms for inspiration.

We couldn't have asked for a more stellar staff at Avalon Travel. Thank you Grace Fujimoto for offering me the job, Kevin Anglin for managing the maps, and Naomi Adler Dancis for months of insightful editing and encouragement.

On the home front, Mom, I appreciate all your help with research, and Dad, thanks for convincing Mom that our family needed dogs in the first place way back when Paul and I were in elementary school. Ganesh, your sister Denali is grateful for your tail-wagging from afar and says "Arf! Arf!" (Meaning: Come visit soon!) To my husband Mike, thank you for your endless supply of patience and support as Denali and I tromped dirt into the house and fussed over synonyms for "mutt." And thanks to friends and family for your prayers and encouragement as I wrote my first book, and the reminder to, ahem, "Man up and eat my f-in' oatmeal."

Finally, a special thanks to everyone at my office job, ERG, who put up with my dogged (though not always successful) attempts at multitasking while writing this manuscript. You're the best!

# Keeping Current

**Note to All Dog Lovers:**
While our information is as current as possible, changes to fees, regulations, parks, roads, and trails sometimes are made after we go to press. Businesses can close, change their ownership, or change their rules. Earthquakes, fires, rainstorms, and other natural phenomena can radically change the condition of parks, hiking trails, and wilderness areas. Before you and your dog begin your travels, please be certain to call the phone numbers for each listing for updated information.

**Attention Dogs of Washington DC:**
Our readers mean everything to us. We explore Washington DC and the surrounding areas so that you and your people can spend true quality time together. Your input to this book is very important. In the last few years, we've heard from many wonderful dogs and their humans about new dog-friendly places, or old dog-friendly places we didn't know about. If we've missed your favorite park, beach, outdoor restaurant, hotel, or dog-friendly activity, please let us know. We'll check out the tip and if it turns out to be a good one, include it in the next edition, giving a thank-you to the dog and/or person who sent in the suggestion. Please write us—we always welcome comments and suggestions.

*The Dog Lover's Companion to Washington DC*
Avalon Travel
1700 Fourth Street
Berkeley, CA 94710, USA
email: atpfeedback@avalonpub.com